Grounds for Assurance and Hope

Selected Biblical and Historical Writings of Bryan W. Ball

An 80th-Birthday Commemorative Selection
Including Several New Chapters not Previously Published

Edited by Bryan W. Ball and Robert K. McIver

Avondale Academic Press
2015

Avondale Academic Press would like to extend thanks to the Clarendon Press, E.J. Brill, James Clarke and Company Ltd, the Oxford University Press, the Pacific Press Publishing Association, Peter Lang, the Review and Herald Publishing Association, and the the Signs Publishing Company, for permission to republish selections of previously published works by Bryan W. Ball. Further details are listed in the Acknowledgments at the end of this book.

Avondale Academic Press
PO Box 19 Cooranbong NSW 2265
Australia

The chapters in this book have been peer-reviewed.

Cover design: Ann Stafford. The cover image is "Rembrandt The Three Crosses 1653" by Rembrandt - www.rijksmuseum.nl : Home : Info : Pic. Licensed under Public Domain via Commons - https://commons.wikimedia.org/wiki/File:Rembrandt_The_Three_Crosses_1653.jpg#/media/File:Rembrandt_The_Three_Crosses_1653.jpg"

National Library of Australia Cataloguing-in-Publication entry
Creator: Ball, Bryan W. (Bryan William), 1935– author, editor.
Title: Grounds for assurance and hope : selected biblical and historical writings of Bryan W. Ball /
Bryan W. Ball and Robert K. McIver, editors, authors.
ISBN: 9780958159142 (paperback)
ISBN: 9780958159159 (ebook)
Subjects: Bible–Commentaries.
        Bible. Revelation–Commentaries.
        Eschatology–History of doctrines.
        Puritans–History.
Other Creators/Contributors:
McIver, Robert K. (Robert Kerry), 1953– author, editor.
Dewey Number: 220.6

With gratitude and affection to
Dawn
Loyal companion and supporter for fifty-six years
and
My Family and Friends
All of whom have greatly enriched my life beyond measure

Foreword

A few months ago an acquaintance of many years wrote to me, "I find it difficult to think of you as an octogenarian". My own feelings exactly, I thought at the time. Fortunately or unfortunately there are documents to prove that it will soon be real enough. This selection of my writings, taken from several of my books and conference papers written over the past forty years, is a commemoration of the fact that this particular milestone is in sight. While I cannot say that this will be my last book, it is also a grateful acknowledgment of a long and rewarding life.

It is also intended for those who may not have seen the original books, to bring to their attention certain ideas and beliefs that, for one reason or another, I feel are still relevant and necessary. I hope it will appeal both to those who are already believers but who, in this age of unbelief and uncertainty, are reassured by being reminded of why they believe, and also to those who do not believe or are not sure if they can reasonably do so but are open-minded enough to consider at least some of the evidence.

The process of selection has not been easy. Space limitations have meant that much has been omitted that to my mind still has value. Two factors determined the final choice. Chapters and topics have been included that fell naturally into some clearly discernible structure. This seemed preferable to what otherwise would have looked like a random collection of disconnected topics. The result is a collection of sixteen chapters from my own writings, in three sections which are more or less cohesive and self-explanatory. Even so, it is not difficult to detect some overlap between the contents of the three sections.

I have also attempted in the main to include topics that are of fundamental importance to Christian identity and that reflect unwavering fidelity to the biblical revelation. This is particularly true of those chapters dealing with Puritan theology and belief, chapters 5, 11 and 14, which although expressive of the thinking and language of the times, are in my view as relevant now as when first propounded. Together they are a salient reminder that history can play a part in the divine processes of revelation and the preservation of truth.

That said, hopefully it will be evident that everything in this selection is included for a reason, including chapters 6 and 11, which could perhaps be regarded as provocative, although for different reasons, as well as the chapters that are largely historical. Chapter 16, which relates specifically to the times in which we live and which reflects a point of view I have come to regard as undeniable, has been written specifically for this book and has not been published previously. Six chapters, directly or indirectly, address the fundamental Christian and biblical theme of hope, justifying the claim in the book's title that it provides grounds for renewed assurance and hope, both defining characteristics of authentic Christianity and both in short supply at the present time.

If a theological or biblical formula would clarify the foregoing, perhaps it could be set out as both a logical and existential continuum:

Revelation – Faith – Assurance – Hope – Reward

Revelation comes through the Word, written and incarnate, and the New Testament variously describes the reward as prize, crown, eternal life, heaven, glory and a new earth "in which righteousness dwells". It aptly summarises the substance of the Christian proclamation and the implicit message of this book. If words express reality, there are indeed grounds for assurance and hope, as much now as in centuries past.

Finally, I am most grateful for the contributions of other biblical and historical scholars, specifically Robert McIver, Steven Thompson and Daniel Renaud, which introduce and conclude my own writings. They give a context and a richness to the book as a whole which would without question be incomplete without them.

Bryan Ball
Martinsville
New South Wales
April, 2015

Contents

8

1. Bryan W. Ball: Academic, Administrator, Apologist

Robert K. McIver

Avondale Seminary

Bryan William Ball was born in July 1935 in the Devonshire village of Bere Ferrers, just across the river Tavy from the historic naval city of Plymouth. Descended from an old Devon family which has been traced back to the early 1700s, his father was an ex-naval officer who had served on several ships in the British Navy between World War I and World War II, including the new battleship H.M.S. *Rodney*, on which he visited Sydney in 1925 as part of the *Rodney's* year-long 'courtesy' cruise to distant parts of the British Empire. Bryan was the eldest of four children born to Cecil and Norah (nee Beardsell) Ball, an Adventist family which during Bryan's early years and in World War II lived in several different parts of England, a fact which influenced his education and outlook on life.

At various times in his working life, Bryan filled a number of different roles: pastor-evangelist; a historian of English Puritanism whose works have been published by prestigious publishing houses; an administrator of two tertiary educational institutions, and a church administrator at a very senior level. Each of these roles is challenging for a variety of reasons, and Bryan has made a significant contribution in all of them.

Bryan's professional life took place in the context of the Seventh-day Adventist Church. In 1950, two years before Bryan began his training to become a minister at Newbold College, the Adventist Church had a worldwide membership of 755,712, of which the largest single component was in North America.[1] In the British Isles, the Church reported a membership of

---

1 In 1950 the North American Division had 250,939 members, or 33% of the church's world membership. The next largest Division of the Church, the Southern European Division, had at that time 78,167 members (equal to about one third of the North American membership) and included "unions" in Angola, Austria, Czechoslovakia, Franco-Belgium, French-speaking West and Equatorial Africa, Hungary, Indian Ocean, Italy, North Africa, Portugal, Romania, Switzerland, Yugoslavia, Bulgaria, Greece, Portuguese East Africa and Spain. The official statistics of the Adventist Church may be found at http://docs.adventistarchives.org//documents.asp?CatID=11&SortBy=2&ShowDateOrder=True

6,666 distributed across 102 churches.[2] Within the United States, in 1950 the ratio of members of the Adventist Church to the general population was 1 to 629, while in the United Kingdom this figure was 1 to 7593.[3] Thus the English branch of the Seventh-day Adventist Church in which Bryan grew up and trained to serve could only be described as small. Today, although it has grown in numbers in comparison to 1950, the Adventist Church is still rather small in England.[4] On the other hand, the membership of the world-wide church has grown to over 18 million, and it has become truly international.[5]

Bryan describes himself as a third-generation Adventist, since his parents and three of his grandparents were Seventh-day Adventists. Until the age of 14 he lived in places where there was no easily accessible Adventist Church—Bere Ferrers in Devon, Potton in Bedfordshire, and Carlisle in Cumbria. When aged from 12 to 14 years, he was able to attend a small church having only 3 or 4 members in Bedford once every 5 to 6 weeks. Bryan accompanied his grandmother and reports that his earliest memo-

---

2 In 1950, the British Union Conference included the Eire Mission (34 members); the North England Conference (2,018), (the Northern Ireland Mission (161), the Scottish Mission (323), the South England Conference (3,663) and the Welsh Mission (467). The South England Conference reported 48 churches for its membership of 3,663, or one church for 76 members.

3 The population figures used in these calculations were found at http://www.photius.com/rankings/world2050.html.

4 According to the most recent statistical report available at the time of writing, the "2014 Annual Statistical Report: 150th Report of the General Conference of Seventh-day Adventists for 2012 and 2013," the church membership at the end of 2013 in the British Union Conference was 34,512, of whom 22,811 were in the South England Conference. Immigration has contributed significantly to this growth throughout the British Isles.

5 The official membership at the end of 2013 stood at 18,143,745. During the last quinquennial period the Secretariat of the Adventist Church at General Conference headquarters has made a concerted effort to ensure that the figures reported in the Annual Reports are representative of those actually attending church regularly. In those parts of the world where denominational affiliation is gathered as part of census data, those who identify themselves as Seventh-day Adventists in the census returns are much greater in number than the official church statistics. Furthermore, the membership of the church was no longer concentrated in North America. At the end of 2013, the largest Division of the Adventist Church was the Inter-American Division (with 3,686,255 members), followed by the Southern Africa-Indian Ocean Division (3,167,259), the East-Central Africa Division (2,856,708), the South American Division (2,263,194), the Southern Asia Division (1,510,326), and the Southern Asia-Pacific Division (1,222,546). All these Divisions of the Church now have a greater membership than that of the North American Division (1,184,395).

ries of the Adventist Church were of "a very small and somewhat peculiar church composed mostly of old ladies who met at the Oddfellows Hall in Bedford and usually had a lay preacher."[6] When Bryan was 14 years old, his family moved back to the Plymouth area and they, with him, began regularly attending Plymouth Church, which then had about 100 members, making it one of the larger churches by the standards of the Adventist Church in England at the time. It was there that the teenaged Bryan became active in his local church. When the local members heard his speaking ability at MV meetings,[7] he was urged by them to consider a career as a Gospel minister. He was able to attend a "meet Newbold" weekend in the spring of 1952, and recalls that he "… felt that Newbold was for me rather than a secular university. After much deliberation, and discussion with a rather disappointed father," he went to Newbold in the September of that year to study in preparation to become an Adventist minister. Early in his time at Newbold the structure and content of the ministerial training course underwent significant change through an affiliation with Columbia Union College in Washington, which enabled Bryan and his fellow classmates to graduate with a BA in Theology.

In 1956 Bryan was in the first group of Newbold students to graduate with this new qualification, and was appointed as a ministerial intern at the New Gallery Centre in London.[8] While there, he worked with such church luminaries as the Australian Roy Allan Anderson and the Americans H. M. S. Richards and Elman Folkenberg.[9] Bryan claims that the preaching of An-

---

6 Unless otherwise indicated, quotations from Bryan Ball are from an email interview between Robert K. McIver and Bryan W. Ball, 13–15 July, 2015. The full text of this interview may be found at the Adventist Heritage Centre, Avondale College of Higher Education, Cooranbong, NSW 2265.

7 MV meetings, or "Missionary Volunteer" meetings, were afternoon meetings, usually designed to interest youth aged in the late teens and young adults and to involve them in the life of the church.

8 The New Gallery Centre at 123 Regent St in London's West End was established first as an art gallery in 1888. It is a Grade II listed building, and has been used as a restaurant (1910–1913), a cinema (1925–1953), a Seventh-day Adventist Centre (1953–1990s), a Habitat Furniture Store (2006–2010), and a flagship store for Burberry (from 2011).

9 Roy Allan Anderson (1895–1985), an Australian Adventist Evangelist, worked in Australia, England and the United States, and published a number of books, including "The Shepherd Evangelist" which influenced Bryan's type of ministry for several years. Anderson was later editor of *Ministry Magazine* (1950–66), one of the most influential publications of the Adventist Church throughout the world. One interesting source for Anderson is http://www.auspostalhistory.com/articles/1826. php. H. M. S. Richards (1894–1985) was a prominent American Adventist Evangelist, who established "The Voice of Prophecy" a radio program that in its heyday

derson and Richards in particular convinced him of the necessity and efficacy of biblical preaching, both in pastoral and evangelistic ministry. It was
while working at the New Gallery that he met his future wife, Dawn, and
they were married in 1959 by Russell Kranz, who was then musical director
at the New Gallery. From 1958 to 1967 Bryan worked as a successful pas-
tor/evangelist, first in North London and later in the West Midlands, which
was part of the North England Conference.

When he was a student at Newbold, Bryan already had the conviction
that the Church "needed people with advanced degrees if it was to make
an impression on the growing secular culture of the day," a conviction that
was only strengthened by his work as an evangelist. He was one of the first
to take advantage of the Andrews University summer extension schools offered at Newbold (with a final quarter spent at Andrews University) and
gained an MA in Religion, *summa cum laude,* from that institution in 1966.
He was soon able to use this award to gain entry into a PhD program at the
University of London.

Bryan says it was rather a "struggle" at the time to get authorization, especially from some senior administrators, to enrol in a PhD program. Given
the circumstances and prevailing attitudes of the Church, this should not be
considered surprising, as he was unique in his generation in seeking a PhD
qualification from an English university. When asked whether he was aware
of any other Adventist students studying for a doctoral degree at the time he
was doing so, Bryan answered, "Not in England," although he was aware
that other European Adventists had completed PhDs in the recent past.[10]

---

was aired on stations across the United States. Elman J. Folkenberg (1920–1986)
developed the so called "Five-day Plan" to help stop smoking, a pioneer public
health program associated with the Seventh-day Adventist Church. The importance
of the program no doubt was instrumental in the decision by the Washington Post
to publish his obituary. http://www.washingtonpost.com/archive/local/1986/01/22/
elman-j-folkenberg-dies/aec711bb-0d89-4a02-ae98-1020a34aebad/

10   Bryan specifically mentions V. Norskov Olsen and Leslie Hardinge (who
both had PhDs) in comments quoted later in this chapter. It should not be forgotten
that the Scot, W. G. C. Murdoch, who had been principal of Newbold College for 16
years and then president of Australian Missionary College (now Avondale College
of Higher Education) for six years, before his appointment in 1953 to the Seventh-
day Theological Seminary at Andrews University in Michigan, held a PhD before
he arrived in Australia. Furthermore, Edward E. Heppenstall (1901–1994), was
born in Rotherham, Yorkshire, UK, so should also be considered an Englishman.
He moved to the USA in 1931 and completed his tertiary study there, eventually
receiving a PhD in Religious Education from the University of Southern California
in 1951. Both Murdoch and Heppenstall taught Bryan while he was studying for his
MA through Andrews University.

Finally having received authorization to begin his PhD study, albeit initially on a part-time basis, Bryan enrolled at the University of London, which at that time had a very good church history department, working under the guidance of the Rev Dr Geoffrey Nuttall who was recognised as one of the leading authorities in the world on Puritanism and English Nonconformity and was himself a prolific writer, having published at least one book or journal article every year for 50 years until his retirement. Bryan believes he was very fortunate to have Geoffrey Nuttall to guide him through the PhD programme, despite Nuttall's reputation as a rigorous supervisor. When asked why he chose the English Reformation to study (rather than OT, or NT, or Systematic Theology, or some other area), Bryan replied:

> I soon learned after graduation that many English people generally regarded Adventism as a nineteenth-century American sect. I felt it was essential to change that perception if the church was to make any impression on the English population, both those who were already Christian as well as the growing numbers of secular people, and that it might be done through tracing the roots of Adventism in all its essentials to the Reformation. My mentor at this period was V. Norskov Olsen, first my Bible and Church history teacher, later principal of Newbold, and then president of Loma Linda University. Olsen's book, *John Foxe and the Elizabethan Church*, was like a beacon of light to me. It was one of the first books by an Adventist scholar published by a secular university press (University of California Press, 1973), and it was widely acclaimed in England. Much the same could be said of Leslie Hardinge's book, *The Celtic Church in Britain,* published in England by SPCK only a year before Olsen's book. Both these books confirmed my conviction that good, scholarly studies by Adventist scholars could, and should, be published by recognised non-denominational publishers. Otherwise, it seemed to me, as it still does, that we are largely talking to ourselves. So it seems that my *A Great Expectation* was the second work to be published in English by an Adventist scholar in Europe. Interestingly, all three of these early studies were in the field of Church History, maybe because in those tentative years it seemed less likely to be confrontational and would therefore help to bring Adventist scholarship to the attention of the scholarly world.

These comments reveal that the younger Bryan Ball felt uncomfortable with the perception of the Adventist Church as a North American sect to such an extent that countering that impression became a significant aspect of his future vision. However, given the counter-cultural nature of Seventh-day Adventism in the 1950s and 1960s, its emphasis on the prophecies of Daniel and Revelation, its view of itself as the proclaimer of the three angels' messages of Revelation 14, its small numbers, and the dominance of the denomination by North Americans at the time, to characterise the English Seventh-day Adventist Church of the time as a North American sect could be defended. The Adventist Church of that era could even be said to have felt a certain level of tension with its social environment, a characteristic sometimes used to identify a sect as distinct from a church.[11] Yet by the 1950s the Adventists had already been on the journey described by sociologists as the progression from sect to denomination to church for at least 50 years.

There are many factors that have led the Adventist Church in this direction. Prominent amongst these causes are the vigorous development of schools and colleges and the establishment and maintenance of a large and high-profile hospital system. In doing so, the Church has inevitably embraced the changes that flow from running and staffing institutions that become leaders in their field by meeting the most stringent accreditation standards set by society as a whole.[12] There have been and still are many communities where the influence of Adventist educational and health institutions contribute markedly to the general good of society. Evidence of this came in 2001 when, at the centenary of Australian Federation in that year, Bryan received the Centennial Medal from the Australian Government "for services to Australian society through the Seventh-day Adventist Church". Today, 60 years or so after the time described by Bryan, the Seventh-day Adventist Church is a global church, and in many parts of the world would more likely be classified as a denomination rather than as a sect.[13] In other words, it should no longer be considered a North American sect. Bryan Ball has himself contributed to that change in perception, both within the Adventist Church itself and by many of the cultures in which it functions.

True to his goal of tracing the "roots of Adventism in all its essentials to the Reformation," Bryan has had the results of his research published by

---

11 Rodney Stark and Roger Finke, for example, use the degree of tension between a religious group and its sociological environment as the key to defining whether or not a religious group is a sect: "Definition 26. Churches are religious bodies in relatively lower tension with their surroundings. Definition 27. Sects are religious bodies in relatively higher tension with their surroundings." Rodney Stark & Roger Finke, *Acts of Faith: Explaining the Human Side of Religion* (Berkeley, CA: University of California Press, 2000), 143–44.

12 The Adventists' establishment and expansion of school and hospital systems is traced in Richard W. Schwarz and Floyd Greenleaf, *Light Bearers: A History of the Seventh-day Adventist Church* (Nampa, ID: Pacific Press, 2000), 100–129, 191–206, 293–312, 478–498. See also Malcolm Bull and Keith Lockhart, *Seeking a Sanctuary: Seventh-day Adventism and the American Dream* (2d ed.; Bloomington and Indianapolis: Indiana University Press, 2007), 302–332.

13 "A nineteenth-century religious sect that observes a seventh-day Sabbath, proclaims the imminent end of the world, and practices health reform, Seventh-day Adventism is now on the way to becoming a major world religion." So Bull and Lockhart, *Seeking a Sanctuary*, xiii.

recognized academic publishers rather than by the publishing houses operated by the Adventist Church.[14] Over the span of his writing career Bryan has published the following books, with, it should be noted, prestigious academic publishers:

A Great Expectation: Eschatological Thought in English Protestantism to 1660, Leiden: E. J. Brill, 1975; Vol. XII in 'Studies in the History of Christian Thought', ed. Heiko A. Oberman.

The English Connection: The Puritan Roots of Seventh-day Adventist Belief. Cambridge, UK: James Clarke, 1981; 2^d ed., revised, Cambridge, UK: James Clarke, 2014

The Seventh-day Men: Sabbatarians and Sabbatarianism in England and Wales, 1600–1800, Oxford, UK: Clarendon, 1994; 2^d ed., revised and expanded, Cambridge, UK: James Clarke & Co, 2009.

The Soul Sleepers: Christian Mortalism from Wycliffe to Priestley, Cambridge, UK: James Clarke, 2008.

All of that of course was in the future for Bryan when he graduated with his PhD from the University of London in 1971, having written a dissertation on the topic, "Eschatological Thought in English Protestant Theology, 1640–1660: With Special Reference to the Second Coming of Christ and the End of the Age", four years later published by Brill as *A Great Expectation.*

Fifteen years after graduating from Newbold, and having served in pastoral and evangelistic roles in both English conferences, Bryan was elected as President of the North England Conference, and served the Church in that role between 1971 and 1975. Soon after this he was invited to move to Newbold College as Chair of the Religion Department, a role he filled between 1976 and 1983. In the early 1980s Bryan also took on the role of Co-ordinator of Theology and Church History in the newly established European Seminary. He was subsequently invited to become the Principal of Avondale College in Cooranbong NSW, in Australia, where he served from 1984 until 1990.

---

14 It is interesting to compare Bryan's choice of publishers with that used by Le Roy Froom (1890–1974). Froom wrote several works, including a major work tracing the history of prophetic interpretation, and another tracing those espousing conditional immortality, topics which Bryan Ball has explored in two of his books. Froom published his through the Review and Herald, a publishing house owned and operated by the Seventh-day Adventist Church (*The Prophetic Faith of Our Fathers: The Historical Development of Prophetic Interpretation,* 4 volumes [Washington, DC: Review and Herald, 1946–54]; and *The Conditionalist Faith of our Fathers: The Conflict of the Ages Over the Nature and Destiny of Man,* 2 volumes [Washington, DC: Review and Herald, 1965–66]. Bryan published his books through the publishing houses of Brill of Leiden; Oxford University Press, and James Clarke of Cambridge.

During his time as Principal of Avondale, a new girls' dormitory was built (Ella Boyd Hall), an extension to the gymnasium was added (including squash courts) and re-accreditations were negotiated in many disciplines.[15] Towards the end of his presidency much time was taken up with a legal case which was taken to the Industrial Tribunal Court in Sydney, over the matter of whether the wages paid to Avondale lecturers should be tied to the salary system of other tertiary institutions rather than to the Church's own salary system. The case was eventually decided in the Church's favour, but the judgement of the court was not passed down until Bryan had moved on to be President of the South Pacific Division of the Seventh-day Adventist Church.

Bryan's professional career is remarkable in many ways, not least because of his move from College Principal or President to Division President. Given that the presidents of Conferences, Unions and Divisions are appointed by an elective process, usually at a "session" of delegates, career paths within the Adventist Church are not always predictable. But one pattern emerges – it is highly unusual for an existing College President to be appointed as a Division President.[16] No doubt Bryan's work with the General Conference on his research into the Reformation backgrounds of Adventist belief, his previous experience as a conference president, his undoubted abilities as a preacher when representing Avondale at camp meetings and other large venues, together with his sensible approach to administrative tasks, all played a part in his appointment. Bryan served as Division President between 1990 and 1997. During that time significant changes took place at all of the institutions of which Bryan was chair of the governing board: the Sydney Adventist Hospital (e.g. opening a 24-bed Emergency Care Department and an intensive care unit),[17] the Sanitarium Health Food Company (restructuring),[18] and Pacific Adventist College (which became

---

15 See further on developments at Avondale College during this time period, Milton Hook, *Avondale: Experiment on the Dora* (Cooranbong, NSW: Avondale Academic Press, 1998), 312–316.

16 Bryan has pointed out to me that Jan Paulsen had a career that also moved from the academic world to Church administration. "He [Paulsen] had been head of Religion at both Newbold and the Adventist Seminary of West Africa before being Newbold principal, then Division Secretary and President, and finally General Conference President [i.e. President of the World-wide Adventist Church]." While it is not unknown for talented individuals to move from academic Administration to the broader church administration in the Adventist Church, it is very unusual.

17 See Arthur N. Patrick, *The San: 100 Years of Christian Caring, 1903–2003* (Wahroonga, NSW: Sydney Adventist Hospital, 2003), 139–256.

18 See Robert Parr and Glyn Litster, *"What Hath God Wrought!": The Sanitarium Health Food Company Story* (Berkeley Vale, NSW: Sanitarium Health Food, 1996), passim.

Pacific Adventist University).[19] While he was chair of Avondale's governing board negotiations were opened to take the college to university status, possibly the single most important step in the College's long history. Bryan also was heavily involved in reviewing and developing the strategic plan for the Division during this period.

Bryan retired in 1997. As he says:

> I retired relatively early[20] in order to return to research in my specialty field, English Puritan and Nonconformist history, and also to broaden my writing base by addressing other wider theological issues. I still felt a strong conviction that the church could benefit from my writing in both areas. As the list of my publications shows, many of them, especially if second editions are included, have appeared since I retired. *Can We Still Believe the Bible?* has been particularly useful in many parts of the world and continues to be so, having sold upward of 25,000 copies in two editions in English as well as being translated into Spanish, Latvian and is in preparation for translation into Russian.
>
> I have also completed another longstanding ambition of a quite different nature — walking the South-West Coast Path in the UK, a distance of 1014 kms, and calculated to involve climbs equivalent to three times the height of Everest over its entire length! I have also been much involved in preaching on Sabbaths, most of it in the North New South Wales, South New South Wales and Greater Sydney Conferences — in more than 50 different churches, as well as presentations at Camp Meetings and Ministers' Meetings. But there is still much to do, God willing!

Retirement has allowed Bryan to return to his work as an apologist for biblical Christianity as well as for distinctive Adventist beliefs. In retirement he added to his list of academic publications relating to aspects of English Reformation thought and Puritanism with the publication in 2008 of *The Soul Sleepers: Christian Mortalism from Wycliffe to Priestley*, published by James Clarke of Cambridge, UK. He has also produced major revisions of two of his other books. As well as this, he has written, edited or contributed to a number of volumes on issues that he considers important for the Seventh-day Adventist Church members to consider. These publications include:

As sole author:

Living in the Spirit, Warburton, Victoria: Signs Publishing Co., 1997.

Can We Still Believe the Bible? And Does it Really Matter? Warburton, Victoria: Signs Publishing Co., 2007; Spanish edition, Buenos Aires, Argen-

---

19 See S. R. Tarburton, *A Place Chosen by God: Pacific Adventist University* (np: np, 2005), passim.

20 Bryan retired at age 62.

tina: Asociacion Casa Editora Sudamerica, 2010; Latvian edition, Riga, LV: Patmos, 2010; 2nd Edition, revised and enlarged, Warburton, Victoria: Signs Publishing Co, 2011.

As [Joint] Editor and Contributor:

The Essential Jesus: The Man, His Message, His Mission, Boise, ID: Pacific Press, 2002; second edition, Nampa, ID: Pacific Press, 2011, in the Adventist Heritage Library.

In The Beginning: Science and Scripture Confirm Creation, Nampa, ID: Pacific Press, 2012; Portuguese Edition, Tatui, SP, Brazil: Casa Publicadora Brasileira, 2014.

The Adventist Church in which Bryan W. Ball served changed much during his years of service, and can no longer be described as a small North-American sect. Many contributed to that change, although Bryan has perhaps been more influential than many others. His career has taken him literally half-way across the globe, working in two countries with distinct histories and cultures. He sought education to doctoral level at a time when it was unusual for leaders of the Adventist Church to seek such qualifications.[21] He began his ministry as an evangelist and has worked as an administrator. He has been tireless in pursuing his objectives to reveal the connection between the distinctive doctrines of the Seventh-day Adventist Church and their roots in English heritage and to enable his readers to see those beliefs in the context of historic Christian doctrine. The writings selected for inclusion in this book represent his many interests, ranging from biblical and theological studies, historical backgrounds, to origins and sociological observations. Many of them, naturally, come from his great interest in English religious history and the light that it throws on the development of Puritan and Adventist doctrine.

This year Bryan reaches his 80th birthday. This book is a celebration of his long and remarkable career.

---

21 One is conscious of a change in this as in many areas in the Adventist Church. David Trim, Director of Archives, Statistics, and Research at the General Conference of Seventh-day Adventists, pointed out to me in a private conversation that the General Conference president and all the vice presidents that served in 2010–2015 had earned doctorates.

Revelation and the Bible

"Revelation is not concerned with knowledge we once had but have forgotten for the time being. Nor does it refer to the kind of knowledge that we might attain by diligent research. It is knowledge that comes to us from outside of ourselves and is beyond our own ability to discover".
Leon Morris, *I Believe in Revelation* (1976), p.10.

2. Revelation and the Authority of Scripture[1]

Bryan Ball

Revelation may be defined as the self-disclosure of God to humankind. Any knowledge that human beings may have of God, therefore, is not the result of their own diligent enquiry but is the outcome of God's gracious initiative and of his will to be known. Without revelation, God would remain hidden and incomprehensible. G.S. Hendry says, "Knowledge of God must be given by God himself".[2] That which is thus revealed is the foundation of all Christian understanding of the present and the future, of God and of mankind. The significance of such revelation to Christianity and to Christian belief and witness can hardly be overstated. Paul Helm correctly observes, "Revelation is central to Christianity, and it is hard to see how Christianity could proceed without appealing to it". [3]

Until relatively recently most theologians have in general agreed with this historic view of revelation. Many also accept the proposition that revelation is "the ultimate question" underlying many contemporary issues in society and in the Church.[4] For example, Edward Heppenstall suggests that revelation is the "crucial question" for theology today, making the important point that the Bible's primary claim is not simply to inspiration, but to revelation.[5] Raoul Dederen has related the issue to the whole church, stating, "Few issues are of more crucial significance for Christians than the nature and purpose of God's self-revelation".[6] In his study of revelation and in-

1 An earlier version of this chapter first published in Bryan W. Ball, ed., *In the Beginning: Science and Scripture Confirm Creation* (Pacific Press, Nampa, ID, 2012), 18-32. Reprinted with permission.

2 G. S. Hendry, 'Reveal (and) Revelation', in Alan Richardson, ed., *A Theological Word Book of the Bible* (London: SCM, 1957), 196.

3 Paul Helm, *The Divine Revelation* (Westchester, IL: Crossway, 1982), xi.

4 Leon Morris, *I Believe in Revelation* (London: Hodder and Stoughton, 1977), 11.

5 Edward Heppenstall, 'The Nature of Revelation' (Centre for Adventist Research, Andrews University, 1960s, ref. 001419), 1.

6 R.F. Dederen, 'The Revelation-Inspiration Phenomenon According to the Bible Writers', in Frank Holbrook and Leo Van Dolson, eds., *Issues in Revelation and Inspiration,* vol. 1 (Berrien Springs, MI: Adventist Theological Society Publications, 1992), 9.

spiration Fernando Canale even argues the importance of the topic because "Christian theology is in crisis".[7]

This high view of revelation underlies the defining claim of Christianity to be a revealed religion. That the Judaeo-Christian God is a God who actively seeks humankind is Christianity's distinguishing characteristic. This seeking God is known through his self-revelation, principally in Christ but also in Scripture. This historic understanding of God and revelation has in recent years come under attack, and we do well to heed Leon Morris's warning, "We can no longer take the traditional idea of revelation for granted".[8] The debate continues to simmer and is not likely to go away. The evangelical theologian J. I. Packer said of revelation, "The real subject under discussion is the essential nature of Christianity".[9] The significance of that observation should not escape us, particularly at the present time.

These matters give rise to a series of related questions: What is revelation? Can it be understood? Has it actually occurred? Does the Bible itself have anything to say on the matter? Is the Bible the result of divine revelation? If it is, then what is an appropriate response? Not least are questions relating to revelation and reason, whether or not revelation occurs in propositional form, that is to say through words, or if God's self-revelation is just that – a disclosure of himself and not also of information about him. Within the confines of this chapter we shall attempt to answer some of these questions in the hope that we can determine whether or not Scripture should continue to have authority in the life of the Church, in the formulation of belief, and in the lives of individual believers, as it has done for the best part of two millennia.[10]

---

7 F. Canale, *The Cognitive Principle of Christian Theology: A Hermeneutical Study of the Revelation and Inspiration of the Bible* (Berrien Springs, MI: Andrews University Lithotec, 2005), 22.

8 Morris, *Revelation*, 9. That the issue has also impinged on Adventist thinking is evidenced in the Adventist Theological Society's publication, edited by Frank Holbrook and Leo Van Dolson, *Issues in Revelation and Inspiration* (Berrien Springs, MI: Adventist Theological Society,1992), a response to Alden Thompson's book *Inspiration: Hard Questions, Honest Answers* (Hagerstown, MD: Review and Herald, 1991).

9 J. I. Packer, 'Contemporary Views of Revelation', in C. F. Henry, ed., *Revelation and the Bible* (Grand Rapids, MI: Baker, 1976), 89.

10 The related question of inspiration lies beyond the parameters of this essay, except to note that it is a critical aspect of the revelatory process that has resulted in a book that is both human and divine. The divine-human nature of Scripture makes careful interpretation essential. Interpretation, inerrancy and illumination are also not considered due to limitations of space.

Revelation Historically Understood

An adequate understanding of revelation and the issues surrounding it is best obtained in the context of the historical background and the continuing debate over revelation that has developed through the centuries.

The Early Church. It is clear from the New Testament that the first Christians accepted totally that God had revealed himself in Christ and also through Scripture. For them Scripture was the corpus of Old Testament writings which Christ himself had frequently cited and to which he appealed to authenticate his own identity and mission (Luke 24:25–27, 44–47). That God had come to earth in the person of Christ and that Jesus was the fulfilment of Old Testament Messianic prophecy was undoubtedly the keynote of apostolic proclamation, as is apparent from even the most cursory reading of Acts. But the emphasis on Scripture as witness to the facts concerning Christ and as being revelatory and with redemptive purpose itself, is equally clear (*e.g.,* Acts 13:32–34; 17:1–3; 18:28).

When Paul wrote to Timothy, *c.* AD 64, concerning "Scripture", noting that Timothy had known from childhood "the sacred writings"[11] and claiming "All Scripture is breathed out by God"(2 Tim 3:16),[12] he wrote initially to Timothy himself without thought of those in centuries to come. Similarly, when Peter (*c.* AD 67/68) declared that in "Scripture … men spoke from God" (2 Pet 1:20–21) he was addressing first-century Christians. Peter's recognition of Paul's epistles as "Scripture" (2 Pet 3:16) endorses both Paul's writings and the status of Scripture itself. Paul's final evangelistic endeavours in Rome focused on Jesus and the "kingdom of God" and were based on frequent appeal to "the Law of Moses and the Prophets", and his quotation from Isaiah (Acts 28:23–28) is incontrovertible evidence of his respect for the Old Testament Scriptures as a revelation of the divine purpose. Christianity spread rapidly across the first-century Roman world primarily as a result of the proclamation of both Christ and of Scripture's witness to Christ. It seems incontrovertible that early Christianity maintained a high view of Scripture for several centuries.

The Medieval Church. That major changes in Christian thinking occurred from the third century onward is widely recognised. Many of these changes related to beliefs about Christ, the virgin Mary, apostolic authority and therefore about Scripture itself. As the medieval period developed, the view came to prevail that Scripture of itself was insufficient, especially for ordinary people, and that it needed to be interpreted and authenticated by

---

11 Or 'Holy Scriptures', NKJV; *hiera,* 'sacred', is in the Greek.

12 Biblical quotations are from the English Standard Version unless otherwise indicated.

the church. Tradition came to assume an ever-increasing role in the life and teachings of the Church.

Tradition includes customs and practices that arose in various places and which were later accepted as norms of Christian belief and practice, often formally endorsed by the Church. During the medieval period the chief source of tradition became conciliar pronouncements and church decretals – *ecclesia docens,* Church teaching – that assumed the same, or even a superior, authority to that of Scripture. In the view of the medieval Church itself "unwritten traditions formed a second, independent, original, authentic source of information and doctrine alongside Scripture", a position that was always unacceptable to historic orthodoxy.[13] The original revelation in Scripture had become perceived as insufficient and consequently devalued.

The Reformation. The sixteenth-century European Reformation was in essence a reaction against tradition and the subsequent errors and abuses that crept into the Church as the medieval era unfolded. The defining call of the Reformation became *Sola Scriptura,* the Bible only, reaffirming the foundation of authentic Christian belief. Diarmaid MacCulloch says of that era, "Authority was to be respected … This was particularly the case with the greatest authoritative text of all, the Christian Bible".[14] One of the enduring achievements of the Reformation was the translation and printing of the Bible in the vernacular languages of Europe. Luther's German Bible and Tyndale's English New Testament shaped the language and cultures of their peoples, ensuring that Reformation principles continued to prevail for centuries.

A significant outcome of the Reformation emphasis on the Word of God was recovery of the notion concerning the "sufficiency of Scripture" – the conviction that man's knowledge of God and everything necessary for salvation should be derived from the Bible. Packer says that as a result of this rediscovery, "The Bible was set up, according to its own demand, as judge of those traditions which previously had been supposed to supplant it".[15] The Reformation cannot be understood fully unless the desire to return to apostolic Christianity with its fundamental convictions about Scripture and divine revelation is grasped. Protestantism was thus born and from it the

---

13 R. P. C. Hanson, 'Tradition' in Alan Richardson, *A Dictionary of Christian Theology* (London: SCM, 1969), 342. Burn-Murdoch included the dogma of the immaculate conception, substitution of the Lord's Day for the Sabbath, and baptism by affusion as examples of tradition that have superseded the teaching of Scripture, H. Burn-Murdoch, *The Development of the Papacy* (London: Faber and Faber, 1954), 378–379.

14 Diarmaid MacCulloch, *Reformation: Europe's House Divided 1490–1700* (London: Penguin, 2004), 71.

15 Packer in *Revelation and the Bible,* 91.

Nonconformist Churches later emerged with their uncompromising insistence on Scripture as the normative guide for all religious belief and practice.

The Enlightenment. For three hundred years or more the Reformation view of Scripture dominated Protestantism and much of the civilised world. Alister McGrath states that the Bible was "central to the life of Western European society in a way that we cannot begin to imagine today".[16] It was, in fact, the single most formative influence in the final development of Western civilisation. But that was to change dramatically in the eighteenth century with the coming of the Enlightenment, or the Age of Reason, resulting in the secularisation of Western European thought.[17]

Under the influence of the Enlightenment principles of rationalism, individualism and subjectivism, many thinkers of the time, such as Voltaire and Hume, came to believe that they had been emancipated from the "tyranny" of the Church and Scripture. Intellectual objections were raised against Christianity and the Bible. Louis Berkhof speaks of the "chill winds of Rationalism" that swept over Europe, under which "Man became intoxicated with a sense of his own ability and goodness, refused to listen and submit to the voice of authority that spoke to him in Scripture, and reposed complete trust in the ability of human reason to lead him".[18]

This humanistic attitude led to rejection of the biblical revelation as traditionally understood and reflects an unjustified confidence in the unaided human mind and its ability to discover religious truth for itself. The Bible became devalued and was to be interpreted just as any other book. Divine revelation and biblical authority were replaced by human wisdom and personal judgement. History has repeatedly demonstrated the persistent attraction of this viewpoint and its devastating consequences for the individual and for society.

The Contemporary Scene. Much could be said of the prevailing eclectic scene with its divergent and often conflicting views of revelation,[19] but space restricts us to only two observations.

---

16 Alister McGrath, *In the Beginning: The Story of the King James Bible* (London, Sydney and Auckland: Hodder and Stoughton, 2001), 2.

17 Enlightenment thinking began to appear in Europe from the mid-seventeenth century onwards, reaching its high point during the early decades of the eighteenth century.

18 L. Berkhof, *Systematic Theology* (London: Banner of Truth, 1963), 38.

19 'Contemporary' is a relative term, here used mainly of the twentieth century and up until the present time. The complexity of contemporary views of revelation is illustrated in publications such as Paul Helm, *Divine Revelation: The Basic Issues* (London: Marshall, Morgan and Scott, 1982) and Colin Gunton, *A Brief Theology of Revelation* (Edinburgh: T & T Clark, 1995).

We note firstly the continuing influence of Enlightenment thinking, especially in academic circles where in many institutions it prevails across most disciplines, including theology and biblical studies. Here it first led to a radically critical view of the Bible, resulting in the reinterpretation of Scripture according to Enlightenment principles.[20] The so-called Documentary Hypothesis, according to which the Pentateuch is a late compilation (*c.* sixth century BC) from several different sources rather than the work of one author or compiler, Moses, is a classic example. The New Testament has also been radically reinterpreted. Much of the life and teachings of Jesus have been rejected as myth, especially his miracles and the resurrection, and Jesus himself widely regarded, not as the Son of God as historically understood, but as an itinerant peasant preacher or a social revolutionary intent on undermining Roman authority in Palestine.[21]

Secondly, revelation itself has been redefined. It is now widely held that revelation is not a phenomenon that occurs through words *about* God, that is, in the Bible, but that it is a disclosure of God *himself,* an encounter of the human with the divine. Martin Buber, an Austrian Jewish philosopher (1868–1965), encapsulated encounter theology with his now-famous dictum "I-Thou" that succinctly represents this point of view – revelation principally as encounter. It has to be said that there is an important truth here. If the purpose of revelation is redemptive, then it must ultimately lead to some kind of interaction between God and humans at a personal level. But is it only this Buberian-type of encounter that is the authentic revelation of God? Or does revelation also occur at another level? Do words, spoken or written, play any part in the revelatory process of bringing about personal contact between God and human beings? The remainder of this chapter will attempt to answer this most fundamental question.

The Biblical Witness to Revelation

It has been asserted that the Bible itself has relatively little to say about revelation, indeed that revelation is a concept imposed on Scripture, and that what it does say, particularly in the New Testament, refers mainly to the revelation of Christ at the last day.[22] We must, therefore, allow the Bible to speak for itself to determine if such claims are sustainable.

The Old Testament. Consideration of the Old Testament text at many points tells us explicitly that revelation occurred at various times throughout

---

20 Michael Green states, "It is one of the three basic assumptions of the modern critical method that the Bible is in all respects to be treated exactly like any other ancient book", in Morris, *Revelation,* 8.

21 See, *e.g.,* the views referenced in Bryan W. Ball and William Johnson, eds., *The Essential Jesus* (Boise, ID: Pacific Press, 2002), 12–14.

22 See, *e.g.,* Richardson, ed., *Dictionary of Christian Theology,* 294.

Old Testament history and that it is a basic idea in Old Testament theology. Such texts confirm our basic understanding of what revelation is – disclosure of that which otherwise would be known only to God: "The secret things belong to the Lord our God, but the things that are revealed belong to us and to our children forever"(Deut 29:29). The experience of the prophet Samuel further affirms revelation and recognises the fact that it occurs through the words of the Lord, and at a time of God's choosing: "The Lord revealed himself to Samuel at Shiloh by the word of the Lord" (1 Sam 3:21). David claimed that he had been the recipient of divine revelation, "For you, O Lord of hosts, the God of Israel, have made this revelation to your servant, saying, 'I will build you a house'" (2 Sam 7:27). Centuries later the Babylonian king Nebuchadnezzar acknowledged that Daniel's God was a "revealer of secrets" (Dan 2:19, 22, 28–30, 47, NKJV; cf. 10:1). The repeated emphasis on revelation throughout this entire passage is impossible to ignore. Amos 3:7 reaffirms that revelation undergirds God's communication with the prophets, when it says, "The Lord God does nothing without revealing his secret to his servants the prophets". On the basis of these texts alone it seems difficult to avoid the conclusion that revelation occurred throughout the Old Testament era, and that it was so recognised, and that it frequently involved communication by word.

Many scholars recognise that the God of the Old Testament is portrayed consistently as "active" and as "speaking" and that these two characteristics are definitive of the Judaeo-Christian God. This understanding is confirmed by the text of Genesis 1 and 2, seminal chapters of the Bible by any criteria. The Creation account in Genesis 1 and 2 testifies to the "active" God of the Old Testament by the use of several verbs denoting action, including 'created', 'made', 'separated', 'formed', 'blessed', 'breathed', 'planted', 'caused' and so on. Beyond the various activities ascribed to God by these verbs, they also imply intention, planning, oversight and, not least, sovereignty. This early representation of the "active God" in the opening chapters of the Bible is foundational to a correct understanding of God and is frequently reiterated throughout the Old Testament.

But God also appears in Genesis 1 as the "speaking" God, who uses words to explain himself and to bring about his purpose. The repeated use of the phrase "God said" in the Creation account not only indicates the manner in which Creation took place, thereby providing the Psalmist with the basis for his assertion, "By the word of the Lord the heavens were made … For he spoke and it came to be; he commanded, and it stood firm" (Psa 33:6, 9), but also fittingly introduces us to the God who will continue to speak throughout the Old Testament. The verbs 'to say' and 'to speak' appear more than any other verbs in the Old Testament text, most frequently

with reference to God. They repeatedly underline the fundamental nature of
the Old Testament God as a God who makes known his will and his wishes
in verbal form.

It is often claimed by those who are attracted to the idea of encounter
revelation that God's principal method of revelation in Old Testament times
was through various acts at specific points in history and in his encounters
with specific individuals at times of crisis in their lives. "The central feature
of the biblical revelation is that it was given in real history, among real men
in the crises of their national and individual lives".[23] While revelation is undoubtedly communicated within the context of history and indeed includes
God's acts in history, many would question that this personal dimension was
its "central" feature.

Ned Stonehouse draws an important conclusion from the role of Moses
during the Exodus and in the wilderness experience of Israel. Noting the
"greatness" of Moses in biblical and Israelite history, his "distinctive place
in the history of revelation" and "the historical character of the Old Testament revelation", Stonehouse remarks:

> The word of the Lord which came by Moses could be and was, because
> of its historical character, handed down to the people from generation
> to generation. It is obvious that in the transmission of this special rev-
> elation the fact of its being so largely committed to writing was highly
> significant. The fact of its inscripturation assuredly did nothing to mod-
> ify its essential character as revelation.[24]

The resultant writings were incorporated in the Pentateuch, and the word
thus written then became God's revelation of his past dealings with his people for succeeding generations.

Morris cites several Old Testament prophetic passages, all of which refer
specifically to the word of the Lord as it came to the prophets, including
"The Lord said to me" (Isa 8:1); "The word that came to Jeremiah from the
Lord" (Jer 7:1); "I heard the voice of one speaking" (Ezek 1:28). Morris
argues convincingly against the view that revelation does not occur through
the words of the prophets, for time after time that is precisely what the
prophets themselves claim, and in view of the repeated use of such terms it
is difficult to reach any other conclusion:

> I cannot see why men should write in this way if what they wanted to
> tell us was that they had given the matter thought and were now pre-
> pared to let us have their considered conclusions. If words mean any-
> thing they are reporting disclosures. They are saying that God spoke to
> them, revealed himself to them, if you like.[25]

23 *Ibid.*, 295.

24 Ned B. Stonehouse, 'Special Revelation as Scriptural', in Henry, ed., *Revelation and the Bible*, 77–78.

25 Morris, *Revelation*, 21.

So when we allow the Old Testament writers to speak for themselves, we find that they insist that they are communicating what God first communicated to them. "They may not use our term, but they are recording what we call revelation".[26]

The New Testament. The New Testament Greek words that are translated "reveal" and "revelation" in English versions are the verb *apokalupto*, to unveil or uncover, and the related noun *apokalupsis*, an uncovering, or an unveiling. That which is "unveiled" already exists prior to any *apokalupsis* and without being unveiled would remain hidden. This, as we have seen, is precisely what the basic Christian concepts of God and revelation contain. But it is more than God himself who is unveiled through the revelatory process. Knowledge and facts relative to God's redemptive purposes are also revealed.

The verb *apokalupto* is attributed to Jesus twice in Matthew 11:25–27, once of his Father and once of himself, thereby claiming for him an equal authority to reveal what is normally hidden. Elsewhere, while the Old Testament continually uses phrases like "Thus says the Lord" (*e.g.,* Jer 31:2,7,15,23,35,37), the New Testament records the repeated declarations of Jesus, "I say to you" (*e.g.,* Matt 5:18,22,28; John 5:19, 24–25). Here, surely, is the reason why his words elicited such astonishment, "For his word possessed authority" (Luke 4:32). It was the authority of divine revelation, equal to the authority of the Old Testament prophets. Jesus further asserts that "knowledge of the secrets of the kingdom of heaven" had been given to the disciples, indicating that revelation imparts understanding (Matt 13:11, NIV). And in response to Peter's confession of Jesus as the Christ, he said to Peter, "This was not revealed to you by man, but by Father in heaven" (Matt 16:17, NIV).

Similarly, the Pauline epistles demonstrate the crucial significance of revelation in Paul's thinking and experience. Romans 1:16–17, 1 Corinthians 2:20, Galatians 1:12, Ephesians 1:17–18; 3:3–5, Philippians 3:15 and Colossians 1:26–27 all require careful consideration since they testify explicitly to revelation and since none of them refers to the revelation of Christ at the end of the age. Most of them relate specifically to Paul's own experience. Space restricts extended discussion of these texts, but Galatians 1:11–12 deserves mention on account of its unambiguous witness to revelation in Paul's own experience. Paul says that the Gospel he preached was not a human message, "For I did not receive it from any man, nor was I taught it, but I received it through a revelation [*apokalupsis*] of Jesus Christ". These texts alone confirm that revelation was a defining factor in Paul's life and therefore in the development of the Christian message.

---

26 *Ibid.,* 22.

In addition to these specific references there are numerous passages in which revelation is clearly assumed or implied, both in the Pauline writings and in other New Testament passages, for example, 1 Corinthians 11:23; 15:3; 2 Corinthians 4:3–6; 1 Thessalonians 2:13–14; Acts 26:12–18 and so on. How, in the face of all this textual evidence, it is possible to doubt that revelation is a fact in the New Testament record, completely unrelated to the revelation of Christ at the *parousia* is almost beyond comprehension.

We are thus confronted with a mass of evidence from both Old and New Testaments to the reality of revelation, to its immense significance in the divine purpose and to the fact that it is more than simply 'encounter', important though that is. Moreover, it frequently includes words that signify the impartation of knowledge and understanding and that necessarily have revelatory significance themselves. Morris summarises the import of the biblical witness to revelation rather neatly when, having argued at some length that revelation occurs through the words of the prophets, he says, "I do not see how it is possible for a Christian to reject the idea that God has disclosed at least something of himself and still be authentically Christian".[27]

General and Special Revelation

The significance of revelation as a key concept for understanding the Bible and even for the survival of Christianity in an ever-increasingly secular culture has been recognised for some time. The terms "general revelation" and "special revelation" have been used in the attempt to explain and clarify the concept of revelation and it is necessary to consider these terms and their implications more carefully.

General Revelation. General revelation is the more recent term for what in the medieval period was usually called "natural revelation". It refers to the fact that there are evidences in nature and within human experience that testify to God's existence and that are evident for all to see. These evidences are generally held to include the cosmos that surrounds us, certain aspects of the natural world in which we live and the innate sense of right and wrong that exists in all human beings. Kant's memorable phrase "the starry heavens above me and the moral law within me"[28] is still a useful summary of the scope of general revelation.

The Old Testament, for example in Psalm 19:1–6, and the New Testament, in Romans 1:18–20, bear witness to the fact that God has revealed something of himself in nature. Paul seems to be quite clear on this, saying that God's power and his divinity "have been clearly perceived, ever since the creation of the world, in the things that have been made" (Rom 1:20). Such revelation, however, has generally been held to be limited, perhaps

---

27 *Ibid.*, 28.
28 From the conclusion to his *Critique of Practical Reason* (1788).

awakening the conscience, an awareness of God and a desire to know more of him, but inadequate for a full understanding of either God or humanity and hence for salvation.[29] Gordon Clark says, "The planets above and the plants below show some of the wisdom and power of God", but argues that the cosmos and the creation do not reveal the full wisdom and power of God and that neither omnipotence nor righteousness are necessarily conclusions to be drawn from the stars.[30]

Special Revelation. Special revelation refers to God's self-disclosures in Christ and in Scripture, both necessitated by humanity's natural alienation from God, the result of fallen human sinfulness with its "ignorance" and "darkened understanding" (Eph 4:18; Col 1:20). The symbiotic relationship between Christ and Scripture is so close as to be in some respects virtually inseparable. Both are expressions of the divine "Word", the very *logos* of God,[31] Christ the incarnate Word and the Bible the inscripturated Word, each bearing witness to the other, Christ testifying repeatedly to the role of the written Word[32] and the written Word clearly and consistently bearing witness to the incarnate Word.[33] We are concerned here particularly with the function of Scripture, the written Word, as God's special revelation.

While it is undeniable that natural human alienation from God is the fundamental reason for all revelation, it is also true that special revelation is necessary on account of human finitude as well as fallenness. Revelation akin to what we now term special revelation began in Eden before the writing of the Old Testament commenced and before human sin. Clark argues that the necessity of special revelation became apparent as soon as humans were created, in other words on account of their creatureliness as well as, and before, their sinfulness:

> When Adam was created and placed in the Garden of Eden, he did not know what to do. Nor would a study of the Garden have led to any necessary conclusion. His duty was imposed upon him by a special divine revelation. God told him to be fruitful and multiply, to subdue nature, to make use of animals, to eat of the fruit of the trees, with one

---

29 Some are reluctant to concede that "general revelation" amounts to revelation at all. John Macquarrie prefers to think of it as providing "a general possibility of revelation", *Principles of Christian Theology* (London, SCM, 1966), 51.

30 Gordon Clark, 'Special Divine Revelation as Rational' in Henry, ed., *Revelation and the Bible*, 28.

31 On the depth of meaning inherent in *Logos*, the 'Word' of God, as an appropriate word to communicate the idea of revelation, see ch.16.

32 See, *e.g.,* the chapter by Pierre Marcel, 'Our Lord's Use of Scripture' in Henry, ed., *Revelation and the Bible.*

33 This is not to overlook the distinctions between the two or the supremacy of the incarnate Word, as set forth for example in Hebrews 1:1–3.

fateful exception. Thus moral norms, commands and prohibitions were
established by a special … revelation. Only so could man know God's
requirements …[34]

There is therefore a twofold necessity for special revelation: human ignorance and human sinfulness. That this Edenic revelation to the first humans
occurred through verbal communication is clear. The record states, "God
said to them, 'be fruitful and multiply' and 'God commanded'" (Gen 1:26;
2:16). Here is the speaking God in verbal communication with the first man
and woman.

From then on, as Old Testament history unfolded and as its text shows,
God revealed himself through a succession of remarkable acts. But it is
equally clear that he also revealed himself through the written account of
those mighty acts. How else could succeeding generations know about those
deeds and their significance? It is so obvious from a thorough reading of the
Bible, especially in the case of the Old Testament, that one wonders why it
has ever been disputed. Morris criticises the artificial distinction between
the deeds of God and his words, the more recent view that revelation occurred in the acts of God but not in verbal form or through the written record. His comments are worth noting:

> We have no access to the deeds except through the record. If the record
> is unreliable then we do not know what God did and accordingly we
> do not know how he revealed himself. We have lost the revelation …
> It is impossible to be rid of the words if we are to find revelation in
> the deeds. It is the words and the deeds together which make up the
> revelation.[35]

With reference to the New Testament, Stonehouse declares that by its very
nature this new revelation, "no less surely than the old, was virtually crying
out for inscripturation in order that the Church might be provided with assured knowledge of the fulfilment of the divine purpose of redemption".[36]

Concerning special revelation Morris speaks of "the scandal of particularity that we cannot evade".[37] It is a protest against those who dislike the
idea of special revelation or who deny it altogether. Enlightenment thinking,
still very much evident today, rebels against the view that mankind needs
assistance to discover truth, let alone to counter the effects of fallenness and
sin and the consequent need for salvation. The "scandal of particularity" is
a reflection, perhaps an extension, of Paul's "scandal of the cross" – "we
preach Christ crucified, to the Jews a stumbling-block [Greek skandalon, an
offense] and to the Greeks foolishness" (1 Cor 1:23). To the Jews the idea

---

34 Clark in Henry, ed., *Revelation and the Bible*, 29.
35 Morris, *Revelation*, 44.
36 Stonehouse in Henry, ed., *Revelation and the Bible*, 84.
37 Morris, *Revelation*, 47.

that the death of a common criminal crucified under Roman law could have any religious significance was abhorrent. To the Greeks the idea that the death of any man for the salvation of others was irrational foolishness, "so much silliness", as Lenski puts it.[38] The scandal of the cross was universally offensive in the pagan Greco-Roman first-century world, as it and the record that bears witness to it still are to many.

Part of that offense, that "scandal", lies in its particularity. Caiaphas thought it was "expedient" for one man to die for the people (John 18:14). In the divine purpose it was essential: "By one man's obedience, many will be made righteous" (Rom 5:19). Special revelation was necessary to explain the meaning of that astonishing act of grace and to make it universally known. Humans could not have discovered it or understood it without such assistance. But in our time, under the baneful influence of radical Enlightenment thinking pushed to its limits, both the act and the explanation are offensive. The scandal of the cross has become the scandal of particularity in our time. One special man, the one of God's own choosing, and the special revelation that testifies to the meaning of his life, death and resurrection are equally offensive to the "Greeks" of our day.

Morris argues that this scandal of particularity cannot be avoided because particularity was in the divine purpose from the beginning:

> It is what God has done in Israel that matters, not what he did in the nations generally, what he did in Jesus that is important, not his action in men in general. It is in the death of Jesus that the atonement for men's sins was wrought out not in the deaths of martyrs who through the ages have lived and died for the truth.[39]

Authentic Christians can never deny the uniqueness of Christ or his atoning death, for they are integral to the Christian proclamation. Neither can they deny the uniqueness of the special revelation through which the record and the meaning of that life and that death have been made available, the "particularity" of Scripture. The Bible *is* a reality, and it *is* unique. It holds a special place in the literature of the world because it is the product of divine revelation. Nothing ever written is comparable with it. It is incontrovertibly special. Morris is undeniably correct when he says, "We do not do justice to the facts ... unless we see the Bible as unique".[40]

Special Revelation as Rational Proposition

We must now address two crucial aspects of the revelatory process, particularly as they relate to special revelation: the extent to which reason is

---

38 R. C. H. Lenski, *The Interpretation of I and II Corinthians* (Minneapolis, MN: Augsburg, 1963), 67.

39 Morris, *Revelation*, 47.

40 *Ibid.*

involved, and whether or not special revelation is at any time propositional, that is to say, occurs through words and statements.

Revelation and Reason. The centuries-old debate concerning revelation and reason has generally resulted in acknowledgment that reason is an important factor in human response to revelation. In other words, revelation would be pointless if those for whom it occurred did not know about it or understand it. In recent discussions of revelation the emphasis on revelation as 'encounter' has been seen by many as unbalanced, misleading and contrary to the biblical revelation itself. Archbishop William Temple spoke for many, as his words still do, when he stated, "Revelation can, and in the long run must, on pain of becoming manifest as superstition, vindicate its claim by satisfying reason".[41] More recently John Macquarrie has argued strongly in defence of reason as being necessary to understanding the revelatory process, declaring that he "must part company with the many theologians who in recent times have claimed that the content of revelation is a personal encounter".[42]

The importance of reason appears in the Old Testament through the repeated claims that the prophets declared "the word of the Lord" in texts such as Isaiah 1:18, with God's invitation to fallen man to "reason together", and the many references to understanding and knowledge throughout the Old Testament text. It is, however, in the New Testament, notably (although not exclusively) in the epistles, that the mind and reason are most stressed, perhaps in view of the prevailing emphasis on reason and rational discourse in the Greco-Roman world, which early Christianity sought to reach with the Gospel. Frequent use of such words as mind (*nous*), understanding (*sunesis* and *nous*), knowledge (*gnosis* and *epignosis*), to make known (*gnorizo*) and to consider (*katanoeo,* literally meaning to perceive thoroughly) is sufficient to make it abundantly evident that reason is an essential element in the human response to revelation.

The New Testament evidence is particularly impressive. In Colossians 2 Paul's hope that believers may have "full assurance of understanding" and "knowledge of God's mystery" (v. 2) follows the revelation already made of that mystery, Christ and the Gospel (1:25–27). In Ephesians 1 the "spirit of wisdom and of revelation in the knowledge of him [Christ]" and the 'enlightenment' of the believers at Ephesus (1:17–18) is contrasted with the "darkened understanding", "futile minds" and "ignorance" of the as yet unenlightened Gentiles (4:17–19). Paul's plea that Christians offer "reasonable"[43] service and be transformed by the "renewing" of their

---

41   William Temple, *Nature, Man and God* (Edinburgh: T & T Clark, 1934), 396.

42   Macquarrie, *Christian Theology*, 96.

43   The rare Greek word *logikon* translated 'reasonable' in many English ver-

"minds" (Rom 12:1–2), his own testimony to serving God with his mind (Rom 7:25) and his exhortation that Christians should be "fully convinced" in their minds (Rom 14:5) illustrate just how crucial reason is in the experience of New Testament Christians. It seems indisputable that God's revelation in Scripture is cognitive, addressed to the mind and leading to knowledge and understanding that otherwise would not be attainable.

Reason itself requires objective consideration of all relevant data, and while space does not permit further investigation of this defining human faculty and its role in the revelatory process enough has been said to underline its critical significance. Centuries of theological reflection on the biblical witness and on normal human experience strongly indicate that revelation comes to human beings through words that convey knowledge, that impart understanding and that ultimately lead to self-knowledge and a radical life-changing 'encounter' with God. It may be claimed, therefore, that reason, among other things, is necessary to

- Understand what revelation is;
- Perceive how it takes place;
- Determine whether or not it has occurred;
- Interpret what it means;
- Communicate to others its content and consequences.

It is impossible to conceive of any meaningful self-disclosure of God to humans that bypasses the mind and the understanding. Through the special revelation in Scripture, "God stoops to make himself known in ways we can grasp and understand. He comes to us in categories of thought and action which make sense to us".[44]

The more recent understanding of revelation as 'encounter', a nebulous, mystical concept, is the outcome of post-Enlightenment existentialism, itself an unbalanced and unbiblical reaction to reactionary Enlightenment rationalism. Ironically, the revelation to which Scripture and reason bear witness and which conveys knowledge and understanding also leads to a personal, inner experience that far surpasses the mystical, ill-defined 'encounter' of existential theology. It asserts "Christ in you, the hope of glory" (Col 1:27) and "It is no longer I who live, but Christ who lives in me" (Gal 2:20) and "the Spirit of him who raised Jesus from the dead dwells in you" (Rom 8:11). We note that Joseph Scriven wrote the immensely popular hymn "What a Friend We Have in Jesus" under the influence of the strongly biblical preaching of the Second Great Awakening in North America some

---

sions signifies rationality; see A. Souter, *A Pocket Lexicon to the Greek New Testament* (Oxford: Clarendon Press, 1960), 147; *cf.* the marginal notes in ESV and NKJV.

44 Clark Pinnock, 'Revelation' in S. B. Ferguson and D. F. Wright, eds., *New Dictionary of Theology* (Leicester, UK and Downers Grove, IL: IVP, 1996), 587.

seventy years before Buber published *Ich und Du*. The biblical revelation is rational, cognitive and informative; it is also redemptive and ultimately relational.

Revelation as Propositional.[45] For at least the past hundred years the belief that revelation occurred through words and statements has come under sustained attack. Due largely to the influence of 'encounter' theology, the concept of propositional revelation became widely regarded as out-dated and even misleading. Paul Helm notes that in the twentieth century the idea was "fiercely controverted", even though it had been regarded as "commonplace" in the earlier centuries of Christianity.[46] While the attack has abated more recently, the underlying antipathy to it lingers in certain quarters, evident for example in the suspicion with which doctrine is regarded, even rejected, by some and also in the tendency to be selective with regard to which words of the biblical revelation to accept.

Bernard Ramm regarded the phrase "propositional revelation" as "inept"[47] – we might at least agree that it is insufficient – yet the idea it is intended to convey is unequivocally fundamental to the divine-human dialogue. Simply stated – and at risk of being repetitious – it is that God has revealed himself and his purposes through words. We have already seen substantial evidence of the fact that from the beginning God has addressed human beings verbally, firstly through the spoken word and subsequently through the written word. We here make the point that propositional revelation, correctly understood, is a consequence both of the "speaking God" of history and Scripture and the "hearing man" of God's own creation. It is necessary both on account of God's own determination to use words in the revelatory process and on account of man's singular ability to reason, an inherent and defining rationality. Noting the "spiritual importance of the word", Morris states that "rational intercourse depends on the use of words" concluding that it is "not easy to see" how propositional revelation "can be resisted".[48]

G. E. Ladd asserts that both God's deeds and his words constitute revelation, but argues that the deeds require the words in order to become of revelatory significance to future generations. "God did not act in history in such a way that historical events were eloquent in and of themselves", he says.

---

45 Proposition in the sense in which it is generally used in discussions of revelation means, of course, more than 'assertion' or 'proposal' but 'words' in the broader sense. Thus Scripture, while a verbal revelation, is more than bald theological assertions.

46 Helm, *Divine Revelation*, 21–22.

47 B. Ramm, *Special Revelation and the Word of God* (Grand Rapids, MI: Eerdmans, 1971), 154.

48 Morris, *Revelation*, 117–118.

"The historical events are revelatory *only when they are accompanied by the revelatory word*".[49] The prime example is God's supreme self-revelation in the death of Christ. That Christ died is a simple historical fact. But propositional revelation informs us why he died, emphasising in so doing the love of God. Ladd explains:

> The cross by itself did not speak of love and forgiveness. Proof of this may be found in the experience of those who watched Jesus die. Were any of these witnesses overwhelmed with a sense of the love of God, conscious that he [or she] was beholding the awesome spectacle of atonement being made for [human] sins? Did John, or Mary, or the centurion, or the High Priest throw himself in choking joy upon the earth before the cross with the cry, 'I never knew how much God loved me'?[50]

Ladd then states: "It was only after the interpretive word was given to the disciples that they came to understand that the death of Christ was revelatory of the love of God".[51] The event required explanatory words, propositional statements, indeed a whole series of propositional statements. These statements were incorporated into the New Testament, which became the substance of divine revelation for generations to come. Without them, the greatest single revelatory act of God in history would have been lost in antiquity and Christianity would probably not have survived.

Propositional revelation is a logical and necessary consequence of the fact that God has spoken to mankind. It is also an inevitable consequence of inherent human rationality and the use of words in normal discourse. Far from being out-dated, misleading and irrelevant, propositional revelation demonstrates the shallowness of the ill-defined 'encounter' concept, the Enlightenment alternative to the historical reality. Revelation through word and speech, propositional revelation as traditionally understood, is also the necessary corollary to God's will to be known by rational human beings. Morris concludes, "We need not, accordingly, be surprised at the place words occupy in revelation. They are God's way of making his truth known to people" and again, "It is only in the measure that we can trust the record that we can apprehend the revelation".[52]

Revelation and Authority

It remains to consider briefly the ultimate question, that of authority. Should God's revelation in Scripture, the "Word of God" as traditionally

---

49 G. E. Ladd, *A Theology of the New Testament* (Guildford and London: Lutterworth, 1974), 30–31, emphasis in the original.

50 *Ibid.*

51 *Ibid.*, 31.

52 Morris, *Revelation*, 118.

understood, still be regarded as authoritative, particularly in the areas it specifically addresses?

Historically, the answer is clear and unequivocally affirmative. The
phrase "Word of God" arises from the Bible's own testimony about itself
and ever since the Reformation, Protestant creeds and confessions of faith
have affirmed the authority of the Word in the life and belief of the Church
and in the lives of individual believers. Two such documents that have articulated Protestant belief in the English-speaking world are the Anglican
Thirty-Nine Articles of Religion (1562) and the Presbyterian Westminster
Confession of Faith (1643). The former refers to the authority of Holy Scripture, the "canonical books of the Old and New Testament" that "contain all
things necessary to salvation".[53] Article 1 of the Westminster Confession
specifies "the divine authority" of Holy Scripture, to which "the Church is
finally to appeal".[54] These two documents alone have shaped Protestantism
around the world and reflect the deep conviction of millions of Christians
throughout the centuries as well as the nature of historic Protestantism itself. Only the most liberal of liberal theologians would deny any authority
to Scripture, although many appear to have come perilously close to doing
so in our time.

Of more immediate relevance, however, is that reason requires a similar
conclusion. If the Bible is a special divine revelation, to be received therefore as the Word of God, it would be irrational to deny it the authoritative
status it has been accorded throughout Christian history. If God has spoken,
rational man must listen. Morris insists that since revelation has occurred in
and through the Bible, "it is a book which has authority".[55] There is no logical way of avoiding this conclusion. To think otherwise would be contrary
to reason. The attribution of authority to Scripture "follows from the fact"
that the Bible provides evidence of its status as divine revelation.[56] Packer
refers to "the normative authority of Scripture", explaining that unless "we
have direct access to revelation normatively presented, by which we may
test and correct our own fallible notions", we are left "to drift on a sea of
speculations and doubts".[57]

An insidious challenge to the notion of biblical authority arises from
the prevailing contemporary mind-set. It is not merely rejection of biblical
authority that concerns us, although in the context of the present discussion
this is clearly the major issue, but the rejection of authority *per se*. Colin

53 E. Cardwell, *Synodalia* (Oxford: OUP, 1842, reprinted 1966), 56.

54 H. Bettenson, ed., *Documents of the Christian Church* (Oxford: OUP, 1963),
245.

55 Morris, *Revelation*, 138, 136.

56 *Ibid.*, 136.

57 Packer in Henry, ed., *Revelation and the Bible*, 96, 99.

Gunton identifies "the heart of the modern offence with revelation". It is, he says, "rooted in the problem of authority and the way it appears to violate human autonomy".[58] It is, in short, the pervasive influence of humanistic, Enlightenment thinking, the authority of Scripture being its most notable casualty, certainly from a Christian standpoint. The enthronement of "reason only" over revelation has led to a significantly unreasonable conclusion. In her justly acclaimed analysis of the global battle over God, truth and power in modern society, *The World Turned Upside Down*, Melanie Phillips concludes that the present decline of Western culture results from the Enlightenment and post-Enlightenment assault on the authority of the Judaeo-Christian Scriptures. "The attack on Western civilisation at its most profound level is an attack on the creed that lies at the very heart of that civilisation".[59]

Nor is Phillips a lone voice crying in a modern wilderness. Half a century ago Harry Blamires began his perceptive analysis of contemporary Christian thought, *The Christian Mind*, an acknowledgement that Western civilisation was already in deep trouble by the mid-twentieth century, with the startling assertion, "There is no longer a Christian mind", arguing that contemporary Christianity had "succumbed to secularisation".[60] The heart of Blamire's argument is that the true Christian mind is defined by its orientation to the supernatural, its conception of truth and its acceptance of authority.[61] "Our age", he declared, "is in revolt against the very notions that are crucial to Christian thinking and acting".[62] Contemporary secularism, he argued,

> ... heavily biased as it is towards individualism, subjectivism and atomistic intellectualism, is quickly eroding what remains of the Christian mind, ... oriented towards a truth revealed, demanding, and divinely guaranteed, whose objective certitude and authoritativeness are alike distasteful to a secularism deeply committed to self-culture as opposed to self-discipline, and to a destiny of mastery as opposed to rigorous service.[63]

In explaining that the Christian mind is defined by its acceptance of the authority of revelation, Blamires further wrote,

> One cannot seriously contemplate the first elementary truths of Christianity – the doctrine of the divine creation of man and his world, the

---

58 Gunton, *Theology of Revelation*, 32.

59 Melanie Phillips, *The World Turned Upside Down* (New York and London: Encounter, 2010), 316.

60 H. Blamires, *The Christian Mind: How Should a Christian Think?* (Ann Arbor, MI: Servant Books, 1963), 3.

61 He also includes its awareness of evil and its concern for the person.

62 Blamires, *Christian Mind*, 132.

63 *Ibid.*, 130.

doctrine of redemption, and the doctrine of the church, without realis-
ing that here is something which is either authoritative and binding or
false, deserving of submission or of total neglect.[64]

More recently David Wells has reminded us that churches with roots in
the Protestant Reformation accept that truth is revealed in the Word of God.
"There is unanimous agreement", he says, "that this authoritative truth lies
at the heart of Christian life and practice, for this is what it means to live
under the authority of Scripture".[65] Such is the very essence of Protestant
identity. All this, and much more, underlines the binding claims of this special revelation that tells us so clearly of the eternal Christ, the creative Word
and the redeeming Saviour, and explains what it means to believe in him
and to be his disciple. It is an authority that cannot be avoided or evaded for
those who claim discipleship. As Blamires so poignantly puts it, "It is either
the bowed head or the turned back".[66]

The claims of biblical authority apply at every level of Church life and
to each individual Christian. Indeed, Christian authenticity is determined, in
part at least, by the response to God's authoritative revelation in Scripture.
Christian leaders, Christian professionals, doctors, teachers, lawyers, writers, pastors and preachers, academics in all disciplines, tradesmen, business
executives, parents and students – indeed every professing member of the
body of Christ – are all, by virtue of their claim to be Christian, inescapably
subject to the authority of Scripture. It is as inevitable and consequential as
a citizen being subject to the law of the land. Difficult as it may be at times,
the constant eroding pressure of secular, humanistic, culture must be recognised for what it is and resisted in the name of authentic Christianity.

At a time when the challenge to biblical authority was becoming increasingly obvious in the Protestant world, the influential Dutch theologian G.
C. Berkouwer pointed out that the authority of the Bible was threatened not
only from without, but also from within, by those who "really do not subject
themselves to this authority and do not manifest the reality of their confession in their daily lives".[67] It is a sobering call to reflection and reaffirmation.
Recognition and re-emphasis of the twin concepts of revelation and biblical
authority in the life of the Church may be the single most pressing challenge
of our time, to recapture and re-establish them in areas where the insidious

---

64 *Ibid.,* 132. See also David F. Wells, *No Place for Truth, or Whatever Happened to Evangelical Theology?* (Grand Rapids, MI and Cambridge, UK: Eerdmans, 1993), *passim* but especially 99–106, 279–282.

65 Wells, *No Place for Truth,* 99.

66 Blamires, *Christian Mind,* 132.

67 G. C. Berkouwer, *Studies in Dogmatics: Holy Scripture* (Grand Rapids, MI:
Eerdmans, 1975), 35.

infiltration of humanism and liberalism have eroded them in the name of progress and enlightenment. The sure consequences of reaffirmed biblical authority are certainty, hope and motivation. Such commitment is essential for a healthy and vibrant church.

3. The Birth of the English Bible[1]

Bryan Ball

No book has had such a widespread and lasting impact on history or has touched the lives of so many people as the Bible, particularly the Authorised or King James version. First published in 1611, it profoundly influenced the entire English-speaking world for more than 300 years. Yet the story of the English Bible really began much earlier. In one sense 1611 marked the end of the story, rather than its beginning. That story began centuries previously, and for reasons it is important for those who live so much later to understand.

The Times and the Tensions

When the Authorised Version first appeared, Europe in general and England in particular had not long emerged from centuries of medieval ignorance and superstition. It was widely believed at the time – and has since been repeatedly confirmed – that the domination of the medieval Catholic Church throughout Europe in virtually all matters of public and private life was the underlying problem.

There had been various protests at papal excesses and inconsistencies through the centuries, but by the early 16th century a major revolt was inevitable. It came in the form of the Protestant Reformation. Led initially by Martin Luther in Germany, it rapidly spread across much of Europe. The significance of this unprecedented upheaval has since been widely recognised. The distinguished historian Hans Hillerbrand described the Reformation as 'one of the great epochs in the history of Western civilisation'.[2]

During the long medieval period the Bible was literally a closed book, unknown to the vast majority of European people, most of whom were illiterate in any case. Before the invention of the printing press in c. 1439/1440, the Bible was available only in manuscript form, only in Latin and only to the few better-educated priests. Church services were also conducted in

---

1 An earlier version of this chapter was published in *Can We Still Believe the Bible? And Does it Really Matter?* (2nd revised edition; Warburton, Vic: Signs, 2011), to coincide with the 400th anniversary of the Authorised Version. Reprinted with permission.

2 Hans J. Hillerbrand, ed., *The Protestant Reformation* (London and Melbourne: Macmillan, 1968), xi.

Latin and were unintelligible to almost all parishioners. The widespread ignorance and frequent corruption of the parish clergy made matters worse. Not without reason have the Middle Ages also been known as the Dark Ages. By the time the Reformation arrived, it was long overdue.

Perhaps Luther's greatest contribution to the Reformation in his homeland and to the development of German culture was his translation of the Bible into the German language – finally in 1533 but first with the New Testament in 1522. Although there had been some translations of parts of the Bible into German before Luther, his translation was a masterpiece which for "the next two or three hundred years was to mould the German language".[3]

Rather than translating from the Latin Vulgate, the only available printed Bible at the time, Luther used the best available Greek and Hebrew manuscripts. He expressed the hope that as a result of his work, "the German lark would sing as well as the Greek nightingale".[4] History confirms that indeed it did. Much the same could be said of many other European countries where the Bible was translated into the language of the people. Roland Bainton, another authority on Reformation history, commented, "The Reformers dethroned the pope and enthroned the Bible".[5]

A similar situation had already been developing in England. Widespread unhappiness with the ignorance and immorality of the clergy and the perceived excesses of the church had surfaced much earlier. John Wycliffe, 'the morning star of the Reformation' and an Oxford doctor of theology, had voiced his revolutionary concerns in the 1370s. Tried as a heretic in 1377 and again in 1382, Wycliffe was forced to leave Oxford. His chief offence was that he had challenged the basis of papal teachings. He claimed that the Bible was the only true source of Christian belief and the standard of life in the church and for each individual. He argued that every person should be able to read the Scriptures in their native tongue. Claire Cross, a noted Wycliffe scholar, says that after he retired to his parish of Lutterworth in 1381, Wycliffe continued to write against papal teachings, advocating a return to apostolic simplicity, "contrasting the Church of Christ with the Church of Antichrist ... and supporting the opening of the sacred scriptures to the laity".[6]

Wycliffe died in 1384, having "created a hunger for the Bible in the tongue of the common man"[7] and also having attracted a considerable num-

---

3 Richard Friedenthal, *Luther* (London: Weidenfeld and Nicholson, 1970), 310.

4 James Atkinson, *The Great Light: Luther and the Reformation* (Grand Rapids, MI: Eerdmans, 1968), 71.

5 See S. L. Greenslade, ed., *The Cambridge History of the Bible* (Grand Rapids, MI: Baker, 1963), vol.3, 1.

6 Claire Cross, *Church and People, 1450 –1660* (London: Fontana, 1976), 15.

7 Donald Brake, *A Visual History of the English Bible* (Grand Rapids, MI:

ber of followers in many parts of the country. They were known as Lollards, from the old Dutch word *lollen* meaning to 'mumble, or 'murmer', because as they travelled from place to place they would sing quietly or mumble the words of Scripture they had committed to memory, sharing what they had learnt of the Bible with many willing hearers. The Lollards recognised a hunger for the Scriptures among the common people and the desire to have it in their own language that later moved the German people to support Luther.

Since Wycliffe's teachings had taken hold across much of the country, legislation was enacted by Parliament in 1401 with the ominously worded anti-heresy Act, *De Haeretico Comburendo,* "Concerning the Burning of Heretics". Thereafter a steady stream of Lollards from many parts of the country appeared before the courts, many ending up in prison or at the stake. They persisted in large numbers well into the next century and were always known principally for their emphasis on the Bible. A few examples must suffice. Foxe's famous *Book of Martyrs*, as well as several other sources, contains many more.

- William Smith of Leicester had taught himself to read and write in order to produce manuscripts based on the Bible to share with others. He was brought before the courts in 1398.
- William Scrivener, from Amersham, was put to death for 'heresy' in 1511. He owned a copy of the Ten Commandments and the Gospels of Matthew and Mark.
- A Richard Collins owned a copy of the Gospel of Luke, the book of Revelation and one of Paul's epistles. Alice, his wife, could recite the Ten Commandments and the Epistles of James and Peter, which she did frequently at Lollard gatherings.
- Another convicted 'heretic', John Pykas, had taught others the Ten Commandments and the Lord's Prayer in English and knew of other Lollards who could recite the Epistles of James and John.[8]
- Thomas Bilney was burned at Norwich in 1531 as a 'relapsed heretic' for preaching and for distributing copies of Tyndale's New Testament.

It is recorded that many Lollards sat up all night reading or listening to the words of Scripture. Cross states that many of the more illiterate among them learned to read "with the express purpose of reaching the kernel of the Scriptures for themselves".[9] At a time when manuscripts were costly to purchase, many were willing to pay large sums for just small portions of the

---

Baker, 2008), 49.

8 For these and other Lollards with similar views, see Cross, *Church and People,* 32– 42.

9 Cross, *Church and People,* 34.

Bible. Some gave a load of hay for a few chapters of the New Testament. As we have seen, some were willing to pay with their lives.

Lollard enthusiasm for the Bible persisted throughout the fifteenth century, until the beginnings of the English Reformation in the reign of Henry VIII. This same passion for the Bible undergirded the Reformation in England, the dismantling of the corrupt medieval church and the establishment of Protestant England, greatly helping them on their way. Lollard faithfulness to Scripture was, in reality, a significant factor in the early development of Western civilisation.

Three things in particular, then, characterised the people of England in the times leading up to the first printed translations of the Bible:
- A great respect for Scripture;
- A great desire to be able to read it in their own language;
- A great thirst to understand its meaning and message for themselves.

In his beautifully illustrated book, *A Visual History of the English Bible*, Donald Brake stresses the vital place of the Bible in the success of the Reformation in England. He says that without the Bible "the English Reformation would have languished in the dungeons of Henry VIII", and points out that "for the first time, every literate person could read and understand God's Word".[10]

Early English Translations

The story of the English Bible actually begins centuries before Wycliffe and the 14th- and 15th- century Lollards. In his history of the English Bible, Donald Coggan reminds us that "the beginnings of the Bible in Britain must forever be wrapped in the mists of obscurity".[11] While this is undeniably true, notable peaks can be discerned through those ancient swirling mists. No account of the origins of the English Bible is complete without at least a glimpse of them.

First, chronologically if not for literary merit, is **Caedmon of Whitby**, an illiterate cowherd attached to the great monastery at Whitby in the county of Northumberland. A fascinating story concerning Caedmon has persisted through the centuries, even finding its way into the *Oxford Dictionary of National Biography*. In about the year AD 670 Caedmon, it is said, received a vision in which he heard a voice calling him by name. That night, it was widely believed, Caedmon suddenly became proficient in music and poetry. F. F. Bruce tells us that Caedmon, previously "ungifted in poetry and song",

---

10 Brake, *English Bible*, 50.

11 Donald Coggan, *The English Bible* (London: Longmans, Green and Co., 1963), 13.

began to turn the biblical record, told to him by the Whitby monks, into melodious verse.[12]

The monk and early English historian, Bede, in his renowned *Ecclesiastical History of England*, written shortly after Caedmon's experience, tells it like this:

> He sang of the creation of the world, the origin of man and all the history of Genesis, the departure of the children of Israel out of Egypt, their entrance into the promised land, and many other histories from Holy Scripture; the incarnation, passion and resurrection of our Lord, and his ascension into heaven; the coming of the Holy Ghost, and the teaching of the Apostles.[13]

Professor Bruce contends that through his verse, Caedmon created a "people's Bible", unwritten but sung and shared in a Northumbrian dialect of the Anglo-Saxon tongue. A later manuscript of more than 200 pages of Caedmon's verse is now housed in the Bodleian Library in Oxford.[14] Without committing a word to parchment or vellum, Caedmon became the first 'translator' of large portions of the Bible into the Old English language.[15]

Aldhelm of Sherborne is next discernible through the mists of antiquity. He was the first bishop of this historic Dorset town in south-western England and was regarded as one of the most prominent scholars of his day. In about AD 700 Aldhelm translated some of the Psalms into Anglo-Saxon, thus providing the first known written translation of any part of the Bible into Old English.

Shortly thereafter **Bede**, "the father of English history", whose learning was renowned throughout Western Europe, translated parts of the Bible into the Anglo-Saxon of his day, including the Lord's Prayer and the Gospel of John. He completed the latter on the day he died in AD 735. According to another respected scholar, Sir Frederic Kenyon, Bede was driven by the same vision that compelled the Lollards 700 years later: "That the Scriptures might be faithfully delivered to the common people in their own tongue".[16]

Mention must also be made of **Aelfred** or **King Alfred the Great** who, in an age of widespread illiteracy, was one of the few literate English monarchs up to that time. Alfred is remembered for his desire to reform the

---

12 F. F. Bruce, *History of the Bible in English* (Oxford: OUP, 1978), 2–3.

13 A. M. Sellar, tr, *Bede's Ecclesiastical History of England* (London: George Bell & Son, 1907), 279.

14 Bruce, 3; David Marshall, *The Battle for the* Book (Grantham: Autumn House, 1991), 101.

15 Old English prevailed between the mid-5th century (c. AD 450) to the mid-12th century (c. AD 1150); Middle English from about 1150 to about 1500, and modern English from about 1500 onward.

16 F. G. Kenyon, *Our Bible and the Ancient Manuscripts* (London: Eyre and Spottiswoode, 4th edit., 1939), 195.

church of his day and to promote learning throughout his kingdom. This latter goal was, it is widely recognised, "the most distinctive feature of his rule".[17] He introduced a noted code of law which contained a translation of the Ten Commandments, passages from Exodus and the book of Acts, and a notation that Christ "had come not shatter or annul the commandments but to fulfil them". He had begun translating the Psalms when he died in AD 901.

More distinct peaks can now be seen through those ancient mists. The world-famous and intricately beautiful **Lindisfarne Gospels,** originally written or copied in about AD 698 in Latin, are attributed to the monk **Eadfrith**. In about 970 a literal translation into Anglo-Saxon of many passages was added beneath the Latin, making the meaning of the text clear in the vernacular tongue. These later translations or explanations, known as glosses, became increasingly popular with scholars working with older manuscripts.

At about the same time, the first known translation of the four gospels, now known as the **Wessex Gospels,** appeared in Old English. Attributed by some to **Aelfric of Bath**, this historic manuscript can be seen in the British Library, together with many other priceless manuscripts and documents relating to the history of the English Bible. Aelfric also translated parts of several Old Testament books, including passages from the Pentateuch, Kings, Job and Daniel.

It is possible, then, to discern several significant attempts to translate the Bible, or parts of it, into the Old English or Anglo-Saxon language before AD 1000. All were important contributions to the story of the English Bible. However, the Norman invasion of 1066 brought an abrupt halt to the use of Anglo-Saxon by imposing French and Latin as the spoken and written languages of Church and State. Thus Old English became merely the language of the common people. Only after another 300 years or more did English reappear as the language of scholarship as well as the language of ordinary communication. By then it had been transformed by the addition of thousands of new words and phrases from Latin and French, and the stage was set for a new chapter in the story of the English Bible.

The 'Wycliffe' Bible

The 'Wycliffe' Bible is one of two early translations that had a profound influence on the Authorised Version of 1611. As the first complete Bible in the English language, albeit in the Middle English of the late 14th and early 15th centuries, it was a milestone in the development of both social and religious history. It was produced against a background of heated theological controversy and we can only fully understand Wycliffe and his followers if

---

17 S. Lee, ed., *Concise Dictionary of National Biography,* under 'Aelfred'.

we first understand why they reacted so strongly to the medieval Church of the day.

As previously noted, Wycliffe was much concerned by the ignorance and immorality of many priests, as well as the general condition of the Church in the 1370s and 1380s. His Lollard followers shared the same convictions – but there was more. In 1378 the papacy had been split by two rival popes, Clement VII, who resided at Avignon in France, and Urban VI, located in Rome. Known now as the 'Great Schism' in the medieval papacy, this situation lasted until 1417. It was made even more ludicrous by the election of a third pope at Pisa in 1409, all three claiming to be the true successor of St Peter. As this undignified scenario unfolded, Wycliffe himself was already writing and speaking against the wealth of the papacy, the ostentatious lifestyle of many church dignitaries, and the sale of indulgences to raise further income from already over-burdened working people.

Wycliffe thus called for the Bible to be translated into English and for its teachings to be recognised as the standard for the corporate life of the Church. This included the daily life of individual members and all church dignitaries. A. G. Dickens says, "He accepted the Bible as the sure basis of belief, and demanded that it should be freely placed in lay hands".[18] Wycliffe himself said,

> Holy Scripture is the faith of the Church, and the more widely its true meaning becomes known the better it will be. Therefore since the laity should know the faith, it should be taught in whatever language is most easily comprehended. Christ and his Apostles taught the people in the language best known to them.[19]

And so it happened. The 'Wycliffe' translation of the New Testament first appeared in 1380, followed in 1384, the year in which Wycliffe died, by the rest of the Bible. It is known as the 'Early Wycliffe Bible'.

An important clarification needs to be made here. Although known since as 'Wycliffe's' Bible, it is almost certain that Wycliffe did not translate most of it. He may have been responsible for certain parts of the New Testament but the majority of it was the work of his followers at Oxford, careful scholars who shared Wycliffe's convictions and aspirations. Chief among them was John Purvey, who became leader of the Lollards after Wycliffe's death. This first Wycliffite Bible was a strict and literal translation from Jerome's Latin Vulgate and did not read easily in English. In some places it followed the Latin so closely that it could hardly be understood. Nevertheless, it was a huge leap forward in making the Bible available to the people, even though still in manuscript form.

---

18 A. G. Dickens, *The English Reformation* (London: Batsford, 1964), 22.
19 Cited in Brake, *English Bible,* 47–48.

Shortly after Wycliffe's death another translation of the complete Bible was produced by Wycliffe's Oxford disciples. Known as the 'Later Wycliffe Bible', it was also produced under the guidance of John Purvey. It appeared in 1388, or soon afterward, and although it was still a translation of the Latin Vulgate – Greek manuscripts were rarely available in the late 14th century – it read much more easily in English. Still in manuscript form, it became the predominant English Bible until the time of Tyndale nearly 150 years later. Its influence was incalculable. In the introduction to the 2002 British Library reprint of the 1388 Wycliffe New Testament, Dr W. R. Cooper describes it as a "magnificent translation, a superior, powerful rendition of the Scriptures",[20] which "truly heralded the dawning of the great English Reformation". It is still, he adds, "a monument to be read and cherished'.[21]

Despite prohibition, confiscation and destruction, the copying, reading and proliferation of Wycliffe's Bible continued for more than a century. Some even preferred it after printed Bibles became available in the 16th century, such were its power and attraction. More than 200 copies of Wycliffe's Bible have survived, in part or in whole, most of them copies of the 'Later' Wycliffe version and many of them showing evidence of great usage. It is clear testimony to the widespread production, distribution and use of the Wycliffe Bible during the 15th and early 16th centuries.

Wycliffe died at Lutterworth in 1384, convinced of his stand to the end. But in the eyes of the Church he was a convicted heretic, excommunicated and lucky to have died in his bed, judging by what happened to many of his followers. In 1415, more than 30 years later, the Council of Constance condemned his writings yet again and ordered that his remains be disinterred and burned. This eventually happened in 1428. His ashes were cast into the river Swift, which carried them into the Avon, thence to the Severn and the sea, a fitting if unintended symbol of the ever-widening influence of Wycliffe's teachings and writings, and of the first English translation of the Bible.

Tyndale's New Testament

William Tyndale has been called "the father of the English Bible" and his 1526 New Testament the "jewel in the crown" of that Bible.[22] It had an immense impact on the English religious scene and its effects are still with us today. The broadcaster and scholar Melvyn Bragg argues that Tyndale's

---

20 W. R. Cooper, ed., *The Wycliffe New Testament* (London: British Library, 2002), vii.

21 *Ibid.*, viii.

22 H. W. Robinson, *The Bible in Ancient and English Versions* (Oxford: Clarendon, 1954), 149; David Daniell, *William Tyndale: A Biography* (New Haven, CN and London: Yale University, 1994), 6.

New Testament is "probably the most influential book in the history of the language".[23] It was, after Wycliffe, the second of those early English translations which profoundly influenced the Authorised Version of 1611. Professor David Daniell even claims that through his New Testament, Tyndale has influenced more people than Shakespeare.

Two world-changing events had occurred in the years between the Wycliffe Bibles and Tyndale's New Testament. Firstly, Johannes Gutenberg had invented the printing press in Germany in c.1439/1440 and soon afterward, in 1455, had produced the first printed book — the famous Gutenberg Bible. Then, in 1453, the 1000-year-old Byzantine city of Constantinople had fallen to the Islamic Ottomans, an event with considerable political, social and religious implications. Though it was seen as a massive blow to Christianity, it was not entirely bad. Many Christian scholars fled to Europe, taking with them old Greek and Latin manuscripts previously unknown in the West. Had these two momentous events not occurred, Tyndale's great work would not have been possible.

Like Wycliffe before him, Tyndale was an accomplished scholar, educated at Oxford and possibly also at Cambridge. He was proficient in eight languages, with particular skill in Hebrew, Greek and Latin, all of which were essential for accurate Bible translation. He was regarded by many as England's best Greek scholar of the time. But Tyndale was unhappy with the Oxford scene — especially its emphasis on Greek and Roman authors and the philosophical rationalisation that undergirded the study of theology. Alister McGrath points out that for Tyndale "theology was worthy of the name only when it took its lead directly from the Bible".[24] Moreover, in the early 1500s Oxford was still intent on eliminating the Wycliffite 'heresy'.

Reacting against all this, and the sorry state of the English clergy that had changed little since Wycliffe's day, Tyndale's life work began to take shape in his mind. After university, Tyndale found employment for a short time in the home of Sir John Walsh of Little Sodbury in Gloucestershire as tutor to the Walsh's two young sons. While there, Tyndale's conviction of the pressing need for a Bible in the English language found expression. In a discussion with a Gloucestershire priest whose knowledge of the Bible was minimal, Tyndale uttered the famous words that have come down to us across 400 years: "If God spare my life, ere many years I will cause a boy that driveth a plough shall know more of the Scripture than thou dost". History testifies to the unquestionable fulfilment of this compelling vision.

23 Melvyn Bragg, *The Adventure of English*, TimeLife DVD, SBS 2008, Disc One, Episode 3.

24 Alister McGrath, *In the Beginning: The Story of the King James Bible* (London: Hodder and Stoughton, 2001), 69.

Tyndale had wanted to undertake his work in England, with the blessing of the Bishop of London, Cuthbert Tunstall. It was, perhaps, a naive hope given that his initial approach to Tunstall took place in 1523, thirteen years before the formal beginning of the English Reformation. Whilst a moderate and a scholar himself, Tunstall was also one of the leaders of the prevailing Catholic Church. Tyndale had few remaining options. He left England and went first to Germany, arriving in Cologne in 1525. While there, he finished the work of translation and the printing of the New Testament began. But being discovered by his enemies, Tyndale and his friends were forced to leave, taking everything with them to Worms. There the printing of the entire New Testament in English was completed by February 1526.

Perhaps the most important fact about Tyndale's New Testament is that it was translated directly from the best available Greek manuscripts of the day, and not from the Latin Vulgate. It was not a translation of a translation but a translation from the original — the first in the history of the English Bible. It was as true to the original as possible, presented in gripping but straightforward English. McGrath states that there is evidence to suggest that many people used it to learn to read "as well as to learn about the Christian faith".[25] F. F. Bruce noted Tyndale's "honesty, sincerity and scrupulous integrity", commenting on the "magical simplicity of phrase" that gave his work an "authority" that has lasted until today.[26]

Some 3,000 copies were printed in a small, pocket-sized edition that was soon available in London and other places in southern and eastern England. It had to be smuggled into the country in bales of cloth or bags of flour, or concealed in the false bottoms of wine casks. The translation was immediately popular — and immediately banned. Efforts to suppress and destroy it were intense. Boats were requisitioned to guard the south-eastern shores of England to prevent it being landed in the country. W. R. Cooper tells us that even listening to it being read was punishable by death. Many copies, perhaps most, were burnt on the orders of Bishop Tunstall. Only three copies are known to have survived. One of them, complete but for the title page, is now in the British Library, bought from Bristol Baptist College for a reported one million pounds.

Two leading authorities, Alister McGrath and David Daniell, both describe the printing of Tyndale's New Testament as a "landmark". McGrath says it was a landmark "in the history of the English Bible" and Daniell calls it a landmark in "the history of all English-speaking peoples".[27] It was,

---

25 *Ibid.*, 78.

26 Bruce, *History of the Bible*, 44

27 McGrath, 1; David Daniell in W. R .Cooper, ed., *New Testament, 1526* (London: British Library, 2000), v.

of course, both — and more. It eventually played a major role in shaping the Authorised Version and through it the social and religious history of the English-speaking world. It helped chart the course of Western civilisation for at least three centuries. Its first arrival in England has been described as "arguably the most important single event … of the English Reformation".[28] It is equally arguable that it was the catalyst for the spread of Protestantism throughout the entire English-speaking world, thus impacting the lives of untold millions for nearly five centuries. Yet it had almost been wiped out within a few months of its appearance.

This remarkable book was so popular and demand so great that supplies of the first edition quickly ran out. Soon unauthorised pirated editions were being printed in Europe and shipped to England. Two such editions of about 5,000 copies each were hastily printed in Antwerp, but proved to be full of errors. And there were others, including at least one unauthorised edition printed in England. In 1534 Tyndale decided to publish a revised edition himself, which he did, in even better English than the original. His name was added to the title page and many improvements were made in the text. Another printing was issued in 1535. This edition was, in Daniell's words, "the glory of his lifework" and the New Testament "as English speakers have known it until the last few decades of the twentieth century".[29] It was the text of this edition that eventually found its way almost verbatim into the Authorised Version.

Many have written about Tyndale's New Testament through the years, reminding successive generations of its immense significance. The following comment by Dr Cooper, from his introduction to the British Library's reprint of the 1526 Tyndale New Testament, is as good a summary as any:

> Its impact on arrival in England was immediate, and almost impossible to calculate in terms of spiritual revival and political upheaval. Every effort was made to suppress and destroy the 'perfidious' work, but to no avail. The more it was suppressed, the more it was read. And the more it was read, the more people's eyes were opened, and the sooner was brought about the downfall in this land of the mediaeval Papacy, and the pretensions of a hopelessly corrupt church.[30]

If influence is to be judged by popularity and readership, we should remember that between 1526 and 1566 at least 40 editions of Tyndale's New Testament were printed, with an estimated circulation of more than 50,000 copies.

Mention must also be made of Tyndale's important work on the Old Testament, since his original aim had been to translate the entire Bible into Eng-

---

28 Cooper, *New Testament,* ix.
29 Daniell, *Tyndale,* 331.
30 Cooper, *New Testament,* ix.

lish. By 1530, working from the Hebrew text, he had completed translating the Pentateuch, again succeeding in putting it into language that could easily be understood. Compared to some other translations, to read Tyndale's Old Testament has been described as like "seeing the road ahead through a windscreen that has been suddenly wiped".[31]

Tyndale's Pentateuch was published in 1530 and again in 1534. By the time of his death in 1536 he had translated at least ten more books of the Old Testament. Most of this also went straight into the Authorised Version. Bishop Westcott wrote in 1868 that Tyndale directly contributed to the Authorised Version "half of the Old Testament, as well as almost the whole of the New".[32] There can be little doubt that Tyndale was indeed "the father of the English Bible".

But it was all accomplished at a terrible price. While still working on the Old Testament in Antwerp in 1535, Tyndale was betrayed to the authorities by English spies. He was arrested and imprisoned in Vilvorde castle near Brussels. After more than a year in prison, he was eventually tried and condemned to death as a heretic. Dr Daniell tersely notes that "in netting Tyndale the heresy-hunters had their largest catch".[33] In October, 1536, after a perfunctory trial, Tyndale was brought to the stake, bound and then strangled. His body was then burned, but his last words have persisted through more than four centuries: "Lord, open the king of England's eyes".

Tyndale would have been amazed at how soon that fervent prayer was answered. Within a year of Tyndale's death, Henry VIII's eyes had indeed been opened, his mind changed and two versions of the English Bible officially approved. The course of English history, and ultimately that of other English-speaking peoples, had been radically and irreversibly changed.

Other Early English Translations

Tyndale's New Testament precipitated something of an avalanche. Between 1535 and 1611, less than eighty years, at least seven new complete translations of the Bible were produced in English, most of them also printed in England. They all played an important part in the developing story of the English Bible and together they are undeniable evidence of great interest, great activity, and a new and more enlightened England.

Prior to Tyndale's death, one of his disciples and helpers, Miles Coverdale, later Bishop of Exeter, another competent scholar and reformer, produced a translation of the Bible in 1535 while exiled in Europe. **Coverdale's Bible** was the first complete printed English Bible. It was, however, a sec-

---

31 Daniell, *Tyndale,* 312.

32 B. F. Westcott, *The History of the English Bible* (London: Macmillan, 1927), 158.

33 Daniell, *Tyndale,* 375.

ondary translation, based on Luther's German Bible and the Latin Vulgate as well as all Tyndale's Old Testament translations and his New Testament. It was printed in Europe and dedicated to Henry VIII. After taking advice, Henry approved Coverdale's work. Although this Bible was never 'authorised' by royal decree, it was officially licensed. Coverdale's English was often smoother than that of Tyndale and, for the first time, the books of the Apocrypha were separated from the rest of the Old Testament. A note was included, explaining that they did not appear in the Hebrew Scriptures and therefore did not have the same authority.

Just two years later, in 1537, **Matthew's Bible** was published in London, although probably printed in Antwerp. 'Matthew' was a pseudonym for the translator John Rogers, another Tyndale supporter. His Bible consisted of Tyndale's Pentateuch and other Old Testament translations, the remainder of the Old Testament from Coverdale's Bible, and Tyndale's New Testament. The bulk of Matthew's Bible was thus the work of Tyndale, a point not to be missed, for it later turned out to be the foundation of all later English versions. It has been calculated that 65 per cent of Matthew's entire Bible was straight from Tyndale, and all later Protestant translations were essentially revisions of this text. It was licensed by Henry VIII and was circulating in England within a year of Tyndale's death. Rogers, however, was to meet a similar fate as Tyndale, and became the first victim of persecution under the Catholic Queen Mary. He was burnt at the stake at Smithfield in London in 1555.

In 1539, Richard Taverner, another noted Greek scholar, published what was basically a minor revision of Matthew's Bible with only a few changes. **Taverner's Bible** introduced some new Saxon words into the English text, though his New Testament remained essentially Tyndale and his Old Testament a combination of Tyndale and Coverdale. Its influence on later versions was minimal and some accounts of the English Bible do not even include Taverner's translation. Taverner spent some time in the Tower of London for his work on the Bible but he survived the persecutions under Mary and was later favoured by Elizabeth I.

In that same year, a more substantial and influential Bible appeared in England. It was known as **The Great Bible**, since it was larger than any previously printed English Bible. It carried on its title page the announcement "This Bible is appointed to the use of the churches", meaning that it was authorised by Henry VIII to be read in church as well as privately. It was intended that a copy be placed in every church in the land. Wherever this happened, people flocked to see the Bible publicly displayed and to hear it read. It was the first Bible many of them had ever seen, and it was also eagerly bought and read at home.

Described as both "evangelical" and "scholarly", the Great Bible went through six printings before the end of 1541, with an extensive revision in 1540 and many later editions and reprints. Its translation and production was overseen by Coverdale and was a revision of Matthew's Bible, which in turn had been a revision of Tyndale's work, although it excluded most of the controversial strongly Protestant notes that had been included in Matthew's Bible. Toward the end of Henry's reign, an anti-Protestant reaction set in, and more Bibles were burnt. The Great Bible was the last of the English Bibles printed before the return of Catholicism under Queen Mary.

During the years of suppression and persecution, particularly those of Mary's reign (1553–58), hundreds of English believers sought refuge in Continental Europe. Many of them found a temporary home in Geneva, a strong Protestant centre. It was there that the next English Bible was prepared, translated by William Whittingham. The complete **Geneva Bible** was first published in 1560 and rapidly became popular throughout England, where it was the most widely read Bible for the next fifty years. It ran to one hundred and forty printings between 1560 and 1644. It was also read widely in Scotland, where the parliament made it compulsory for all householders with adequate income to buy a copy. It too was based largely on Tyndale and also the Great Bible, revised with particular attention to those parts of the Old Testament that Tyndale had not translated.

The Geneva Bible was the first English Bible to divide the text into verses. It soon became known as the 'Breeches Bible' on account of its rendering of Genesis 3:7, where it was recorded that Adam and Eve sewed together fig leaves "and made themselves breeches". Its most distinctive features were the copious marginal notes of a strongly Calvinistic nature, which greatly influenced the rise and development of English Puritanism. Of this Gerald Hammond wrote, "Of all English versions the Geneva Bible had probably the greatest political significance, in its preparing a generation of radical Puritans to challenge, with the Word of God, their tyrant rulers".[34] He had in mind the long struggle against the Church/State alliance, the English Civil Wars, the eventual overthrow of royal and ecclesiastical domination and, perhaps even the founding of the American colonies.

Although popular with the people, the Geneva Bible was not regarded as suitable for the churches on account of its marginal notes. As Elizabeth's reign began to develop, a new version was deemed necessary to replace the Great Bible that had been authorised for this purpose. Under the guidance of Matthew Parker, Archbishop of Canterbury, and with the assistance of the English bishops, **The Bishops' Bible** was first published in 1568, and

---

34 Gerald Hammond, *The Making of the English Bible* (Manchester: Carcanet, 1982), 136.

in 1571 all parish churches were ordered to obtain a copy. It remained the official English version until the introduction of the Authorised Version in 1611. The result was one Bible for church — the Bishops' Bible, and another Bible for home and the people — the Geneva Bible. The latter remained in print until 1644, long after the last edition of the Bishops' Bible had been printed in 1602.

Apart from following the Geneva Bible in dividing the text into verses, the Bishops' Bible was based entirely on the Great Bible. Parker gave instructions to the translators to follow that version closely, except "where it varieth manifestly from the Hebrew or Greek original".[35] There were relatively few changes of any significance in the text but the new Bishops' Bible contained only a few marginal notes, the offending Calvinism of the Geneva Bible having been removed. One interesting feature of the Bishops' Bible was that the New Testament was printed on thicker paper, since it was believed that it would be read more than the Old Testament — "because it should be more occupied", to use the quaint words of Archbishop Parker's instructions. It has been suggested this directive completely misunderstood the spirit and tradition of English Bible reading, and this is probably correct.

All the English Bibles surveyed to this point were Protestant Bibles. They were of the Reformation and for the Reformation. However, by the end of the 16th century, with Protestantism well established in the land and Catholicism on the defensive, the Catholic Church recognised the need for a Bible acceptable to those of the Catholic faith, "free from the heretical renderings in the earlier English Bibles".[36] The result was the **Rheims-Douai Bible,** the New Testament translated first by scholars from the English Catholic College in Douai and published in Rheims in 1582. The Old Testament was based on the Latin Vulgate rather than from the original language manuscripts and retained much of the old Latin vocabulary of the medieval church.

The Rheims-Douai Version was intended to reflect the old faith and remained in use among English Catholics for three centuries. The article in the *Oxford Dictionary of the Christian Church* on this Bible refers to the "dogmatic intentions of its authors", while another writer points out that the marginal notes rather than the text "made the book so strongly sectarian".[37] In its favour was the fact that the Vulgate was based on Greek manuscripts older than any available to the translators of any of the other English versions, including the Authorised Version. A. W. Pollard concluded neverthe-

35 Greenslade, ed., *Cambridge History of the Bible,* 3, 159.

36 F. L. Cross and E. A. Livingstone, eds., *Oxford Dictionary of the Christian Church* (Oxford: OUP, 3rd edit., 1997), under 'Douai-Rheims Bible'.

37 Elizabeth Eisenhart, ed., *A Ready Reference History of the English Bible* (New York: American Bible Society, 1976), 25.

less that it was "a devoted attempt by the Jesuits to win back England to the faith".[38] He was most likely correct, even though the Rheims-Douai Bible did not enjoy wide circulation at any time during its long life.

The Authorised Version

When James I came to the throne of England and Ireland in 1603, it was evident that no existing version of the English Bible was acceptable to all parties in the English Church. A new version was needed which perhaps would bring unity to the Church and the nation. The decision to proceed was made in 1604 at the famous Hampton Court conference, on a proposal by Dr John Reynolds, the Puritan president of Corpus Christi College, Oxford. It was endorsed by King James, who was a keen and accomplished Bible student and who firmly believed that earlier versions were inadequate since they were not in all respects true to the original languages.

Work eventually began in 1607, in accordance with a process that was to set the pattern for future major translations. It was to be undertaken by a large and representative team of well-qualified scholars, rather than as previously by one or two individuals. In this way bias would be eliminated or countered and the objective of the enterprise assured. This team set out to produce a version of the Bible that was moderate, leaning neither to the left nor the right, neither to Puritanism nor Catholicism.

James himself specified that "the best learned in both universities" should make up the translation team. Accordingly, most of the leading biblical and oriental scholars from Cambridge and Oxford were appointed, together with a few suitably qualified laymen. There were in total 47 (perhaps 48), Anglican and Puritan, carefully chosen for their skills and all "notably competent", in the words of one record. They were divided into six groups, each responsible for a section of the Bible, with their work to be submitted for final approval to a team of 12, composed of the two leading members of each of the six teams. The final revision was to be approved by the king and his council.

The six groups were to work in accordance with guidelines drawn up by Richard Bancroft, the new Archbishop of Canterbury, and approved by the king. The first and most important rule stipulated that the new version was to be based on the Bishops' Bible, "as little altered" from it "as the truth of the original will permit".[39] In other words, it was to be a revision rather than a new translation, a fact frequently forgotten. Reference to earlier English versions was permitted, even encouraged. Rule 14 specified which of the previ-

---

38 A. W. Pollard, 'The Earlier English Translations' in *The Holy Bible, King James Version* (Peabody, MA: Hendrickson, 2000), 25.

39 Cited in McGrath, *In the Beginning,* 173.

ous English versions might be consulted and all were named, except that of Taverner. Reference to available original Hebrew and Greek texts was also encouraged. German and French translations could also be consulted, and the influence of the Rheims New Testament can also be detected.

The guidelines further laid down that existing chapter and verse divisions should be retained, only marginal notes that explained difficult Hebrew and Greek words should be included and the widest possible consultation should take place at every stage in order to ensure the accuracy of the text and its faithfulness to the original languages. The outcome of this well-structured and well-supervised process was exactly what had been intended — a better version of the English Bible than any previously issued. When work on the Revised Version began in 1881, the revisers wrote of the Authorised Version:

> We have had to study this great version carefully and minutely, line by line, and the longer we have been engaged upon it the more we have learned to admire its simplicity, its dignity, its power, its happy turns of expression, its general accuracy, and, we must not fail to add, the music of its cadences and the felicities of its rhythm.[40]

The passing of time has not altered the essential accuracy of this generous assessment.

The Authorised Version was what is now known as a 'formal' translation, the most distinguished in a long line of such translations that has continued until the present day. Wherever possible, it attempted to ensure that every word in the original was translated by an equivalent English word. This word-for-word approach requires careful balancing. While the meaning of the original language takes precedence, the receptor language must also be accurate and intelligible. Words in the translation that were not in the original were generally shown in italics in the translated text. One writer observes:

> Such understanding is found in the King James Bible, which retains the word order of the original to a remarkable extent, while still making allowances for the resulting text to be, in the first place, recognisably English and in the second, intelligible.[41]

An important result of this way of translating is that a large number of Hebrew and Greek words and idioms have passed into the English language, and thence into all succeeding English literature. It is just one way in which the Authorised Version has influenced the development of the Western world.

We have now returned to the starting point of this chapter — the influence of the Bible in general and of the Authorised Version in particular.

---

40 Preface to the *Revised Version,* 1881.
41 McGrath, *In the Beginning,* 252.

All who have seriously considered the story of the Authorised Version in any depth have commented on this amazing influence. Quotations could be multiplied to prove this point. Let it simply be noted here again that this version of the English Bible made a significant impact on the development of Western civilisation. When we acknowledge the Authorised Version, we acknowledge who we are and where we have come from, perhaps without even knowing it.

A few tributes, then, of many which could be cited. The American scholar, Laura Wild, called the Authorised Version 'our English classic' and observed,

> Out of the fire came this book, so simple and direct, so beautiful and resonant in rhythm, so majestic and inspiring in tone that as literature it is said even to surpass the original, and no one influence has been so great in the life of English-speaking people, religiously, morally, socially, politically, as has this version.[42]

The twentieth-century English scholar, Sir Frederic Kenyon, to whom all later biblical scholars owe such an immense debt, wrote of the Authorised Version,

> It has been the Bible, not merely of public use, not merely of one sect or party, not even of a single country, but of the whole nation and of every English-speaking country on the face of the globe. It has been the literature of millions who have read little else, it has been the guide of conduct to men and women of every class in life and of every rank in learning and education ... It was the work, not of one man, nor of one age, but of many labourers, of diverse and even opposing views, over a period of ninety years. It was watered with the blood of martyrs, and its slow growth gave time for the casting off of all imperfections and for the full accomplishment of its destiny as the Bible of the English nation.[43]

Alister McGrath has recently put it more succinctly, "Our culture has been enriched by the King James Bible. Sadly, we shall never see its equal, or even its like, again".[44]

Postscript: Beyond 1611

It might be thought that what has been said to this point leads to the conclusion that the Authorised Version is the best — perhaps the only — acceptable English translation of the Bible. Indeed, as an earlier writer noted, the Authorised Version has "become so sanctified by time and use that to many people it has come to be regarded as *the* Bible". He discerningly points out

---

42 Laura Wild, *The Romance of the English Bible* (New York: Doubleday, 1929), 195–196.
43 Kenyon, *Our Bible,* 234.
44 McGrath, *In the Beginning,* 310.

this view reflects an attitude "comparable to that taken toward the Latin Vulgate by the mediaeval church".[45] So, significant and influential though the Authorised Version unquestionably was, we do not intend to suggest either that it brought to an end the history of the English Bible or that it alone constitutes the available Word of God, "the original Bible" which, if "good enough for the apostle Paul", should also be good enough for us. There are at least three reasons why this is not so.

Firstly, despite the great care taken in its production, there were many mistakes and errors in the 1611 Authorised Version. A revised edition was printed in 1613 that contained more than 300 corrections to the original edition. Further corrected revisions were published in 1629, 1638 and 1657, and new revisions continued to appear. By the mid-18th century extensive variations in the many printed editions "had reached the proportions of a scandal",[46] resulting in two further major revisions, one in 1762 at Cambridge and another in 1769 at Oxford. The latter reflected more than 24,000 corrections to the 1611 edition and came to be the standard text, more than 150 years after the original.

Most corrections were of minor a nature but the 1769 edition also corrected the so-called 'Wicked Bible' of 1631, which had inadvertently printed the seventh commandment as 'Thou shalt commit adultery'. A 1717 edition was known as the 'Vinegar Bible' because in Luke 20 it mistakenly used the word 'vinegar' instead of 'vineyard'. Many other mistakes are on record, a few more substantial than either of the two just mentioned. New manuscript discoveries and a better understanding of biblical history, geography and social customs still continue to throw light on the format and meaning of the original Hebrew and Greek texts.

Secondly, the Authorised Version of 1611 contained the Apocrypha, and continued to do so until 1782, when it was excluded from an edition published in America and authorised by Congress. The apocryphal books were originally intermingled with the books of the Old Testament in the Latin Vulgate and were not separated from it until Coverdale's Bible in 1535. This distinction between Old Testament and Apocrypha reflected the views of most of the Protestant Reformers both in Europe and in England that the books of the Apocrypha were not of equal status with the books of the Old Testament, since they were not part of the original Hebrew Scriptures. Even now, however, the Apocrypha is retained in some English versions such as the New English Bible, reflecting the continuing influence of the Authorised

---

45 H. G. May, *Our English Bible in the Making* (Westminster, CO: Westminster, 1952), 48.

46 www.wikipedia.org, 'Authorised King James Version', see 'Standard Text of 1769'.

Version as a theological *via media* between the extremes of medieval Catholicism on one hand and the more radical Puritanism of the later English Reformation. Today, most Bibles from the Protestant tradition do not contain the Apocrypha.

A third and more practical reason for avoiding the mistake of regarding the Authorised Version as the one and only true translation of the Bible is the fact that English is still a language in flux. Old words are constantly disappearing from use and new words are constantly being added. As McGrath says, "The English of 1611 is not the English of the twenty-first century".[47] In fact, by 1611 the Authorised Version was already linguistically obsolete in some respects. If the Bible is indeed the Word of God, then that Word must be communicated in the language of the people. This principle has been understood by all translators of the Bible since Wycliffe's time and it still holds true today. It explains in part why there have been so many new translations in recent times and why they continue to roll from presses and publishing houses throughout the English-speaking world.

While the influence of the Authorised Version can never be diminished and should never be forgotten, its meaning can often be clarified with the help of more recent translations. Those who wish to read and understand God's word from its pages can, of course, still do so. Others find recent translations more easy to read and understand. They, too, have access to the Word of God. That the Bible is available today in so many translations and versions is a great advantage, and that in most parts of the world we are free to read it is one of the great benefits of living in a democratic society. And the fact remains that no other book has had such a widespread impact on world history or has influenced for good the lives of so many people in so many countries as the Bible, especially through its many English-language versions.

---

47 McGrath, *In the Beginning,* 309.

4. The Enduring Influence of the Authorised Version[1]

Bryan W. Ball

It is almost impossible to overstate the widespread and lasting influence of the King James Bible, or the Authorised Version, as it is better known in the land of its origin.[2] Referring specifically to this much-loved 1611 version of the Bible, TV presenter and academic, Melvyn Bragg, states it has had "more impact on the ideology of the last four centuries than any other creed, manifesto or dogma".[3]

Others are quick to agree. Alister McGrath, Professor of Theology at the University of London's Kings College, says that its influence "has been incalculable".[4] Gordon Campbell, a world authority on the English language and Professor of Renaissance Literature at the University of Leicester, claims it is "the most important book in the English language".[5] Professor David Daniell argues that any attempt to understand the literature, politics, art and social history of England and the English-speaking world of the past 400 years without knowledge of the Authorised Version "is to be crippled".[6] Perhaps the fact that more than 10 million copies of all versions are sold every year in more than 1,700 languages is the most compelling evidence of the Bible's continuing worldwide influence and of the persisting impact of the version which dominated the English-speaking world for more than three centuries.

---

1 An earlier version of this chapter was published in Nikolaus Satelmajer, ed., *The Book That Changed the World: The Story of the King James Version* (Nampa, ID: Pacific Press, 2012), 61-70. It is here expanded, with 'Authorised Version' generally replacing 'King James Version'. Used with permission.

2 Some of the material in this chapter has been adapted and expanded from the author's *Can We Still Believe the Bible?* (Warburton: VIC: Signs Publishing Co., 2nd ed., 2011). Used with permission.

3 Melvyn Bragg, *12 Books That Changed The World* (London: Hodder & Stoughton, 2006), 282.

4 Alister McGrath, *In The Beginning: The Story of The King James Bible* (London: Hodder & Stoughton, 2001), 1.

5 Gordon Campbell, *Bible: The Story of The King James Version* (Oxford: OUP, 2010), 2.

6 David Daniell, *William Tyndale: A Biography* (New Haven and London: Yale University, 1994), 3.

The Authorised Version profoundly influenced the entire English-speaking world and Western culture for more than three hundred years. As McGrath states, "It changed a Nation, a Language, and a Culture". And it did so in many ways.

At a most fundamental level it has had an immense impact on *the English language*. In his fascinating study of the Authorised Version, *In The Beginning, the Story of the King James Bible*, McGrath says that it was one of the two "greatest influences on the shaping of the English language", stating that its publication was "a landmark in the history of the language".[7] Melvyn Bragg, in his equally important account of the Authorised Version, *The Book of Books: the Radical Impact of the King James Bible*, describes it "as a hoarder and breeder of language" and says it is "without parallel in our culture".[8]

Many of the words and phrases that first appeared in Tyndale's New Testament and then flowed on into the Authorised Version are still part of the every-day language of millions who speak English: "the salt of the earth", "the powers that be", "a law unto themselves", "highways and byways", "a word in season", "lick the dust", "the root of all evil", "the heat of the day", "coals of fire", "fight the good fight", "from strength to strength", "like a lamb to the slaughter", "the signs of the times", "how are the mighty fallen", "the skin of our teeth", "no rest to the wicked", "nothing new under the sun" and many more. Spoken and written English were unquestionably shaped by the vocabulary and imagery of the Bible. In his study of the Authorised Version's influence on our language, English specialist and honorary professor of linguistics at the University of Wales, David Crystal, examines in detail many of these expressions. With specific reference to the words and phrases coined by Tyndale and others who contributed to the Authorised Version, Crystal says "no book has had greater influence on the English language".[9]

Many other outstanding scholars over the last century have also recognized the immense influence of the Authorised Version on the development of English. They include Sir Arthur Quiller-Couch of Cambridge University, Professor Albert Cook of Yale University and more recently, as already noted, Professor Alister McGrath of Oxford and London. McGrath states quite categorically that the Authorised Version exercised a "substantial and decisive influence over the shaping of the English language".[10] In assessing

---

7 McGrath, *In the Beginning,* 1. The other significant influence on the English language identified by McGrath was the works of Shakespeare.

8 Melvyn Bragg, *The Book of Books: The Radical Impact of the King James Bible 1611–2011* (London: Hodder & Stoughton, 2011), 129.

9 David Crystal, *Begat: The King James Bible and The English Language* (Oxford: OUP, 2011), 261.

10 McGrath, *In The Beginning,* 258.

the significance of all this we should remember that English is the first language of many countries, including Australia, Canada, India, New Zealand, South Africa and the United States of America. It is also the international language of politics, commerce, industry, communication, medicine and aviation. The influence of the Authorised Version on the language used in much of the world today has been far greater than King James or his translators could ever have imagined.

From language flows literature and it is hardly surprising that the Authorised Version of the Bible had a profound and lasting impact on **English literature**. We tend to think of the Bible as the source of religious truth, forgetting its inherent value as literature. Yet the Bible is great literature in its own right. The Authorised Version is itself an outstanding example of the best in English literature according to Sir Arthur Quiller-Couch who, in a lecture at Cambridge University, stated that it was "the very greatest literary achievement in the English language".[11] Another description cited by McGrath calls the Authorised Version the "noblest monument of English prose".[12] This is one reason that the Authorised Version is still so popular four hundred years after it was first published.

But there is more. The Authorised Version has influenced other writers, beginning with those who wrote at the same period in history. For example, Shakespeare quoted directly or alluded to at least forty-two books of the Bible of his day[13] — the Authorised Version. One writer says it is impossible to understand many passages in Shakespeare's works without knowledge of the Bible. The same is true of Milton's *Paradise Lost* and *Paradise Regained*, of Bunyan's *Pilgrim's Progress* and of the works of dozens of other great writers whose works are still regarded as classics. Such authors include Spenser, Addison, Wordsworth, Tennyson, Coleridge, Dickens, Thackeray, the Brontes, and Longfellow. We have already spanned more than two centuries.

Mention must also be made of Ruskin. It has been calculated that an index of biblical references in the writings of Ruskin, one of the acknowledged masters of English literature, would make a book of more than three hundred pages. The same writer concludes, "For over twelve hundred years [back to the time of Alfred the Great] the Bible has been an active force in English literature", having moulded the thinking of successive generations of authors.[14] Alister McGrath states that up until the end of World War I "the King James Bible was seen not simply as the most important English trans-

11   *Ibid.*, 1.

12   *Ibid.*

13   W. Graham Scroggie in R. T. Kendall, ed., *The Word of the Lord* (Basingstoke: Marshall Pickering, 1996), 27.

14   *Ibid.*, 28.

lation of the Bible but as one of the finest literary works in the English language". "It did not follow literary trends", he adds, "it established them".[15]

The Authorised Version has influenced *music*. In his book *The Word of the Lord*, Dr W. Graham Scroggie asks a question: "What if there had never been a Bible?" By way of answer the author points to many of the truly great musical compositions that are the heritage of Western culture and reminds us that they owe their very existence to the Authorised Version of the Bible. He mentions Haydn's *Creation*, Handel's *Messiah*, Mendelssohn's *Elijah*, Purcell's *Jubilate*, Bach's *St. Matthew's Passion*, Sullivan's *Light of the World* and Stainer's *Crucifixion* and says, "All this would never have been if the Bible had never been written".[16] He could have mentioned many more, all of which have inspired millions for centuries as they still do. Were Handel's much-loved *Messiah* the only great musical masterpiece to have survived it would by itself be enough to substantiate the claim that the Bible has influenced the composition of the world's great music. Its words are taken only from the text of the Authorised Version.

To this may be added an incalculable number of Christian hymns, all coming as they do from this same great textual tradition. Isaac Watts wrote more than six thousand. Charles Wesley, Philip Doddridge, Fanny Crosby, Toplady, Newton, Cowper, Heber and a host of others wrote thousands more. These hymns all drew their inspiration directly from the words of the Authorised Version and owe their existence to it. They have been sung by many generations and have expressed the hopes, fears, longings and beliefs of untold millions across the English-speaking world.

Many of these great hymns of the Christian faith also resound with non-believers. They have been sung at great sporting occasions and at times of national tragedy as well as in church. For years at English football cup finals the famous old Wembley Stadium in London resounded with the words of "Abide with Me", "Guide Me O Thou Great Jehovah" and many other well-known hymns. Their words and sentiments are rooted in the Bible, Dr Scroggie reminds us.

Melvyn Bragg says that the Authorised Version "made its way everywhere", specifically, of course, "in the hymns of the Anglican Church and in the hymns of the Methodist church and other Nonconformist churches". But more than that, memorable lines and melodies "carried words from the Bible across hills and fields the world over", the ripples still flowing onwards and outwards. "The laments of the early Afro-Americans and their liberationist spirituals use the words and deeds in the Bible [AV] all the time, and these flowed into soul music, into the blues, even into pop music".[17]

---

15 McGrath, *In The Beginning*, 3.
16 Scroggie in R. T. Kendall, ed., *Word of The Lord*, 25–26.
17 Bragg, *12 Books*, 279.

What if there had never been a Bible? Well, for one thing, most of the great hymns in the English language and much of the most sublime music in the world would never have been composed.

The Bible has also influenced **art**. By art, we usually mean painting. In this chapter we mean specifically the paintings of the great masters, known and appreciated around the world. Art in the broader sense, however, includes sculpture and architecture, etching and engraving, all of which have reflected in their own way the Christian message drawn from the Bible. The great medieval cathedrals of Europe have been called "symphonies in stone". Standing before Michelangelo's *Pieta*, his *David* or his *Risen Christ*, or before the works of many other Renaissance sculptors, we see and feel the powerful influence of the Bible.

It is, however, in the magnificent paintings of so many of the great masters that we most clearly see the influence of the Bible once again. These paintings can be found in many of the world's great museums, art galleries and cathedrals and have captured huge sums of money through the centuries. The works of Rembrandt, Rubens, Raphael, Michelangelo and Titian, to mention only a few of the better-known artists of the Renaissance, are all heavily indebted to biblical themes. As one writer says:

> But for the Bible these works would never have existed, and art galleries in London, Dresden, Florence, Venice, Paris, Antwerp and Milan would never have housed these great creations of Christian art. It is not too much to say that some of the finest work that has ever been done by pen, and brush, and chisel, and trowel, has been done in the presentation of themes and scenes which only the Bible can supply.[18]

One of these "great creations" appeared in the nineteenth century when the English artist Holman Hunt added to the world's masterpieces his serene and moving painting *The Light of the World*, based specifically on texts in the Authorised Version. It has been described as "a painted text, a sermon on canvas".

The title page of the first edition of the Authorised Version is itself an impressive work of art, designed by the Dutchman Cornelius Boel who had settled in England and had previously painted members of the Royal family. The work is full of symbolism, much of it drawn directly from the biblical text and, as McGrath rightly notes, was intended "to stress the centrality of Jesus Christ to the message of the Bible".[19]

Much might be said concerning the considerable influence of the Authorised Version on **education**. It has elsewhere been noted that since the days of the Wycliffite Bibles people have learned to read for themselves by

---

18   Scroggie in Kendall, *Word of the Lord*, 23.
19   McGrath, *In The Beginning*, 210.

reading the Bible.[20] But the impact of the Authorised Version on education in general has been much wider, and has been well documented in Melvyn Bragg's *The Book of Books: The Radical Impact of the King James Bible 1611–2011*. Professor Bragg explains that the Authorised Version was, for the first three centuries of its existence, "the prime educating force in the English-speaking world",[21] pointing out that the Bible had many "educative functions" beyond those of religion and moral instruction in that world. The Protestant churches of the English-speaking world of the eighteenth and nineteenth centuries in particular, "through the Bible … opened the doors of education to millions who had been shut out from learning until this book of faith brought them their enlightenment".[22]

The Bible, specifically the Authorised Version, has also influenced **social reform.** It is easy to forget that many of the great social reforms of the past three centuries have come about, not only through political initiative and government policy but initially as a result of principles enshrined in Scripture. It has been pointed out more than once that the British Labour Party owes its social conscience to the Methodist church and to biblical teachings. Keir Hardie, one of the primary founders of the British Labour movement, was a lay preacher in the Evangelical Union Church in Scotland. He testified, "The impetus that drove me first into the Labour movement and the inspiration which has carried me on in it, has been derived more from the teachings of Jesus of Nazareth than from all the other sources combined".[23]

It cannot for a moment be doubted that many reformers of recent centuries, perhaps most, were practising Christians who believed in the humanitarian teachings of the Bible and who, as the eighteenth and nineteenth centuries unfolded, found these principles directly in the pages of the Authorised Version. We may note the following:

John Howard (1726–1790) — prison reform
William Wilberforce (1759–1833) — abolition of slavery
Elizabeth Fry (1780–1845) — prison reform
The Earl of Shaftsbury (1801–1885) — reform of working conditions
George Mueller (1805–1898) — establishment of orphanages
Florence Nightingale (1820–1910) — nursing reform
Sir Wilfrid Lawson (1829–1906) — liquor and drinking reform
Thomas Barnado (1845–1905) — homes for destitute children.

---

20   See Claire Cross, *Church and People: 1450–1660* (London: Fontana, 1976), 32–34.
21   Bragg, *The Book of Books,* 279.
22   *Ibid.,* 260, 270.
23   Bragg, *The Book of Books*, 233. See also www.spartacus.schoolnet.co.uk/PRHardie

In 2009, David Simpson, the member for a Northern Ireland constituency in the British Parliament, pressed the government to approve formal commemoration of the 400th anniversary of the Authorised Version. His speech included recognition of the influence of that version on social welfare achievements of past years: "Hospitals were built and charities created as a result of its influence. The hungry were fed, the sick nursed, the poor given shelter [and] lives that lay in ruins were made whole and souls that were in bondage were set at liberty".[24] It is hard indeed to argue otherwise.

If we had to choose just one or two outstanding social reformers who were driven by Christian, biblical principles we might well settle for William and Catherine Booth, founders of the Salvation Army, whose followers still carry their convictions around the world with great effect. These were all men and women whose lives were "deeply rooted" in the Authorised Version and it is impossible to separate their actions from their beliefs.

Democracy itself, as we know and cherish it today in the Western world, owes an immense debt to the Authorised Version. According to Melvyn Bragg, its followers "provided the vocabulary, the seedbed and construction model for the early development of democracy". And again, "Democracy eventually clawed its way up and over that high wall [illiteracy and ignorance which characterized the populace during the medieval and early modern periods] as a result of the determination of thousands of individual men and women, who in many instances drew inspiration from the New Testament".[25]

This would almost certainly have been true of John Pym, the early English parliamentarian who, in the seventeenth century, was the driving force behind many of the initiatives to curb the old ideas and practice of royal absolutism in favour of parliamentary democracy. Pym's strong Puritan views matured just as the Authorised Version was by usage claiming its place as the 'national Bible'. Certainly the freedoms which characterise modern democracy — freedom of speech, freedom of assembly, freedom of the press, freedom of religious belief, to mention only a few — were being forged in the struggle between royal authority and the democratic process in mid-seventeenth-century England. And it is worth noting again that the initiative for a new translation of the Bible which arose at the famous Hampton Court conference in 1604 and which led directly to the King James or Authorised Version, was proposed by one of the leading Puritans of the age, Dr John Reynolds, president of Corpus Christi College, Oxford.

George Washington, first president of the United States of America, is credited with saying, "It is impossible to rightly govern the world without

---

24 Cited in Bragg, *The Book of Books*, 11.
25 Bragg, *The Book of Books*, 6, 87. See also ch. 25, *passim*.

God and the Bible".[26] He would have had in mind the Authorised Version, the only version available at the time. The self-evident truth of that assertion can be seen today in virtually every country where the values of the Bible, once cherished, have been ignored or rejected and where democracy is all too often prostituted by corruption, greed, minority agendas, self-interest and the lust for power.

Those who have written recently about the Authorised Version in North America where the AV/KJV is still widely favoured, have noted its influence in several other areas of life, including social mores, women's rights, and even in early modern science. Its impact on religious life and belief in every continent and upon untold millions of individual lives requires no comment for it is indisputable. Writing of the science-religion nexus, Professor Bragg contends that in the formative years of scientific enquiry and experiment, the latter part of the seventeenth century, religion and science were "mutually re-affirming" and concludes his chapter on the formation of the Royal Society in London and the relationship of early modern science and the Bible with this interesting comment: "In the formative years of the seventeenth century it could be said that the King James Bible joined religion and science together in a marriage which has just about held despite massive bombardment".[27] The comment deserves further exploration, as do many of the other aspects of life mentioned above. Unfortunately limitations of space prevent us from pursuing them here.

What can be said, however, is that everything we have examined in this chapter, together with those aspects of contemporary thought and life mentioned above, can be summed up in one word — 'culture', or perhaps 'civilization', in our case Western civilization. So it will perhaps be appropriate to conclude this chapter with some reflections on the influence of the Authorised Version **on Western civilization** in general.

Literature, language, music, art, social conscience, education and democracy all help to define culture. But Western culture is more than these vibrant expressions of the human soul. Culture is also defined by values and beliefs and by the social and political mechanisms that make a society cohesive and functional. In the Western world, the Bible has played a key role in developing these values and structural processes.

Alister McGrath, whose incisive mind and voluminous writings are increasingly seen as a beacon of light in our time, points out that during the 16th and 17th centuries, a defining era in the development of Western culture, the Bible was seen "as the foundation of every aspect" of that culture.[28] This was especially true in England where the foundations were already being

---

26 *Ibid.,* 7.

27 *Ibid.,* 109, 118.

28 McGrath, *In The Beginning,* 3

laid for an empire, then a Commonwealth, which — with all their shortcomings — would in many respects inherit and perpetuate the values and beliefs of that nascent culture. Of course, the United States of America, only then emerging as a national identity and very much indebted at the time to English values and beliefs, has since played a major role in the development of the West. So McGrath can say:

> Without the King James Bible, there would have been no *Paradise Lost,* no *Pilgrim's Progress,* no Handel's *Messiah,* no Negro Spirituals, and no Gettysburg address. These, and innumerable other works, were inspired by the language of the Bible. Without *this* Bible [the King James Version] the culture of the English-speaking world would have been immeasurably impoverished.[29]

Only the most bigoted mind would deny that the beliefs and values inherent in the Bible have, until relatively recently, characterized and defined Western culture. They have been transmitted to much of the world via the English language, itself to a marked degree a result of the powerful influence of the King James Bible. These ideals were established in England and other parts of Western Europe and later in the United States of America as the Bible became available to the people and as its principles took root in individual lives and in the collective consciousness of the nations. Indisputably, without the Authorised Version "the culture of the English-speaking world would have been immeasurably impoverished".

Amidst all this quite justifiable affirmation, a more sombre note may not be out of place, for the times have changed. It is hard to believe that our culture, Western civilization, undoubtedly the most advanced civilization of all that have arisen through history, might one day disappear. Yet that is what many are now telling us is already happening. Since Oswald Spengler's acclaimed book *The Decline of the West* was published in 1926, a mounting chorus of voices has been telling us that our civilization is coming to an end. A more recent title tells it as *The Wreck of Western Culture,*[30] a compelling account of the rise, influence and ultimate failure of humanism written by John Carroll, professor of sociology at La Trobe University, Melbourne. These writings and many others of a similar nature will be explored more fully in a later chapter of this collection of writings.[31]

Yet this is not merely a warning, or a necessary counter-balance to the recent upbeat celebration of the 400th anniversary of the 1611 Au-

---

29   *Ibid.,* 2. Final emphasis supplied.

30   John Carroll, *The Wreck of Western Culture: Humanism Revisited* (Melbourne: Scribe, 2nd edit., 2010).

31   See ch. 16, '*The Decline of the West: Myth or Reason for Hope?*

thorised Version and all versions that have followed. It is also another affirmation of the incalculable influence of the Bible in the formulation of Western civilization and its various cultural characteristics that can still be seen in many parts of the world. It should encourage us to cherish, defend, promulgate and exemplify the values and ideals of this quite amazing book that lies at the heart of our civilization and of our national and individual identities.

5. The Sufficiency of Scripture [1]

Bryan W. Ball

English Protestantism in its entirety, from the earliest appearance of Anglicanism in the reign of Henry VIII, through Puritanism and on to the various manifestations of Nonconformity in the seventeenth and eighteenth centuries, was thoroughly and unequivocally based on the Bible. It could not have arisen, existed or multiplied as it did without its unambiguous commitment to what it believed was the divinely revealed Word of God. When the Anglican Thirty-Nine Articles of Religion (1571) referred to the "sufficiency of Scripture"[2] they spoke for all English Protestants then and for at least three hundred years to come. A distinguished Puritan theologian, William Perkins,[3] used identical language in explaining the claims of 2 Timothy 3:16–17. He, too, spoke of "the sufficiency of Scripture". The phrase seems an appropriate title, then, for this account of early English Protestant belief in the Bible.

Perkins was a fellow of Christ's College, Cambridge, from 1584 to 1595 and for much of that time a regular preacher at Great St Andrews, a church frequented by many from the university fraternity. His influence in perpetuating the biblical emphasis among succeeding generations of English preachers is beyond question. His fame abroad as a writer was scarcely less than his reputation at home as a teacher and preacher. Many of his works were translated into various European languages and most of them, particularly those published in English, were read long after his untimely death in 1602. We may be certain that what Perkins said about Scripture fairly represented the view of mainstream English Protestantism for many years to come. Some fifty years later, John Ball, who was deprived of his Staf-

---

1 Earlier versions of this chapter were published in *The English Connection: The Puritan Roots of Seventh-day Adventist Belief* (Cambridge: James Clarke, 1981); and in its revised 2nd edition, also published by James Clarke, 2014. Used with permission.

2 "The Thirty-Nine Articles of Religion" (1571), Article 6. The place of publication of all seventeenth-century English works is London, unless otherwise stated. Names of publishers are usually unavailable.

3 Vignettes of Perkins and many of the Puritan preachers and writers cited in this chapter can be found in J. R. Beeke and R. J. Patterson, *Meet the Puritans* (Grand Rapids, MI: Reformation Heritage, 2006).

fordshire living and who more than once was imprisoned for his Puritan sympathies, declared plainly, "the Word of God is the ground of all our faith, whereby we live, be directed, and be upheld in our trials".[4] The influential Thomas Adams, chaplain to Sir Henry Montagu, the Lord Chief Justice and Lord High Treasurer of the realm, described Scripture as "a perfect and absolute rule".[5] It would not be difficult to find a hundred such restatements of the position Perkins had outlined earlier. Puritanism, as Protestantism as a whole, held that the entire Bible, Old and New Testaments together, was "sufficient to prescribe the true and perfect way to eternal life".[6]

Authority

The question underlying the European Reformation in general and the English Puritan movement in particular, as the preceding comments suggest, was that of authority. From what source did the Church and the individual believer receive the faith, and against what standard could that faith be measured? Who formulated doctrine and on what grounds? And who defined duty? The insistence within Puritanism on Scripture as the answer to these fundamental questions and many others like them cannot be understood without reference to the centuries of tradition and prescribed religion from which the Church had so lately emerged. John Owen and Richard Baxter, perhaps the two greatest seventeenth-century Puritan theologians, both drew attention to the subordination of Scripture to tradition which had characterised medieval Catholicism.

Owen's defence of the Bible, published in 1659 with the cumbersome title, *Of the Divine Originall, Authority, Self-evidencing Light, and Power of the Scriptures,* stated openly that it had been written principally as a corrective to renewed attacks by Roman Catholic scholars on Scripture. Owen was particularly concerned to refute suggestions that the Bible was only a partial revelation of God's will (and hence, by implication, not wholly sufficient), and that Scripture was not valid unless accepted and interpreted by the Church.[7] No self-respecting Protestant theologian of the day could allow such claims to go unchallenged, and the gist of Owen's reply, conveyed in the title of his book, is that the authority of Scripture is above that of the Church, since in Scripture God speaks authoritatively and directly to the individual. Baxter similarly argued that the subjection of Christian belief to

---

4 John Ball, *A Treatise of Faith* (1632), 198.

5 Thomas Adams, *The Workes of Tho. Adams* (1630), 903.

6 William Perkins, *The Workes of that Famous and Worthy Minister of Christ ... Mr. William Perkins* (1626), I, 581.

7 See John Owen, *Of the Divine Originall, Authority, Self-evidencing Light, and Power of the Scriptures* (Oxford, 1659), Ep. Ded., sig. A4v.

the authority of the Church rather than to Scripture was the most injurious of all doctrines emanating from Rome.[8] In making this assertion, Baxter clearly understood how crucial the question of authority was to the whole structure of belief, as well as to the freedom of the individual before God.[9]

Perhaps the case was stated most clearly by the learned James Ussher who, prior to his elevation to the archbishopric of Armagh in 1625, had for the previous fourteen years held the chair of Divinity at Dublin. There is no doubt in this thoroughly Protestant mind about the place of Scripture:

> The books of Holy Scripture are so sufficient for the knowledge of Christian religion, that they do most plentifully contain all doctrine necessary to salvation ... It followeth that we need no unwritten verities, no traditions or inventions of men, no canons of councils, no sentences of Fathers, much less decrees of popes, to supply any supposed defect of the written Word, or to give us a more perfect direction in the worship of God and the way of life, than is already expressed in the canonical Scriptures.[10]

The "doctrine necessary to salvation" of which Ussher here speaks, points to the dual nature of the authority held by Protestantism to reside in Scripture. It is an authority which extends equally to the formulation of doctrine by the Church and to the regulation of the life of the individual believer. For Puritans, the two cannot be separated. Those who become impatient with the doctrinal controversies which characterised Puritanism fail to understand this relationship. Doctrine is important precisely because in the end it is concerned with salvation and with the individual. Sound doctrine is therefore to be pursued and false doctrine to be avoided and Scripture is the final court of appeal, the objective standard by which the faith of both Church and individual believer are to be measured. So Ussher adds, "From them only [the Scriptures] all doctrine concerning our salvation must be drawn and derived".[11] The Baptist pastor, Henry Denne, concurs: "Wheresoever the Protestant confessions do go hand in hand with Holy Scripture, we do rejoice to follow them". On the other hand, if the Church, even the Protestant Church, has deviated from this authoritative rule, "their example must not be our precedent".[12] Quite clearly, most shades of opinion within the

---

8   Richard Baxter, *The Saints' Everlasting Rest* (1669), 199.

9   The question of biblical authority remains a critical factor in the determination of Christian authenticity, if revelation and inspiration are foundational to Christian identity.

10   James Ussher, *A Body of Divinitie, or the Summe and Substance of Christian Religion* (1647), 18.

11   *Ibid.*

12   Henry Denne, *Antichrist Unmasked in Two Treatises* (1645), 52.

English Church of the seventeenth century agree that the Bible, as opposed to tradition and to creed, is the final source of authority.

It is at this point that Richard Baxter registers a note of disquiet. Baxter, learned, moderate and devout, and widely regarded as one of the most eminent divines of his age, was a prolific writer and an indefatigable preacher. Later generations have acknowledged his profound influence on the religious life of the times. *The Saints' Everlasting Rest* must be regarded as one of the most significant works of Puritanism, if not of Protestantism as a whole. Published first in 1650, and re-issued in numerous editions well into the nineteenth century, this book, written 'by a dying man to dying men', has exerted a lasting influence on countless thousands of readers. The *Saints' Rest* is an admirable example of Puritanism's concern with the salvation of the individual and with practical godliness rather than with institutional and creedal Christianity. Coming as it did a century or more after the beginnings of the English Reformation, it points out the danger, as real to established Protestantism as to established Catholicism, of assigning authority to the establishment rather than to Scripture. Baxter sees clearly the paradox of Protestantism's continuing protest against Rome's subjection of the authority of Scripture to that of the Church, while at the same time being guilty on a similar count. "The Papists believe Scripture to be the Word of God, because their Church saith so", he maintains. Yet Protestants have adopted a similar attitude to Scripture, "because our Church or our leaders say so".[13]

Baxter's argument, of course, is that it is not sufficient for any Christian to accept the authority of the Bible merely on the basis that this may be the official position of the Church as a whole, or of that section of the Church to which he may have given his allegiance. There must be a personal conviction, a personal knowledge of the issues involved. George Lawson, a contemporary and often a critic of Baxter, pressed this particular point further. Assent to the authority of Scripture is a fundamental article of faith, yet no Christian should accept that authority blindly "further than he hath certain reason so to do".[14] It is a matter, not merely of faith, but also of reason, of understanding. It is necessary for the believer as an individual to know for himself why he should accept the authority of the Bible and why he should regard it as an inspired revelation.

The ground for accepting the authority of Scripture is its own claim to be the Word of God, and it is therefore desirable to understand the "certain reasons" which led English Protestants of the sixteenth and seventeenth centuries to accept without hesitation the Bible's claim to inspiration, and hence

---

13   Baxter, *Saints' Rest*, 199.
14   George Lawson, *Theo-Politica or, a Body of Divinitie* (1659), 7.

its authority in dogma and in life. Why was the Bible so strongly held to be the Word of God rather than a collection of mere human writings? What precisely did William Perkins have in mind when he stated that the evidences for the divine origin of the Bible were "not to be found in any other writings in the world"?[15]

Inspiration

We may begin, as Puritanism itself began, with the fact of the Bible's existence. There was nothing fortuitous in the fact that the Bible had survived through centuries of history. It was, in fact, little short of a miracle. No other book had aroused such universal antipathy. No other book had outlived such sustained and rigorous opposition. Richard Baxter asks rhetorically if there was ever a time when all the Bibles in the world had been destroyed?[16] If the blood of martyrs was the seed of the Church, so too were the ashes of Scripture. "They could burn these witnesses by thousands, but yet they could never either hinder their succession or extinguish their testimonies",[17] Baxter writes in *The Saints' Rest*. It may be difficult for those who live in the twenty-first century, with the Bible translated into hundreds of languages and dialects and with free access to an almost bewildering variety of versions, to understand the force of this argument to those who lived so much nearer the age of Bible-burning and persecution. John Goodwin, whose *Divine Authority of Scriptures* (1648) proved to be an able defence of the traditional Protestant doctrine of Scripture, saw the position clearly enough. History bore witness to the fact that the best brains, the strongest hands and the most plausible eloquence had united in sustained attempts to eradicate the Scriptures and to counter their influence:

> And yet we see that they stand, and are as mighty, and as like to stand still in the world, as ever; all their enemies, with all their councils, imaginations, attempts, and machinations against them, from first to last, are fallen, and ready to fall before them; whereas many other books and writings, which had no enemies, no opposition, either from devils or men, nay, which had friends in abundance which loved them and looked after them, are wholly perished and lost.[18]

The continuing existence of the Bible, despite the repeated and determined attempts of its enemies to destroy it, spoke strongly of a providential care.

Not only had the Bible itself been guarded from destruction, but its message similarly had been preserved from corruption. To demonstrate this par-

---

15   Perkins, *Workes*, I, 484.

16   Baxter, *Saints' Rest*, 222.

17   *Ibid.*, 226.

18   John Goodwin, *The Divine Authority of the Scriptures Asserted* (1648), 251–52.

ticular truth was the object of John Owen's *Divine Originall*, the title page of which declared it to be a "vindication of the purity and integrity of the Hebrew and Greek texts". Owen's learning well suited him for this task, and it is to his credit that he recognised the importance of textual accuracy to any respectable defence of scriptural authority. It is of more than passing interest that the reliability of the text was questioned long before the nineteenth century. Owen castigates those who "with a show of learning have ventured to question almost every word in the Scripture",[19] and among the reasons which he presents for accepting the received text of Scripture as authentic and reliable are the following:

1. The concern of the original writers to be accurate;
2. The care taken by the Jews, before and after Christ, to preserve authentic copies of the Old Testament;
3. The concern of the Masoretes[20] to preserve the textual accuracy of the Old Testament;
4. Christ's attitude to the Old Testament, thereby giving it the final seal of approval;
5. The determination of the Christian Church to preserve accurate copies of Scripture;
6. The care taken by copyists to ensure accuracy;
7. The concurrence of available manuscripts.[21]

Time has not diminished the combined strength of these arguments, and we can understand what Owen means when he says that in all this the providence of God may be seen in preserving his Word and ensuring its essential accuracy. Of course, variations do appear in the texts of differing manuscripts, but these are of no great significance as they do not affect the Bible's essential message. In this Baxter agrees with Owen that any errors caused by copyists or printers are "of no great moment, as long as it is certain that the Scriptures are not *de industria* corrupted, nor any material doctrine, history, or prophecy thereby obscured or depraved".[22] As Baxter further somewhat dryly remarks, God had not taken it upon himself to supervise every printer to the end of time; what did matter was that the text had survived without material corruption.

Further testimony to the unique character of the Bible could be found by those who were willing to read it and consider its message. John Owen contended that sufficient internal evidence could be seen within Scripture it-

---

19 Owen, *Divine Originall*, 220.

20 Rabbinical scholars working between the 7th and 11th centuries, who took great care to ensure the accurate transmission of the text of the Hebrew Bible.

21 Owen, *Divine Originall*, 175–78.

22 Baxter, *Saints' Rest*, 206.

self to convince the honest reader of its divine origin. "The authority of God shining in them, they afford unto us all the Divine evidence of themselves",[23] Owen wrote of the collected books of Scripture. William Perkins had put forward a similar arguments years earlier. Let any discerning person read the Bible, let him duly note the content, the style and the purpose of each part and of the whole together, "and he shall be resolved that Scripture is Scripture, even by the Scripture itself".[24] The intrinsic character of the Bible is better appreciated in the light of its design, its unity, its "sweet concord and perfect coherence", as James Ussher described it, which stood out as a more objective testimony to its supernatural origin. Referring to the unity of theme and purpose evident in the various books of the Bible, Ussher pointed out that they had been written by some forty men of different backgrounds, under different circumstances, and at different times. Yet, as Ussher says, "There is a most holy and heavenly consent and agreement of all parts thereof together, though written in so sundry ages, by so sundry men, in so distance places".[25] It was difficult to disregard the unique character of the Bible when considering the question of its origin.

One of the most telling arguments in favour of the inspiration of the Bible was fulfilled prophecy. The capacity to foretell the course of future events "whilst there is yet nothing at all in being ... likely to produce them, or to contribute towards their being"[26] is beyond human ability, and is a mark of divine foreknowledge. Human beings are unable to predict future events with any degree of detailed accuracy. Yet the Bible contains such predictions, many of them concerning events which were to occur hundreds of years in the future, and which have been accurately fulfilled. Richard Baxter mentions in this respect the Old Testament prophecies concerning Christ. "There is scarce any passage of the birth, life, sufferings, death, resurrection, ascension, or glory of our Saviour", he says, "which are not particularly prophesied of in the Old Testament".[27] It is the verifiable fulfilment of these and other prophecies that gives confidence in Scripture, and also of course in those prophetic utterances which have yet to be fulfilled. The knowledge of fulfilled prophecy led William Perkins to declare:

> Now there is no man able of himself to know or foresee these things to come. Therefore this knowledge must rest in Him alone who is most wise, that perfectly understandeth and beholdeth all things that are not, and to whom all future things are present, and therefore certain.[28]

---

23   Owen, *Divine Originall,* 34.
24   Perkins, *Workes,* I, 582.
25   Ussher, *Body of Divinitie,* 9.
26   Goodwin, *Divine Authority,* 320.
27   Richard Baxter, *The Reasons of the Christian Religion* (1667), 263.
28   William Perkins, *The Whole Treatise of the Cases of Conscience* (1651),

John Goodwin adds that only He who can "read the long roll of time from the one end of it unto the other" can truly foretell the future.[29] The conclusion which Puritanism drew from the fulfilment of prophecy was that God had spoken to man through his Word.

A further consideration which brought strength to the other arguments supporting inspiration was found in the inherent power of the Bible. Here was a living force over the minds and lives of men and women such as no other book or collection of books could provide. "No writings of man", says John Ball, however persuasively set forth "with wit, words, orders, or depth of learning, can so enlighten the mind, move the will, pierce the heart, and stir up the affections, as doth the Word of God".[30] Although contrary to man's nature and disposition, the Bible, when preached and explained under the power of the Spirit, "convinceth and condemneth men of sin, it turneth and converteth them to itself, and causeth them to live and die in love and obedience thereof".[31] This it could never do were it simply of human origin — so argues William Perkins. John Goodwin is even more specific: "The covetous man it makes liberal, the oppressor it makes merciful, the earthly-minded it makes heavenly, the fearful it encourageth, the proud it humbleth, the unclean it purifieth, the profane it sanctifieth … it takes away the heart of stone, and gives men an heart of flesh".[32] Such testimonies to the intrinsic and unique power of Scripture are to be found in abundance on the pages of Puritan doctrine and devotion. They are the testimonies of experience and of observation. We may pause to note one more. John Flavel, cast in the mould of the true spiritual shepherd, and bound with invisible ties of concern for the eternal welfare of his people in Dartmouth, had seen the power of this living Word at work in the lives of his congregation:

> Can the power of any creature, the word of a mere man so convince the conscience, so terrify the heart, so discover the very secret thoughts of the soul, put a man into such trembling? No, no, a greater than man must needs be here. None but a God can so open the eyes of the blind, so open the graves of the dead, so quicken and enliven the conscience that was seared, so bind over the soul of the sinner to the judgement to come, so change and alter the frame and temper of a man's spirit, so powerfully raise, refresh, and comfort a drooping, dying soul.[33]

126.

29 Goodwin, *Divine Authority*, 320.

30 John Ball, *A Short Treatise Containing all the Grounds of Christian Religion* (1654), 26.

31 Perkins, *Workes*, I, 484.

32 Goodwin, *Divine Authority*, 148–149.

33 John Flavel, *The Whole Works of the Reverend Mr. John Flavel* (1716), I, 325.

We sense Flavel's conviction, and understand his conclusion. This must be the power of God and if there were no other arguments to bring forth, "yet this alone were sufficient to make full proof of the divine authority of the Scriptures".[34]

For such reasons English Protestants believed in the inspiration of the Bible and hence in its authority as the living Word of the living God. This did not lead, as some have suggested, to bibliolatry. That might have been the case if the dominant concept of inspiration had been that which later became known as "verbal inspiration". It was widely agreed in Puritan theological circles, however, that this view, which held that each word of Scripture had been given directly to the original writers, was too narrow. "The true and proper foundation of Christian religion is not ink and paper, not any book or books, not any writing or writings whatsoever, whether translations or originals", John Goodwin argued. The Christian faith, he continued, was "that substance of matter ... concerning the salvation of the world by Jesus Christ which [is] represented and declared both in translations and the originals but [which is] essentially and really distinct from both".[35] Baxter made a distinction between the basic doctrine of Scripture and the words which gave that doctrine expression: "The one is as the blood, the other as the veins in which it runs".[36] To Goodwin, again, the concept of Scripture means, "The matter and substance of things contained and held forth in the books of the Old and New Testament", but not "all the letters, syllables, words, phrases, sentences, and periods of speech" found either in manuscript or translation.[37]

A favourite expression with Puritan theologians was that the original writers of the Bible were God's "penmen".[38] This conveyed the thought that their role in the formulation of Scripture was not entirely passive, in the sense that they received the words of God in much the same way as a secretary might receive a dictated letter. Rather, the mind of each writer had been subject to the operation of the Holy Spirit, thereby receiving in thought-form the message of God, with the freedom to transmit that message in words and phrases of his own choosing. The message was then wholly the message of God, transmitted through human personality in human language. The Puritan theologians readily saw that this in no way detracted from the doctrine of inspiration, and John Goodwin representatively declares without

---

34   *Ibid.*

35   Goodwin, *Divine Authority*, 17.

36   Baxter, *Saints' Rest*, 201.

37   Goodwin, *Divine Authority*, 13.

38   E.g., Ussher, *Body of Divinitie*, 8; Richard Baxter, *More Reasons for the Christian Religion* (1672), 56. The same phrase was used by Ellen White in her frequently-cited essay, 'The Inspiration of Prophetic Writers', *Selected Messages* (Washington, D.C.: Review and Herald, 1958), I, 21.

hesitation, "I fully and with all my heart and all my soul believe them to be of divine authority".[39]

In practice, this meant that no particular version of the Bible could claim to be the Word of God more than another. The Authorised Version of 1611, the Geneva Bible of 1560, Coverdale's version of 1535 and, beyond them, translations in other languages, all contained what Goodwin described as the "substance" of Christian faith, and were therefore equally to be esteemed as "the Word of God". It was the authority of this Word, prized above that of priest or prelate, which gave character and meaning to English Protestantism, and John Flavel spoke intelligibly to both Church and believer when he advised "Keep the Word, and the Word will keep you".[40]

The Purpose of Scripture

In offering this advice Flavel makes it clear that he is thinking more of the individual believer than of the church corporate: "As the first receiving of the Word regenerated your hearts, so the keeping of the Word within you will preserve your hearts".[41] Flavel captures in this sentence the two fundamental purposes of Scripture. The Word of God led a man initially to the experience of salvation and then enabled him to proceed in that experience. It converted him and kept him. The emphasis in both cases is on that personal religion for which Puritanism strove and which is one of its chief characteristics. The authority of Scripture was only worked through to its logical conclusion as it was demonstrated in the lives of people, and that demonstration was to be seen in both unbelievers and believers. It was to be seen in leading the unbeliever to faith and in leading the believer to greater faith.

To the unbeliever, Baxter addressed one of his best-known and influential works, *A Call to the Unconverted*, in which he explained that the normal method by which God worked to bring a man to the saving knowledge of himself was through the Bible. "If you will be converted and saved, attend upon the Word of God", he advises. "Read the Scripture, or hear it read and other holy writings that do apply it. Constantly attend on the public preaching of the Word".[42] In this way the purpose of Scripture is to be fulfilled and men will be "born again ... by the Word of God, which liveth and abideth forever" (1 Peter 1:23). Perkins says that the Word "being preached by the Minister appointed by God, converteth nature, and turns the heart of man".[43] To those who have already responded to the saving Word of Scripture, Fla-

---

39   Goodwin, *Divine Authority*, 13.
40   Flavel, *Works*, II, 39.
41   *Ibid.*
42   Richard Baxter, *A Call to the Unconverted* (1660), 231.
43   Perkins, *Cases of Conscience*, 133.

vel offers similar counsel: "Let the Word of Christ dwell richly in you; let it dwell, not tarry with you for a night, and let it dwell richly or plentifully; in all that is of it, in its commands, promises, threats; in all that is in you, in your understandings, memories, consciences, affections and then "twill preserve your hearts".[44] There can be little doubt that the lives of countless Englishmen and their families were ennobled and enriched by the preaching ministries of Baxter and Flavel who sought to confront saints and sinners alike with the living, saving truths of Scripture.

The desire to convince men and women of their need of the Bible and its message understandably resulted in certain emphases. Chief among these, if we analyse Puritan theology aright, was that the main design of Scripture is to reveal Christ and to lead men and women to a personal knowledge of the salvation which God had provided in Him. Flavel declared, "The knowledge of Jesus Christ is the very marrow and kernel of all the Scriptures", and went on to show how both Old and New Testaments were "full of Christ", how "the blessed lines of both Testaments meet in Him".[45] Thomas Adams, who on account of his preaching and writing later came to be known as 'the Shakespeare of Puritan theologians', maintained that Christ was "the sum of the whole Bible; prophesied, typified, prefigured, exhibited, demonstrated; to be found in every leaf, almost in every line".[46] The great characters of sacred history were types of the Christ who was to come, stars shining in a light borrowed from the sun which was, in the fullness of time, to arise on a darkened world. And William Perkins, whose theology, though expressed with less rhetoric, was good theology nonetheless, succinctly concluded, "The scope of the whole Bible is Christ with His benefits, and He is revealed, propounded, and offered unto us in ... the Word".[47]

The relationship between doctrine and salvation in Puritan theology has already been noted. The repeated emphasis on sound doctrine in the Pauline epistles did not pass unnoticed in the seventeenth century. Those who remembered their Church history were reminded of many who had made shipwreck of the faith and who had wrought havoc in the Church through doctrinal deviation, particularly concerning Christology or those doctrines relating to the person and work of Christ. If it was necessary to believe in Christ for salvation, it was equally necessary to believe correctly. And since the practice of religion depended upon a correct understanding of duty and obedience as set forth in Scripture, it was also necessary that the specific doctrines relating to the Christian life should be clearly understood. Flavel,

---

44 Flavel, *Works*, II, 39.
45 Flavel, *Works*, I, 12.
46 Adams, *Workes*, 1209.
47 Perkins, *Workes*, I, 484.

again, speaks of "many honest, well-meaning, but weak Christians ... easily beguiled by specious pretence of new light" and "pliable to many dangerous errors".[48] The seventeenth century undoubtedly had its share of such "well-meaning" believers — Ranters, Muggletonians, Seekers, Diggers, Levellers, Fifth Monarchy Men, to name a few — whose sincerity could not generally be questioned, but whose interpretations of Scripture were at the best doubtful and whose Christology was generally distorted. It was to guard the feet of the saints from such slippery paths that moderate religious opinion in the seventeenth century expressed its concern for sound doctrine. Thus, in answer to a question about the purpose of a written revelation such as the Bible, John Ball replied, "That it might be an infallible standard of true doctrine, and ... that it might be the determiner of all controversies".[49] It must be conceded that had the Church at all times stood by that axiom there might have been less division and less misunderstanding.

One cannot read far into Puritan theology, or for that matter into Puritan history, without recognising the importance accorded to individual conscience in the outworking of salvation and the application of doctrine. Much has been written about freedom of conscience and the freedom of the individual in matters of faith, and of the contribution made in the seventeenth century to human progress in this respect. Without detracting in any way from what is certainly a basic human freedom, it must be understood that in moderate Puritan eyes the conscience was only truly free as it was captive to the Word of God. Conscience was that inner light given to every man, as part of the general revelation of God in the world, to prompt him to seek and follow ways of truth and goodness, yet insufficient of itself to lead to a saving knowledge of Christ. Conscience can only be completely effective in the context of knowledge, that is to say in spiritual terms, when enlightened with truth. The light within, Joseph Alleine specifically states, is incapable of leading a man to salvation "without the direction of God's Word". On the other hand, "a well informed conscience", Alleine argues, "instructed in the Scriptures, and well studied in the mind of God ... may be a great help to a Christian".[50] The Bible, therefore, finds a further important function as a guide to conscience. A Christian instructed in Scripture will not only know in general terms that he ought to do right, but he will know from the Word of God what to do. Flavel says, "If Scripture and conscience tell you such a way is sinful, [you] may not venture upon it".[51] It is Scripture and conscience together which provide constraint. Alleine, prevented from serving

48 Flavel, *Works*, I, 626.
49 Ball, *Short Treatise*, 7.
50 Joseph Alleine, *Remains of that Excellent Minister of Jesus Christ, Mr. Joseph Alleine* (1674), 76.
51 Flavel, *Works*, II, 185.

his congregation by the harsh legislation which followed the Restoration of the Monarchy in 1660, therefore declares, "My brethren, if God deprive you of the preacher in the pulpit, take the more earnest heed to the preacher in your bosom".[52]

Understanding the Bible

Given that the Bible is the inspired Word of God, the most important question of all comes at the level of personal understanding. How shall the Bible be interpreted? By what method is the water of life to be drawn from the well of salvation? Thomas Adams, with a characteristic turn of phrase, chides those who are willing to accept the applications of Scripture pressed upon them by the preacher, without understanding the reasons thereof for themselves, "as if they had only need to have their hearts warmed, and not to have their minds warned, and enlightened with knowledge. But alas, no eyes, no salvation".[53] One writer complains bitterly of "the prattling housewife and the old dotard" taking it upon themselves to interpret Scripture, "readily teaching that they never learned, and abundantly pouring out that which was never infused into them".[54] He is, of course, making the observation that false conclusions can be reached as a result of incorrect and uninformed methods of interpretation. Hence the need for a ministry trained, among other things, in the principles of biblical interpretation and with knowledge of the original languages in which the Bible was written. Hence the need for preachers to expound Scripture to the people of God and for the Church to expect such exposition.

Children of the English Reformation believed, then, that God speaks to man immediately in the Bible and mediately by those who understand Scripture and who are called to teach and expound it. George Lawson, a moderate Anglican, says for example, that God speaks "immediately" to the Prophets, "mediately" by the Prophets who are inspired and "mediately" by those appointed to teach Scripture but who are not inspired.[55] For all that, however, the Bible was essentially an open book and each individual believer could attain to "that knowledge of the mind and will of God revealed in the Scripture, which is sufficient to direct him in the life of God, to deliver him from the dangers of ignorance, darkness, and error, and to conduct him into blessedness".[56] For this reason personal Bible study must complement the public preaching of the Word.

---

52   Alleine, *Remains*, 76.

53   Adams, *Workes*, 663.

54   Daniel Featley, *The Dippers Dipt* (1647), sig. B3r.

55   George Lawson, *An Exposition of the Epistle to the Hebrews* (1662), 3.

56   John Owen, *The Causes, Waies and Means of Understanding the Mind of God as Revealed in His Word* (1678), 5.

Two factors, the Holy Spirit and reason, combine in bringing honest seekers and willing listeners to a saving knowledge of Scripture. The great importance of the Holy Spirit in the study of the Bible must never be forgotten. "The Word alone, though never so excellently preached, conduces no more to the conviction and salvation of a sinner than the waters of Bethsaida did, when the angel came not down to trouble them", but when one is under the tutelage of the Spirit mediating the written word, "then Christ speaks to the heart".[57] Thus John Flavel explains the relationship of Word and Spirit. "The Word and Spirit go together ... the Word is dead without the Spirit", argues Richard Sibbes, "Therefore attend on the Word, and then wait on the Spirit to quicken the Word, that both Word and Spirit may guide us to life everlasting".[58] The inspiration of Scripture had been directly effected by the working of the Spirit on the minds of the original writers. Now that same Spirit illuminates the minds of those who read and hear the Word. So the Spirit becomes both author and interpreter, ensuring that the divine message contained in Scripture is both available and intelligible. The illumination of the human mind by the Spirit is therefore crucial in the process of understanding the Bible.

Yet the Spirit does not supersede reason. Human beings are rational creatures and God approaches them through their rationality, the Spirit enlightening the mind in a manner that does not dispense with the normal processes of human thought. So John Flavel speaks of those "natural qualifications" necessary to arrive at an understanding of the Word, "clearness of apprehension, solidity of judgement, and fidelity of retention".[59] Those who would deny us the use of reason in understanding the Scriptures "would deal with us", says John Owen, "as the Philistines did with Samson, first put out our eyes, and then make us grind in their mill".[60] Richard Sibbes, one of the great Puritan devotional preachers, points out "There is strong reason in all divine truth ... and it is a part of wisdom to observe how conclusions rise from principles, as branches and buds do from roots".[61] It is the free access of the Spirit to the mind and the full use of reason which together result in the understanding of Scripture.

In practice, however, the tendency to lean to one's own understanding in seeking to arrive at a correct interpretation of the Bible is always present. It is easier, even for the regenerate, to think their way through to a conclusion than to consciously seek, or wait for, the enlightenment of the Spirit. We have previously noticed Thomas Adams' strictures against those who

---

57 Flavel, *Works,* II, 72.
58 Richard Sibbes, *A Fountaine Sealed* (1639), 98–99.
59 Flavel, *Works,* I, 613.
60 Owen, *Causes, Waies and Means,* 10–11.
61 Richard Sibbes, *Christs Exaltation Purchast by Humiliation* (1639), 47–48.

submissively accept suggested interpretations without taking the trouble to examine for themselves the scriptural evidence. John Flavel is equally anxious over those who come to the Bible in order to substantiate views already held. "They bring their erroneous opinions to the Scriptures ... and force the Scriptures to countenance and legitimise their opinions",[62] he says. John White offers appropriate counsel:

> We must be very careful that we bring with us our minds free, and not prepossessed with any opinion which we have either framed in our own fantasy, or received from others. A mind forestalled by an erroneous conceit is no fit judge of any truth, or of any testimony concerning truth, but as coloured glass transmits the light, and represents it to the eye infected with the same colour with which itself is dyed ... so happens it with a mind prepossessed with any fantasy, it apprehends and judgeth all things according to that opinion which itself hath entertained.[63]

The quest for spiritual truth is impeded by coming to Scripture with prejudice and pre-conceived opinion. John Owen speaks more strongly yet, contending that most of the heresy which has infected Christian doctrine through the ages has arisen from men "lighting on some expressions in Scripture, that singly considered seem to give countenance to some such opinion as they are willing to embrace".[64] The clear implication is that coming to the Bible with pre-conceived opinions results in less than an objective study of the text, and hence in the perpetuation of error. The Bible must always be approached with an open mind to seek the consensus of Scripture as a whole, with a willingness to learn and to change one's opinion if the honest study of all the relevant textual evidence leads in that direction.

Puritans in general were particularly disturbed by two influences from the past which tended to shape biblical interpretation in a manner likely to restrict the full discovery of truth. The first of these influences was tradition, that immense body of comment and exposition which had been handed on from generation to generation and which found its fullest expression in the writings of the Church Fathers. It must not be thought that Puritanism wanted to discard these writings altogether. On the contrary, it was generally agreed that much truth and wisdom could be found in patristic literature. But the Fathers also had been human, and on that count liable to error and their writings must be read with discernment. Humphrey Hody, an outstanding Oxford professor of the late seventeenth century, who was not a Puritan at all, stated the case as clearly as any Puritan writer could have done. "I desire

---

62 Flavel, *Works*, I, 615.

63 John White, *A Way to the Tree of Life* (1647), Ep. Ded., sigs. A3v, A4r.

64 John Owen, *An Exposition of the Two First Chapters of ... Paul ... unto the Hebrews* (1668), 111.

as much as any man to pay a just deference and regard to the judgements of the ancient Fathers", he said, "but it must be confessed that though their authority be great in matters of tradition, yet the reasons and arguments which they produce to confirm their doctrines are not always convincing".[65] John Owen spoke with equal clarity for Puritanism when he argued that an exaggerated deference to the opinions of the past had been the major weakness in Judaism at the time of Christ and in Catholicism at the time of the Reformation.

> What their forefathers have professed, what themselves have imbibed from their infancy, what all their outward circumstances are involved in, what they have advantage by, what is in reputation with those in whom they are principally concerned, that shall be the truth with them and nothing else. Unto persons whose minds are wholly vitiated with the leaven of this corrupt affection, there is not a line in the Scripture whose sense can be truly and clearly represented ... If men will not forego all pre-imbibed opinions, prejudices and conceptions of mind however riveted into them by traditions, custom, veneration of elders, and secular advantages ... they will never learn the truth, nor attain a full assurance of understanding in the mysteries of God.[66]

Tradition, therefore, may be given its due place, but no more, in the interpretation of Scripture.

The related danger to correct interpretation from which Puritanism withdrew was that of philosophy. It recognised the threat to sound doctrine contained in a system of interpretation which was influenced by the presuppositions and methods of Greek philosophical speculation. There was little doubt in thorough-going Protestantism that influences of this nature had been brought to bear on biblical interpretation in the past, and the significance of Puritanism's desire to be free of all such doubtful influences and to achieve a purer understanding of the Word must not be underestimated. We turn here to Francis Bampfield, yet another learned and godly Nonconformist divine who, after the Restoration, was frequently imprisoned for preaching without the required authorisation and who died in Newgate gaol in 1683. Seven years before his death Bampfield had published an unusual treatise on Scripture as the revelation of God's will, applicable to all aspects of human learning and experience, in which he argued that the divisions in the Christian Church were a consequence of human interpretations placed on the Bible and that ministers and preachers were responsible for perpetuating such error. Concerning the influence of philosophy on the interpretation of the Bible, Bampfield writes:

> What an enemy to the doctrine of salvation by faith in Christ was the Grecian philosophy! What a disfigured face has it put upon religion by

---

65 Humphrey Hody, *The Resurrection of the (same) body Asserted* (1694), 210.
66 Owen, *Causes, Waies and Means*, 146.

its mythologising vanity! ... And what is yet further matter of more
lamentation, those who have the name of the scholastic learned among
Christians, do still pertinaciously adhere unto many of the philosophic
errors ... subjecting theology to philosophy and Christianity to soph-
istry.[67]

The argument that underlies the whole of Bampfield's interesting treatise
is that the principles and presuppositions of pagan philosophy have been allowed to mould the interpretation of the Bible and hence the formulation of
Christian doctrine. Possibly nothing characterised Puritanism as a whole so
much as its desire to come to grips with the real meaning of Scripture and to
submit to its authority, and in order that this might be achieved, the dangers
inherent in both traditional interpretations and philosophical principles were
to be avoided.

Progressive Revelation

One final factor of immense significance must be mentioned if we are
fully to appreciate the desire for truth which so characterised the Puritan
quest. The possibility, noted earlier, that the Fathers of the Christian Church
might have erred in their understanding of the Bible unavoidably implied
that later interpreters, Puritan theologians among them, could also reach
erroneous conclusions. No individual or generation could claim to have
arrived at a perfect knowledge of Scripture. Truth, or more correctly, the
understanding of truth, is progressive. God reveals himself and his will to
human beings as He sees fit and in accordance with the divine purpose. Men
and women must seek continually for further light, their minds must ever be
open to receive more knowledge, deeper insights. Thus the future continually beckons those who desire to progress in the way of truth. "Well may it
be conceived", wrote John Goodwin, "not only that some, but many truths,
yea and those of main concern and importance, may be yet unborn and not
come forth out of the mother's womb (I mean the secrets of the Scriptures)".
Goodwin goes on to speak of the "endless variety of the riches" contained in
Scripture, of "the unknown abyss of truth" to be found in the Bible.[68] All this
is but the fuller expression of the conviction voiced by John Robinson to the
Pilgrim Fathers on their departure for the New World in 1620 that God had
more truth and light yet to break forth from his Holy Word.

This belief that the future would bring greater understanding of the truths
of the Bible was deep-rooted in Puritan theology and fundamental to its
very existence. It is found in writings representative of all shades of opinion, but few express it as forcefully as Goodwin. At the beginning of time,

---

67   Francis Bampfield, *All in One* (1677), 59–61.

68   John Goodwin, *Imputatio Fidei, or a Treatise of Justification* (1642), sig.
b3v.

Goodwin argued, truth made its entry into the world "like the first dawning of the day". The light, though perceptible, was barely so, shrouded yet by darkness. Again, it was "like the corn, [which] when it first sprouts and peers above ground, hath nothing of that shape and body which it comes to afterwards". In such an undeveloped manner the Gospel had been first proclaimed to man. Then, as time passed, God's message to humanity became clearer, further editions of the truth appeared, revised and enlarged, as for example in the time of Noah and in the time of Abraham and notably in the time of Moses, until eventually God revealed himself more fully than in any previous age in the person of his own Son "to be published and preached throughout the world".[69] Yet even this, the ultimate revelation of God, confronts men and women in himself with undiscovered truth, calling each succeeding generation to a richer and more enlightened faith. "The knowledge of Christ is profound and large ... a boundless, bottomless ocean", says John Flavel. In seeking to arrive at this knowledge in its fullness men go through an experience akin to that of discovering and inhabiting a new and unexplored country. At first they colonise the coastal region, gradually penetrating further inland until at length the whole land is traversed and occupied.[70] So with the knowledge of Christ, suggests Flavel. But there is a difference: "The best of us are yet on the borders of this vast continent ... Though something of Christ be unfolded in one age, and something in another, yet eternity itself cannot fully unfold Him".[71]

So, too, with the knowledge of Scripture in its challenging and beckoning fullness. The redemptive truths of the Bible are not completely comprehended at one time, or even by one individual, but rather as God chooses to reveal their significance to those who seek. Thus, in the age succeeding Constantine, marked as it was by Christological controversy, the truth to be asserted concerned the deity of Christ. At the Reformation, when the emphasis had for so long been placed on works and merit as the way of salvation, the time had come to emphasise the redemptive work of Christ and justification by faith. In the latter ages the emphasis was to be placed on the hope of the coming kingdom of God.[72] Thus at no time in the past or in the present had the Church possessed an absolute knowledge of truth. Only as she remembers her fallible humanity and responds to the promise of the future will she move forward towards a complete understanding and fulfilment of Scripture.

---

69   Goodwin, *Divine Authority*, 48, 51.

70   Flavel, writing from Dartmouth in Devon, would have understood the hopes of those who in his day left England's shores, perhaps from Dartmouth itself, in search of conditions in distant lands more conducive to the practice of religion.

71   Flavel, *Works*, I, 2.

72   See Nathaniel Homes, *The Resurrection Revealed* (1661), 278–79.

For those who lived in the latter ages of world history — in the immediate context, this applied to those living in the seventeenth century, who believed that theirs was the last age and that Christ would soon establish his kingdom — the doctrine of progressive revelation and progressive understanding had a special significance. At that time truth was to come to ultimate fruition. "God's people went into mystical Babylon gradually", argued Henry Danvers, referring to the medieval suppression of the Bible and the ensuing decline in biblical theology. "So must their coming out be, some at one time, and some at another",[73] he continued. Goodwin believed that the Bible itself foretold a discovery of truth and sound doctrine before the final consummation. Commenting on Daniel 12:4, which refers to an increase of knowledge at the end of time, Goodwin explained that the text promised a greater understanding of Daniel's prophecies in particular and a deeper knowledge of the Scriptures as a whole in the last days.[74] "All spiritual light is increasing light, which shineth more and more unto the perfect day",[75] said Flavel. Each generation within the Church, therefore, must be open to the future, open to the Word of God and open to the guidance of the Holy Spirit. Thus led, both the Church as a body and believers as individuals, may rightfully anticipate a deeper knowledge of the Word, written and incarnate, continuing growth towards maturity in Christ and lasting satisfaction and enlightenment in the pursuit of truth.

---

73   Henry Danvers, *Treatise of Baptism* (1674), sigs. A3*v*, A4*r*.
74   Goodwin, *Treatise of Justification*, sigs. b4*r*,*v*.
75   Flavel, *Works*, I, 392.

6. The Origins of Genesis Reconsidered[1]

Bryan W. Ball

Genesis, we are frequently reminded, is the book of origins. It sets before us the beginnings of the world and of humankind, of life and death, sin and the first promises of salvation, the Sabbath and marriage, society, civilisation and, through the stories of Abraham, Isaac and Jacob, the beginnings of God's chosen people, Israel. Genesis is the foundation upon which the rest of the Bible is built and, as many have correctly claimed, it is an essential cornerstone of historic Christian theology. There is, as one Genesis specialist remarks, "No work known to us from the ancient Near East that is remotely comparable in scope".[2]

But what of the origins of Genesis itself? Where did it come from? Who wrote it? When was it written? Is it the work of one author or many? Is the Genesis text reliable? Is it to be understood literally and historically or, as many would now claim, is it largely myth which must be 'demythologised' in order to be understood? And are the first eleven chapters of an entirely different *genre* from the rest of the book, resulting in a dichotomy rather than a unity? These are all important questions, not only for Genesis itself, but also for the rest of the Bible.

For most of the last three and a half thousand years it has been held that Moses wrote Genesis, together with the other four books of the Pentateuch. While this view prevailed virtually unchallenged for so long, nowhere in the Bible is the Mosaic authorship of Genesis actually asserted although, as we shall see, there may be good reason for this. Many competent Jewish and Christian scholars still hold that Moses did write Genesis, either just before or just after the Exodus, *i.e.* at some point *c.*1445 BC.[3] It means that events outlined in the early chapters of Genesis were as ancient to Moses as he is to us, even older by a further three or four thousand years if we accept the chronology of many conservative scholars, and it raises the legitimate question of the source, or sources, of Moses' information. Is it really feasible to think that all the information in Genesis — extensive, detailed genealogies

---

1 First published in *In the Beginning: Science and Scripture Confirm Creation* (Nampa, ID: Pacific Press, 2012), 81-96. Reprinted with permission.

2 Derek Kidner, *Genesis* (Nottingham: IVP, 1967), 15.

3 The *Seventh-day Adventist Bible Commentary*, ed. Francis D. Nichol (Washington, DC: Review and Herald, 1953), I:203–4, takes the former view.

and names of cities and places that had already been lost for centuries by Moses' time — had been handed down orally without loss or corruption through countless generations? Or is it more reasonable to think, without in any way compromising an informed understanding of inspiration, that Moses worked from written sources? The main purpose of this essay is to attempt a coherent, credible answer to these latter questions.

Meanwhile, in the critical atmosphere which arose following the Enlightenment, another theory concerning the origins of Genesis was conceived, a theory seriously at variance with the traditional view of Mosaic authorship. Known either as the Graf-Wellhausen theory, after the two German scholars who articulated it in its classic form in the 1860s and 1870s, or the Documentary Hypothesis (DH), since it postulated that Genesis as we now have it was actually composed of various earlier fragmentary documents written much later than Moses, this theory quickly came to dominate Old Testament scholarship and has remained a major influence in biblical scholarship ever since. It will be necessary to outline this theory in more detail shortly. Suffice it to say here that from its early days it has attracted a steady stream of well-informed and articulate critics, among them the archaeologist and biblical scholar, P. J. Wiseman.

On the basis of considerable archaeological evidence and a careful analysis of the Genesis text, and reacting against the DH which he believed to be seriously flawed, Wiseman proposed that Genesis had originally been written on tablets, by the patriarchs themselves or their appointed scribes, in chronological sequence and in the manner in which it was customary throughout the ancient Near East to record important events or to write literary compositions. Wiseman contended that Moses had then compiled Genesis from these ancient and original texts, arguing that the structure of Genesis proves this to be the case. As we shall see, Wiseman's Tablet Theory is supported at various points by an astonishing amount of archaeological evidence and is presented in a convincing manner and by a sequence of persuasive arguments.

Wiseman first published his views in 1936 as *New Discoveries in Babylonia about Genesis.* The book was reprinted six times by 1953 and was then revised before his death and re-issued with a new title, *Clues to Creation in Genesis*, in 1977.[4] It was republished again in 1985 as *Ancient Records and the Structure of Genesis.* Of the 1977 edition the *Inter-Varsity Magazine*

---

4   *New Discoveries in Babylonia about Genesis* (London: Marshall, Morgan and Scott, 1947). The 1977 edition also included Wiseman's other book *Creation Revealed in Six Days*, first published in 1948 by Marshall, Morgan & Scott (London and Edinburgh). The present study focuses on Wiseman's first book which has the sub-title "Ancient Records and the Structure of Genesis" in the 1977 *Clues to Creation in Genesis* (London: Marshall, Morgan & Scott, 1977)

commented, "We can recollect few books so startlingly convincing or so helpful in clearing up many difficulties concerned with the Old Testament … It is one of the best books we have seen".[5] Similar sentiments have been expressed by many who have read the book in any of its editions.

In this essay we shall attempt to explain the Tablet Theory with sufficient detail to convey the strength of its arguments and demonstrate how many of its main features are supported by archaeological evidence and by other biblical scholars and Ancient Near Eastern specialists. We note here two prominent scholars who have endorsed the tablet proposal, D. J. Wiseman, the author's son and editor of later editions of the book and R. K. Harrison, author of *Introduction to the Old Testament*.[6] Wiseman, the son, was himself a distinguished Assyriologist at the British Museum and professor of Assyriology at London University, and General Editor of the Tyndale Old Testament Commentary series. It need not be said that his conclusions were based on the arguments and the evidence rather than on any filial relationship. Harrison's *Introduction to the Old Testament* is clearly the work of an able and erudite scholar. Among several other works Harrison co-edited the *New International Dictionary of Biblical Archaeology* and until 1993 served as first General Editor of the *New International Commentary on the Old Testament*. Conclusions reached by scholars of this calibre cannot lightly be dismissed or simply ignored.[7]

The Documentary Hypothesis

Wiseman's Tablet Theory originated in part from his own profound misgivings concerning the DH and at a time when that hypothesis dominated Old Testament scholarship in general and the origins of Genesis in particular. He regarded it as "misconceived", "unenlightened", "a series of suggestions" already in his opinion obsolete on account of substantial archaeological discoveries in the ancient Near East.[8] In order to appreciate Wiseman's criticisms and reservations and perhaps also for the benefit of readers not well-acquainted with the DH, we briefly recount its main features here.

The essence of the theory is that Genesis is not the work of a single author but consists of fragments of several earlier documents of different and unknown authorship and date of origin. These earlier sources were designated J, E and P and two of them (J and E) were said to reflect the differ-

---

5 Wiseman, *Clues to Creation in Genesis*, back cover.

6 R. K. Harrison, *Introduction to the Old Testament* (London: Tyndale, 1970)

7 The French scholar Jean Astruc (1684–1760) was one of the first to propose that Moses compiled Genesis from original documents, but this cannot be regarded as anticipating the DH since Astruc regarded his thesis as supportive of the Mosaic authorship of Genesis.

8 Wiseman, *Clues to Creation in Genesis,* 75–77.

ent names for God (*Jahweh* and *Elohim*) used in the original text by various authors. Later versions of the theory claim to have discovered yet more sources for the Pentateuch with the consequent addition of D, L and R and the subsequent origin of Genesis, or parts of it, is put as late as the sixth century BC with the resulting conclusion that much of Genesis was myth rather than history. As one critic claims, "the stories of the patriarchs were sagas or legends", Genesis containing "no historical knowledge about the patriarchs", for they were "stories" that arose later among the Israelite people.[9] The theory is bluntly, but not unfairly, summarised by K.A. Kitchen:

> During the later 19th century, rationalistic Old Testament scholarship in Germany decided that the Old Testament accounts of Hebrew history did not fit 'history' as it '*should*' have happened, according to their preconceived ideas. Therefore, its leading representatives rearranged the Old Testament writings ... until Old Testament history, religion and literature had been suitably manipulated to fit in with their philosophical preconceptions.[10]

Yet up to now no-one knows who J or E or P really were or even if they or their documents ever existed. Astonishing as it may seem, not one document or fragment has ever been discovered. It was all theoretical speculation.

Although Wiseman and others protested vigorously against the DH it remained the dominant influence in Old Testament scholarship for much of the twentieth century. Victor Hamilton's stimulating commentary on Genesis in the New International Commentary series recognises the dominating influence of Wellhausen, stating that "Even to this day [1990] he remains one of the 'founding fathers' of biblical studies", being to modern biblical scholarship "what Abraham is to the Jew, the father of the faithful".[11] Derek Kidner, who wrote the commentary on Genesis in the Tyndale Old Testament Commentary series (with an introduction by D. J. Wiseman to the 2008 printing of the original 1967 edition), notes "The old literary analysis of the Pentateuch is in fact still treated as substantially valid".[12] However, since the 1970s and 1980s opposition to the DH has grown, Rendsburg in his study of Genesis concluding that it is "untenable" and should be "discarded".[13] It will be helpful to note the reasons which have contributed to its decline, since they reflect many of the concerns which led P. J. Wiseman to first propose the Tablet Theory.

---

9   J. Wellhausen and H. Gunkel, cited in K. A. Kitchen, *The Bible in its World* (Exeter: Paternoster, 1977), 57.

10   Kitchen, *The Bible*, 56.

11   Victor P. Hamilton, *The Book of Genesis, Chapters 1–17* (Grand Rapids, MI: Eerdmans, 1990), 13.

12   Kidner, *Genesis*, 21.

13   G.A. Rendsburg, *The Redaction of Genesis* (Winona Lake, IN: Eisenbrauns, 1986), cited in Hamilton, *Genesis*, 31.

Fundamental to an understanding of the Graf-Wellhausen theory is the fact that its development coincided with the rise and spread of Darwinism. Many writers recognise the underlying evolutionary nature of the DH, but we note here only the representative comments of R. K. Harrison. Pointing out that Wellhausen himself held "evolutionary concepts characteristic of the philosophy of Hegel", Harrison reminds us that the intellectual climate of the time was dominated by theories of evolution and that Wellhausen's theory itself "bore all the marks of Hegelian evolutionism" and revealed a "completely unwarranted confidence in the evolutionary Zeitgeist".[14] Harrison also recorded that before his death in 1918 Wellhausen conceded that the critical rationalism he had embraced so readily in earlier years "had made havoc of his own faith in the authority and authenticity of the Old Testament".[15]

In that sobering context a more specific criticism was that the theory lacked any objective basis. Harrison commented on the "conjurations" of those who "postulated the documentary and fragmentary theories of Penta- teuchal origins",[16] but it was another distinguished scholar, the Egyptologist and biblical scholar K. A. Kitchen, who stated plainly what he and many others recognised, that even "the most ardent advocate of the documentary theory must admit that we have as yet *no single scrap* of external, objective evidence for either the existence or the history of 'J', 'E' or any other alleged source document".[17] The strength of this argument should not be allowed to escape us. The DH was just that, an hypothesis, for which there was no documented, objective evidence whatsoever. It was all conjecture, "conjura- tion", as Harrison had put it.

An equally substantial criticism is that the theory was developed and promulgated in almost total ignorance of the ancient Near East and its long literary tradition and literary customs. Kitchen complained strenuously that the prevailing theories in Old Testament studies had been "mainly estab- lished in a vacuum with little or no reference to the ancient Near East" and went on to argue that the information available from the Mesopotamian and eastern Mediterranean region better fitted the existing "observable structure of Old Testament history, literature and religion" than the prevailing "theo- retical reconstructions" inherent in the DH.[18] Wiseman himself was in no doubt that the DH "originated in an age of ignorance concerning the earliest patriarchal times" and believed that the theory would never have been con-

---

14 Harrison, *Introduction to the Old Testament*, 21–22, 41.

15 *Ibid.,* 26.

16 *Ibid.,* 94.

17 K. A. Kitchen, *Ancient Orient and Old Testament* (London: Tyndale, 1966), 23.

18 *Ibid.,* 172.

ceived in the first place had the wealth of archaeological information now available been known at the time.[19] The wealth and weight of archaeological evidence is, in fact, a fundamental argument for Wiseman's Tablet Theory as a whole.

Convincing as are the criticisms of the DH mounted by Harrison, Kitchen and others — and they should be read in context and in whole in order to be fully appreciated — it is the careful work of an earlier scholar that perhaps remains the most impressive *exposé* of the theory. It would still be difficult to find a more scholarly and thorough demolition of the DH than that undertaken by the Hebrew scholar Umberto Cassuto, Professor of Biblical Studies at the Hebrew University in Jerusalem. Cassuto's work, written originally in Hebrew, did not come to the attention of the English speaking world until 1961, when it was translated as *The Documentary Hypothesis and the Composition of the Pentateuch*. The book was a careful textual and linguistic analysis of the theory in its entirety, in which Cassuto examined the five pillars on which, in his view, the theory rested. He recognised that its builders had created "an imposing edifice", noting that in his day they were "still busy decorating its halls and completing its turrets". But upon examination, the kind of scrutiny to which he himself had subjected it, it would be found that "there was nothing to support it". The DH was "founded on air". It was "null and void".[20] As his translator remarked in the introduction to the English edition, Cassuto "examines the basic arguments of the prevailing Higher Critical view one by one, and proceeds to rebut them with compelling logic supported by profound learning".[21] It was a masterpiece in literary deconstruction and set a course for the many who would follow, Harrison, Kitchen and Wiseman among them.

Cassuto's work anticipated the end of the DH, and although the end may not yet have finally arrived, many contemporary Old Testament scholars admit that the DH is now *passé*. Indeed, with the decline of the DH one even speaks of the present "methodological crisis" in Genesis studies.[22] Although it remains to be seen just how that "crisis" will be resolved, the Tablet Theory, with its recognition of the importance of both archaeological evidence and the Genesis text itself must at least merit consideration as a legitimate explanation of the book's origins. It will be prudent at the same time to remember that Wiseman's theory is rejected *a priori* by many modern scholars

---

19   Wiseman, *Clues to Creation*, 5.

20   Umberto Cassuto (trans. Israel Abrahams), *The Documentary Hypothesis and the Composition of the Pentateuch* (Jerusalem: Hebrew University, 1961), 100–101

21   I. Abrahams in Cassuto, *Documentary Hypothesis*, v.

22   James McKeown, *Genesis* (Grand Rapids, MI and Cambridge, UK: Eerdmans, 2008), 8.

who still cling forlornly to the DH, including some who would otherwise be thought of as conservative.

The Tablet Theory

Wiseman was convinced that Genesis should be allowed to speak for itself in the light of archaeological discoveries which had revealed significant information concerning methods of writing used in ancient times. He thus proposed that

> The book of Genesis was originally written on tablets in the ancient script of the time by the Patriarchs who were intimately concerned with the events related, and whose names are clearly stated. Moreover, Moses, the compiler and editor of the book, as we now have it, plainly directs attention to the source of his information.[23]

This is the Tablet Theory in essence. Wiseman argued that the sheer amount of evidence demanded that Genesis be considered in the ancient environment in which it came into existence.[24]

The evidence came principally from the thousands of cuneiform tablets discovered at many sites all across the ancient Near East, beginning with the discovery of Ashurbanipal's famed library at Nineveh in the early 1850s. It is estimated that since archaeological excavations began in earnest in the mid-nineteenth century as many as 500,000 cuneiform tablets have been unearthed at many different sites, most of which are over four thousand years old.[25] They contain a wealth of information concerning virtually every aspect of ancient life and culture and are now scattered in museums all over the world, the majority located in Europe and the United States. Twenty-two thousand tablets from Nineveh alone are now housed in the British Museum.

Wiseman believed that lack of this knowledge had led to major errors in the DH and its underlying presuppositions, four of which he discusses at length:

1. That civilisation had developed gradually and appeared late in history;
2. The late development and use of writing;
3. No understanding of ancient literary customs and procedures;
4. The imposition of unfounded theories on the Genesis text.[26]

As a corrective to these errors, Wiseman argued that the cuneiform literature revealed:

1. The antiquity of civilisation;
2. The early development of writing;

---

23 Wiseman, *Clues to Creation*, 4.
24 *Ibid.*, 5.
25 S. Dalley, *Myths from Mesopotamia* (Oxford: OUP, 1991), xv.
26 *Ibid., passim*

3. The need to understand ancient literary customs;
4. That Genesis should be understood in the light of ancient literary practices which had prevailed in patriarchal times.

Many scholars now support all the above propositions and the important corollary that Genesis as it now stands was probably based on earlier written material. Cyrus Gordon, Professor of Near Eastern Studies at Brandeis University, stated that the sources for Genesis and possibly other Pentateuchal texts "were definitely in written form" before they were incorporated into the present biblical text, and with specific reference to Genesis 5:1 stated that it could only come from "a pre-biblical written source because sefer (or *sepher*)", the original word translated in the text as 'book', designated "only an inscribed text".[27] Several other writers have followed Gordon at this point.

The Antiquity of Civilisation

Working from the evolutionary assumption that human society developed slowly over long eras of time, proponents of the DH believed that civilisation was a recent phenomenon and that any evidence of it, such as writing, was also of late origin. Wiseman was convinced that precisely the opposite was the case. As ground for his understanding of Genesis he refers repeatedly to the great age of civilisation, "the high state of civilisation in early times", stating,

> It was confidently expected that excavation would support the widely held view of a gradual development of civilisation. But the cumulative evidence to the contrary has grown to such substantial proportions ... that it seems that soon after the Flood, civilisation reached a peak from which it was to recede. Instead of the infinitely slow development anticipated, it has become obvious that art, and we may say science, suddenly burst upon the world.[28]

In support of this assertion Wiseman cites other contemporary Near Eastern historians, including H. R. Hall, who wrote in his *History of the Near East,* "When civilisation appears it is already full grown", and "Sumerian culture springs into view readymade".[29] Kitchen succinctly confirms the foregoing, stating, "By 2000 BC the civilised world was already ancient".[30] It is now widely recognised, at least by archaeologists, Assyriologists and other informed ancient Near Eastern authorities, if not by evolutionists, that civilisation is considerably older than has been widely believed under the influence of evolutionary theory. As Wiseman himself put it, Sumerian civi-

---

27 C. H. Gordon, *Before the Bible* (London: Collins, 1962), 282.
28 Wiseman, *Clues to Creation*, 21.
29 *Ibid.,* 19.
30 Kitchen, *The Bible*, 25.

lisation, the oldest now known, "had reached its zenith" centuries before Abraham lived.[31]

Few have attempted to bring this reality to the attention of a generally uninterested world more than Professor S. N. Kramer. In two books in particular, *History Begins at Sumer* and *The Sumerians, Their History, Culture and Character*,[32] Kramer established beyond any possible doubt that the history of the Sumerian peoples proved that civilisation existed much earlier than had been supposed previously and that it had spread widely. Kramer wrote:

> By the third millennium BC, there is good reason to believe that Sumerian culture and civilisation had penetrated, at least to some extent, as far east as India and as far west as the Mediterranean, as far south as ancient Ethiopia and as far north as the Caspian.[33]

Kitchen writes of "the brilliant third millennium BC", the period between approximately 3200 and 2000 BC, stating that during this period "the civilisations of Egypt and Sumer reached their first peak of maturity and brilliant achievement", noting specifically "the emerging brilliance of Mesopotamian culture" as far back even as 5000 BC.[34] Sir Leonard Woolley wrote in *The Sumerians* that already c. 2000 BC, after the fall of the third Sumerian dynasty at Ur, Sumerian scribes "took it in hand to record the glories of the great days that had passed away".[35] It appears that Wiseman's belief in the great antiquity of civilisation was well founded.

The Early Development of Writing

It is not too much to claim that writing is the single most evident mark of civilisation, the final indicator that civilisation has arrived. Writing, of course, presupposes the ability to read. Wiseman knew that writing had developed early and that its use was widespread long before patriarchal times. He claims it as "one of the most remarkable facts that has emerged from archaeological research", noting specifically that although the general view has been to insist on the late appearance of writing, "now (*i.e.* from the mid-twentieth century) the pendulum has swung in the opposite direction, and the present tendency is to thrust back the period for which written records are claimed to about 3500 BC".[36] The early development and widespread use of writing in the ancient world is a crucial factor in Wiseman's tablet

---

31 Wiseman, *Clues to Creation*, 102.

32 S. N. Kramer, *History Begins at Sumer* (London : Thames & Hudson, 1958); *idem, The Sumerians, Their History, Culture and Character* (Chicago, IL: University of Chicago, 1964).

33 Kramer, *The Sumerians, Their History, Culture and Character*, 5.

34 Kitchen, *The Bible*, 23.

35 C. L. Woolley, *The Sumerians*, cited in Wiseman, *Clues to Creation*, 21.

36 Wiseman, *Clues to Creation*, 25.

thesis since it opens up the possibility that Genesis 1–11 could be largely a transcript from a very old series of written records. It is helpful, then, to know that many other respected authorities testify to the antiquity of writing as well as to the antiquity of civilisation itself.

Kramer stated that the Sumerians developed writing into "a vital and effective instrument of communication" pointing out that by the second half of the third millennium BC, Sumerian writing techniques could "express without difficulty the most complicated historical and literary compositions".[37] Harrison also noted "the immense antiquity of writing", arguing that the composition of Genesis should be studied "against the background of ancient Near Eastern literary activity".[38] Kitchen correctly pointed out, "Throughout the ancient biblical world, not one but several systems of writing were in use, often at the same time", specifying that "a rich and considerable literature" has survived from Mesopotamia and that cuneiform tablets discovered in profusion in the ancient Hittite capital at Hattusas prove that at least seven different cuneiform languages were used by the Hittites in formulating their records.[39] W. G. Lambert confirmed that cuneiform writing was used widely "for international communication" throughout Mesopotamia.[40] There is, then, ample confirmation of Wiseman's claim that writing developed before the time of Abraham and for his assertion that in view of the prevailing literary customs of antiquity it would be surprising if the patriarchs had *not* caused the information now recorded in Genesis to be set down in writing.[41]

Ancient Literary Customs

Wiseman also understood that the cuneiform literature revealed that ancient scribes used certain literary devices, notably in connecting successive tablets in a series. There were two such practices, the use of catch-lines and colophons, which it is necessary to understand. A catch-line was a sentence or phrase from the last line of a tablet which was repeated at the beginning of the next tablet to ensure continuity and, if a series of tablets became disordered, to enable the reader to rearrange them correctly. Sometimes the catch-line could be the title of the document, in this case usually the first few words of the opening tablet. Sometimes a numbering system was added. In his study *The Babylonian Genesis*, Alexander Heidel examined the contents of the now well-known Babylonian creation epic, *Enuma Elish*, dating from the early second millennium BC, which had been written on a series of

---

37   S. N. Kramer, *History Begins at Sumer* (London: Thames and Hudson, 1956), 19.

38   Harrison, *Old Testament*, 58, 543.

39   Kitchen, *The Bible*, 17–18.

40   W. G. Lambert, "A New Look at the Babylonian Background of Genesis", *Journal of Theological Studies,* 16 (1965), 300.

41   Wiseman, *Clues to Creation*, 56.

seven tablets, noting the catch-lines as they appeared on successive tablets.[42] It is one of many examples that could be cited. We can perhaps compare catch-lines to the running heads and page numbers of a modern book.

The other frequently used literary device in ancient literature was the colophon. A colophon was the concluding statement on a document and it normally included the name of the scribe or owner of the tablet (not always the same person) and frequently a reference to the time of composition. Thus the colophon took the place of the title-page in a modern book, but appeared at the end of the document rather than at the beginning. Colophons did not always contain the same amount of information, and the cuneiform literature reveals that the content often varied from scribe to scribe. Occasionally no colophon was used at all. Heidel also referred to the use of colophons in the Assyrian recension of the *Atra-hasis* epic found in the library of Ashurbanipal at Nineveh, as did Lambert and Millard in their study of the same story. They note that in this case a colophon appears at the end of each tablet "giving such details as we expect on a title-page".[43]

Wiseman recognised the significance of catch-lines and colophons in ancient texts and referred to them frequently, claiming that a careful analysis of Genesis revealed their recurring presence in the Genesis text and concluding, "There can be little doubt that initially much of the book of Genesis would have been written on tablets (for) on examining the book of Genesis we find that some of these ancient literary usages are still embedded in the present English text". Referring to the scribes of Nineveh who in the second millennium BC copied tablets which had been written a thousand years earlier using these ancient literary techniques, he argued that the compiler of Genesis had done "precisely the same".[44] This writer is persuaded that Wiseman conclusively proved his case.

The Structure of Genesis

The foregoing is all necessary background to the central idea in Wiseman's Tablet Theory — that much of Genesis was originally written on tablets in ancient times, using the literary customs then current. In the foreword to the 1977 edition of Wiseman's book, D. J. Wiseman summarised his father's approach, "Taking his cue from the recurrent catch-lines or colophons in Genesis, he examines them as clues to the literary structure of Genesis

---

42　A. Heidel, *The Babylonian Genesis* (Chicago, IL: University of Chicago, 2nd edn, 1968), 18–20.

43　W. G. Lambert and A. R. Millard, *Atra-hasis: The Babylonian Story of the Flood* (Oxford: Clarendon, 1967), 5.

44　Wiseman, *Clues to Creation*, 33. On the use of catch-lines and colophons in ancient texts see also Dalley, *Myths from Mesopotamia,* 20, 29, 71, 77 etc.

and as indicative of its origin and transmission".[45] So the structure of Genesis, understood in the light of ancient scribal techniques, lies at the heart of the Tablet Theory. We must follow Wiseman closely at this point. He maintained that the phrase, "These are the generations of ..." (KJV), used eleven times in Genesis 1–36,[46] was "the master-key" to understanding its structure. These eleven uses of the *toledot* phrase indicated eleven colophons in the text and thus eleven original tablets on which primeval and patriarchal history had been successively recorded over many centuries.[47]

Perhaps the best way to grasp Wiseman's argument is to imagine that we have in front of us an original Genesis text as it might have appeared to those who first read it — without chapter or verse divisions and without sub-headings in the text to alert us to a change of direction or subject matter — just pages of continuous Hebrew text. How would we know where such changes took place? How would we make sense of it all? Wiseman argued, and virtually all modern scholars now concur, that the phrase "These are the generations of ..." was the point of transition or change throughout the book. Wiseman was working from the KJV but most modern versions translate the phrase differently. Rather than confusing the issue these modern versions are actually helpful, as we shall note, since many of them clarify the meaning of the phrase while maintaining its overall structural significance.

This key phrase is now widely referred to as 'the *toledot* formula' since the Hebrew word translated "generations" in the KJV is the word *toledot* (or *toledoth*). Harrison strongly supports Wiseman's assertion that the use of the *toledot* phrase indicates the presence of a colophon and thus constitutes "part of the concluding sentence of each section, thereby pointing back to a narrative already recorded". He therefore argues that it is "eminently possible to regard its incidence as indicating the presence of a genuine Biblical source in the text".[48] These sources, in the view of both Wiseman and Harrison, were the original tablets on which Genesis had been written. In a section entitled '*Toledot* and the Origins of Genesis' in his *Introduction to the Old Testament*, Harrison also asserts that it was "the clue to the underlying sources" of Genesis and therefore the key to understanding the book.[49] It is, perhaps, of more than passing interest that even advocates of the DH had long recognised that the *toledot* phrase was a distinguishing feature of Genesis. S. R. Driver, the early twentieth-century Old Testament and Hebrew

---

45   D. J. Wiseman, in Foreword to *Clues to Creation*, vi.

46   Gen 2:4; 5:1; 6:9; 10:1; 11:10; 11:27; 25:12; 25:19; 36:1; 36:9; 37:2. Unless otherwise indicated the KJV is cited in all biblical references since this was the version Wiseman worked from.

47   Wiseman, *Clues to Creation*, 34–35.

48   Harrison, *Old Testament*, 547.

49   *Ibid.,* 543.

scholar, stated that Genesis was cast in a framework "marked by the recurring formula 'these are the generations of ...'", and that the "entire narrative as we now have it is accommodated to it".[50] Harrison notes that many other earlier Genesis scholars believed similarly.

But what does *toledot* actually mean? The KJV translates it as "generations", but many modern versions translate it differently. The NKJV, for example, translates it "history" or "genealogy" (in the usual sense of family history), and the NIV translates it "account of". Wiseman points out that *toledot* is not the normal Hebrew word for 'generations' which is *'dor'*, so translated 123 times in the Old Testament. Following the early Hebrew scholar Gesenius, Wiseman argues that the true meaning of *toledot* is "history", especially "family history" or "'origins of'".[51] The equivalent phrase in English would then be "these are the historical origins of" or "these are the beginnings of", which leads us to Wiseman's fundamental point, *"it is therefore evident that the use of the phrase in Genesis is to point back to the origins of family history and not forward to a later development through a line of descendants".* [52] Harrison also insists that the term "is used to describe history" and particularly in Genesis "family history in its origins".[53] This history was initially recorded on tablets, and the transition between each tablet was marked by a colophon which contained the *toledot* phrase. It points backwards to that which precedes it rather than forwards to that which follows.

Wiseman and Harrison both provided tables illustrating the structure of Genesis based on the *toledot* colophons, and noting the eleven source tablets on which Genesis had originally been written. Harrison's table follows:

Tablet 1: Gen.1:1–2:4: The origins of the cosmos;
Tablet 2: Gen 2:5–5:2: The origins of mankind;
Tablet 3: Gen 5:3–6:9a: The history of Noah;
Tablet 4: Gen 6: 9a–10:1: The history of Noah's sons;
Tablet 5: Gen.10:2–11:10a: The history of Shem;
Tablet 6: Gen 11:10b–11:27a: The history of Terah;
Tablet 7: Gen 11:27b–25:12: The history of Ishmael;
Tablet 8: Gen 25:13–25:19a: The history of Isaac;
Tablet 9: Gen 25:19b–36:1: The history of Esau;
Tablet 10: Gen 36:2– 36:9: The history of Esau.
Tablet 11: Gen 36:10–37:2: The history of Jacob.[54]

50 S. R. Driver, *The Book of Genesis* (London: Methuen, 1904), ii.

51 Wiseman, *Clues to Creation*, 36. *Cf.* also L. Koehler and W. Baumgartner, eds., *The Hebrew and Aramaic Lexicon of the Old Testament* (Leiden: E. J. Brill, 1999), vol. 4, 1700.

52 Wiseman, *Clues to Creation,* 37.

53 Harrison, *Old Testament,* 546.

54 *Ibid.,* 548.

These tablets were written successively as history unfolded, providing an accurate account "of primeval and patriarchal life written from the standpoint of a Mesopotamian cultural milieu".[55]

Most contemporary commentators do not follow Wiseman and Harrison, holding instead that the *toledot* phrase introduces the section in the text which follows. Wiseman was aware of this view and drew attention to the first use of the phrase in Genesis 2:4a, "These are the generations of the heavens and the earth", or as in the NKJV, "This is the history of the heavens and the earth", pointing out that in this instance the phrase could not possibly refer to the narrative which followed, but must summarise the creation account which preceded it. Almost all modern authorities concede that this is so, as do many recent translations of the Bible (*e.g.* NEB, NRSV, NLT). It would seem then more logical and consistent to think that the phrase would be used in the same way in succeeding instances and Wiseman comments:

> The phrase is only appropriate as a concluding sentence. So most commentators, notwithstanding their usual opposite interpretation of the words, make the story of the creation *end* with them. Had they seen that *all* sections of Genesis are *concluded* by the use of this formula they would have recognised the key to the composition of the book.[56]

This understanding of the *toledot* phrase is vital to Wiseman's argument, and his detailed explanation of it deserves careful attention.

Wiseman makes one further important point regarding the *toledot* phrase. He contends that the name recorded at the end of the phrase on each occasion it is used "refers to the owner or writer of the tablet rather than to the history of the person named".[57] This again is in harmony with the content of colophons in ancient usage. As already noted, many authorities recognise the widespread use of colophons in ancient literature, and the enlightening study by E. Leichty summarises much of what we have to this point observed. Leichty states that a colophon was "frequently used in ancient Mesopotamian literature", that a tablet with a colophon was "often part of a series", and that in earlier documents the colophon tended to be simple, giving only a name, a date, and sometimes, if part of a series, a catch-line.[58] Wiseman and Harrison both argue persuasively that the name could be either the name of the scribe or the owner of the original tablet. Thus 'These are the origins of Noah' (Genesis 6:9a), does not necessarily mean 'this is the history about Noah', but the history written or possessed by Noah. Wiseman notes that when in chapter 11:27 we read, "These are the generations of

55 *Ibid.*

56 Wiseman, *Clues to Creation*, 37.

57 *Ibid.*, 41.

58 E. Leichty, 'The Colophon', in *Studies Presented to A. Leo Oppenheim* (Chicago, IL: University of Chicago, 1964), 147–148

Terah", we do not read much subsequently about Terah, for it simply records that he was the son of Nahor. Wiseman says "The phrase is intended to indicate that Terah either wrote, or had written for him, the list of his ancestors found in verses 10 to 27".[59]

The colophon, then, concluded the tablet and it included the final *toledot* phrase which referred to the history or origins of the preceding narrative and the name of the writer or the original owner of the tablet. The eleven tablets were written successively in accordance with the literary norms of the times and as patriarchal history developed, and were eventually edited or compiled by Moses shortly before or shortly after the Exodus, in order that the Israelites would never lose the knowledge of their history. Referring to the characteristics of ancient Near Eastern literature, Harrison remarks:

> As with all similar ancient literature, these tablets constituted highly valuable sources for the delineation of patriarchal origins, and it is testimony to their antiquity and to the esteem in which they were held that they have survived in the Hebrew text in something which in all probability approximates to their original form.[60]

Wiseman and Harrison agree that Moses did not compose Genesis, but that he compiled it from a series of ancient tablets recorded as primeval and patriarchal history developed. This is why nowhere in the Bible, let alone in Genesis itself, is it claimed that Moses was the author of the book. Wiseman's own summary fittingly concludes this brief survey of the Tablet Theory:

> The more rigid the tests applied to Genesis, the more minute the examination of its contents in general and the words in particular, the more it is read in the light of the newer facts of archaeology, the more irresistibly does it lead us to the conclusion that Moses ... compiled the book, using the pre-existing records, which the Patriarchs had named, or he has named, at the end of each section of family histories.[61]

Internal Evidence for the Antiquity of Genesis

If the Tablet Theory is correct and the early chapters of Genesis were first written in antiquity, we would expect to find evidence of its great age in the text of those early chapters and evidence of subsequent history in later chapters. Wiseman presents several such lines of evidence, although limitations of space prevent us from exploring most of them in any detail. We note four:

1. *The presence of Babylonian words in the first eleven chapters.* Wiseman states "only definitely Babylonian words are to be found in the earlier chapters of Genesis" and claims that some linguistic experts believe that the

---

59 Wiseman, *Clues to Creation*, 41.
60 Harrison, *Old Testament*, 551.
61 Wiseman, *Clues to Creation*, 74.

entire atmosphere of these chapters is Babylonian. Harrison also mentions the "large number of Babylonian words that occur in the earlier part of the book".[62]

2. *The use of Egyptian words and reference to Egyptian customs in the later chapters.* The argument here is that when the narrative reaches the point at which Joseph arrives in Egypt "the whole environment changes". Wiseman cites several examples, then concludes "the person who wrote these chapters was intimately acquainted with Egyptian life and thought", emphasising "the irresistible testimony" that these later chapters must have been written in Egypt.[63]

3. *References to towns and places which either had ceased to exist or whose original names were already ancient by Moses' time.* Wiseman explains that Moses, as editor/compiler of Genesis, was obliged to add new names to some ancient places so that they could be identified by the Hebrews living in his day. He lists several instances in Genesis 14 alone, a chapter which was part of tablet 7 and written in the time of Abraham. Even in the four hundred or so years between Abraham and Moses some of these names had been lost, so Moses adds explanatory notes at the appropriate points:

> vv. 2, 8: Bela ('the same is Zoar')
>
> v. 3: The vale of Siddim ('which is the Salt Sea')
>
> v. 7: Enmishpat ('which is Kadesh')
>
> v. 15: Hobah ('which is on the left hand of Damascus')

Another instance is the reference to Hebron in Genesis 23:2 where it is recorded that Sarah died in Kirjath-arba with the explanation "the same is Hebron in the land of Canaan". Not only was the name by which the place was known in Moses' day recorded, but it was also necessary to state that Hebron was in Canaan. Wiseman comments "this surely indicates that the note was added at a very early date, before the children of Israel had entered the land. No-one in later times would need to be told where Hebron was".[64]

4. *Catch-lines in the text.* We have previously noted the use of catch-lines as an ancient literary device to connect successive tablets in a series. Wiseman lists the catch-lines that are evident in the Genesis text, claiming the fact we still find them embedded in the text confirms "the purity with which the text has been transmitted to us". It is further confirmation that the text had originally been inscribed on tablets.

---

62   *Ibid.*, 46; Harrison, *Old Testament*, 552.

63   Wiseman, *Clues to Creation*, 47, 103.

64   *Ibid.*, 48.

The catch-lines are as follows:

1:1 God created the heavens and the earth
2:4 Lord God made the heavens and the earth
2:4 When they were created
5:2 When they were created
6:10 Shem, Ham and Japheth
10:1 Shem, Ham and Japheth
10:32 After the Flood
11:10 After the Flood
11:26 Abram, Nahor and Haran
11:27 Abram, Nahor and Haran
25:12 Abraham's son
25:19 Abraham's son
36:1 Who is Edom
36:8 Who is Edom
36:9 Father of the Edomites (lit. father of Edom)
36:43 Father of the Edomites (lit. father of Edom)

Wiseman points to "the striking repetition of these phrases exactly where the tablets begin and end" and says that this repetition "cannot possibly be a mere co-incidence". The catch-lines had remained buried in the Genesis text, their "significance apparently unnoticed", until illuminated by the relatively recent understanding of the ancient cuneiform literary practices.[65]

External Evidence for the Antiquity of Genesis

Internal evidence of the antiquity of Genesis is complemented by a vast amount of external evidence, much of which has been summarised and documented in the works of Kitchen, Harrison and others, and also in the book, *I Studied Inscriptions from before the Flood*.[66] This rather unique title is actually a quotation from the writings of Ashurbanipal, the seventh-century BC king of Assyria whose vast cuneiform library was discovered at Nineveh and was found to contain various early Mesopotamian creation and flood accounts, many of them copies of much older texts. The book is a collection of articles first published in scholarly journals in the latter half of the twentieth century, all of which focussed on various aspects of Genesis 1–11 in the light of archaeological discovery, cuneiform literature and related ancient Near Eastern studies.

---

65 *Ibid.*, 51–52.

66 R. S. Hess and D. T. Tsumura, eds., *I Studied Inscriptions from before the Flood* (Winona Lake, IN: Eisenbrauns, 1994), 255.

The book contains a paper by D. J. Wiseman entitled 'Genesis 10: Some Archaeological Considerations', in which he examines aspects of the so-called Table of Nations in Genesis 10, a highly-condensed account of the three sons of Noah, Shem, Ham and Japheth, their descendents and the re-population of the earth after the flood. Wiseman remarks that the text of Genesis 10 "is in little doubt" since it is essentially confirmed in I Chronicles 1:4–23.[67]

We note here two of D. J. Wiseman's conclusions, the first concerning the descendents of Japheth. Recognising the difficulties in attempting to establish precisely where the Japhethites eventually settled, Wiseman supports the view, based on a "comprehensive survey", that they inhabited Anatolia and the north-eastern Mediterranean region.[68] He states, "Recent archaeological discoveries, especially the inscriptions found, support the view that the Japhetic list covers the north-eastern Mediterranean-Anatolian region". He then investigates the geographical boundaries within which the descendents of Ham and Shem eventually settled, as indicated initially in Genesis 10 by "the Hebrew historian". Reading this chapter, or indeed the preceding study on the Table of Nations, it is impossible to avoid the conclusion that the geographical, archaeological, ethnological and linguistic information under consideration collectively point to historical reality. Wiseman concludes the paper by stating that it is becoming "increasingly clear that the geographical information in Genesis 10 could have been available to the Egyptian court when Moses received his education there in the fifteenth or fourteenth century BC".[69]

Wiseman also draws attention to a significant aspect of Sumerian civilisation. Using phrases such as "literary evidence", "an increasing number of cuneiform texts" and "contemporary documents" he discusses what may be regarded as the central feature of early postdiluvian civilisation, outlined specifically in Genesis 10:10–12. Here are recorded the existence of a number of ancient cities, a reality not generally thought of as characteristic of the early 'hunter-gatherers' in the evolutionary chain. It is that the earliest known peoples of the Mesopotamian region were city-dwellers, rather than nomadic tribesmen. Wiseman says:

> The predominant feature of Sumerian civilization is that men dwelt in large walled cities. Archaeological investigation has produced no proof for a gradual evolution from village to town and then city. This means that they were industrialists and exported their varied wares, while importing other things necessary for their economy.[70]

---

67   D. J. Wiseman, "Genesis 10: Some Archaeological Considerations", in Hess and Tsumura, eds., *I Studied Inscriptions*, 255.

68   *Ibid.,* 258.

69   *Ibid.,* 265.

70   *Ibid.,* 263.

It is almost impossible in this context not to think of the Tower of Babel in Genesis 11. Hamilton, in his commentary on Genesis, remarks that it was "the building of the city, and not the tower per se, that provoked the divine displeasure".[71] Be that as it may, there is accumulated evidence from at least 2000 BC of trading in sophisticated merchandise throughout Mesopotamia, Asia Minor, India and Egypt, evidence in itself of urban rather than agrarian life. In describing the archaeological evidence from early Mesopotamia, Harrison recounts excavations at Uruk, the biblical Erech of Genesis 10:10, noting that Mesopotamia "saw the development of an increasingly complex urban life" with corresponding widespread commercial activity.[72] Wiseman himself concludes that such diversified and widespread trading "is abundantly attested by contemporary documents and implies a knowledge of the very areas outlined in Genesis 10".[73] It becomes increasingly difficult to ignore the factual content of Genesis 1–11, however condensed and sometimes obscure these early records undoubtedly are.

One further piece of external evidence should also be noted, the Sumerian King List (SKL) as it has come to be known, and the light it throws on Genesis 5. The SKL is a list, part fact and part fiction, of rulers from very early Sumerian times. There are now at least fifteen different versions of the list discovered in several locations and of varying age, but it is generally agreed that the list goes back to at least 2000 BC, and possibly earlier. This list has attracted the attention of many scholars, and features in at least nine of the studies included in *I Studied Inscriptions from before the Flood,* in addition to several other works. Later versions of the list divide these early kings into two categories, antediluvian and postdiluvian. It is the antediluvian list which is of most interest, since its earliest versions list ten successive rulers of the antediluvian world.

Two ancient tablets in particular, WB444 and WB62, both located in the Ashmolean Museum in Oxford, have given rise to much discussion, since WB444 lists only eight antediluvian kings, while the earlier WB62 lists ten. J. J. Finkelstein, an acknowledged authority on the SKL, states that on the evidence of WB62 "a case can be made out for the existence already at a relatively early date of the ten-king tradition" and argues persuasively that "the scribe of WB62 would not have presumed" to list ten kings if in fact there was "no precedent for a ten-king antediluvian tradition".[74] That the ten-king

71   Hamilton, *The Book of Genesis*, 356.

72   Harrison, *Old Testament*, 97–8.

73   D. J. Wiseman, 'Genesis 10', 264.

74   J. J. Finkelstein, 'The Antediluvian Kings: A University of California Tablet', in *The Journal of Cuneiform Studies* 17 (1963): 50.

tradition was of early date is confirmed by Lambert and Millard who argue that "the conclusion becomes inescapable that these ten kings were at first an independent tradition only secondarily prefixed to the king list".[75] It will have become apparent by now to the thoughtful reader that we are dealing here with an account that is in some respects parallel to that of Genesis 5, which lists ten generations between creation and the flood, giving the names of the heads of each generation. Ancient Near-Eastern specialists have been studying these ancient texts since the early twentieth century, frequently observing the recurrence of "ten rulers" who reigned before the flood. Wiseman himself states, "It is quite possible that the latter corresponds to the ten patriarchs mentioned in Genesis 5."[76] It is also quite possible, in the minds of some even probable, that the number of ten antediluvian kings is derived from the biblical account and thereby verifies its essential veracity and antiquity.

Umberto Cassuto wrote at great length on the topic, reminding us among much else and with much insight that a tradition regarding "*ten* heads of primeval generations" is to be found in many ancient Oriental cultures, including the Babylonian, Egyptian, Persian and Indian, among others, and that this tradition was reflected in the SKL.[77] He speaks of "the world's ten founding fathers", affirmed by the Genesis text but in contrast at many points with the SKL account. Commenting on the Genesis 5 record and the SKL, Cassuto said that there was between them "a similarity that cannot be fortuitous" and arguing that while the Sumerian accounts confirmed the biblical account, the latter "purified" and "refined" the diverse and often conflicting accounts of the Sumerian, Mesopotamian and Oriental traditions.[78] It is also worth noting that the third-century BC Babylonian historian, Berossus, recorded the ten-king antediluvian tradition in his *Babylonaica,* written in Greek *c.*278 BC, Cassuto commenting that "even the late testimony of Berossus" is sufficient to make us aware of "remarkable parallels" between the biblical record and the Babylonian tradition.[79] It seems that of all the various lists that had proliferated in antiquity, the ten-king version was the earliest and the one that had prevailed by the time Berossus came to write his history or it was the one which he believed retained the most credibility. The antediluvian section of the SKL in its earliest form reminds us once again of the antiquity, integrity and historicity of the Genesis text.

---

75 Lambert and Millard, *Atra-hasis*, 15.

76 Wiseman, *Clues to Creation*, 17.

77 U. Cassuto, *Commentary on Genesis* (Jerusalem: Hebrew University, 1961), 254, emphasis in the original.

78 *Ibid.,* 255, 263.

79 *Ibid.,* 254 ff.

In Conclusion

In *Clues to Creation in Genesis* P. J. Wiseman set out to demonstrate that:

1. Genesis had originally been written on clay tablets in ancient times by the patriarchs or their scribes,
2. In accordance with ancient literary customs.
3. Moses later compiled the book as it now stands and
4. That he clearly directs attention to his sources, evidence of which can still be seen in the Genesis text.

Wiseman believed that he had provided ample evidence in support of all the above. We have traced his arguments and observed that many of them and most, if not all, his various lines of evidence have been endorsed by respected scholars from many disciplines. He considered that the evidence *in sum* confirmed his proposal with such "strength and substance" that it required a decision in favour of the writing of Genesis in antiquity in harmony with the customs and techniques of ancient scribes.[80] If Wiseman was correct then it clearly requires that the historicity of the early chapters of Genesis be treated with more respect than is frequently the case today.

D. J. Wiseman referred to a number of professionals from various disciplines who had been persuaded, as he himself was, that his father's approach to Genesis was "the most rational, the most true to the text of Scripture and the most free from difficulties".[81] As noted, R. K. Harrison also endorsed that view. The arguments, the reasoning, the evidence from archaeology and from the Genesis text itself, the gaping flaws in the discredited Documentary Hypothesis and the unity the proposal brings back to the frequently dissected book of Genesis, all combine to call for the careful reading and objective evaluation of Wiseman's Tablet Theory. It also illuminates our understanding of the processes of revelation and inspiration. While for various reasons, including the lingering influence of the DH,[82] the thesis has until now remained a minority viewpoint, it should not be forgotten that objectivity and the continuing quest for truth do not allow arbitrary rejection of any proposal if the arguments and the evidence are sufficiently compelling, or if they lead to greater understanding.

---

80   Wiseman, *Clues to Creation*, 10.

81   *Ibid.,* viii.

82   Hamilton does not support Wiseman's theory or the general view that the first use of the *toledot* formula in Genesis 2:4a refers to the creation account which precedes it. He argues that the formula here introduces what follows as it does in all other uses in the subsequent text, but his appeal to the DH in support of this view is as significant as it is surprising, *The Book of Genesis*, 4.

Puritan History and Belief

"The greatness of Puritanism was its fidelity to the Word of God as the only source of true doctrine and right practice".
Edward Hindson, *Introduction to Puritan Theology* (1976), p. 23.

7. Puritans and Puritanism[1]

Bryan W. Ball

In his classic account of the early development of the English Puritan movement, William Haller makes the following observations:

> To the modern mind, judging hastily and with animus irrelevant to the facts, the sixteenth-century Puritan may seem a morbid, introspective, inhibited moral bigot and religious zealot. To the common man of the time this was not so ... In spite of the restrictions placed upon their activities, they incessantly preached the Gospel and published books ... and no one can wisely ignore them who desires to understand what Puritanism was and what it came to mean.[2]

It should be noted at the outset that Haller's comments relate specifically to the early Puritan movement in the latter years of the sixteenth century. He was describing the rise of Puritanism. We know, of course, as Haller himself did, that Puritanism only came to its maturity in the seventeenth century and that to understand it more fully we must read what seventeenth-century Puritans wrote and preached about. This we shall attempt to do, at least to a limited extent, in the chapters immediately following.

It is also worth noting that people were still reading Puritan books in the nineteenth century and finding them relevant to their day. One such reader was Ellen G. White, one of the early pioneers of the Seventh-day Adventist Church, who in her book *The Great Controversy Between Christ and Satan,* which was widely read in the nineteenth and early twentieth centuries, numbered among the outstanding English religious leaders of the past three eminent Puritan divines, Richard Baxter, John Flavel and Joseph Alleine.[3] We shall find occasion to refer to each of these three noted writers as we examine some of the biblically based beliefs of mature Puritanism and Nonconformity as they were taught and practised in England in the seventeenth and early eighteenth centuries. But it is first necessary to address more basic issues.

1 Adapted from *The English Connection; The Puritan Roots of Seventh-day Adventist Belief* (Cambridge: James Clarke, 2nd edition, 2014 [1st edition, 1975]). Used with permission.

2 William Haller, *The Rise of Puritanism* (New York: Harper, 1957), 5, 36.

3 Ellen G. White, *The Great Controversy Between Christ and Satan* (Mountain View, CA: Pacific Press, 1950), 252–53.

Who precisely were the Puritans? And what was Puritanism? Why did it exist, and what did it seek to accomplish? These are questions that are still debated by historians and although the answers given vary according to viewpoint, one thing is beyond question. The word 'Puritan' has been persistently misunderstood and misused. Even after the careful efforts of scholars to provide a more objective understanding of Puritanism, it is difficult to dissociate the term in the popular mind from the implications of John Pym's neat phrase 'that odious and factious name of Puritan'. Plainly speaking, Puritans were early regarded as dour, straight-faced kill-joys, opposed to pleasure of any kind and intent on shaping the unwilling majority of their fellow-citizens according to their own narrow whims and fancies. They have become accordingly and understandably unpopular. This image has persisted to the present even though it was less than objective, and frequently cried up by those with their own agendas.

This concept of narrowness, bigotry, even hypocrisy, is far from the true character of Puritanism, as those who are familiar with Puritan thought in its wholeness continue to point out. Inevitably, this jaundiced view owes something to the origin of the term, which it will not be amiss to recall. Like many names which have come to have a lasting religious significance, Quaker and Methodist among them, the term 'Puritan' arose as a derisive comment on the attitudes and actions of a small and vocal group in the Anglican Church during the latter part of the sixteenth century. It was initially applied to those within the Church of England who were dissatisfied with the extent to which the Reformation in England had been carried and who wanted a more thorough-going reform of the national Church. Their chief concern appears to have been with the structure and liturgy of the Anglican Church and with the desire that it should be remodelled according to the Presbyterian pattern of the Calvinistic Reformed Church at Geneva. Few historians would now insist on such a narrow definition of Puritanism, although it is true that at this early stage the concern of the Puritan faction was less with Christian life and doctrine than it was with the structure and organisation of the Church.

This early emphasis was soon to give way to something more fundamental, and as the seventeenth century began to unfold it is clear that there existed in England a much wider body of opinion, both within and without the Anglican Church, whose chief concern was for purity of doctrine and holiness of life. A concern over the nature of the Church remained, as we shall shortly observe, but with this broader group it was not an end in itself, but rather a means for the recovery of true doctrine and the preservation of the true Christian way of life. As such, Puritanism came into its own early in the seventeenth century and continued with remarkable vigour through many vicissitudes for a hundred years or thereabouts, thereafter to be disseminated in various channels, of which some would persist until the present time. Haller, whose *Rise of Puritanism* is indispensable for all who would truly understand the Puritan impetus, points out that Puritanism "was nothing new or totally unrelated to the past but something old, deep-seated, and English, with roots reaching far back into mediaeval life".[4] That comment must be allowed its due place in our thinking if we are to understand Puritanism in its essence, grasp its fundamentally English character and what is undoubtedly of greater importance, sense its significance to the later development of religious and political thought in the Western world.

If a date is required for the formal beginnings of Puritanism, it will not be inappropriate to suggest 1570, when Thomas Cartwright, Lady Margaret Professor of Divinity at the University of Cambridge, was removed from his chair for advocating the abolition of the Episcopal system of government in the Church of England in favour of Presbyterianism.[5] What may appear on the surface as a technical matter of little consequence was, in fact, a matter of some considerable significance at the time, particularly for those whose main court of appeal was the Bible. In Puritan eyes it was a question of whether the Anglican Church was willing to accept a more scriptural form of Church organisation, or persist with a system which could not be supported from the Word of God and which savoured too strongly of Rome and Antichrist. Matters of worship and liturgy were also far from satisfactory to the Puritan mind, since they retained too many features of the Roman system. Again, it was a question of origin and authority. If Scripture supported such practices, let them be retained. If not, they should be rejected and replaced by practices more in harmony with the Bible. The debate over organisation and worship was to continue for a good many years into the future and although it was always fraught with the question of national sovereignty, it would always come back in the end to the more basic question of biblical authority.

These issues went back to the earliest days of the English Reformation. Henry VIII had finally broken with Rome in 1534, although many historians feel that this was essentially a political and personal move,[6] and that compared with what would transpire later, it scarcely affected the doctrine of the Church or the life of the individual believer. There were changes, of course, and research has shown that there were evidences of genuine reformation during Henry's reign and earlier. A. G. Dickens has described the work of

4 Haller, *Rise of Puritanism*, 5.

5 Patrick Collinson, *The Elizabethan Puritan Movement* (London & New York: Methuen, 1967), 124.

6 E.g., M. Powicke, *The Reformation in England* (London: OUP, 1961, 1–3; W. Walker, *A History of the Christian Church* (Edinburgh: T. & T. Clark, 1959), 358–60.

Wycliffe and the Lollards as "the abortive reformation" and demonstrated that Lollard influence persisted well into the sixteenth century.[7] For all that, it is probably true that the formal Reformation which took place in the reign of Henry VIII was largely political and that the religious life of the age saw little practical improvement.

The reigns of Edward VI and Mary were accompanied by more definite changes, with a move towards more thorough-going Protestantism under Edward and a severe return to Rome under Mary. By the time Elizabeth I came to the throne in 1558 the country was bewildered and torn. Some preferred the old way and wanted to retain the Catholic faith and its manner of worship. Others wanted reformation and wanted it to be as thorough as that which had taken place at Geneva under John Calvin. Here, from the Puritan viewpoint, was a true Utopia, a practical demonstration of godly rule in action. Many, perhaps the majority, had no strong convictions, except that they be left in peace to live a life of their own choosing.

Elizabeth's religious policy was to follow the *via media* between these two extremes, with the object of maintaining a united kingdom at the expense of returning to Rome or going on to a more thorough form of Protestantism. The Elizabethan Settlement, as it has come to be known, was her attempt to establish a national Church which would appeal to the majority of her subjects and keep in subjection the extremists on either wing.

It was with a similar compromise in the reign of Henry VIII that Thomas Cartwright and his followers in the 1570s showed their dissatisfaction. They had waited impatiently for ten years or more for the changes which they believed necessary. When it became clear that such changes were not going to materialise, they took matters into their own hands and began in earnest a war of words which manifested itself in sermons, tracts and other forms of literature calculated to demonstrate the strength of their arguments and the need for true reformation. Increasingly thereafter the call for reformation in England was heard in pulpit and press. Although time revealed that it would not be until 1643, with the calling of the Westminster Assembly, that Presbyterianism would be seriously considered, albeit briefly, as an alternative to the Anglican Church, seeds had been sown which would take firm root and which would grow and bear fruit of a kind which even Cartwright could not have foreseen. Before the turn of the century, advocates of total separation from the Anglican Church had arisen, and little groups of Separatists met secretly for worship, or emigrated to Holland where they were able to meet freely to pursue their religion according to the dictates of conscience. By the time Elizabeth came to the end of her illustrious reign in 1603, the Puritan tide was well on its way in.

---

7 A. G. Dickens, *The English Reformation* (London; Batsford, 1964), 22, 27.

What had taken place under the Tudor monarchs in the sixteenth century, momentous as it undoubtedly was, served merely as a prelude to what would transpire under the Stuarts in the century which followed. Now the nation was to witness civil war, the execution of an archbishop and a king, a republican government, the Protectorate under Cromwell, the Restoration of the Monarchy and severe religious persecution, all to some extent consequences of religious convictions, to say nothing at this stage of the nature of those convictions themselves. Not without reason may the seventeenth century be regarded as the most momentous era in the history of England and as seminal to the subsequent development of Western society as a whole.

The accession of James I in 1603 was an event which Puritans in general heralded with some expectation. In Scotland, James had presided over the establishment of a Presbyterian system, in theory at least, and many hoped that he would be favourably disposed to the Puritan cause in England. On his journey south to take up residence in London, he was met by a large delegation of Puritan clergymen who petitioned him to press on at once with the re-organisation of the English Church. But, as Haller says, although James continued to champion Calvinistic theology,[8] "he had had more than enough of Presbyterianism".[9]

Those who had clung to the hopes of a Puritan breakthrough were soon to be disillusioned and we are left with the unhappy record of James threatening to harry Puritans out of the land. From then until 1640 the Puritan impetus was driven to seek expression in less conspicuous ways. It did so through preaching and notably through the production of a vast corpus of literature which grew in quantity, and generally in quality, as the seventeenth century continued to unfold. It is this body of literature — largely books, but also sermons and pamphlets — that we shall refer to in the chapters which immediately follow and which, if nothing else, will surely convince us of the essentially spiritual and irenic nature of mainstream Puritan thought and, of course, of the biblical basis on which it was all founded.

With the events which began in 1640, it seemed as though an avalanche had been precipitated which no man or group of men could contain. In that year, Parliament impeached the Archbishop of Canterbury, William Laud, for high treason and committed him to the Tower of London from where, five years later, he was led out and beheaded. A similar fate awaited Charles I, whose execution in 1649, following the verdict of a court constituted by the House of Commons, was an event of unprecedented boldness. Charles had declared war on the Parliamentary ar-

8   Puritans in general followed the theological system of John Calvin, which required a measure of commitment to the doctrine of predestination.

9   Haller, *Rise of Puritanism,* 49.

mies in 1642 and for some six years civil conflict was waged up and down the land. It was a traumatic time for Englishmen and their families. In 1643 a summoned body of Puritan divines, mostly Presbyterian by conviction but still nominally Anglican, met at Westminster for the purpose of advising Parliament in the matter of reforming the Church. They produced the well-known Westminster Confession of Faith[10] and two catechisms, all of which in their own way influenced Puritan doctrine and devotion in succeeding years. Before they met for the last time in 1649, they also produced a Presbyterian directory for worship which, though approved by Parliament, was never put into practice. That all this could transpire whilst Royalist and Parliamentary forces confronted each other on the battlefield is some indication of the religious nature of the age and of the undertones which ran through the conflict itself.

With the cessation of armed hostilities, the imprisonment of the king and the demise of high churchmanship, the way was opened for a unique experience in English history. For twelve years from 1648, with no ruler claiming as his authority the divine right of kings, the government of the land proceeded by a succession of experiments, which Oliver Cromwell, to give him his due, attempted to guide for the good of the nation as a whole. From the broad Puritan position, the experiment reached its high-point in July 1653 when the Nominated Parliament met for the first time. It consisted solely of members appointed by Cromwell and his advisors for their religious convictions and evident godliness — "saints" to use the contemporary word. It was known more generally as the 'Barbones' Parliament, after Praise-God Barbones, one of its members. Cromwell addressed the new Parliament in significant terms as they began their work: "Truly you are called by God to rule with Him, and for Him, ... I confess I never looked to see such a day as this ... when Jesus Christ should be so owned as He is, at this day".[11] It was, many felt, the beginning of the long-awaited reign of the saints on earth, prior to the glorious coming of Christ and the promised millennium.

But, alas, it was not to be. For reasons which it is not possible to examine here, the experiment ended in failure, the Nominated Parliament lasting less than six months and giving way to Cromwell's Protectorate, itself a form of government which in principle was less than ideal and which in practice proved less than popular. By 1660 most Englishmen were ready for Anglicanism and the monarchy to be restored and a return to stable government. Perhaps the greatest lesson which these years re-emphasise is that the

---

10   For an outline of the thirty-three articles of the Westminster Confession, see Henry Bettenson, ed., *Documents of the Christian Church* (London and Oxford: OUP, 2nd edition, 1967), 244–27.

11   W. C. Abbott, *The Writings and Speeches of Oliver Cromwell* (Cambridge, MA: 1937–1947), III, 61.

kingdoms of this world are not to be confused with the kingdom of God. It was a lesson, nonetheless, that many at that time were unwilling, or unable, to learn.

Many of the religious developments of these years were of equal significance to the subsequent growth of Protestantism in England and in America as they were to the Church in their own day. This is particularly true of the years between 1640 and 1660, which beyond question were the high-water mark of pre-Restoration Puritanism. From the beginning of the seventeenth century, Puritanism, in both senses in which it has been defined, became a powerful and growing force in the religious life of the nation. The ecclesiastical Puritans, intent as always on reforming the structure of the national Church, pressed on with their aims until, as we have observed, they formed a majority in the Westminster Assembly called to advise Parliament on Church reform. Only with the restoration of the monarchy in 1660 did it finally become clear that there was not to be a Presbyterian Church in place of the Episcopal Anglican Church. The more spiritual Puritans, both inside the established Church and among the independent, separatist groups which had sprung up throughout the land, while not ignoring the importance of correct discipline and order, were chiefly concerned to find the way of salvation for themselves and for their families, and to lead a godly life while on earth. Although prior to 1640, owing to the repressive measures of Archbishops Bancroft and Laud and the antipathy of James I and Charles I, both streams of the Puritan movement were held in check, Puritan preachers, as they were permitted, continued to make use of the pulpit and the press to propagate their ideas, so laying a foundation for the tumultuous years which lay just ahead.

Between 1640 and 1660 this outwardly stable situation changed almost beyond recognition, not only in the political arena but, more significantly for our purposes, in the realm of religious belief and religious activity. Ideas which had lain dormant for decades, or which had been discussed in secret, suddenly burst forth with amazing vitality. Mention must be made in this respect of the eschatological convictions which came to play such an important role in the religio-political events of the 1640s and the 1650s. From the earliest days of the English Reformation men had looked forward to the second coming of Christ and the kingdom of God on earth. An increasing interest, during the latter part of the sixteenth century, in the books of Daniel and Revelation, which grew to intensive study during the seventeenth century,[12] provided new eschatological understanding and gave fresh hope for the future.

---

12   See later, chapter 11, 'Early English Apocalyptic Interpretation'.

It is hardly necessary to point out that many of the interpretations of these prophetic books were incorrect and many of the conclusions reached unfounded, particularly among the less qualified expositors. What is beyond doubt is that eschatological expectation ran high for much of the first half of the seventeenth century, reaching its zenith between 1640 and 1660, and affecting during those years not only the religious views of the population as a whole but also the political activity of men in high office. Combined with these hopes of a coming millennium and the kingdom of God were revived fears and convictions concerning the Papacy and the Antichrist. Few doctrines had been more calculated to propel Englishmen in the direction of Protestantism than those which identified the Papacy with the Antichrist, particularly at times when the sovereignty of the state was threatened by papal decrees and intrigue. With Foxe's *Book of Martyrs* always available and read avidly and with the reported Romanising tendencies of Laud and Charles I realities with potentially serious consequences, it is not surprising that in the years we are considering those who studied Scripture carefully found justification for a renewed preoccupation with the dreaded Antichrist.

These years also saw the emergence of religious groups hitherto unheard of, many of which were to pass into obscurity as rapidly as they had arisen, but some of which, containing elements of a more enduring nature, were destined to influence the religious scene in Europe and America for centuries to come. From the beginning of the seventeenth century the Independents grew in strength as the century unfolded and although never numerically as strong as the Presbyterian party, nonetheless counted among their adherents some of the most influential clergy of the day. These early years had also seen the beginnings of a movement towards complete separation from the national Church. Guided by bold spirits who saw an irreducible connection between Rome, the Church of England and Antichrist, little groups of believers, impatient with the slow progress towards reform, sought to make a thorough break with the establishment by instituting a Church and pattern of worship totally divorced from that of the Church of England. These were the Separatists and from them and their Independent brethren, religious communions such as Presbyterians, Congregationalists, and Baptists were to arise, reaching down to the twentieth century and out into the whole world.

It is quite impossible, in the limited space available, to give an account which would be less than confused of the bewildering number of sects which mushroomed almost overnight from 1640 onwards, to say nothing of their equally bewildering beliefs. If we mention only the Fifth Monarchy Men, who were in their own day and have since been recognised as one of the extreme religio-political groups of the time, and say that judged by the views of some of the other sects their opinions were comparatively sane, we have said much.[13] The Fifth Monarchists believed that the four kingdoms of Daniel chapters 2 and 7 had already been fulfilled in history and that the kingdom of the stone, the fifth kingdom of prophecy, was about to be established on earth. They were also convinced that they had been called by God to bring that kingdom into existence by political activism, even by the use of the sword, should that prove necessary. Bizarre as that may seem today, in comparison with groups such as Muggletonians, Behmenists, Ranters, Diggers and the Family of Love, their ideas were not extreme. The existence of these groups serves as a reminder of the new freedom which now prevailed, and which was equally appreciated and exploited by the wider and more sober body of Puritans.

For our immediate purposes the most significant religious development after 1640 was, perhaps, in the area of literature. When William Laud succeeded to the archbishopric of Canterbury in 1633 he set himself the task, among others, of rectifying the laxity which had crept into the regulations which controlled printing and publishing, especially those concerning censorship. It was too late to prevent the dissemination of Puritan ideas by the press, but not too late to make a determined stand against anything which savoured of heresy or of an attack on the existing order. As one writer points out Archbishop Laud, like most of his contemporaries, did not distinguish between words which merely expressed ideas and words which actually incited rebellion or violence. To Laud and his colleagues words were words, whether spoken or written, and, if the need was such, should be punished for what they were.[14] It was this understanding, or lack of it, which prompted Laud to direct his keenest attention to the Puritan preachers and pamphleteers, who ever sought to go into print. As a consequence, the years immediately preceding 1640 are noticeably lacking in printed material other than strictly devotional works by established Puritan preachers and similar works by Anglican authors. This should not be taken to suggest that prior to 1640 religious works were infrequently published. Any representative bibliography will prove that this was not the case. It is intended to suggest that there was a prodigious increase in the output of literature of all kinds and of Puritan literature in particular, after Laud's removal from the scene in 1640. That, too, will be evident from the publication dates in the footnotes to this and other chapters.

With the accession of Charles II and the Restoration of the Monarchy in 1660, the course of English history took another sharp turn. From the Puritan viewpoint it was decidedly a turn for the worse. The heady days of Cromwell's England were now past and Puritans were soon to learn the

---

13 On the Fifth Monarchy Men see B. S. Capp, *The Fifth Monarchy Men* (London: Faber and Faber, 1972).

14 Haller, *Rise of Puritanism*, 235.

harsh realities of a system intolerant of nonconformity, to say nothing of open dissent. In 1662 Parliament passed the Act of Uniformity which required all clergymen to take an oath of loyalty and non-resistance and to declare their total assent to the Book of Common Prayer. It was a cruel dilemma for hundreds of clergymen throughout the land who had espoused Puritan ideals, particularly as the date for compliance was set to coincide with the anniversary of the infamous St. Bartholomew's Day massacre of French Protestants. The outcome must have been predictable to the government and is known in English religious history as the Great Ejection, when between 1,700 and 2,000 clergymen, many of them the cream of the nation's spiritual and intellectual leadership, refused to abjure their consciences and were summarily ejected from their livings. It is estimated that in London alone at least forty graduates of Oxford or Cambridge, including six doctors of Divinity, were removed from their pulpits and forced to eke out a living for themselves and their families as best they could, in common with their ejected brethren throughout the land. The sufferings of the ejected clergy have been variously described, but C. E. Whiting's brief account is probably as near the truth as any: "Some lived on little more than brown bread and water, many had eight or ten pounds a year to maintain a family ... One went to plough six days a week and preached on the Lord's day".[15] Even that was a privilege which was soon to be denied.

Further legislation against Puritan and Nonconformist dissent quickly followed. Collectively known as the Clarendon Code, after the Earl of Clarendon, Charles II's Chancellor and chief minister, it included the Corporation Act, which effectually excluded from national or local public office all who refused to conform; the Conventicle Act, which prohibited all private meetings for worship which were attended by more than four persons beyond the immediate family; and the Five Mile Act, which prevented ejected clergy from living within five miles of a corporate town or any town in which they had preached in recent years. The Test Act of 1673 reaffirmed that every Nonconformist, whether dissenter or recusant, should be excluded from all public office, stipulating that those who wished to be considered eligible should receive the sacrament according to the Anglican rite at his parish church. It is quite clear that the years between 1660 and 1690 brought the most severe restrictions upon the Puritan ministry and laity alike. These were the years of real hardship and active persecution, particularly between 1681 and 1687 and notably under the notorious Judge Jeffreys, following the accession of James II in 1685.

---

15   C. E. Whiting, *Studies in English Puritanism, 1660–1688* (London, 1931), 20.

According to one contemporary record, Jeffreys executed hundreds of Dissenters in Dorset and Somerset and sent hundreds more as convicts to the West Indies.[16] While it is true that these punishments were inflicted for rebellion rather than for religious belief for its own sake, and that not all who were involved in the rebellion were Dissenters, it is also true that many acted from religious motivation and that the effects of Jeffreys' directives were felt most keenly among dissenting communities. Whole congregations were decimated, some reduced virtually to non-existence. Mercifully, circumstances compelled James to adopt a change in policy and the Declaration of Indulgence of 1687 and also the Toleration Act of 1689, effectively brought to an end the various repressive measures which had been levelled against Puritan dissent in the preceding thirty years. Thenceforward, freedom of worship was guaranteed to Protestants who found themselves unable to confirm to the doctrine, liturgy or constitution of the Anglican Church.

These latter years may be regarded as the time of Puritanism's maturity and nowhere is this more evident than in the literature of that era. The bulk of Richard Baxter's enormous output belongs to this period. John Bunyan's immortal *Pilgrim's Progress* and his scarcely less renowned *Grace Abounding to the Chief of Sinners*, both came from these years. John Flavel's works of divinity and devotion, six volumes in all, warm and practical to the end, were also the product of Puritanism's later years. And Joseph Alleine's *Alarm to Unconverted Sinners*, which appeared in a modern edition as recently as 2000, was first published in 1672, selling 20,000 copies. So popular did this book prove to be that another edition in 1675 reached 50,000 copies and numerous further editions continued to appear throughout the following two hundred and fifty years. Many of these writings we shall have occasion to sample as our investigation of selected Puritan beliefs proceeds. It has been argued that the literature of Puritanism's mature years holds the secrets of England's past greatness, the principles of a free society, the motivation for the Church's world mission and, some would add, the key to a revived Protestantism and a completed Reformation.

It is not possible to offer an exhaustive account of any of the Puritan beliefs which are surveyed in the next few chapters. To provide that would almost certainly require a separate volume for each doctrine and, in any case, some of the topics examined have in fact received more extended treatment elsewhere, as, for example in E.F. Kevan's *The Grace of Law* and the present author's *A Great Expectation: Eschatological Thought in English Protestantism to 1660*.[17] In examining the Puritan beliefs selected for inclu-

16 *The Western Martyrology or The Bloody Assize* (1705), *passim*, cited in W. T. Whitley, *A History of British Baptists* (London: Charles Griffin, 1923), 149.

17 E. F. Kevan, *The Grace of Law: a Study in Puritan Theology* (London:

sion in this book, emphasis has been placed on the reasons for those beliefs which exegesis of the biblical text clarified and necessitated. This has often been at the expense of their historical and chronological development and of personal biographical information concerning the men who advocated those beliefs.[18] These omissions are readily acknowledged and they will no doubt disappoint some readers. The nature of these studies suggests, however, that it is more important to understand the doctrines themselves than the men who proclaimed them, and that in order to understand the men it is necessary first to understand the ideas which made them what they were. Having understood the beliefs of the men and women who were called Puritans, it is hoped that we shall then be able to understand Puritanism itself, why it existed and why it came to be such a force in English history in the seventeenth century and in the development of later Nonconformity in much of the English-speaking world.

Carey Kingsgate Press, 1964); B. W. Ball *A Great Expectation: Eschatological Thought in English Protestantism to 1660* (Leiden: E.J. Brill, 1975).

18   Information concerning many of the individuals referred to can be found in Beeke and Pederson, *Meet the Puritans* (Grand Rapids: Reformation Heritage, 2006) as well as the *Oxford Dictionary of National Biography*.

8. 'Puritan' Profiles

Bryan W. Ball

The *Oxford Dictionary of National Biography* (*ODNB*) was published in 2004 and in an online edition in 2008. The *ODNB* contains entries on every significant person who has influenced British history from as far back as records have been kept. The print edition consists of 55 volumes, written by over 10,000 contributors, all specialists in their fields. It replaced the older 50-volume *Dictionary of National Biography* that, for more than a century, had provided similar information on individuals who had lived before the end of the nineteenth century. The *ODNB* was the biggest publishing endeavour ever undertaken by Oxford University Press, and it is difficult to imagine that there will ever be another like it. Following are three entries of the six contributed to the *ODNB* by the present author. They all deal with individuals who lived and worked in the Puritan era. While none of these men was actually Puritan in a strictly defined sense, they belonged unquestionably to the seventeenth century — two Anglicans, Mede and Bold, who held Puritan sympathies, and Writer, who was well to the left of Puritanism and best described as a typical radical. Each of them is related in some way to other chapters in this book, Mede to ch.11 and Bold and Writer to ch.15, through its derivation from *The Soul Sleepers*. The articles are reproduced here *verbatim* by permission of Oxford University Press.

Joseph Mede

Mede [Mead], Joseph (1586–1638), Hebraist and biblical scholar, was born in October 1586 at Berden, Essex, of unknown parents 'of honest rank', according to the 'Life' contained in his collected works, and was related through his father to Sir John Mede (or Mead) of Wenden Lofts, near Bishop's Stortford. When Mede was ten his father died of smallpox and his mother married a Gower of Naseing, Essex, by whom he was sent to school, first at Hoddesdon, Hertfordshire, and later at Wethersfield, Essex. While at Wethersfield, and on a trip to London, he purchased a copy of Bellarmine's *Institutiones linguae Hebraicae* and by the time he left school had, without any instruction, obtained a considerable working knowledge of Hebrew. In 1603 he matriculated as sizar at Christ's College, Cambridge, where he studied first under Daniel Rogers and then under William Addison, before graduating BA in 1607 and proceeding MA in 1610. In 1613 he was elected to succeed Hugh Broughton to the King Edward VI fellowship through the influence of Lancelot Andrewes, then bishop of Ely, after having been passed over several times on suspicion of having 'too much ... tenderness to the Puritan faction' (Mede, 850). Valentine Cary, master of Christ's, may eventually have been disposed to view him more favourably on account of his friendship with Sir Martin Stuteville of Dalham, who was also a friend of Mede. In 1618 Mede was appointed Mildmay Greek lecturer, holding both fellowship and lectureship for the rest of his life. He did not marry, and lived modestly in a chamber at ground level beneath the college library.

Mede was a man of wide interests and considerable attainment. In addition to his skills in Hebrew, Greek and Latin and his knowledge of the biblical text in English and the original languages, he was proficient in several other disciplines. His early biographer describes him as 'an acute logician, an accurate philosopher, a skilful mathematician, a great philologer, and an excellent anatomist' (Worthington, ii). By invitation he frequently attended dissections at Gonville and Caius College. He was also proficient in botany, physics, and history, and was interested in astrology. He is said to have been as deeply versed in ecclesiastical antiquities and knowledge of the Greek and Latin fathers 'as any man living' (Brook, 429). His pursuit of knowledge and his scholarly achievements, including his biblical studies, were marked by a love of truth for its own sake. 'I cannot believe', he is reported as saying, 'that truth can be prejudiced by the discovery of truth' (ibid., 431). A period of scepticism early in his reading of philosophy, which led towards Pyrrhonism, gave way to devout belief. As has been observed, 'escaping the jaws of atheism, he fled towards faith' (Firth, 214).

Despite his profound erudition, Mede was a man of great modesty and humility. John Worthington, who is generally credited with the 'Life' of Mede prefixed to later editions of his *Works*, says he was 'studiously regardless' of formal academic attainment, ecclesiastical preferment, and worldly advantage (Worthington xv). He eschewed higher degrees beyond the BD, which he took in 1618, and in 1627 and again in 1630 declined the provostship of Trinity College, Dublin, an opening made possible on the recommendation of Archbishop James Ussher, who is said to have sought Mede's assistance in the determination of his own great work on sacred chronology. Among Mede's pupils, whom he treated with great consideration, were several who achieved distinction, including John Milton and Henry More. Although his income was meagre Mede regularly gave one-tenth to charitable causes. He maintained good personal relationships and was known for his openness and generosity towards those who opposed him. He suffered throughout life from a speech impediment which, particularly in the early years, led him to decline many invitations to speak in public. He persevered with the defect, however, and was able to preach without noticeable hesitation.

Mede's theological and ecclesiological allegiance was finally settled in favour of moderation and episcopacy, although he was included in Benjamin Brook's *The Lives of the Puritans* (1813) and had some puritan sympathies. Worthington notes his 'reverential regard to the established government and discipline of the Church' (Worthington, xxx), and Ussher's support and, more strikingly, Andrewes's invitation to him to become his chaplain cannot be ignored. Brook refers to Mede's correspondence with several eminent nonconformists and his fear that Roman rites would prevail again in the Church of England. Mede's view of Rome as the Antichrist and his conviction of the necessity of a godly life were both puritan emphases. They were balanced, however, by his concern that some puritan arguments opened the door to Socinianism and by his condemnation of a book by John Eastwick in a letter to Samuel Hartlib. He also opposed presbyterian discipline and practice. It would be incorrect to denominate him a party man in any strict sense, since a spirit of fraternal ecumenicity marked his outlook. He sought charity and mutual forbearance, 'the owning of each other as brethren and members of the same body whereof Christ is the head' (ibid., xvii). Remaining loyal to the Thirty-Nine Articles and prayer book liturgy, he expected that more would be achieved from mutual respect and toleration than by any attempt to legislate or impose uniformity.

Mede is notable for his works on biblical eschatology, and especially for *Clavis Apocalyptica* (1627), translated into English posthumously by Richard More and published as *The Key of the Revelation* (1643). It enjoyed the almost universal praise of contemporaries in England and on the continent and deeply influenced the development of eschatological thought in seventeenth-century England. Despite being intended originally only for private circulation among a select academic audience, it was published three times in Latin and in English between 1627 and 1650. The second Latin (1632) and subsequent English editions included Mede's *In sancti Joannis Apocalypsin commentarius*, a commentary on the Apocalypse, and the *Key* and the commentary, together with his other eschatological works, sufficiently emphasized the coming millennium to justify Mede being regarded as the father of English millenarianism. Given the radical nature of much of the ensuing millenarian activity, it was a reputation that Mede would have sought to avoid almost at any cost. He claimed to have reached his own moderate millenarian convictions with reluctance, having honestly endeavoured to locate the millennium in the past as had other interpreters, including Thomas Brightman and Hugo Grotius. His study of the biblical text, however, would not permit that conclusion. In anticipating a future millennium Mede did not consider that he was proposing extreme or heretical doctrine, but rather a return to the belief of the early church. The view that Mede derived his millenarianism from continental sources, particularly Alsted and Pareus, is outweighed by his own testimony and that of contemporaries. His biographer comments, 'He proceeded upon grounds never traced by any, and infinitely more probable than any laid down by those who before him undertook that task' (Worthington, vii). Fuller remarked that the Fifth Monarchists had driven the nail 'which Master Mede did first enter further than he ever intended it' (Fuller, 335). It remains fair comment on Mede's own millenarian position, and is supported by the later view that it was due to the efforts of others after his death that Mede was 'transformed from scholar to prophet' (Firth, 228). Most of his works were first published posthumously.

The distinctive element of the *Clavis Apocalyptica*, and Mede's unique contribution to contemporary and subsequent prophetic studies, was the noted synchronisms, which he argued were essential to a correct understanding of the book of Revelation. Within the context of the prevailing historicist interpretation of apocalyptic prophecy, the thesis underlying the synchronisms was that the major prophetic outlines in the books of Daniel and the Revelation were inter-related, contingent on each other, and that at many points they overlapped in scope, depicting the same era or events with different emphases. This was Mede's 'Law of Synchronistical necessity' (Mede, 583). It proposed to unlock the mysteries of apocalyptic prophecy making them accessible and relevant to the present age. Mede's standing as a careful scholar ensured that it was to have a profound effect on the religious life and outlook of the time and on the immediate course of English history over the next three decades. In addition to placing the millennium firmly in the future, thus opening the way for speculative interpretations and extreme millenarianism, Mede's exegetical scheme had at least two further consequences: it confirmed historicism as the fundamental principle of prophetic interpretation in English eschatological thought for several succeeding generations, and it unhesitatingly identified Rome as the Antichrist and the predicted latter-day apostasy. In an age which vividly remembered the Gunpowder Plot and its associated fears, Mede's considered and clearly articulated view of Rome as the 'the unfaithful and treacherous spouse, the Christian Jezebel' (J. Mede, *The Apostasy of the Latter Times*, 1641) was staple diet for English minds which cherished Protestantism and valued their religious freedom. Mede's work underpinned such intrinsic aspects of the religious outlook which prevailed in English post-Reformation thought for another 300 years or so.

Chronology and eschatology formed the basis for much of Mede's extensive correspondence, published in the later definitive editions of his works, edited by John Worthington (3rd edn. 1672; reprinted, 1677). Between 1626 and 1638 Mede's correspondents included Samuel Hartlib and John Durie, and his friends William Ames, professor of theology at Franeker in the Netherlands, and Sir William Boswell, ambassador to The Hague, each of whom was instrumental in bringing Mede and the *Clavis Apocalyptica* to the attention of potential readers abroad, and conveyed to Mede the comments and criticisms of some of his overseas readers. He also corresponded with James Ussher, William Twisse — later prolocutor of the Westminster assembly, who provided the preface for *The Apostasy of the Latter Times* - and Samuel Ward, master of Sydney Sussex College, Cambridge. Between 1620 and 1631 Mede also wrote regularly and at length to his friend Sir Martin Stuteville. This extensive series of letters, filling two folio volumes in the British Library (Harleian MSS 389 and 390), deals largely with current university issues and matters of local and public interest in England and abroad, throwing additional light on Mede as a man of his time, willing and able to comment on contemporary issues. The correspondence was brought to an end by Sir Martin's death in 1631.

Mede himself died prematurely, and in some discomfort, on 1 October 1638 at Christ's College, his death precipitated by the application of inappropriate medication which caused an internal blockage. His will, drawn up the day before his death, reveals that he was a man of only modest means, worth in all no more than 500 British pounds. He left 100 pounds to 'the master and fellows' of Christ's College, 100 pounds to the poor of Cambridge, and, after various smaller bequests to his sister and her children, to the children of a deceased sister, and to a pupil, the residue of his estate to Christ's College, 'towards the adorning of the College Chapel', where he was buried on 2 October. A delayed memorial service was held at Great St Mary's in February 1639 at which the preacher was John Alsop, also a fellow of Christ's and Mede's executor. A monumental inscription to Mede in Christ's College chapel, preserved in Latin (Mede, 35) and English, recalls his interest in philosophy, mathematics, chronology, history, and Near Eastern antiquities, and contains the words,

> He studied all languages, cultivated all the arts, ... and above all things, theology, the queen of all sciences ... He was a bigot to no party, but loving truth and peace, he was just to all; candid to his friends, benignant to others: holy, chaste, and humble in his language, wishes, and habits. (Brook, 433)

It remains a fitting tribute to one of the more notable English scholars of the seventeenth century.

Bryan W. Ball

Sources: J. Peile, *Biographical register of Christ's College, 1505–1905, and of the earlier foundation, God's House, 1448–1505, ed.* [J. A. Venn], 1 (1910); J.

Mede, *The works of the pious and profoundly-learned Joseph Mede* (1677); J. Worthington, 'The life of the reverend and most learned Joseph Mede', in *The works of ... Joseph Mede,* ed. J. Worthington, 4th edn (1677); B. Brook, *The lives of the puritans,* 2 (1813); Venn, *Alum. Cant., V*3; E . Middleton, ed., *Biographia evangelica,* 4 vols. (privately printed, London 1779–86); D. Neal, *The history of the puritans or protestant nonconformists,* ed. J. Toulmin, new edn, 2 (1822); K. R. Firth, *The apocalyptic tradition in Reformation Britain, 1530–1645* (1979); B. W. Ball, *A great expectation: eschatological thought in English Protestantism to 1660* (1975); Fuller, *Worthies* (1662); J. van den Bergh, 'Continuity within a changing context: Henry More's millenarianism, seen against the background of the millenarian concepts of Joseph Mede', *Pietismus und Neuzit,* 14 (1988), 185–202; J. van den Bergh, 'Joseph Mede and the Dutch millenarian Daniel van Laren', *Prophecy and eschatology,* ed. M. Wilks (1994), 111–22; J. Hunt, *Religious thought in England from the Reformation to the end of the last century,* 1 (1870); D. A. Cockburn, 'A critical edition of the letters of the Reverend Joseph Mead (1626) 27, contained in British Library Harleian MS 390', PhD diss., U. Cam., 1994; *DNB;* will, TNA: PRO, PROB11/179, fol. 142r; J. Heywood and T. Wright, eds., *Cambridge University transactions during the puritan controversies of the 16th and 17th centuries,* 2 (1854); A. J. Gilsdorf, 'The puritan apocalypse: New England eschatology *in* the seventeenth century', PhD diss., Yale U., 1965; F. S. Plotkin, 'Sighs from Sion: a study of radical puritan eschatology in England, 1640–1660', PhD diss., Columbia University, 1966.

Archives: BL, Harley MSS 389, 390; BL, Harley MSS, letters to Sir Martin Stuteville; BL, Add. MSS 4276, 4254, 4179.

Wealth at death approx. 500 British pounds: will, TNA PRO, PROB 11/1/179, fol. 142r

Samuel Bold

Bold, Samuel (1648–1737), Church of England clergyman, is of obscure origins. He was brought up and educated in Chester by William Cook (1611/12–1684), curate of St Michael's parish there. Cook was ejected in 1662 and served as nonconformist minister in the city thereafter. Bold later paid tribute to Cook's widow, Mary, for her 'great love' and 'motherly affection' from his infancy through childhood and youth (Bold, *Man's Great Duty,* sig. A2r). A Samuel Bold, according to the university register, matriculated from Jesus College, Oxford, on 3 November 1671, aged nineteen; if this is our subject, he was the son of Edward Bold (1603/4–1654/5), rector of Hawarden, Flintshire, and was born in 1651 or 1652 rather than 1648 or 1649, the dates derived from his reported age at death. However, Bold's name does not appear in the college's admission records, and there is no evidence of his graduation in either the college or university archives. Bold is notable principally on three counts: as an advocate of religious toleration, for his defence of John Locke, and for his later views on human nature and immortality.

In 1674 Bold was instituted vicar of Shapwick in Dorset, from which pulpit in March 1682, following the required reading of a brief on behalf of persecuted Protestants in France, he preached against intolerance and persecution in general. He decried both the repulsive nature of persecution and its perpetrators with equal clarity and zeal. The sermon was shortly published as *A Sermon Against Persecution,* specifically for 'the consideration of violent and headstrong men' (Bold, *Sermon,* title-page). It aroused much local indignation, particularly in view of Bold's defence of dissenters personally known to him as men 'of great learning, exemplary piety, strict devotion, and extraordinary loyalty' and his denunciation of those responsible for persecution as the 'devil's agents' (ibid., sig. A2v, 4) inflicting on the church 'unspeakable injury' (ibid., 23, 28) and who, having 'a great affection for Popery, are hastening towards Rome as fast as they can' (ibid., 6). Given the political climate — of the failure to exclude the Catholic James, duke of York, from the succession and the intensified persecution of dissenters during the Tory reaction — it was, to say the least, injudicious.

Bold sought to justify his position and avert retribution with *A Plea for Moderation towards Dissenters* (1682) but the damage had already been done. He only succeeded in further alienating popular and ecclesiastical opinion. *A Plea for Moderation,* although couched initially in more conciliatory language, deploring 'mutual animosities and contentions' and pleading for 'mutual forbearance', did so in view of the perceived papal threat and the fear 'that Hannibal [Rome] is at our gates' (Bold, *Plea,* 5, 6). Bold concluded by protesting again at the 'immoderate heat and peevishness of those fatuous and headstrong bigots' who attacked dissenters (ibid., 36). At a time when English gaols, particularly in the West Country were filled with dissenters on account of the efforts of local informers and magistrates it was more than the authorities, civil and ecclesiastical, could take. Bold was presented to the assizes in Sherborne in August 1682 and shortly afterwards to the court of William Gulston, bishop of Bristol, accused of 'scandalous libel' and sedition. The civil court imposed fines, and Bold was imprisoned for seven weeks until the fines were fully paid. The ecclesiastical prosecution was terminated following Gulston's sudden death.

Bold resigned from Shapwick later that year, possibly on account of the furore raised by his defence of dissenters, but probably also because he had already accepted the more comfortable living at Steeple in the Isle of Purbeck. To the chagrin of his successor at Shapwick, Obadiah Beane, Bold remained popular with the former parishioners and was frequently requested to officiate at marriages and baptisms. Beane recorded such events in the parish registers as married or baptized 'by an unlawful priest' (Sparkes, 19). Bold's views on sovereignty and allegiance and his advocacy of toleration may all have derived from his early association with William Cook, a 'zealous royalist' who before coming to Chester about 1651 had been deprived of the living of Ashby-de-la-Zouch for refusing to take the engagement, thereby withholding his allegiance from the Commonwealth, and had been charged with treason in 1659 for his support of Sir George Booth's royalist rising, only at the Restoration to become a victim of persecution under the so-called Clarendon code (*Nonconformist's Memorial*, 1.327). 'Besides [,] many of those you prosecute', Bold reminded his audience:

> have given greater demonstrations of their loyalty, having suffered more in the late times of usurpation, for the king, than many, if not all of you have, and contributed much more to the bringing of him back to his crown and his just right. (Bold, *Sermon*, 27)

In 1688 Bold published anonymously *A brief account of the first rise of the name protestant ... by a professed enemy to persecution,* a tract urging protestant unity in the face of the popish threat perceived in the policies of James II. In 1690 Bold took issue with Thomas Comber in *An Examination of Dr. Comber's Scholasticall History* which he perceived, probably mistakenly, had been written to justify persecution of dissenters.

Bold was installed as rector at Steeple, also in Dorset (from 1721, Steeple-cum-Tynham) in April 1682, through the influence of William Churchill. It was from there, in 1697, that he commenced the work for which he is chiefly remembered, his defence of John Locke. Locke's *The Reasonableness of Christianity* had appeared in 1695 and was immediately attacked as Socinian by the Calvinist John Edwards in *Socinianism Unmasked* (1696). Lock's own *Vindication* (1695) and *Second Vindication* (1697) of the *Reasonableness of Christianity* against Edwards were supported by Bold who, in 1697, entered the field with *A Short Discourse of the True Knowledge of Christ Jesus* in which he contended with Locke that Christ and the apostles considered it sufficient for a Christian to believe that Jesus was the Christ. Bold published two further works in that year, contra Edwards, in defence of Locke and his own *Short Discourse,* and in 1698 added *Observations on the animadversions ... on a late book entituled, the Reasonableness of Christianity,* again in defence of Locke.

In 1699 Bold turned his attention to the vindication of Locke's other great work, the *Essay Concerning Humane Understanding* (1690) which by then was already in a second edition but which had attracted unfavourable comment. Bold's *Some considerations on the principal objections and arguments ... against Mr. Locke's essay of humane understanding* (1699), together with his earlier work in support of *The Reasonableness of Christianity* drew the comment that Bold was 'one of the ablest advocates of Mr. Locke' (Hutchins, 1.612), as well as Locke's own unstinted gratitude. Bold was frequently mentioned in Locke's correspondence with great regard and

Locke wrote to him in 1699 'everything must be welcome to me that comes from your pen' (*N&Q*, 137), although in 1703 when Bold visited Locke at Otes (or Oates) he was dissuaded by Locke from further publication.

In 1706, however, after Locke's death, Bold's earlier publications in defence of Locke were republished, together with some of his more recent works, in *A collection of tracts publish'd in vindication of Mr. Locke's Reasonableness of Christianity*. One of these later works, *A Discourse Concerning the Resurrection of the Same Body* (1705), seems to have been generated by Bold's assimilation of Locke's views on human existence, resulting in a major shift in Bold's own thinking regarding the nature and destiny of man. In 1696 Bold had published *Meditations Concerning Death* in which he had upheld the traditional view of the soul's immortality and immediate felicity in heaven after death. 'We have immortal souls', he had declared. Death is 'the departure or separation of the immortal soul from the body' to receive either eternal 'happiness or misery' (Bold, *Meditations Concerning Death*, 4, 6).

But there are already hints of a move away from this traditional eschatology in the *Observations* of 1698 and *Some Considerations* of 1699, where in defending Lock's mortalist views Bold asserts that 'the truth of the case' is that immortality, lost by all through Adam's transgression, is restored by Christ 'in that he will raise them all from death' (Bold, *Observations on the Animadversions*, 86), and that 'after the Resurrection man will be immortal' (Bold, *Some Considerations*, 25). In the 1705 *Discourse Concerning the Resurrection*, contra Daniel Whitby and Samuel Parker, who had opposed Locke's view of human nature, contending that death means only the death of the body, Bold predicated a more defined mortalist view, arguing that death 'happeneth to the [whole] man' rather than to the body alone, and confessing that the belief that after death 'man is not dead' was beyond his comprehension. Bold otherwise appears to have been doctrinally orthodox, despite later inclusion in Wallace's *Antitrinitarian Biography* where the author concedes that there was 'no ground for suspecting his orthodoxy' concerning the Trinity (Wallace, 315).

Most of Bold's more than twenty published works appeared during his years at Steeple and in addition to his appeals for tolerance, his defence of Locke, and his own modified theology of the soul and immortality, included a number of sermons and devotional pieces, notably *Man's Great Duty* (1693), *The Duty of Christians* (1717), and *Help to Devotion* (1736), the latter containing a short prayer on every chapter in the New Testament. Bold died at Steeple in August 1737 after a ministry there of more than fifty-five years, aged eighty-eight, and greatly respected.

Bryan W. Ball

Sources: 'Neglected biography, no. 1: some account of the writings, correspondence and persecution of Rev. Samuel Bold, rector of Steeple, in the county of Dorset', *The Christian Reformer* (Aug 1860), 466–78; G. D. Squibb, *Dorset incumbents, 1542–1731* (c.1946); J. Hutchins, *The history and antiquities of the county of Dorset,* 4 vols. (1861–70), vol. 1; *N&Q,* 11 (1855), 137–9; *DNB;* R. Wallace, *Antitrinitarian biography, or, Sketches of the lives and writings of distinguished antitrinitarians,* 3 vols. (1850), vol. 3; Foster, *Alum. Oxon.; The nonconformist's memorial ... originally written by ... Edmund Calamy,* ed. S. Palmer [3rd edn], 1 (1802); S. Sparkes, *St. Bartholomew's Church, Shapwick* (1996); J. Gorton, *A general biographical dictionary* (1841); J. Watkins, *The universal biographical dictionary* (1821); Watt, *Bibl. Brit.;* [C. B. Heberden], ed., *Brasenose College register, 1509–1909,* 2 vols., OHS, 55 (1909); S. Bold, *Man's great duty* (1693); S. Bold, *A sermon against persecution* (1682); S. Bold, *A plea for moderation towards dissenters* (1682)

Clement Writer

Writer, Clement (d. 1659x62), religious controversialist, was one of three known surviving children of unidentified parents. Given his prolonged association with Worcestershire it is possible that he descended from the county. He claimed to have received little formal education, and never married. He first appears in 1627 in conjunction with Captain Edward Spring and an unspecified debt of eight pounds. The state papers indicate that pecuniary difficulties and related litigation dogged him for much of his remaining life. In 1631 an adversary, John Racster, requested Sir Dudley Carleton, secretary of state, to use his influence on his behalf with Sir Nathaniel Brent, judge of the prerogative court, against Writer. In protracted litigation against his uncle, George Worfield, Writer petitioned unsuccessfully for compensation for seven years' remuneration and expenses incurred in conducting Worfield's lawsuits, later claiming that Lord Keeper Sir Thomas Coventry had unjustly decreed against him to the extent of 1500 pounds. In 1640 he sought redress against Coventry from what he called 'the grand committee of the courts of justice' (Writer, *Case,* 1), but the committee was dissolved before his case could be considered. In 1646 his complaint was heard by the Commons committee for petitions, and a subcommittee was appointed to deal with the matter, but the committee itself was suspended before it could receive a report. Frustrated by this succession of disappointments, Writer published *The Sad Case of Clement Writer* (1646) in his defence, arguing that the failure to hear his case in 1640 was a miscarriage of justice that had denied him the opportunity to present his evidence; copies were distributed to MPs. In 1652 Thomas Fowle, solicitor for the Commonwealth, referred his case against Coventry to the Worcester committee for sequestration, but the dissolution of parliament once again prevented the matter from being resolved. Writer ultimately petitioned Cromwell, and the council of state delegated the case to yet another committee in October 1656. It is not known if he ever obtained redress.

Legal problems notwithstanding, Writer was actively involved in the affairs of the day. He was in business as a clothier in Worcester, where he owned property, during the 1630s, and by the early 1640s was trading in London and living in Blackwell Hall. Although he had rejected Presbyterianism for Independency about 1638 after reading the works of John Robinson, he became a prominent member of Thomas Lambe's London General Baptist congregation. In 1641 he accompanied Lambe on an evangelistic mission in Gloucestershire, and his name appears in association with other known General Baptists. On the outbreak of civil war he enlisted horse for the support of the parliamentary army; he himself took up arms, but by 1645 had seemingly returned to civilian life when he attended meetings concerning the issue of religious toleration between the sects, the Independents, and the Presbyterians.

Repeated attempts to determine precisely Writer's religious sympathies have proved difficult, and he remains elusive. Contemporaries were provoked by his departure from theological orthodoxy and reacted accordingly. Thomas Edwards, with some spleen, called him an 'Anti-scripturalist', 'arch-heretique', 'fearfull apostate', even an 'atheist' (Edwards, 1.27), a depiction which has persisted in some modern historiography. Richard Baxter also thought he was both 'apostate' and 'infidel' (*Reliquiae Baxterianae*, 1.116), and in 1655 published *The Unreasonableness of Infidelity* with Writer in mind. However, these assessments by more moderate figures were obviously polemically motivated, and neither Edwards' early view of 1646 or Baxter's later judgement should be taken as the last word. More recently Writer has been portrayed as a General Baptists, a 'Seeker,' even a Leveller, the latter on account of his acquaintance with William Walwyn, who has also been designated a Seeker. The truth probably lies somewhere here, with the term 'Seeker". Baxter believed that this was Writer's own estimation of his position, although after two meetings and correspondence, Baxter himself remained uncertain. Writer's defection from Presbyterianism, his antipathy to ceremony and dissatisfaction with all organized churches, including ultimately those of the General Baptists, and his enquiring mind and emphasis on the Spirit's immediacy were all marks of a Seeker outlook. He could probably be accommodated in the last of Baxter's six categories of Seeker, those who had 'over-grown the Scripture, Ministry and Ordinances' (McGregor and Reay, 126).

Writer's publications reveal his matured thought. He is said to have contributed to Richard Overton's *Man's Mortalitie* (1644), a provocative work which denied the immortality of the soul, a position which his own works subsequently substantiated. Mortalism is thus added to the long list of heresies of which Writer was suspected, the most serious being his liberal view of scripture and the nature of revelation. He was concerned over textual variations of the Bible, questioned Moses' authorship of the Pentateuch, recognized the Bible's openness to conflicting interpretation, and contended that the history of the canon raised difficult questions about inspiration. In the eyes of many this amounted to an attack on biblical infallibility. Such views would not have been approved by most General Baptists and this suggests that by the later 1640s he had moved away from the sect's theological position. Writer's doubts were raised in *The jus divinum of presbyterie* (1st edn, 1646) and *Fides divina: the ground of true faith asserted* (1655), and some of them were discussed at meetings with Baxter in 1653 and 1657. Writer maintained that Baxter had misrepresented him in *The Unreasonableness of Infidelity*, and eventually replied to his charges in 1658 in his *An Apologetical Narration, or, A Just and Necessary Vindication of Clement Writer.*

Writer's questions, however, substantial though they were, do not provide grounds for dismissing him as an 'anti-scripturist'. Despite his reservations, he did not reject outright the authority of scripture. Rather he believed that doctrine was necessary and should be based on 'Scripture and weight of sound reason' (Writer, *Jus divinum*, 1646, 18). The *Jus divinum* itself attempts to demonstrate 'by Scripture' the nature of true ministry, and both it and *Fides divina* repeatedly call on scripture for support. The *Apologetical Narration* displays a thorough knowledge of the biblical text and relies heavily upon it, identifying its author with radical contemporary eschatology. Writer's apparent ambivalence may be explained in part by his insistence on the Spirit's enlightenment. He commended Samuel How's *The Sufficiencie of the Spirit's Teaching without Human Learning* (1st edn, 1639), and insisted that scripture must be interpreted in light of the Spirit's primacy in the believer's personal experience. Thus he suspected learning, the religious establishment, particularly Presbyterianism, and a formally trained ministry in which the individual call is not evidently endorsed by the Spirit: 'For the Ministry of the Gospel is a divine office. So it must necessarily be derived from a divine power, and bring with it suitable evidence' (Writer, *Jus divinum*, 1646, 53). This opposition to ecclesiastical structures and those who maintained them, in addition to his bold criticisms of the Bible, explains the antagonism he received from those who regarded themselves as defenders of orthodoxy. He was, in fact, far more typical of the radical sectarian and Seeker mentality than Edwards or Baxter, and others, have been prepared to allow.

By his will dated 2 August 1659 (proved in 1662), it appears that at the time of Writer's death he was comfortably placed with assets valued at several hundred pounds, including several houses, two mills, and adjoining lands in the city and county of Worcester. Most of his assets were distributed in small bequests to relatives and friends, notably to the children of his brother, Thomas Writer, and to various cousins, with a bequest of 20 pounds to his friend William Walwyn. The will also made provision for sundry debtors, mostly tenants, to be excused their obligations and for the poor of Worcester and other adjoining localities to receive some relief, evidence perhaps that one Seeker, at least, had discovered the essence of true religion, a generous spirit.

Bryan W. Ball

Sources: *CSP dom.,* 1627–9, 1631–3, 1635–6, 1656–7; T. Edwards, *Gangraena, or, A catalogue and discovery of many of the errours, heresies, blasphemies and pernicious practices of the sectaries of this time,* 3 vols., in 1 (1646); *Reliquiae Baxterianae, or Mr. Richard Baxter's narrative of the most memorable passages of his life and times,* ed. M. Sylvester, 1 vol. in 3 pts (1696); C. Hill, *The world turned upside down: radical ideas during the English revolution* (1972); repr. (1975); *DNB*; *Calendar of the correspondence of Richard Baxter,* ed. N. H. Keeble and G. F. Nuttall, 1 (1991), 1638–60; C. Writer, *The sad case of Clement Writer* (1646); [C. Writer], *An apologetical narration, or, A just and necessary vindication of Clement Writer, against a four-fold charge laid on him by Richard Baxter* (1658); 'Writer, Clement', Greaves & Zaller, BDBR, 3.344–5; D. Masson, *The life of Milton,* 3 (1873); K. Lindley, *Popular politics and religion in civil war London* (1997); will, TNA: PRO, PROB 11/307, sig. 30; J. F. McGregor, 'Seekers and Ranters', *Radical religion in the English revolution,* ed. J. F. McGregor and B. Raey (1984), 121–40

Wealth at death assets valued at several hundred pounds, incl. several houses, two mills, and adjoining lands in and around Worcester: will, TNA: PRO, PROB, 11/307, sig. 30.

9. The Roots of English Sabbatarianism[1]

Bryan W. Ball

The English seventh-day movement, as it began to emerge early in the seventeenth century, did so within the context of history. The Seventh-day Men, as English Sabbatarians were often known in their day, contended that the seventh day of the week had been observed both in England and on the Continent at various periods in the Church's history. One of them, Thomas Bampfield, a lawyer, even argued that the seventh day had been kept in England in unbroken succession until the thirteenth century, and that there had been no law for the observance of Sunday until the time of Edward VI.[2] Most advocates of the seventh day, however, were content to point to antecedents in the early Church, in medieval and contemporary Europe, or in parts of what is now North Africa, particularly Ethiopia. Later research has revealed clear connections with the Celtic Church in Britain and with the later Lollard movement. The Sabbatarian controversy, originating in the sixteenth century, although initially not concerned with seventh-day obser-vance, undoubtedly provided an immediate background for the emergence of seventh-day convictions, as we shall see. This chapter surveys these ante-cedents of the English seventh-day Sabbatarians, some of which they cited in the numerous works they published in the attempt to persuade others of the essential correctness of their position. The basic argument, of course, was that the seventh-day Sabbath had been observed by Christians from the very earliest times.

The Early Church

The desire of Protestantism in general and of Puritanism in particular to return to the original purity of New Testament teaching and practice has frequently been noted. The clearest expression of this orientation is seen in Independent and Baptist writers who wanted the Church reformed in all re-spects, constitutional as well as theological, according to the first principles

---

1 Abridged from the first edition of Bryan W. Ball, *The Seventh-day Men: Sab-batarians and Sabbatarianism in England and Wales, 1600–1800* (1st edn., Oxford: Clarendon, 1994). Used with permission. Footnotes, including some titles, have been abbreviated.

2 Thomas Bampfield, *An Enquiry ... Whether the Fourth Command be Re-pealed or Altered?* (1692), 117–119.

of Christ. Saturday Sabbatarians, most of whom were both Independent and Baptist, believed that they were working accordingly in pointing out that the seventh day had been widely observed in the early Church. They were supported in this contention, although for quite different reasons, by those within Anglicanism who opposed all forms of Sabbatarianism, maintaining that the requirements of the Sabbath commandment had not been transferred to Sunday as the Puritans argued, but that the observation of the Lord's Day rested on entirely different grounds. Hence many seventeenth-century writers from quite opposite camps testify to the observance of the seventh day in the first four centuries or so of Christian history.

Theophilus Brabourne, whose writings were seminal to the Sabbatarian cause, presented evidence for seventh-day observance in the early Church in reply to the Presbyterian, John Collings, in 1654. Brabourne cited Athanasius and the Council of Laodicea in support of his argument that the seventh day had been observed at least until the middle of the fourth century. Athanasius had urged that the Sabbath should be kept in a manner which freed it from any taint of Judaizing. "We assemble on the Sabbath day, not as if we were infected with Judaism, but ... that we may worship Jesus the Lord of the Sabbath".[3] The Council of Laodicea (AD 364) finally prohibited the observance of the old seventh day under pain of excommunication: "Christians shall not Judaise and be idle on the Sabbath, but shall work on that day; but the Lord's day they shall especially honour, and, as Christians, shall, if possible, do no work on that day. If, however, they are found Judaising, they shall be shut out from Christ".[4] Some twenty years previously Brabourne had been called to account for his earlier writings advocating the seventh day and he now described for the first time how in the discussions between himself and the Archbishop of Canterbury, William Laud, and the Bishop of Ely, Francis White, both the Archbishop and the Bishop had agreed that the Sabbath had been observed in the early Church. Brabourne maintained that it was essentially the evidence presented above which had convinced the prelates.[5] White eventually conceded a degree of seventh-day observance in the post-apostolic Church in his *Treatise of the Sabbath-Day*, written in 1635 as "a Defence of the Orthodoxall [*sic*] Doctrine of the Church of England against Sabbatarian Novelty" — Brabourne being the chief culprit.[6]

James Ockford (or Oakeford) cited Socrates, the fifth-century Greek Church historian, in support of his assertion that the seventh-day Sabbath had been observed in the early Church for about four centuries. Socrates had recorded that for the first two centuries "Almost all churches throughout

3 Theophilus Brabourne, *A Reply to Mr Collings* (1654), 63.
4 *Ibid.*
5 *Ibid, ,* 65.
6 Francis White, *A Treatise of the Sabbath Day* (1635), 189.

the world" had kept the original Sabbath every week, with the exception of Rome and Alexandria which, "on account of some ancient tradition", had ceased observance of the seventh day.[7] Sozomen, a contemporary of Socrates, confirms the early Sabbatarian tradition by saying, "The people of Constantinople, and almost everywhere, assemble together on the Sabbath, as well as on the first day of the week, which custom is never observed at Rome or at Alexandria".[8]

Peter Heylyn, one of Charles I's chaplains, and perhaps the most erudite seventeenth-century historian of Sabbatarianism, agreed that the seventh day had been kept by the early Church and confirmed that some observed both Saturday and Sunday. In support of the claim that "the old Sabbath was kept holy by the primitive Christians', Heylyn offers as evidence the fourth-century Apostolic Constitutions, Theophilus of Antioch and the Council of Laodicea, adding Gregory of Nyssa, whom he cites as rebuking those who had neglected to observe the Sabbath: "With what face ... wilt thou look upon the Lord's Day which hast dishonoured the Sabbath? Knowest thou not that these two days are sisters and that whosoever doth despite the one doth affront the other?"[9] In Heylyn's view observance of the seventh day began to decline in the West towards the end of the fourth century, although in the East the seventh day "retained its wonted credit, little inferior to the Lord's day, if not plainly equal" until Augustine's day. The seventh day was known specifically as the Sabbath, while the first day was referred to as the Lord's Day, both being observed as days of rest, but not, it was to be noted, "infected any whit with Judaisme". Meetings for worship were held on the Sabbath, but the day was not otherwise observed in the strict Jewish sense "like a Sabbath".[10]

Others throughout the seventeenth century, who themselves had no allegiance to the seventh day, recognized that it had been observed in early Christian history. Edward Brerewood, in 1611, emphasized the significance of the seventh day in the Eastern Church "three hundred years and more" after Christ [11]and Edmund Porter, a prebendary of Norwich, put seventh-day observance generally "long after Origen's time".[12] John Ley, who was greatly disturbed that the Sabbath had "become as a ball betwixt two rackets" argued that the Council of Laodicea had failed to curtail observance of the seventh day and that in the time of Pope Gregory the Great there were

---

7   James Ockford, *The Doctrine of the Fourth Commandement* (1650), 27.

8   *Ibid.*

9   Peter Heylin, *Respondet Petrus* (1658), 60–61.

10   *Ibid,* 61; *History of the Sabbath* (1636), 73–74.

11   Edward Brerewood, *A Learned Treatise of the Sabaoth* (1630), 77, 101.

12   Edmund Porter, *Sabbatum: The Mystery of the Sabbath Discovered* (1658), 32.

still advocates of the old Sabbath, despite Gregory's strictures against them as being antichristian.[13] Even Ephraim Pagitt, the heresiographer, "willingly" acknowledged that "the Jewish Sabbath" had been observed by "many primitive Christians", although not persuaded that this included Gentiles.[14]

William Cave, a noted patristic scholar and Canon of Windsor, wrote at length about the prevailing understanding of his day concerning the Sabbath in apostolic and post-apostolic centuries: "Next to the Lord's day", Cave says, "the Sabbath or Saturday ... was held in great veneration, and especially in the Eastern parts honoured with all the public solemnities of religion". He explains:

> They met together for public prayers, for reading the Scriptures, celebration of the sacraments, and such like duties. This is plain, not only from some passages in Ignatius and Clemens his Constitutions, but from writers of more unquestionable credit and authority. Athanasius, bishop of Alexandria tells us, that they assembled on Saturdays, not that they were infected with Judaism, but only worship Jesus Christ, the Lord of the Sabbath; and Socrates, speaking of the usual times of their public meeting, calls the Sabbath and the Lord's day the weekly festivals, on which the congregation was wont to meet in the church for the performance of divine services.[15]

Cave notes that in some parts of the Roman Empire the seventh day was observed to accommodate large numbers of Jewish converts, but insists that great care was taken to avoid any impression of Judaism.[16]

With a few reservations most Seventh-day Men would have concurred. They might have preferred less emphasis on the dual role of the seventh day and the first day, particularly as a universal custom, and less emphasis on the concessionary nature of seventh-day observance to Jewish converts. For all that, it seems beyond doubt that English Sabbatarians in the seventeenth century recognised that the seventh day had been observed in the early Church for several centuries.

The Celtic Church

Various scholars over the past hundred years or so have consistently maintained that a Sabbatarian tradition persisted for several centuries in the Celtic Church. According to Skene, the Scottish historiographer, traces of observing both Saturday and Sunday in the early Irish Church were also found in Scotland, where they lasted until Margaret, in the eleventh cen-

---

13 John Ley, *Sunday a Sabbath* (1641), Pref., 166.
14 Ephraim Pagitt, *Heresiography* (6th edn., 1661), 173.
15 William Cave, *Primitive Christianity* (1673), 173–74.
16 *Ibid*, 175–76.

tury, reformed the Church according "to the rules of the true faith (and) sacred customs of the universal church".[17] Margaret's reforms were aimed, among other things, at prevailing attitudes to the Lord's Day, for which she sought more recognition and more reverence.[18] Both Lang and Moffat refer specifically to the practice of observing the seventh day in the early Celtic Church. Moffat says that in keeping "Saturday the Jewish Sabbath" the Celtic Church "obeyed the fourth commandment literally upon the seventh day of the week". This was "customary in the Celtic Church of early times, in Ireland as well as Scotland".[19] Lang adds that Saturday was kept strictly "in a sabbatical manner".[20] T. Ratcliffe Barnett noted that it was traditional in the ancient Irish Church to observe Saturday instead of Sunday as the day of rest,[21] and A. C. Flick points again to the custom of keeping the seventh day as a day of rest and of holding religious services on Sunday.[22]

More recent studies of the Celtic Church and relevant extant documents have confirmed these earlier conclusions of nineteenth-century historians. In the 1961 edition of *Adomnan's Life of Columba*, edited by A. O. and M. O. Anderson, recognition of Saturday as the Sabbath and the dual role of Saturday and Sunday in the Celtic Church are both noted. Adomnan referred to the first day of the week as "Lord's day" (*'dominica dies' or 'dies dominica'*) and called Saturday the Sabbath (*'Sabbatum'*) or "the day of Sabbath".[23] Another more recent study points out that Adomnan invariably used the name "Sabbatum" when speaking of the seventh day and always referred to the Sabbath "in a manner betokening a respect which is not detected in writers two centuries later".[24] This fits well with the thesis that the complete Romanizing of the Celtic Church occurred much later than it did in the British Church at large. According to Adomnan, Columba himself

---

17 W. F. Skene, *Celtic Scotland: A History of Ancient Alban (Church and Culture)* (Edinburgh: David Douglas, 1877), ii, 346, 349.

18 *Ibid,* 348–349.

19 J. C. Moffat, *The Church in Scotland. A history ... from the earliest recorded times to the first Assembly of the Reformed Church* (Philadelphia: Presbyterian Board of Publication, 1882), 140.

20 A. Lang, *A History of Scotland from the Roman Occupation* (Edinburgh and London: William Blackwood, 1900), i, 96.

21 T. R. Barnett, *Margaret of Scotland* (Edinburgh, London: Oliver and Boyd, 1926), 97. Barnett suggests that Columba's views regarding the Saturday Sabbath had taken root in Scotland.

22 A. C. Flick, *The Rise of the Medieval Church* (New York, London: G. P. Putnam's Sons, 1909), 237.

23 A. O. and M. O. Anderson, eds, *Adomnán's Life of Columba* (Oxford: Clarendon, 1961), 120.

24 L. Hardinge, *The Celtic Church in Britain* (London: SPCK, 1972), 84.

distinguished between the Sabbath and Sunday, although there is no clear evidence here that either Adomnan or Columba themselves kept Saturday or Sunday exclusively.[25]

The deference given to both Sabbath and Sunday is apparent in Adomnan's reference to the Rule of Columcelle, where it is laid down that the allowance of food for Sabbath and Sunday are equal in amount "because of the reverence paid to the Sabbath in the Old Testament". The Sabbath differs from Sunday in respect of work only. Other regulations demonstrate further similarities between Sabbath and Sunday.[26] Harding cites instances from the *Mediaeval Handbook of Penance* and other contemporary sources which indicate a continuing tension between Saturday and Sunday, demonstrating perhaps a reluctance both to let go of the seventh day and to take hold fully of the Lord's Day with the rest of the Romanized Church in the British Isles.[27] That this was a period of transition is clear from Adomnan's reference to early Irish attempts "to persuade Christians to observe Sunday as the Sabbath",[28] although the editors specifically note that "the sabbatical Sunday had not yet been accepted by Adomnan or in Iona at the time when Adomnan wrote".[29]

This lingering ambivalence between Sabbath and Sunday, evident here in the Celtic Church and also at times in the post-apostolic Church, is perhaps one of the stronger evidences of an earlier commitment to the seventh day. Hardinge remarks that "there was a gradual shift from the keeping of Saturday, the seventh-day Sabbath, to the observance of both Saturday and Sunday and then to the celebration of Sunday exclusively".[30]

Given the measure of respect for the Bible evident in Celtic texts, it is not at all surprising that observance of the seventh day occurred in the Celtic Church. Patrick's allegiance to Scripture and his aversion to patristic and conciliar sources are well known.[31] According to one source, the Bible was accorded paramount authority in Celtic theology and practice and was revered "as the voice of the Holy Ghost addressing his people in the character of a king upon his throne".[32] Laistner notes "the pre-occupation of Irish scholars with Biblical exegesis", often following a strictly literal hermeneu-

---

25 Anderson, *Adomnán*, 25.

26 *Ibid*, 120.

27 Hardinge, *Celtic Church*, 84–85, and *passim*.

28 Anderson, *Adomnán*, 27.

29 *Ibid*, 29.

30 Hardinge, *Celtic Church*, 89.

31 E.g., W. Stokes, *The Tripartite Life of Patrick* (1887), ii, 567; Hardinge, *Celtic Church*, 30.

32 W. Stokes and J. Strachan, *Thesaurus Palaeohibernicus* (Cambridge: University Press, 1901–10), i, 389, in Hardinge, *Celtic Church*, 32.

tic.[33] It seems that particular respect was accorded to the Old Testament, in which connection the *Liber ex lege Moisi* played a prominent role. Patrick is said to have left a copy of "the books of the Law, and of the book of the Gospel" wherever he established a church. The *Liber ex lege Moisi* is the only extant Celtic manuscript which fits this tradition.[34] Whether or not this is the case, the *Liber ex lege Moisi* exerted a profound influence on Celtic thought. In fact, the *Liber* commences with the Ten Commandments and Hardinge is probably correct in asserting that the observance of the Sabbath of the Old Testament in the Celtic Church was a material outgrowth of an emphasis on Christian obedience inculcated though usage of the *Liber* in exegesis and pastoral instruction.[35]

The liturgical practices of the early Irish Church as reflected in the seventh-century *Antiphonary of Bangor* may also indicate a lingering devotion to the Sabbath. Hardinge records J. F. Kenney's observation that the *Antiphonary* is "the only record surviving of the old Irish Church services unaffected by the Romanizing movement of the seventh and eighth centuries" and notes that included in it were suggestions for conducting the Divine Office at Easter, on Sabbaths, on Sunday in Eastertide, and on Sabbaths and Sunday throughout the year.[36] Hardinge's own conclusions, based on the Celtic regard for Scripture and the accompanying emphasis on the obedient life, are appropriate:

> There was no Sabbatizing of Sunday during the Celtic period. The seventh day was kept from sunset on Friday until sunset on Saturday, and even until dawn on Sunday in some places. No work was done on it, as the laws of the *Liber ex lege Moisi* stipulate. While Sunday was also held to possess minor sanctity, and religious services were carried out on it, the daily chores, the gathering of food, the washing of hair and taking of baths, the going on journeys and carrying out of regular business transactions were all permitted on the first day.[37]

The Lollards

The most cursory survey of the geographical distribution of seventeenth-century Sabbatarian congregations would suggest an affinity with Lollardy. A Seventh-day presence was established in many areas which previously had been Lollard strongholds. London, East Anglia, Buckinghamshire and the Chilterns, the Severn Valley, particularly around Gloucester, Dorset,

---

33   M. L. W. Laistner, *Thought and Letters in Western Europe, AD 500 to 900* (London: Methuen ,1957), 146.

34   Stokes, *Life of Patrick,* ii, 300 and J. F. Kenney, *Sources for the Early History of Ireland* (New York: Columbia University Press, 1929), i, 250.

35   Hardinge, *Celtic Church,* 210, 203.

36   Kenney, *Sources,* 712; Hardinge, *Celtic Church,* 120–121.

37   Hardinge, *Celtic Church,* 203.

Wiltshire and Hereford and the Welsh Borders may all be mentioned as typical in this respect. Since the Lollard movement persisted in some of these areas well into the sixteenth century,[38] there may have been a much stronger connection than is often granted between Lollard theology and that of the more radical reformed groups which flourished in England during the seventeenth century. Claire Cross describes early Lollards as "characterised first and foremost by their biblical fundamentalism"[39] and this, added to the rapid dissemination of Lollard ideas, the readiness with which they were received, the provision of the Bible or parts of it in the vernacular and the persistence of a Lollard tradition in many parts of the country, are sufficient grounds for concluding that Lollard influence may well have contributed to the later appearance of seventh-day observance.

This tentative conclusion is confirmed by evidence from original sources. Once again it is reverence for the Old Testament and the Ten Commandments which initially delineates the Lollards as setting a precedent for later Sabbatarian theology. Wycliffe himself had stressed the importance for Christians of obeying the Ten Commandments,[40] and although the Wycliffite *Lanterne of Light* may not have been his, it nevertheless may be taken as representative of Wycliffe's thought. *The Lanterne of Light* is typical of Lollard commentaries on the Decalogue. It follows that form of the Ten Commandments used by the medieval Church, citing the third commandment as the Sabbath commandment and referring to the seventh day as the true Sabbath with the injunction: "Have mind that thou hallow this holy day. In six days thou shalt work and do all thine own works, for so the seventh day is the Sabbath of the Lord". Several variations of this exhortation to observe the Sabbath are noted, with the gloss that it is the devil who leads men to break the Sabbath.[41] If the *Lanterne of Light* may be taken as typical of Lollard teaching, it is not difficult to perceive how reverence for the Sabbath would have arisen in Lollard communities.

Robert Pope of Amersham and Thomas Taylor of Newbury are both recorded as owning a suspect book containing the Ten Commandments.[42] Alice Collins, wife of a noted Lollard and herself "a famous woman among them", had memorized large portions of Scripture and was often invited to recite the Ten Commandments, together with the Epistles of Peter and

---

38 See A. G. Dickens, *The English Reformation* (London: Batsford, 1964), 22–37 and Claire Cross, *Church and People, 1450–1660* (Oxford: Blackwell, 1976), 9–52.

39 Cross, *Church and People*, 16.

40 T. Arnold, ed., *Select English Works of John Wyclif* (1869–71), iii, 82ff.

41 L. M. Swinburne, ed., *The Lanterne of Light* (1917), 90–91.

42 Cross, *Church and People*, 33; J. A. F. Thomson, *The Later Lollards* (London: Oxford University Press, 1965), 76.

James, at conventicles in Burford c.1520.[43] In 1469 John Cornewe and John Breche, Lollards from Lydney, Gloucestershire, were called to abjure, among other opinions, the view that the authority of the Old Testament was preferable to that of the New Testament: "*Item quod auctoritas veteris testamenti preferenda et melior est novo testamento*".[44] According to Cross, as late as the early sixteenth century an Essex Lollard confessed to have taught others the Lord's Prayer and the Ten Commandments in English.[45]

The case of William Fuer of Gloucester is one of several specific instances now coming to light of Lollard Sabbatarianism. Fuer abjured under duress in 1448, saying that he derived his views form Bristol Lollards, including William Smith, one of the most noted Lollards of the day, who was eventually burnt for heresy. According to J. A. F. Thomson, who records Fuer's case, a considerable number of heresy trials had been conducted in the Severn Valley in the years preceding 1450, in which some of those tried revealed views more heretical than had previously been detected. Certainly extreme Sabbatarianism would have been so regarded and Fuer confessed to holding such views, saying that the Sabbath should be observed as strictly as commanded in the Old Testament with the preparation of food the only permissible activity.[46] It is not specifically stated that Fuer's Sabbatarianism extended to the seventh day, although given the general direction of Lollard theology, it is not improbable. A movement towards the stricter observance of Sunday appeared in England early in the fifteenth century, arising largely from Lollard convictions which could not overlook the injunctions of the fourth commandment. Gairdner and Spedding observed over a century ago that if Lollards had regarded the observance of Sunday as merely resting on the authority of the Church, they would have classed it with all other "abuses of tradition ... and other noxious superstitions which they were anxious should be thoroughly rooted out".[47] William Fuer was clearly of that mind in maintaining a highly developed Sabbatarianism and his obdurate defence of the Old Testament Sabbath is likely to have included the seventh day.

There is no such ambiguity in the earlier case of John Seygno of London, in the light of which perhaps Fuer's own views should be evaluated. In 1402, only a year after Parliament had assented to the anti-heresy Act, *De haeretico comburendo*, John Seygno and two others, Richard Herbert and

---

43   John Foxe, *Actes and Monuments of John Foxe* (1965 edn.), iv, 238.

44   A. T. Bannister, ed., *The Register of John Stanbury, Bishop of Hereford* (Hereford: Cantilupe Society, 1918), 119.

45   Cross, *Church and People,* 38.

46   Thomson, *Later Lollards,* 36.

47   J. Gairdner and J. Spedding, *Studies in English History* (Edinburgh: David Douglas, 1881), 295–96.

Emmota Wylly, were brought before the courts on a heresy charge. Seygno had apparently been arraigned on a previous occasion at Canterbury and having been convicted on charges similar to those now brought against him again, had sworn that he had never held views worthy of condemnation. Whether or not the earlier charges had included Sabbatarianism is not recorded, but now he admitted that the Sabbath was to be observed "according to what was observed in the Old Testament". Claiming that he wished to observe "a Sabbath of this kind as described in the old law, that is according to the customs and rites of the Jews", he indicated that he intended to do so until he could be persuaded otherwise with sufficient reasons.[48] On the strength of Seygno's case alone, it would seem incontrovertible that seventh-day observance appeared among Lollards within twenty years of Wycliffe's death and, moreover, that a direct connection between Lollardy and the Seventh-day Men is a distinct possibility.

An early fifteenth-century manuscript, now in the British Library,[49] confirms that the Sabbath issue was openly debated two centuries or so before observance of the seventh day was first established in worshipping communities in England and Wales. The tract is described by one palaeographer as "apparently directed against an aberration … that might be expected to follow from principles of Wycliffite scriptural interpretation".[50] The author evidently felt the need to respond to those who questioned the change of the Sabbath from the seventh day to the first, as may be seen from the tract's title: "A litil tretys agens ye opynyon of sum men yt seyn yat no man hath powr for to change ye Saboth fro ye Satirday to ye Sonday. And here is pleynly proved ye contrarie, bi Holi Writt, and Doctouris sentence accordynge herwit". The writer, most probably a priest, begins by referring to questions regarding the authority by which such a change in the day of worship could be made. Since there is no human authority which can change the law of God, some doubt had been cast on the validity of Sunday as a day of special significance: "summen douten sith no man hath leeve for to change ye ten comaundementis of God; how myghte we chaunge our Saboth fro ye Satirday to Sonday".[51] The author explains that the law contains ceremonial as well as moral precepts and that, since observance of the seventh day was ceremonial, it was no longer of binding force. Furthermore, the Church has authority to make what changes she deems necessary. In this instance Christ, who has power over all things, had appointed the

---

48 D. Wilkins, *Concilia Magnae Brittaniae et Hiberniae* (1737), iii, 270–71.

49 British Library, MS. Harl. 2339.

50 A.I. Doyle, 'A Treatise of the Three Estates', *Dominican Studies,* 3 (1950), 353.

51 British Library, MS. Harl. 2339, fol. 104v.

Lord's Day by his own actions.[52] The cases of John Seygno and William Fuer suggest that there were at least some in the Lollard fraternity who were not persuaded.

Continental Sabbatarians

Well before the end of the sixteenth century references to seventh-day observance had begun to appear in English Sabbatarian literature. In1584, John Stockwood published *A Verie Profitable and Necessarie Discourse Concerning the observation and keeping of the Sabboth Day*, extracted from the earlier work of the German theologian Ursinus. Stockwood scathingly referred to Sabbatarians who "obstinately and stiffly" upheld the "ceremonial observation of the seventh day", which they regarded as immutable and completely binding.[53] In 1607 John Sprint explained the two extreme positions in the Sabbatarian controversy. At one end were those who maintained that no Sabbath at all was to be observed as such by Christians, while at the other end were those who held that "the Jewish Sabbath of the seventh day" was to be kept "being no less necessary for us to observe now, than it ever was for the Jews".[54] Neither Stockwood nor Sprint state whether they refer to Seventh-day observance in England, although if the 1874 edition of *Chambers Encyclopaedia* can be taken as a guide, it would have to be concluded that the seventh day had been widely observed in England from Elizabethan times.[55] If, on the other hand, Stockwood and Sprint refer to Continental Sabbatarianism, then they were in good company, for both Erasmus and Luther had drawn attention to the Sabbatarian phenomenon on the Continent, Erasmus to Sabbatarians in Bohemia, "a new kind of Jews",[56] and Luther to similar groups in Moravia and Austria, "a foolish group of people who maintained the observance of the Sabbath according to Jewish manner and custom".[57] Hospinian of Zurich likewise wrote against the Sabbatarians in 1592, showing that the issue was alive on the Continent for much of the sixteenth century.

The Continental Sabbatarian tradition, in fact, went back considerably further, as was known to at least some English seventeenth-century Sabbatarian controversialists. John Prideaux, Rector of Exeter College, Oxford and Vice-Chancellor of the University on three occasions during a distin-

---

52   *Ibid.,* fols. 105r–116r.

53   John Stockwood (tr.), *A Profitable ... Discourse Concerning ... the Sabboth Day* (1584), Ep. Ded., sig. Aiii.

54   John Sprint, *Propositions ... of the Christian Sabbath, or Lord's Day* (1607), 2.

55   *Chambers Encyclopaedia* (1874), viii, 402.

56   Erasmus, *De amabili Ecclesiae Concordia* (1533), sig. F6v.

57   *D.Martin Luthers Werke* (Weimar, 1911), xlii, 520.

guished career, maintained that in the twelfth century the neo-Ebionite Petrobusians, under their founder Peter de Bruis (or de Bruys) had been "Jewish in this point".[58] The eighteenth-century Church historian Mosheim mentions the Pasagini (or Pasagii) of Lombardy who were distinct on account of their teaching that the law of Moses should be kept in all details except the offering of sacrifices, and their Arian views on the nature of Christ. With regard to the former, they were sometimes known as Circumcisii since they practised circumcision. Mosheim notes that they also abstained from unclean meats prohibited by the Mosaic law.[59] The martyrs of Arras in 1420 were also reported to have kept "the complete law of the Jews" and to have "observed Saturday instead of Sunday" and for this reason are said to have been marked with a yellow cross following the custom of designating Jews during the Middle Ages.[60] The charge of Judaizing, fairly or unfairly, was never far from the lips of those who opposed seventh-day observance and it persisted throughout the history of the English Seventh-day movement of the seventeenth and eighteenth centuries. G. H. Williams records that an extreme movement of this nature arose c.1470 in the Kiev area of Russia, which lasted well into the sixteenth century, making the Decalogue the basis of its religious life in much the same way as the later Pentateuchalists of Strasburg.[61] While many English Sabbatarians adopted Mosaic dietary laws, few would have rejected the Messiahship of Jesus or the authority of the New Testament as some of these extreme Continental groups are said to have done.[62]

As the sixteenth century developed there appeared in Europe a more coherent and widespread Sabbatarian movement, identifiable in the main with the Anabaptists of the Radical Reformation,[63] although Luther himself had been embarrassed by the Sabbatarian inclinations of Carlstadt. The year 1527–8 is the date usually given for the appearance of Sabbatarian Anabaptists in the Continental Reformation. At about this time Andreas Fischer adopted the Sabbatarian beliefs of Oswald Glait in Nikolsburg, Moravia and became thenceforth Glait's principal co-labourer.[64] In 1528 they successfully propagated Sabbatarian views in Silesia, where they were opposed in public disputation and in print by Caspar Schwenckfeld. Glait shortly thereafter published *Buchlenn vom Sabbath*, to which both

58   John Prideaux, *Doctrine of the Sabbath*, Pref. sig. A2r.

59   J. L. von Mosheim, *Institutes of Ecclesiastical History* (1841), ii, 510.

60   P. Beuzart, *Les Heresies pendant le Moyen Age ...* (1912), 37–47.

61   G. H. Williams, *The Radical Reformation* (1962), 740, 835.

62   *Ibid,* 252.

63   G. F. Hasel, 'Sabbatarian Anabaptists of the Sixteenth Century', *Andrews University Seminary Studies,* 5 (1967), 101–21 and 6 (1968), 19–28.

64   Williams, *Radical Reformation,* 410.

Schwenckfeld and Wolfgang Capito replied in print.[65] It is possible that Luther's own *Brief wider die Sabbather* (1538) may have been provoked, in part at least, by the Sabbatarians of Silesia and Moravia, since he had known of their existence from 1532, although he also notes the rise of Sabbatarians (*Sabbather*) in Austria during the same period.[66]

English writers of the time were aware of other contemporary Saturday Sabbath-keeping movements, as Cox points out, and references may be found in several well-known seventeenth-century authorities. Samuel Purchas, chiefly known for *Purchas his Pilgrims* (1625), recorded that from the middle of the sixteenth century the Seventh-day Sabbath had been taught in Ethiopia,[67] a fact confirmed by Baratti's travels in that region, an account of which was published in an English translation in 1670. Baratti, an Italian gentleman, described how "chaplains" at the Imperial Court expounded Scripture in the Emperor's presence "on the Sabbath day ... according to the ancient manner of the Jews". Saturday, he explained, was the day appointed for public worship in Ethiopia "because God on that day finished the great work of the creation of the world".[68] In a note on the fly-leaf of his father's *The Insnared Taken in the Work of his Hands* (1677), Joseph Stennett referred to Baratti's account as evidence of contemporary Sabbath-keeping.[69] Stennett further cited Peter Heylyn's *Cosmography* in which the Melchites of Syria were also described as worshipping "as solemnly on the Saturday as on the Sunday".[70] These more remote and obscure observers of the seventh day would understandably have been of interest to a man of Stennett's learning and wide interests.

Other areas in which seventh-day observance appeared in the sixteenth century include Poland, particularly Lithuania, Bohemia (as noted by Erasmus) and especially Transylvania, where some Sabbatarians professed Unitarian views and some adopted Mosaic dietary practices.[71] Williams notes that the Transylvanian Sabbatarians persisted at least until 1618, when they were formally excluded from the Unitarian fold.[72] A widespread

---

65   Hasel, 'Sabbatarian Anabaptists of the Sixteenth Century', 112.

66   *Ibid,* 107.

67   Samuel Purchas, *Purchas his Pilgrims* (1625), 1177.

68   G. Baratti, *Travels into Remote Countries* (1670), 46, 135.

69   Edward Stennett, *The Insnared Taken in the Work of his Hands* (1677), BL 1471 de 11.

70   Peter Heylin, *Cosmography* (1674), iii, 40.

71   Williams, *Radical Reformation,* 414, 686, 730–32; Hasel, 'Sabbatarian Anabaptists of the Sixteenth Century', *AUSS* 6 (1968) 20–21; 5 (1967) 106–7, 114. See also E. M. Wilbur, *A History of Unitarianism* (Cambridge, MA: Harvard University Press, 1952), 106–115.

72   Williams, *Radical Reformation,* 732.

Sabbatarian movement thus found expression across the European continent and beyond for much of the sixteenth century and although a detailed survey of its development and theology is beyond the scope of this work, it may be noted that Glait and Fischer, its two most able proponents in central Europe, both emphasized the perpetuity of the moral law in the Decalogue and the example of Christ, the apostles and the early Church.[73] These were arguments well known to English Sabbatarians of the seventeenth century and it is rather strange that there are so few references in the English Sabbatarian literature to Continental Sabbatarianism. This may support the conclusion that the Seventh-day cause in England was spontaneous and self-contained, rather than being derived from Continental Anabaptism, as has sometimes been suggested, although East Anglia may have been susceptible to some Continental influence. It may also be indicative of a desire not to be too closely identified with a movement which, taken as a whole, was frequently characterized as legalistic, Judaistic, or anti-trinitarian.

The Sabbatarian Controversy

It was inevitable that the Sabbatarian controversy, "peculiar to England of all Christendom" in the view of one contemporary,[74] should give rise to seventh-day observance. This debate, begun in the sixteenth century and extending well into the seventeenth century, frequently vigorous and occasionally acrimonious, continues to be a focus of scholarly attention and although its broad features are sufficiently well known, it cannot be omitted from an objective survey of Seventh-day antecedents. In the light of earlier observations on the Lollard tradition, it is significant to note, as background to the Sabbatarian doctrine defined by Nicholas Bownde in 1595, a consistent emphasis on Sabbath observance, *per se*, from the early years of the English Reformation. In 1548 John Hooper emphasised the Sabbath in *A Declaration of the Ten Holy Commaundements*, explaining that the fourth commandment was essentially moral like all the others and therefore binding, rather than ceremonial, although the specific day of rest had been changed.[75] In 1552 Hugh Latimer reminded a congregation in Lincolnshire that "God is and remaineth still the old God: He will have us keep his Sabbath, as well now as then". The Sabbath day is "God's ploughing day" when the hearts of men are broken up to receive the seed of the gospel.[76] Thomas Becon, the Anglican scholar, could be read for a thoroughgoing Puritan Sabbatarian when he says that God's will is that men "should sanctify the Sabbath day" and upon it "quietly meditate in God's law, read the

---

73 Hasel, *AUSS*, 5 (1967) 116–21; 6 (1968) 22–27.

74 Bodleian Library, MS. Rawl. D. 846 fol. 42r.

75 John Hooper, *A Declaration of ... Almyghty God* (1548), 341–42.

76 G. E. Corrie, ed., *Works of Hugh Latimer* (1844), i, 473.

holy Scriptures, give themselves to divine contemplation, talk of serious matters, pray to God for grace, give him thanks for his benefits, visit the sick and comfortless, and continually be given to works of the Spirit".[77]

Such views were readily incorporated into the doctrine of the Elizabethan Church and found expression, for example, in the 1563 Book of Homilies:

> God hath given express charge to all men, that upon the Sabbath day, which is now our Sunday, they should cease from all weekly and work-day labour, to the intent that like as God himself wrought six days, and rested the seventh, and blessed and sanctified it, and consecrated it to quietness and rest from labour, even so God's obedient people should use the Sunday holily, and rest from their common and daily business, and also give themselves wholly to heavenly exercises of God's true religion and service.[78]

Parker states that this homily "must be acknowledged as the primary source of Sabbatarian teaching in the Elizabethan and early Stuart period".[79]

It was easy thenceforth for preachers and expositors alike to uphold the idea of the Sabbath even though at the time its observance in practice might have left much to be desired. The Elizabethan "merrie England" was so called largely on account of Sunday diversions such as hunting, hawking, fencing, clowning and morris dancing, not to mention trading and other "flagrant abuses of the Sabbath".[80] Such laxness and obvious inconsistency with the professed doctrine of the Church gave rise to strictures such as those of Humphry Roberts, *An Earnest Complaint of divers Vain, Wicked and Abased Exercises Practiced on the Sabbath Day* (1572) and John Northbrooke, *A Treatise wherein Dicing, Dancing, Vain Plays or Interludes, with other idle Pastimes commonly used on the Sabbath are by the Word of God and ancient Writers reproved* (1579). In 1583 Gervase Babington, soon to become Bishop of Llandaff, and later of Exeter and Worcester, published his *Very Fruitfull Exposition of the Commandments*, one of a growing number of works intended to draw attention to the Sabbath problem and encourage more faithful observance of Sunday. In that same year the Puritan John Field took the occasion of an accident at the Paris Gardens near London to press home the gravity of Sabbath-breaking. Many had been killed and several injured in a large audience attending a bear-baiting on Sunday and Field interpreted this as divine judgement on

---

77 J. Eyre, ed., *Early Works of Thomas Becon* (1843), 38.

78 *Certaine Sermons appointed to be ... read for the better understanding of simple people* (1563), ii, fol. 138*r* .

79 K. L. Parker, *The English Sabbath* (Cambridge: University Press ,1988), 46.

80 Attributed to James Gilfillan, *The Sabbath Viewed in the Light of Reason, Revelation and History* (1861), 59.

those concerned.[81] And in 1585 Lancelot Andrewes, later Bishop of Chichester (1603), Ely (1609) and Winchester (1619), delivered a series of lectures at Cambridge in which he expounded the doctrine that the Sabbath (Sunday) should be kept as a day of rest and worship on the grounds of the continuing morality of the fourth commandment.[82]

Thus Nicholas Bownde's *The Doctrine of the Sabbath* (1595), while a classic formulation of the Puritan concept and the immediate cause of the Sabbatarian debate, came from a well-established Sabbath tradition in English Reformation theology. Bownde's work remains of significance and his arguments and those of succeeding advocates of the Puritan view may be summarized as follows. The Sabbath was an ordinance instituted at Creation and thus originated with Adam rather than with the Jews. The fourth commandment of the Decalogue was moral, in harmony with the rest of the Ten Commandments and therefore perpetually binding. The Sabbath was also therefore moral and binding and was not ceremonial since it antedated all ceremonies. Christians were thus obliged to keep the Sabbath in the same way the Jews had been obliged to keep the original seventh day, although now, under the New Testament, the Sabbath institution had been transferred from Saturday to Sunday. The change was justified on the grounds that the Sabbath commandment called for one day of rest after six days of labour. The actual day of rest could therefore be changed without affecting the inherent morality of the commandment. This had occurred under apostolic authority, hence the Sunday Sabbath was equally an institution of divine appointment and was to be observed for the entire twenty-four-hour period. The Sabbath was holy time, to be set aside for rest, worship, prayer, meditation and all profitable spiritual exercises.[83]

Although no Puritan, Richard Hooker epitomizes that view of the Sabbath which, following the Puritan campaign launched with the Dedham debates and the publication of Bownde's book, came to prevail in English religious life for the better part of three centuries:

> The moral law requiring therefore a seventh part throughout the age of the whole world to be that way employed, although with us the day be changed, in regard of a new revolution begun by our Saviour Christ; yet the same proportion of time continueth which was before, ... we are bound to account the sanctification of one day in seven, a duty which God's immutable Law doth exact forever.[84]

To use Hooker's phrase, it was "God's immutable Law" which gave the impetus to Puritan Sabbatarianism. As Patrick Collinson has aptly summarized

81   John Field, A *godly exhortation ... concerning the keeping of the Sabbath day* (1583), *passim.*

82   Lancelot Andrewes, *A Patterne of Catechisticall Doctrine* (1630), 234.

83   Nicholas Bownde, *The Doctrine of the Sabbath* (1595), *passim.*

84   Richard Hooker, *The Lawes of Ecclesiasticall Politie* (1622), 378–79.

it, the whole Sabbatarian controversy was based on "the doctrinal assertion that the fourth commandment is not an obsolete ceremonial law of the
Jews but a perpetual, moral law, binding on Christians".[85] Sabbatarianism,
in particular seventh-day Sabbatarianism, cannot be understood apart from
its nexus in the Decalogue and the continuing authority of the Decalogue as
it was perceived to exist in the New Testament. Bownde had emphasized the
significance of the law in this respect and the Puritan writers who would follow him in asserting the necessity of the Sabbath would do likewise.

Finally, some of the more fundamental aspects of the Puritan understanding of the law are essential to an adequate grasp of the wider Sabbatarian
movement as well as of seventh-day Sabbatarianism. The moral law as set
forth in the Ten Commandments was repeatedly emphasised by Sabbatarian
writers as perpetually binding, an expression of the will of the divine Lawgiver himself. John White wrote, "The Moral Law, seeing it sets down rules
of governing a man as a man ... is therefore universally and perpetually to
be observed".[86] The moral law was to be distinguished from the ceremonial
law, which had been abrogated by the death of Christ. White says again,
"from the Ceremonial Law we are wholly freed by the coming of Christ
into the world, who is the body of those shadows".[87] The same was true, in
general, of the judicial and social laws of the Old Testament, although some
differences of opinion surfaced as to the continuing value for Christians of
some aspects of this code.

The moral law was effective in pointing out sin and then of leading the
penitent and believing soul to Christ. Samuel Bolton speaks of the law "as a
Reprover and Corrector of sin ... not only to discover sin, but to make it appear exceeding sinful".[88] And John Flavel, that powerful exponent of Puritan
spirituality, admonishes: "Learn hence the usefulness of the Law, to bring
souls to Jesus Christ ... It cannot relieve us or ease us, but it can, and doth
awaken and rouse us; its a fair glass to shew us the face of sin; and till we
have seen that, we cannot see the face of Jesus Christ".[89]

The moral law was also the recognized measure of conduct and behaviour in the Christian life. John Ball, speaking of the covenant of faith and the
obedience required in a godly life, explains that "they which believe God to
be their God, must declare the same by obedience to his Commandments".
And further, "This is an inseparable consequent: that if we embrace God by

85   P. Collinson, 'The Beginnings of English Sabbatarianism', *Studies in Church History* 1 (1964), 207.

86   John White, *A Way to the Tree of Life* (1647), 206.

87   *Ibid.*

88   Samuel Bolton, *The True Bounds of Christian Freedom* (1656), 119, 121.

89   John Flavel, 'The Method of Grace', in *Workes of ... John Flavel* (1716), i, 278.

faith, we must and ought to follow his Commandments by our deeds, and he that doth not this latter, bewrayeth [sic] that he hath not with a true heart and faith received the former".[90]

The moral law becomes internalised in the true Christian life, since it is written in the heart of the believer, tending to natural obedience. The law, which after man's sin was written on tables of stone, is "turned to an internal law again" as God "implants it on the heart as it was at first", and so becomes "inbred" and "effectual" once more.[91] Richard Sibbes explains that the dynamic of the new covenant "is that we may expect from this Lordship of Christ, the performance of the covenant of grace in writing his law in our hearts". Otherwise the "covenant of grace should be frustrate as the first was".[92]

And the moral law would be the standard by which all men, Christians included, would be measured in the last judgement. John Seagar states explicitly, "the certainty of this world's dissolution should persuade us to be universal in our obedience", striving "to practise every known duty prescribed in God's Word, after the example of Zacharias and Elisabeth his wife, who walked in all the commandments of God blameless".[93] Baxter says, "Christ, at that great Assize ... as he governed by a Law, so will he judge by a Law ... and the equity of his judgement may be manifest to all".[94]

Such was the scope and strength of moral law in Puritan theology. As a *force majeure* in the emergence of sixteenth- and seventeenth-century Sabbatarianism it was quite irresistible. In retrospect, and given the immense respect for the Ten Commandments across all shades of opinion within the Anglican Church, to say nothing of the earlier and persisting Lollard tradition, it would have been remarkable indeed had the Sabbath not become a prominent issue. It was equally inevitable that, once the Sabbatarian debate had been joined, the question of the seventh day would sooner or later be raised. This possibility seems to have been inherent in an early seventeenth-century comment on the implications of the fourth commandment. "Go through the whole commandment", say Dod and Cleaver in their popular *Exposition of the Ten Commandments* (1615) and "what one word in all of it hath any note of ceremony? What reason savours of any special thing to the Jews that the commandment should be tied only to them?"[95] This was a rejoinder, in part at least, to those who had already begun to attack the Puritan

---

90 John Ball, *A Treatise of Faith* (1632), 32–33.

91 John Owen, *The Nature ... of Indwelling Sin in Believers* (1668), 16–17.

92 Richard Sibbes, *Christ's Exaltation* (1639), 145.

93 John Seagar, *A Discoverie of the World to Come* (1650), 46–47.

94 Richard Baxter, *Aphorismes of Justification* (1649), 318.

95 John Dod and Robert Cleaver, *Exposition of the Ten Commandments* (1615), 126.

Sabbatarian position as an unnecessarily extreme view of the Christian Sunday, the argument being that the ceremonial aspects of the fourth commandment applied only to the Jews. More directly, Francis White remarked that
the "errant" advocate of the seventh day, Theophilus Brabourne, had derived
most of his arguments from "Principles which the Sabbatarian Dogmatists
had lent him".[96] White even conceded that if the fourth commandment was
indeed moral and perpetually binding "then the Saturday Sabbath of every
week must be observed by Christians, and not the Sunday or Lord's Day in
the place thereof".[97]

It seems incontrovertible that there were precedents for the Seventh-day
Men in the Anglicanism of the day as well as in Puritan Sabbatarianism,
as there were indeed in other earlier and contemporary antecedents, all of
which together were the foundation of seventh-day observance in many
parts of England and Wales for the best part of two centuries to come.

96   White, *Treatise,* Ep. Ded., sig. A2v.
97   Francis White, *An Examination and Confutation of a Lawlesse Pamphlet*
(1637), 4.

10. Through Darkness to Light: Post-Restoration Sabbatarianism, Survival and Continuity[1]

Bryan W. Ball

The Seventh-day Sabbatarian movement during the post-Restoration years, like English Nonconformity in general, found itself on the defensive and running for cover. In February 1668, Edward Stennett, patriarch of the prominent Stennett family, wrote from Abingdon, then in Berkshire, to the fledgling Sabbatarian church in Newport, Rhode Island, of the difficulties Sabbatarians in England were experiencing. "We have passed through great opposition, for this truth's sake", he wrote, adding "Many once eminent churches have been shattered in pieces".[2] A month later the church in Bell Lane, London, also wrote to Newport in similar vein. The letter told of their "troubles", "fiery trials", "great opposition", specifying the "persecution of enemies" and the "frowns of friends",[3] the latter a reference to antagonism to the seventh day from believers of other persuasions. It was all indicative of the times. In April 1671 Stennett wrote again, from Wallingford where he was now elder of a Sabbatarian congregation which met in the ruins of Wallingford castle. The situation had worsened. "Thick clouds and darkness are upon us in many places", he said, "we are in jeopardy every hour".[4]

A few months later such fears turned to reality for many members of the Bell Lane congregation. On Saturday 24 June John Belcher, their elder, was reported to the authorities for preaching to an unlawful assembly and he and thirty-four others, "dangerous and seditious persons", were taken into custody. Twenty-six were committed to Newgate, four to Bridewell

1 Paper presented at a conference on religious minorities and pluralism in the UK in 2004, subsequently published in Richard Bonney and D.J.B. Trim, eds., *The Development of Pluralism in Modern England and France* (Oxford, Bern, New York: Peter Lang, 2007). Used with permisison. The post-Restoration period commences with the restoration of the monarchy in 1660.

2   Edward Stennett to the church in Newport, Rhode Island [hereafter cited as Newport], 2 Feb. 1668, quoted in *The Seventh Day Baptist Memorial*, 1:1 (Jan. 1852), 26.

3   Bell Lane to Newport, Mar. 1668, *ibid.*, 24–25.

4   Stennett to Newport, 9 April, 1671, in Samuel Hubbard's Journal, Seventh Day Baptist Historical Society MS 194x.6, 67–68.

and Belcher himself, "a most notorious knave" and three others, including Arthur Squibb, formerly Member of Parliament for Middlesex in the
Nominated Parliament, were sent to the Tower. Three weeks later thirty-one
of them were sent to trial upon refusing the oath of allegiance. They were
found guilty, their goods confiscated and they were imprisoned pending the
King's pleasure. As a final gesture, their meeting place was destroyed.[5] Although Professor Capp is correct in observing that by the time this episode
took place persecution in general was less severe than it had been,[6] the effect
on a single congregation and a small movement was nonetheless traumatic.

These are merely fleeting glimpses of the times. Similar instances could
be recounted from many places in the realm where the penal legislation of
the early 1660s was brought to bear upon individuals and congregations.
And this is to say nothing of the hostile attitudes, for example, of Seth Ward,
Bishop of Salisbury, or John Fell, Bishop of Oxford, in their severe opposition to Dissenters, including Sabbatarians. Nor does it take account of the
merciless activities of the notorious Judge Jeffreys in the West of England
following the suppression of Monmouth's rebellion of 1685. While the specific effects of the so-called "bloody assizes" on Sabbatarians remain largely
un-examined, the *Western Martyrology* of 1705 suggests that they would
have fared no better than Baptists and Dissenters in general, for whom the
decimation of whole families and entire congregations was not uncommon.
Joseph Davis, whose own contribution to the Sabbatarian cause we shall
note shortly, wrote in 1685, "The shadows of evening seem to be streached
[*sic*] out upon Great Britain".[7] G. R. Cragg comments, "This was the period
of the great persecution … Never had their sufferings been so bitter or so
prolonged".[8] We easily forget the harsh historical realities which form part
of the background of many European minorities.

We speak also, however, of survival and continuity. Edward Stennett and
the Bell Lane church are two cases in point. They were survivors. Repressive legislation and its zealous application by the Establishment did not inevitably lead to extinction. Stennett, who first appeared *c.*1655 in Berkshire
and who published his first book advocating the seventh-day Sabbath in
1658,[9] remained a leading figure in the movement until his death in 1705.

5 *CSPD 1671*, 356–57, 386; J. C. Jeaffreson, ed., *Middlesex County Records*,
4(1892), 29–30.

6 B. S. Capp, *The Fifth Monarchy Men* (London: Faber & Faber, 1972), 216.

7 Joseph Davis Snr. to Newport, in Samuel Hubbard's Journal, SDBHS MS
194x.6, 140.

8 G. R. Cragg, *The Church and the Age of Reason, 1648–1789* (London: Penguin, 1960), 57–58.

9 Edward Stennett, *The Royal Law Contended For, or, Some Brief Grounds
serving to prove that the Ten Commandments are yet in full force,* … (London,
1658).

For fifty years, and through two high periods of persecution, Stennett was the guiding light of several Sabbatarian congregations in Berkshire, Oxfordshire and London. Although strangely omitted from the old *Dictionary of National Biography* he was in every sense the patriarch of the nascent Sabbatarian movement and lived to see it through its most difficult years.

Bell Lane typifies the survival of a congregation. Those who were arrested and imprisoned in 1671 comprised almost the entire male membership of the Bell Lane congregation. It has been suggested that Charles II may already have had in mind the Declaration of Indulgence which eventuated in 1672 and the prisoners were shortly released.[10] Although their meeting house had been destroyed, the Bell Lane congregation regrouped and continued for another thirty years until in 1702 it amalgamated with the like-minded Particular Baptist Sabbatarian congregation at Pinners' Hall. In the meantime, Bell Lane had played a significant role in the establishment of the Sabbatarian cause in New England and hence, it may be argued, in the modern world.

Perhaps the most important single testimony to the survival of the seventeenth-century Sabbatarian movement is an account recorded in the Llanwenarth Baptist Church book, dated December 1690. Dr E. A. Payne, the Baptist historian, first drew attention to this remarkable document in the *Baptist Quarterly* in 1951.[11] It is the record of surviving Sabbatarian congregations in England shortly after the cessation of repressive measures against Dissenters which followed James II's second Declaration of Indulgence in 1688. Just why a Baptist congregation in Wales should be so interested in the English Sabbatarian movement is still an unresolved question, but the suggestion that it was itself a mixed-communion congregation and a connection with the Stennett family are two plausible reasons. In any event the account lists twenty-two Sabbatarian congregations in England, together with the names of their elders or ministers. It omits congregations at Braintree, Leominster and Hay-on-Wye, which from other sources are known to have existed at the time, and makes no reference to the strong Sabbatarian interest in the northern counties, or to several small groups which are also known to have existed in other parts of the country. It is, nonetheless, an important historical document in terms of Sabbatarian history and continuity.

We turn, then, to what is perhaps one of the most important questions to arise from the survival in England of the Saturday Sabbath well into the eighteenth century. It is the matter of causation. What enabled a relatively

---

10 Capp, *Fifth Monarchy Men,* 216.

11 E. A. Payne, 'More about the Sabbatarian Baptists', *The Baptist Quarterly,* 14 (1951–52), 165. The document is reproduced in Bryan W. Ball, *The Seventh-day Men: Sabbatarians and Sabbatarianism in England and Wales, 1600–1800* (Oxford: Clarendon, 1994), 228–29.

small movement with an unpopular doctrine to survive such difficult times and the strong and sustained opposition of both friend and foe? The answers are no doubt many and complex and would apply variously to any given congregation, but we can detect four principal factors, each demonstrated in the life and work of a prominent Sabbatarian of the period. Each of these individuals suffered personally in the times of persecution: two of them survived and two of them did not.

Theophilus Brabourne, 1590–1662: Convincing Apologetic Literature

Theophilus Brabourne, a native of Norwich and an Anglican clergyman with Puritan inclinations, was the first English writer to publish an apology for the seventh-day Sabbath. His *Discourse upon the Sabbath Day* (1628) was the forerunner of more than seventy such works of varying size and quality which appeared over the next 120 years.[12] As the only known non-Baptist who published in favour of the Saturday Sabbath during the seventeenth century, Brabourne's influence on the development of the Sabbatarian movement as a whole was considerable. Cox is thoroughly justified in calling him an able writer, although in error in describing him as a Seventh Day Baptist.[13]

Born in 1590, the elder son of a Norwich hosier, Brabourne was one of the relatively few who received episcopal ordination without having first received a university education. According to Alexander Gordon, Brabourne was ordained in 1621 by Thomas Dove, Bishop of Peterborough, licensed for the diocese of Norwich in 1622 and appears a few years later as the curate of Catton in Norfolk.[14] The *Discourse upon the Sabbath Day* came indisputably from an Anglican context. There is equally little doubt that Brabourne remained at heart a loyal Anglican for the rest of his life, although well-disposed to Nonconformists, particularly Baptists, many of whom in coming years gladly espoused the Sabbatarian doctrine he had earlier advocated.

Brabourne's journey to the Court of High Commission and to Newgate gaol began in 1632 with the publication of his second book, *A Defence of ... the Sabbath Day*. This work was boldly dedicated to Charles I who referred it for a response to Francis White, Bishop of Ely. The dedication to Charles I was motivated by the hope that he would initiate a Sabbath reformation

---

12   A chronological bibliography of the English Sabbatarian literature from 1628 to 1750 is given in Ball, *Seventh-day Men,* Appendix IV, 342–50.

13   Robert Cox, *The Literature of the Sabbath Question* (Edinburgh: Maclachlan and Stewart, 1865), I, 157–58.

14   *Dictionary of National Biography,* II, 1047–49.

similar to that undertaken by Old Testament kings such as Hezekiah and Josiah. "The soundness and clearness of my cause giveth me good hope", Brabourne wrote and sent the *Defence* on its way, prepared to defend it as necessary, but aware of the possible consequences and quoting Esther, "and if I perish, I perish".[15] Parker notes that Brabourne was not a schismatic[16] and we may add, neither was he a fanatic as the earlier Sabbatarian John Traske had clearly been. Unfortunately, Brabourne was regarded by the authorities with Traske as one of a kind and they were apparently determined to treat him in a similar manner. White's reply to Brabourne, which Bishop Cox judged to be, after Peter Heylin's *History of the Sabbath*, "the most notable work" in the entire Sabbatarian controversy, appeared in 1635. But this was too late to deal as expeditiously as necessary with Brabourne's views, which White himself admitted already "might have poisoned and infected many people with this Sabbatarian error".[17]

So in April and in June 1634 Brabourne found himself before the Court of High Commission charged with holding and disseminating "erroneous, heretical, and judaical opinions".[18] The trial took place on 16 June, before more than a hundred clergy and several hundred other onlookers. In answer to questioning Brabourne confessed himself a Sabbatarian, "as much bound to keep the Saturday Sabbath as the Jews were before the coming of Christ". It was an injudicious response, for Brabourne was neither a legalist nor a Judaiser, as his published arguments clearly demonstrate. The Court had heard all it needed, however, and Brabourne was pronounced a Jew, a heretic and a schismatic, "worthy to be severely punished".[19] It was ordered that he be deprived of all ecclesiastical privileges, including his living, deposed from holy orders, excommunicated, fined one thousand pounds and required to make a public retraction of his errors at such time and place and in such words as the Court should approve. It was also ordered that he be remanded in custody pending further consideration of his case and the possibility of delivering him to the secular power.[20] The outlook was not bright.

The proceedings against him dragged on for another year, most of which

---

15 Theophilus Brabourne, *A Defence Of that most Ancient, and Sacred ordinance of GOD's the SABBATH DAY* ([Amsterdam], 1632), sig 3Cv.

16 K. L. Parker, *The English Sabbath* (Cambridge: Cambridge University, 1988), 199.

17 Francis White, *A Treatise of the Sabbath Day; containing a Defence of the Orthodoxal Doctrine of the Church of England against Sabbatarian Novelty* (London, 1635), Ep. Ded.

18 *CSPD 1634–35,* 126.

19 See Ball, *Seventh-day Men,* 65.

20 *CSPD 1633–34,* 108, 122, 126–27; W. H. Hart, *Index Expurgatorius Anglicanus* (London, 1872–78), III, 75.

time he spent in the Gatehouse and in Newgate, in conditions he later described as "loathsome" and in the company of "rogues, lousie felons and cheaters". Although the fine of a thousand pounds was eventually remitted, the strong feelings against him should not be underestimated. One of his prosecutors, Sir Henry Marten, moved during the trial that the old anti-Lollard legislation *De haeretico comburendo* should be brought against him, and the message reached Brabourne's wife that he was to be burnt. It is said that only the personal intervention of William Laud prevented it.[21]

Brabourne eventually returned to Norwich, but we hear little of him again until the Commonwealth era, by which time he was no longer an Anglican priest. Then, in 1653, after having kept an appropriately low profile for several years, he resumed publication with a further eight works in the space of nine years which wholly, or in part, advocated the Sabbatarian view. In fact, of the twenty books advocating the Seventh-day Sabbath which appeared in print by 1660 Brabourne was the author of ten.[22] In his *Of the Sabbath Day* (1660), he maintained that the debate over the Sabbath was at that time "the Highest Controversie in the Church of England".[23] Whether or not this claim was valid is difficult to determine, but already in 1635 Francis White, in attempting to defend the orthodox position of the Church of England against "Sabbatarian Novelty", had conceded that Brabourne's arguments were "commonly preached, printed, and believed, throughout the kingdom".[24]

Brabourne produced in total more than one thousand pages in support of the Saturday Sabbath. It was by any standard an impressive output, giving evidence throughout of a keen mind and a thorough grasp of the historical and biblical material involved. It included the forthright apologetic of his early writings and the later controversies involving opponents who had attacked him or the Sabbath doctrine, including Collings of Norwich, Cawdrey and Ives of London and Warren of Colchester. Later Sabbatarian apologists would return frequently to most of the arguments found in his writings, but it was indisputably Brabourne who laid the foundation for the revival of an ancient practice that was to last in the British Isles without break for at least four centuries. While Brabourne passed from the scene of action shortly after the Restoration, the lasting influence of his writings demands recognition of the major role he played in the development of English Sabbatarianism.

---

21 Theophilus Brabourne, A *Reply to the Indoctus Doctor Edoctus* ... (London, 1654), 100–101; *CSPD 1635–36,* 495. The *Reply* was a response to John Collings of Norwich, who had attacked Brabourne on a number of issues, including the Sabbath.

22 See Ball, *Seventh-day Men,* 342–44.

23 Theophilus Brabourne, *Of the Sabbath Day* (London, 1660), title page.

24 White, *Treatise,* Ep. Ded.

John James, d. 1661: Unwavering Commitment

John James is one of the very few Sabbatarians who is mentioned by all the early Baptist historians, including Crosby, Ivimey and Taylor and by many who have added to Baptist and Nonconformist history more recently, notably W. T. Whitley, B. R. White and B. S. Capp.[25] Within a month of his death in 1661 James had established a place of lasting significance in the ranks of seventeenth-century anti-paedobaptists and Sabbatarians. Had he lived a century earlier he might well have featured prominently in Foxe's *Actes and Monuments*, more commonly known as the *Book of Martyrs*.

Little is known of James's early life and he first appears in the late 1650s as the first identifiable pastor of the Mill Yard General Baptist Sabbatarian congregation meeting in Bullstake Alley, Whitechapel.[26] A ribbon weaver by trade and barely literate, he earned his place in the history of the period on account of his trial and execution in 1661, which have been variously described as "grossly unjust", a "judicial murder" and "one of the many blots on the reign of Charles II".[27] In view of the facts, it might even be concluded that such judgements were lenient.

The series of events which led to his death can only be seen properly in the context of the Fifth Monarchy movement, which is today much better understood than it was in its own time. In January 1661, Thomas Venner, a Fifth Monarchist desperado, had led an abortive uprising against the government of Charles II, for which he had been tried and executed. The basis for Fifth Monarchist activism was an interpretation of the prophecies of Daniel and Revelation, which held that the final kingdom in the succession of earthly powers delineated therein, Christ's kingdom, was soon to be set up on earth and that Christ's true followers were to be instruments in its establishment, using force if necessary. Although many Fifth Monarchists were not as radical as Venner and his immediate band of followers, the government was understandably fearful of any Fifth Monarchist tendencies, particularly when Fifth Monarchy language was used indiscriminately by those who were themselves pacifist in their inclinations. The indications are that John James was in this category, particularly since he had publicly disavowed any connection with Venner or support for his activities.[28]

---

25 W. T. Whitley, *A History of British Baptists* (London: Charles Griffin, 1923), 110; B. R. White, *The English Baptists of the Seventeenth Century* (London: Baptist Historical Society, 1983), 99; B. S. Capp, *The Fifth Monarchy Men* (London: Faber & Faber, 1972), 201, 253.

26 R. L. Greaves and R. Zaller, *A Biographical Dictionary of British Radicals in the Seventeenth Century* (Brighton, MA: Harvester,1982–84), II, 138; Capp, *Fifth Monarchy Men*, 253.

27 *A Narrative of the Apprehending, Commitment, Arraignment, Condemnation, and Execution of John James, who Suffered at Tyburn, Nov. 26, 1661* (1662).

28 Ball, *Seventh-day Men*, 83–84.

On 19 October, while preaching at the regular hour of Sabbath worship
at Bullstake Alley, officials interrupted the meeting and ordered James to
come down from the pulpit, accusing him of treason. When he twice ignored the order, he was dragged from the pulpit and taken to Newgate on
the concocted charge of "preaching maliciously and traitorously against the
life and safety of our Sovereign Lord the King". He was accused of being
a Fifth Monarchist and of having been connected with Venner's uprising.
Several members of his congregation who protested his innocence were also
taken into custody, but were subsequently released without charge.[29] It was
deemed advisable to deal with the matter as expeditiously as possible and
accordingly James was brought to trial on 14 November before a jury and
witnesses that, according to an informer, had been hand-picked in order to
ensure a conviction. He was indicted, *inter alia:*

1.   for compassing and imagining the death of the King;
2.   for endeavouring to levy war against the King: and
3.   for endeavouring a change of the government.[30]

The charges were manifestly untrue, if not absurd, but under such circumstances a conviction was inevitable. Despite a personal plea to Charles II by
James's wife he was convicted and sentenced to death.

The view that this was one of the most barbaric acts of the Restoration
government seems fully justified by the wording of the sentence. The nature
of the event and its intended message for those judged to be radical and
dangerous, can only be fully grasped by hearing the sentence as John James
himself heard it from the dock:

> Thou art to be carried from hence to prison, and from thence to the
> place of execution, and there to be hanged by the neck, and being yet
> alive, to be cut down and thy bowels taken out and to be burnt before
> thy face, and thy head to be severed from thy body, and thy body to
> be quartered, and thy head and body to be disposed according to the
> King's pleasure.[31]

And that is precisely what happened. It was a severe blow to the Mill Yard
Church and to Sabbatarianism *per se.*

The days of James's imprisonment prior to execution were mercifully
short. The warders were reported to be grasping and heartless. They stole
his clothes and pressed him continually for money which he did not have
and could not obtain. On the day before his execution, the hangman arrived
and demanded twenty pounds "that he might be favourable to him at his

---

29 Detailed accounts of James's trial and execution can be found in the anony-
mous *A Narrative* (1662) and in T. B. Howell, ed., *Cobbett's Complete Collection
of State Trials,* VI (1810), 72ff.

30 *A Narrative,* 12.

31 *Ibid.,* 24.

death".[32] It was an impossible request and they settled for five pounds, the hangman threatening "to torture him exceedingly" if the five pounds was not forthcoming. The next day he was dragged on a hurdle to Tyburn and executed according to the sentence. His speech at the gallows was in reality a confession of faith which confirmed a non-militant eschatological hope, said nothing of Fifth Monarchism, and owned "the Lord's holy Sabbath, the seventh day of the week".[33]

How do we evaluate John James's contribution to the Sabbatarian cause? What does it represent in Sabbatarianism that ensured its survival through intense opposition and when the prospects were so bleak? The word we use today, commitment, sounds trite against the reality of what took place. Yet it would be difficult to find a better example then or now of what we understand by the word. Certainly he typified commitment to the cause, to the Sabbath, which he saw as an institution of divine origin, enshrined in the fourth commandment which required Christian obedience, and to Sabbatarianism as a vehicle for communicating and perpetuating those convictions. It was what Edward Stennett had in mind when later he said that he and his congregation were suffering for "this truth". James also demonstrated pastoral commitment to his congregation at a time when it might have been better for him to have disappeared until safer days returned. It is easy with hindsight to make such suggestions, yet what Dr B. R. White calls the "paranoia in government circles"[34] which prevailed at the time indicates that it might have been a more prudent option. This is to say nothing of commitment to his own conscience, a characteristic of Nonconformity in general throughout the seventeenth century and critical to its existence and identity. It may reasonably be concluded that all this was very much germane to the survival of English Sabbatarianism.

Joseph Davis Snr, 1627–1707: Considered Beneficence

Joseph Davis Snr is a classic illustration of the fact that the well-being of a congregation depends on the commitment of its members as well as its minister. Born in 1627 at Chipping Norton, his first religious affiliation was with a Baptist church in Coventry where his father was a burgess and chief magistrate. Between 1660 and 1662 Davis found himself in prison briefly on several occasions on charges relating to alleged breaches of the post-Restoration legislation against Dissenters. Then in the spring of 1662 he was again arrested and committed to Oxford Castle where he spent the next ten years. Following the Declaration of Indulgence in 1672 he was

---

32 *Ibid.,* 198.

33 *Ibid.,* 40.

34 B. R. White, *The English Baptists of the Seventeenth Century* (London: Baptist Historical Society, 1983), 100.

released, together with four hundred and eighty-nine others, including John Bunyan. These years of imprisonment, which he later described as being spent mostly "in a cold, high tower", were notable on two counts. In 1665 he was released temporarily to attend his dying wife and arrange for the care of their children and in 1668 he became convinced of the seventh-day Sabbath and forthwith commenced its observance.[35]

An enlightening letter from Davis to the Seventh Day Baptist Church in Newport, Rhode Island, written in 1670, is preserved in Samuel Hubbard's Journal. It tells of his trials and reveals a temperament that no amount of tribulation would easily crush:

> Satan in the present day hath appeared, and operates in the spirits of men, who rage with violence and open force, casting forth waters like a flood, thinking to destroy and swallow us in the sea of their confusion … for which I have suffered the loss of wife and enjoyment of children, trade and public ordinances, in the hope of being of that happy number who shall stand on Mount Zion …[36]

Regarding his "afflictions" as "the appointments of our dear Father" and rejoicing that "the snares which were laid to take away my life" had not prevailed, he continued, "It is my lot to sit here alone in the observation of God's holy Sabbath, yet not without some precious tokens of his presence, which makes a wilderness like an Eden, and a desert like a garden of the Lord".[37]

Soon after his release from Oxford gaol, Davis moved to London and there established a drapery business which, together with other ventures, was to reward him and the Sabbatarian cause beyond expectation in the years to come. The first evidence of his generosity came in 1691 when he purchased a property for the Mill Yard church, consisting of a meeting place, almshouses and a burial ground, which in 1700 was conveyed to nine trustees appointed by the congregation.[38] This became the home of the Mill Yard Sabbatarians for a hundred years. In 1705 he purchased another property, the Manor at Little Maplestead in Essex, and in 1706 he established a charitable trust, under the terms of which an annuity was to be paid in perpetuity to the ministers of nine specified Particular or General Baptist Sabbatarian congregations.[39] We shall return to these congregations shortly.

---

35   [Joseph Davis], *The Last Legacy of Mr. Joseph Davis, Snr* (London, 1720), 5–16, 26–29.

36   Joseph Davis to Newport in *The Seventh Day Baptist Memorial*, 1:2 (April 1852), 74.

37   *Ibid.*, 75

38   W. H. Black, ed., *The Last Legacy of Joseph Davis, Snr.* (London: Mill Yard Congregation, 1869), xii; William Wallen, *The History and Antiquities of the Round Church at Little Maplestead, Essex* (London, 1836), 137–38.

39   *The Case Submitted to the General Body of Dissenting Ministers of the*

When Joseph Davis died in 1707, all his assets were inherited by his son, Joseph Jnr, who himself died without heir in 1731, at which time the entire Davis estate, with the exception of certain specific bequests to be noted below, passed to the Mill Yard Church. The pecuniary benefits flowing to Mill Yard from these dispositions, and the annual disbursements, though modest, from the charitable trust to qualifying Sabbatarian ministers over many decades were together a source of considerable strength to the Sabbatarian cause. It has been claimed that by 1900, one hundred and seventy years after Mill Yard first benefited from the Joseph Davis legacy, the income it generated was more than seven hundred pounds per annum.[40]

The nine endowed Sabbatarian pastorates, which did not include Mill Yard itself, provide further evidence of the continuing effect of Joseph Davis's charitable concerns. Of these nine congregations, six survived for at least fifty years and three for more than one hundred years. Records for these three are scanty, but all continued well into the eighteenth century. The congregation that had coalesced in the Berkshire-Oxfordshire area finally expired in 1806. The last Sabbatarian at Salisbury died in 1844 and at Natton in 1910. Joseph Davis would surely have been gratified to know that his generosity had such far-reaching effects. The benevolence of Joseph Davis Jnr consolidated the impact of his father's provisions. Six beneficiaries of Joseph Jnr's will were known Sabbatarians, five of them members of the congregations specified in his father's will and four of them ministers: Philip Jones of Tewkesbury-Natton, John Ridley of Woodbridge, Daniel Wright of Colchester-Braintree and Edmund Townsend of Mill Yard and Currier's Hall.[41] All but one of them received two hundred pounds. Joseph Stennett II, the minister of South Street Baptist Church at Exeter and Moderator of the Western Baptist Association and a practising Sabbatarian, also received two hundred pounds.[42] It is clear that the consolidation and progress of the whole Sabbatarian movement resulted to a significant degree from the first benefactions of the Davis family and in particular from the dispositions of Joseph Davis Snr. at Mill Yard in 1691, 1700 and 1706.

Francis Bampfield, 1615–1684: Informed and Persuasive Preaching

Francis Bampfield, a graduate of Wadham College, Oxford, was the third son of Sir John Bampfield, sheriff of Devon and Elizabeth, daughter of Thomas Drake of Buckland Abbey. The Drakes, of course, were the

---

Three Denominations (1901), 9. A copy of this rare document is included with the photocopy of the Mill Yard Church Book at Dr Williams's Library.

40 *Ibid.*
41 Black, *Last Legacy,* 72.
42 *Ibid.*

staunchest of English Protestant families, and Sir Francis, Thomas Drake's brother, the most distinguished of them all. Francis Bampfield tells us that he was born of "religious parents", with an inclination to "love books" and "to delight in learning from a child".[43] Joseph Ivimey later described him as "a man of great learning and judgment".[44] Bampfield's scholarship is most evident in his grasp of biblical languages and although he was chiefly known as a Hebraist, his works also give evidence of a thorough acquaintance with Greek. Whitley thought, probably correctly, that some of Bampfield's works pre-figured Hutchinsonianism and the theories of Thomas Burnet.[45] Densham and Ogle more recently commented that he was "one of the most remarkable men of his time — a time when remarkable men were not scarce".[46]

Bampfield was a relative late-comer to the Sabbatarian tradition. He had graduated MA from Oxford in 1638 and was shortly thereafter presented by his father to the living of Rampisham in Dorset, where he remained as rector for several years.[47] In 1655 he accepted an invitation to become Vicar of Sherbourne, a charge he maintained with distinction and with much popular support until 1662 when he was ejected for refusing to take the oath of allegiance. Calamy reminds us of the irony in this, since Bampfield was a staunch Royalist, his objection being to oaths in general. His real troubles began shortly thereafter, when in the following year he was arrested in nearby Shaftesbury for holding an unlawful conventicle and was imprisoned in Dorchester gaol for the next eight years and nine months.[48] This was the longest of several periods of imprisonment Bampfield was to suffer. One source states that he was "more frequently imprisoned and exposed to greater hardships for his Nonconformity than most other Dissenters".[49]

---

43   Francis Bampfield, *A Name, an After-One ... an Historical Declaration of the Life of Shem Acher* (London, 1681), 2.

44   Joseph Ivimey, *History of the English Baptists* (London, 1811–30), II, 480.

45   W. T. Whitley, *A History of British Baptists* (London: Griffin, 1923), 134. Hutchinsonianism refers to the views of John Hutchinson (1674-1737), who disputed Newton's theory of gravity and claimed that a system of natural science was inherent in the Bible, particularly the Old Testament. Thomas Burnet (1635-1715) also attempted to harmonise the Bible with the science of his day in his most well-known work, *The Sacred Theory of the Earth*, the first English edition of which (1684) explained the Flood in the light of Scripture, geology and cosmology. The title of one of Bampfield's major works, *All in One* (1677), suggested that he also believed that all knowledge derived from one source and was evident through a careful and thorough study of the Biblical text

46   W. Densham and J. Ogle, *The Story of the Congregational Churches of Dorset* (Bournemouth, 1899), 245.

47   A.G. Matthews, *Calamy Revised* (Oxford: Clarendon, 1934), 26.

48   *Ibid;* Ivimey, *History,* II, 476.

49   Benjamin Stinton, 'An Account of Some of the Most Eminent and Leading

It was while in Dorchester gaol that Bampfield became a Sabbatarian and commenced observance of the seventh-day Sabbath, to the consternation of many friends and acquaintances. William Benn, the ejected Presbyterian of Dorchester who, some years later in 1672, published Bampfield's *Judgement ... for the Observation of ... the Seventh-day Sabbath*, recalled that his conversion to the seventh day was "the discourse of many, the wonder of not a few, and the grief of some".[50] Dr Geoffrey Nuttall records a letter from Isaac Clifford to John Pinney in 1666 in which he confessed to being "troubled" by Bampfield's new views of the Sabbath, with the fear that "many will make but a sad use of it".[51] In the event Bampfield convinced five or six fellow prisoners of the Sabbatarian position and gathered a congregation around him while in prison. Shortly after his release he was again apprehended and imprisoned for eighteen weeks in Salisbury gaol for preaching without a licence. In the more relaxed atmosphere of 1672 a general licence was issued to him as "a Nonconforming minister" to preach in any licensed place of assembly, a provision he was to use with great effect in the ensuing years.[52]

Bampfield's most effective labours in the Sabbatarian cause began after his removal to London in 1674. Within a year he had gathered a church in his own home in Bethnal Green and a year later, in 1676, a company was organised under a simple covenant which owned "the Lord Jesus Christ to be the one and only Lord and Lawgiver" and "the Holy Scriptures of Truth, as the one and only Rule of Faith".[53] This was the beginning of the famous Pinners' Hall-Cripplegate Sabbatarian Church of Particular Baptists to which several generations of Stennetts would later minister and which would help to sustain the Sabbatarian cause in London and in the provinces for almost two centuries.

Bampfield's final sufferings began in February 1683, when he was arrested on a warrant from the Lord Mayor while preaching at Pinners' Hall on suspicion of having received Jesuit training and the fatuous charge of attempting to re-establish the Catholic faith. The following week the meeting was again disturbed by a constable and officers and Bampfield was pulled from the pulpit while offering prayer, taken before magistrates and ultimately, after months of imprisonment, to the Old Bailey charged with the persistent refusal to take the Oath of Allegiance. He was sentenced in

Men among the English Anti-paedobaptists', Angus Library, Regents Park College, Oxford, MS 36.G.A.e.10, fo. 61r.

50   William Benn, *The Judgement of Mr. Francis Bampfield ...for the observation of the Jewish or Seventh Day Sabbath* (London, 1672), 9.

51   G. F. Nuttall, *Letters of John Pinney, 1679–1699* (London: Oxford University Press, 1939), 2.

52   Matthews, *Calamy Revised*, 26.

53   Bampfield, *A Name*, 26.

January 1684 to be outlawed and detained at the King's pleasure, but died in Newgate a month later, a victim of the circumstances and the conditions.[54] Ivimey's comment points us to Bampfield's singular contribution to the continuity of the Sabbatarian cause. He was, Ivimey says, "a man of great learning, and one of the most celebrated preachers in the West of England".[55] Without doubt, Bampfield combined these two characteristics in his ministry to the Sabbatarian churches over a period of nearly twenty years. Informed and persuasive preaching has always been one of the hallmarks of vigorous Nonconformist church life and in few instances did they come together more effectively than in Bampfield's pulpit ministry. His induction sermon at Sherbourne attracted a congregation of more than two thousand. During his nearly nine years in Dorchester gaol he preached on most days to local townspeople, according to Calamy, and according to his own testimony frequently as often as sixteen times a week.[56] Soon after arriving in London and before the establishment of his own congregation, Bampfield was invited to preach to both existing Sabbatarian congregations at Mill Yard and Bell Lane. Later he was sent by his own people on a preaching tour to strengthen the Sabbatarian churches in Wiltshire, Hampshire, Dorset, Gloucestershire and Berkshire.[57] The *Dictionary of National Biography* noted that he was "repeatedly imprisoned for preaching". His own judgement on effective pastoral ministry was the existence of a "converted, edified, comforted, confirmed people".[58] That such Sabbatarian congregations survived the hard times following the penal legislation of the post-Restoration era is due in no small measure to Bampfield's preaching ministry between 1665 and 1684.

The Wider Picture

We have traced the fortunes of four prominent seventeenth-century Sabbatarians and through them the fortunes of the wider Sabbatarian community as they ebbed and flowed through years of relative freedom and long periods of repression. We have noted the specific strengths of each man and suggested that these strengths were seminal to Sabbatarianism's survival and its consolidation in the eighteenth century. It would be misleading, however, to imply that the movement owed its survival to these four stalwarts alone. The gifts and qualities they demonstrated appeared and re-appeared in Sabbatarianism for the better part of a hundred and fifty years. The literature which began with Theophilus Brabourne serves as an illustration.

---

54   Francis Bampfield, *The Lords Free Prisoner* (London, 1683), *passim*.
55   Ivimey, *History*, II, 480.
56   Bampfield, *A Name*, 21; Matthews, *Calamy Revised*, 26.
57   Bampfield, *A Name*, 7.
58   *Ibid.*, 9.

Not only did that literature exert a considerable influence in its own day, it also set a precedent for later generations. Edward Stennett, who between 1658 and 1677 published three major works advocating the seventh day,[59] and Thomas Bampfield, who for a brief period had been Speaker in the Barebones Parliament, deserve mention. Bampfield's unfinished dialogue concerning the Sabbath with John Wallis, Savilian Professor of Geometry at Oxford, was prematurely terminated by his death in 1693. Others took up the cause. John Maulden of Mill Yard added three further works between 1708 and 1724 and finally Robert Cornthwaite, the last and most articulate and persuasive of all the Sabbatarian writers, contributed another six between 1731 and 1745. It is doubtful whether the Sabbatarian movement would have survived and rallied without its apologists.[60]

There were of course other individuals worthy of note, and other factors in the complex scheme of events which enabled this small and relatively insignificant movement to survive as it did and find a lasting place in the history of English religious thought and practice. Yet the evidence remains strong that the combination of convincing apologetic literature, unwavering commitment, sustained beneficence and informed and persuasive preaching was at the heart of the Sabbatarian impetus. These factors, individually and together, were an effective antidote against the predominating spirit of the age. They dispelled the clouds of darkness and oppression which in earlier years had surrounded Edward Stennett and Joseph Davis, Brabourne, Bampfield and John James and at times the whole Sabbatarian movement. They gave it grounds for hope and enabled it to survive and, for a time, to thrive. Undoubtedly such factors did the same for many other causes that similarly languished under harsh legislation, hostile adversaries and unsympathetic friends. It might reasonably be concluded that they were crucial, not only to the survival of seventh-day Sabbatarianism in England and Wales, but also to the growth and stability of many religious minorities and that singly or together they made a significant contribution to the existence of a confessionally pluralist society.

---

59 In addition to *The Royal Law*, cited in note 8 above, Stennett also published *The Seventh Day is the Sabbath of the Lord* (1664) and, in response to John Cowell's defection from the Sabbatarian movement, *The Insnared Taken in the Work of his Hands, an Answer to Mr John Cowell* (1677).

60 See Ball, *Seventh-day Men*, Appendix IV, for the works of Thomas Bampfield, Maulden and Cornthwaite.

11. Early English Apocalyptic Interpretation[1]

Bryan W. Ball

Ben Jonson, the seventeenth-century poet and playwright, referred in *The Alchemist,* perhaps his best-known play (1612), to "the two legs and the fourth Beast", and to "the stone" which "falls on the other four straight".[2] That a popular contemporary author could allude so obviously to apocalyptic imagery drawn directly from the Bible is some indication of widespread familiarity with those passages of Scripture which today rarely receive much attention. There was certainly nothing strange about this in the seventeenth century. Even the most cursory reading of the literature of the time reveals that it was deemed as proper and necessary to understand the books of Daniel and Revelation as it was to read the Psalms or the Gospels. Nor was Ben Jonson the only prominent man of his age to write about biblical apocalyptic prophecy. King James I, James Ussher, the Archbishop of Armagh, and Joseph Hall, Bishop of Norwich, all published books explaining the meaning of various prophecies in Daniel and Revelation, most of them running to several editions and some being translated into French and/or Latin.

If a king, an archbishop and a bishop could regard the study of prophecy as a serious and necessary matter, it is not surprising that others should come to think likewise. Many, in fact, from all quarters of the ecclesiastical establishment did so, throughout the seventeenth century and beyond. Edmund Hall, a Presbyterian, wrote in 1651 that it was "a sin" to neglect prophecies which gave light to the times:

> in the Revelation there are shallows as well as depths; there the lamb may wade, and the elephant may swim ... not understanding, or neglect of searching to understand the prophetic texts of the Old Testament was the cause of the greatest sin and scandal in the Church that ever was committed, the murdering of Christ.[3]

---

1 Abridged (with a newly written conclusion) from ch. 2 of Bryan W. Ball, *A Great Expectation: Eschatological Thought in English Protestantism to 1660* (Leiden: E.J. Brill, 1975), volume XII in the Brill series 'Studies in the History of Christian Thought', ed. Heiko A. Oberman. Used with permission. Spelling and punctuation in quotations have generally been modernised.

2 Ben Jonson, *The Alchemist* (1612), Act 4, Sc.5: cf. Dan 2:31–35 and 7: 7.

3 Edmund Hall, *Manus Testium Movens* (1651), Epistle to the Reader, sig. A2r.

Edmund's brother, Thomas, also a clergyman, maintained "it is our duty to take notice of the prophecies delivered to us in the Word of God ... they must not by our negligence be as a sealed book to us".[4] With such convictions widely held by preachers and writers of every shade of opinion, it was to be expected that much attention would be given to biblical prophecy, particularly to the apocalyptic prophecies of Daniel and Revelation, and that much paper would be used in the publication of a great number of books and pamphlets throughout the seventeenth century and beyond.

In actual fact, interest in prophetic interpretation predated the seventeenth century by many years, and can be traced back to the earliest years of the Reformation, both on the Continent and in England. Luther had written a commentary on Daniel, and Heinrich Bullinger, his associate in the German Reformation, who was much respected in England, had in 1577 written *In Apocalypsim Iesu Christi*, which was published in English in 1561 as *A Hundred Sermons upon the Apocalypse of Jesus Christ.* John Foxe, best known for his *Book of Martyrs,* which played such an important role in consolidating the English Reformation, also wrote a book on Revelation which for some reason was only published posthumously by his son. William Lamont, a recent authority on the Reformation in England, has noted the influence of Foxe on Thomas Brightman who, to use Lamont's words, "acknowledged his debt to John Foxe for his pioneer labours in the field of apocalyptic interpretation".[5]

With Brightman (1562–1607), we come to one of four men in the early years of the seventeenth century whose efforts to popularise the prophecies of Daniel and Revelation met with notable success and whose work was destined to have a more far-reaching influence than any of them could possibly have imagined. Together with John Napier (1550–1617), Arthur Dent (d.1607) and Joseph Mede (1586–1638), Brightman gave to prophetic study a sense of urgency which it had never previously enjoyed in the history of English religious thought and a respectability which it never wholly regained after the century had passed. While others were also attracted to the fascinating imagery and chronology described by Daniel and John, even making their own significant contributions, it remains true that the foundation upon which all succeeding generations raised their prophetic hopes was laid in the early years by these four learned and articulate men.

The arguments substantiating this assertion are (i) the repeated reprinting of the works of these earlier writers and (ii) continual references to them, particularly to Brightman and Mede, in the writings of later expositors.

---

4   Thomas Hall, *A Practical and Polemical Commentary Upon the Third and Fourth Chapters of the Latter Epistle of Saint Paul to Timothy* (1658), 5.

5   William Lamont, *Marginal Prynne 1600–1669* (London: Routledge,1963), 59.

Napier's book, *A Plain Discovery of the Whole Revelation of Saint John*, had been issued first in 1593 and was reprinted in 1594, 1611, 1641 and 1645 in addition to being published twice in Dutch and four times in French, all between 1600 and 1607. Arthur Dent's *The Ruine of Rome*, also an exposition of Revelation, enjoyed an even greater popularity among English readers, going through at least eleven printings between 1603 and 1662. Brightman's interest in prophecy also included the book of Daniel. His *Exposition ... of the Prophecy of Daniel* appeared first in 1614 and then in 1635 and 1644, while his *Revelation of the Revelation*, which was issued first in Latin in 1609 and again three years later, was published in English in 1611, 1615, 1616 and 1644. The erudite Joseph Mede was undoubtedly the most prolific and influential writer of this early group, perhaps of all prophetic interpreters.[6] His most significant works included *Clavis Apocalyptica* (1627), issued three times in Latin and three times in English between 1627 and 1650 and again in 1833; *The Apostasy of the Latter Times* (1641, 1642, 1650, 1652); and *Daniel's Weeks* (1643). His collected *Works*[7] were published in 1648, 1663–4, 1672 and 1677.

So when in the 1650s Edmund and Thomas Hall stressed the duty of searching into the prophecies, they did not consider this to be an attempt at defending the discredited views of an insignificant, or extreme, minority. They saw themselves rather as custodians of a tradition established early in the century by scholars such as Mede and his predecessors. John Napier had already asked, with a forceful degree of logic, "To what effect were the prophecies of Daniel and of the Revelation given to the Church ... if God had appointed the same to be never known or understood?"[8] Arthur Dent, with characteristic candour, had gone further, laying responsibility for imparting the meaning of Revelation squarely on the shoulders of the ministry: "I hold that every Minister of the Gospel standeth bound as much as in him lyeth, to preach the doctrine of the Apocalypse to his particular charge and congregation".[9]

The premise that the books of Daniel and Revelation were an integral part of inspired Scripture and therefore to be accepted and understood, was as fundamental to the Baptist pastor, George Hammon, as it was to the Anglican scholar, Joseph Mede. When men of the stature of Thomas Goodwin,

---

6   On Mede, who stands out in this early group, if not among all expositors in the seventeenth century, see *supra* ch.8, 'Puritan Profiles'.

7   Mede's 'Epistles', in his *Works* contain further material on prophecy and extensive correspondence with prominent men of his day, again largely on questions of prophetic interpretation and biblical chronology.

8   John Napier, *A Plaine Discovery of the Whole Revelation of Saint John* (1593), 18.

9   Arthur Dent, *The Ruine of Rome* (1603), Epistle to the Reader, sig. aa1*v*.

John Cotton, Joseph Mede, Nathaniel Homes or James Durham wrote at length on the prophecies, expanding and enlarging and sometimes correcting the views of an earlier generation and always seeing fulfilment in their own time, it is not surprising that a host of lesser men arose, of equal sincerity and in many cases, of equal scholarship, to shine forth as lights dispelling the darkness of the "Antichristian world".[10] William Hicks, in *The Revelation Revealed* (1659), a commentary on the Apocalypse expressly intended "for the keeping the saints feet straight, in not stumbling by a false interpreting and applying of this book of prophecies", and as a corrective to "wild applications" of its symbolism, nevertheless maintained that "the things represented in this book are no more mysteries and hidden things, but as clear and accomplished acts unto us".[11] *The Revelation Revealed* was one of the last in a long line of works between Napier's *Plain Discovery* of 1593 and 1660, which attempted to set the study of apocalyptic prophecy fairly within the context of orthodox Christian thought.

Beneath all this, however, lay a deep conviction which gave to these arguments an immediate relevance. It had been expressed by Arthur Dent when he had declared, "For in this age wherein we live, this Prophecy [the book of Revelation] can never be enough opened and beaten upon, that all good Protestants may be armed with it against future times".[12] Richard Bernard had also argued, "It as much belongeth unto us now living, as it did unto others in time past".[13] It was this belief that Revelation, together with the book of Daniel, spoke with meaning and authority to the present generation, which gave to the interpretations of the biblical exegetes an impetus and a vitality which was noticeably lacking in the study of other prophetic books of the Bible. No comparable interest, for example, existed in the writings of Jeremiah, or Ezekiel, or Zechariah, since it was not felt that they spoke with specific reference to the present. With the apocalyptic prophets, however, it is significant that men such as Richard Sibbes and Jeremiah Burroughes, who were not regarded as prophetic interpreters in the strict sense, spoke in terms which indicated an acceptance of this attitude to Daniel and Revelation.[14] David Pareus, the Dutch scholar whose commentary on Revelation had been translated into English, stated the point as succinctly as anyone, "This book is not only worthy to be continually read in the Church

---

10   John Cotton, *The Pouring out of the Seven Vials* (1642), 10.

11   William Hicks, *The Revelation Revealed ... a Practical Commentary on the Revelation of St. John ...* (1659), Preface, sig. C1v.

12   Dent, *Ruine of Rome,* sig. aair.

13   Richard Bernard, *A Key of Knowledge for the Opening of the Secret Mysteries of St John's Mystical Revelation* (1617), 4.

14   See Richard Sibbes, *The Brides Longing,* 2 and Jeremiah Burroughes, *Jerusalem's Glory Breaking Forth into the World* (1675), 86.

and meditated on: but also to contain very profitable and necessary doctrines, especially for this last age".[15] Even the moderate Thomas Hall saw fit
to defend the relevance of Revelation:

> The book of the Revelations is an excellent prophecy of the downfall of
> the Church's enemies, and of the great things which in the latter days
> God will do for his people, even to the end of the world; and therefore
> the Lord would have us attentively to consider, and humbly and accu-
> rately to weigh what is written there.[16]

There were few in the seventeenth century who were disposed to disagree
with that.

There was a caveat, however. The need for care in expounding prophecy
was illustrated in what had been foretold about the first coming of Christ.
Mede had recognised that the Old Testament prophets had often spoken of
the first and second advents of Christ as one event and cautioned:

> For the old Prophets (for the most part) speak of the coming of Christ
> indefinitely and in general, without that distinction of first and second
> coming, which the Gospel out of Daniel hath more clearly taught us.
> And so consequently they spake of the things to be at Christ's com-
> ing indefinitely and altogether, which we, who are now more fully in-
> formed by the revelation of the Gospel of a two-fold coming, must
> apply each of them to its proper time.[17]

It was with this realisation of hermeneutical difficulties and possible misinterpretations that led some of the leading expositors to appeal for restraint
and to sound a note of warning against extreme conclusions. Mede wrote
concerning the millennium, "But here (if any where) the known shipwrecks
of those who have been too venturous should make us most wary and careful, that we admit nothing into our imaginations which may cross or im-
peach any Catholic [universal] tenet of the Christian faith".[18]

Even the moderate Edmund Calamy could agree with his old adversary
Joseph Hall on this point. In the preface to Nathaniel Stephens' *Number of
the Beast,* Calamy wrote of many who "by adventuring into this sea, have
made shipwreck", and who had "built upon such weak foundations ... that
they have deceived both themselves and others".[19] This was entirely in harmony with Thomas Hall's opinion, expressed in *The Revelation Unrevealed,*

15   David Pareus, *A Commentary Upon the Divine Revelation* (Amsterdam,
1644), 15.

16   Thomas Hall, *Commentary,* 5.

17   Joseph Mede, 'A Paraphrase and Exposition of the Prophecy of St. Peter'
(1642) in *Works* (1672), 611.

18   Joseph Mede, 'Remaines on Some Passages in the Apocalypse' (1650), in
Works, 603.

19   Edmund Calamy, To the Reader, in Nathaniel Stephens, *A Plaine and Easie
Calculation of Name, Mark, and Number of the Name of the Beast* (1656).

where he stated that the book of Revelation, being a difficult part of the Bible to understand, had given rise to many strange interpretations.

One factor which appears to have carried some weight with many who attempted to interpret apocalyptic prophecy was the principle of progressive revelation. Not only was it believed that there were certain aspects of truth which God had revealed, and would reveal, at specific key moments in history and which He had even reserved for such times, but also that through a diligent study of Scripture, His servants on earth could proceed from already established beliefs to the knowledge of truths hidden from earlier generations. There is no evidence to suggest that this concept was regarded as licence to depart from the fundamentals of the faith. "Present Truth" was the apt term used by Nathaniel Homes in an attempt to convey the idea to his readers:

> There is in most generations successively a present truth ... Now some believers though they know generally all other saving truths, yet heed not, observe not the present truth, to contend for it in their profession and accordingly to put it into their prayers and supplications.[20]

"What is present truth in any generation?", he asked. Homes' answer to that question is a classic statement of the concept of progressive revelation or, perhaps, we should say, of progressive understanding:

> It is that truth which the corrupt stream of the present times would fain drown, either by doctrine, or disputes, or counter imposition, or persecution, to the great dishonour of the God of truth, and prejudice to Christ ... Thus in the time of the Arian persecution soon after Constantine's time, the present truth was to assert the deity of Christ. In Luther's time, at the beginning of our Henry the 8th, the satisfaction of Christ apprehended by faith, as the full ground of Justification, was the present truth to be asserted. And now Christ's pure worship and Christ's glorious kingdom (which inseparably concur) are the truths now to be asserted.[21]

Fortified by the immediate relevance of the idea of progressive revelation, earnest and devout scholars could approach Daniel and Revelation, aware of the difficulties of interpretation but not daunted by them, and in the assurance that their labours would not be in vain.

The circulation of such views was reason enough to anticipate prophetic interpretations from a host of biblical scholars well versed in the theological disciplines of the day. It was also an open invitation to others, the "mechanic" preachers with little or no formal qualifications, to unburden a variety of interpretations on a seemingly insatiable public. While this study is concerned primarily with the view of those in the former category it will not be

---

20 Nathaniel Homes, *The Resurrection-Revealed Raised Above Doubts and Difficulties* (1661), 278.

21 *Ibid.*, 279.

out of place to remark that, in the context of the prevailing religious mood of the age, which increasingly place the emphasis upon the individual's response to the Spirit's illumination of the Word, it was predictable that men and women from all walks of life should become enthused with the hope engendered by reading Daniel and Revelation and proclaim views which now appear unbelievably naïve. Elizabeth Avery's belief that the feet and toes of Daniel's image represented the State and Church of England,[22] Mary Cary's view that the Little Horn of Daniel's fourth beast symbolised Charles I,[23] and John More's opinion that the second beast of Revelation 13 depicted Oliver Cromwell,[24] were all strained interpretations which might have been avoided had the advice of Richard Bernard been heeded.

Bernard's *Key of Knowledge for the Opening of the Secret Mysteries of St. Johns Mystical Revelation* had been concerned almost entirely with suggesting principles and rules for a serious study of prophecy and abounded with detailed and fascinating counsel for all would-be interpreters of the Apocalypse. He had carefully enunciated the idea that prophecy can only be understood completely in the light of history. Prophecies relating to the future are difficult to understand and become clear only when they have been fulfilled. Of the early Church Fathers he wrote, "so much the more were they further from beholding the things fulfilled and done; and therefore less able to shew the true meaning, then we which have the fulfilling hereof".[25] The great advantage which the present generation held over the Fathers, and even over the Apostles themselves, was time. Within the perspective of history, prophecy could be understood but, by the same token, all prophecy which still pertained to the future must be approached with caution. As Joseph Hall had suggested, prophecy was not to be held as a licence for making wild guesses about the future.[26] It was this precept which, to their own discredit and often, though mistakenly, to the calumny of more sober scholarship, the extremists chose to ignore.

There were other basic principles of interpretation which it is also necessary to understand in order to reach a fair and objective assessment of the entire brotherhood of prophetic interpreters. Some were less vital than others, but all were recognised, and clearly guided the majority of serious expositors in their attempts to explain the prophecies of Daniel and Revelation. Joseph Mede expressed an important idea which became self-evident

---

22 Elizabeth Avery, *Scripture-Prophecies Opened* (1647), 3.

23 Mary Cary, *The Little Horn's Doom and Downfall* (1651), 6.

24   John More, *A Trumpet Sounded, or The Great Mystery of the Two Little Horns Unfolded* (1654), 8.

25 Bernard, *Key of Knowledge*, 93.

26   Joseph Hall, *The Revelation Unrevealed, Concerning the Thousand Years Reign of the Saints with Christ upon Earth* (1650), 13–14.

to all scholars of the seventeenth century when he said, "I conceive Daniel to be *Apocalypsis contracta,* and the Apocalyps *Daniel explicate*, in that ... both treat about the same subject".[27] This premise of the complementary nature of Daniel and Revelation was certainly fundamental to all interpreters of the time. Robert Maton drew attention to another point which others, both before and after him, accepted without question. "It is a currant [sic] axiom in our schools ... that we must not forsake the literal and proper sense of the Scripture, unless an evident necessity doth require it".[28] The significance of this exception, of course, was that the greater part of both Daniel and Revelation were written in highly symbolic language.

The recognition of this particular principle, with its implied necessity for a correct definition of the symbolic imagery used in the prophetic writings, was unquestionably one of the key factors in arriving at a satisfactory exegesis of both Daniel and Revelation. Bernard had realised this and had made it one of his major principles prerequisite to the interpretation of Revelation:

> The words are figurative, the whole prophecy full of metaphors, and almost altogether allegorical; so we must take heed that we look further than into the letter and naked relation of things, as they are set down, otherwise the book should be full of absurdities, impossibilities, falsities, and flat contradictions unto other truths of Scripture ... For who can believe a lamb to have seven eyes, a mountain burning to be cast into the sea, and this thereby in a third part to become blood ... Therefore we must not stick in the letter, but search out an historical sense, which is the truth intended, and so take the words typically, and not literally.[29]

While it is evident that most expositors in the seventeenth century differed from others on many points of interpretation and application, it is also clear that a remarkable unanimity of opinion prevailed regarding what were thought of as the basic symbols of prophetic imagery. Without making an artificial distinction between these varied and numerous representations, it may be said that there were five which were fundamental to even the most elementary interpretations.

In the first place, in symbolic prophecy a day represented a year of literal time. The lead given by John Napier here was followed almost exclusively for years to come and was never wholly to be discarded again: "So then" he said, "a prophetical day is a year, the week seven years, the month thirty years, (because the Hebrew and Grecian month hath thirty days) and consequently the prophetical year is 360 years".[30] Napier's explanation of the thirty-day month as a basis for reckoning time is important for understand-

---

27   Joseph Mede, 'Epistles', *Works,* 787.

28   Robert Maton, *Israel's Redemption* (1642), 47–48.

29   Bernard, *Key of Knowledge,* 130–31.

30   Napier, *Plaine Discovery,* 2.

ing the calculations of the prophetic time-periods which were so germane to the concept of the end of the age.

Secondly, prophetic beasts symbolised earthly kingdoms, or "Civil and Spiritual" rulers.[31] The extension of this symbol to include more than secular powers had implications of far-reaching influence. An important corollary to this second symbol, was that the heads and horns of the various beasts likewise depicted "kinds of governments", again both secular and ecclesiastical.[32]

Thirdly, the seas or waters, out of which nearly all prophetic beasts were seen to arise, symbolised peoples or nations.[33] Thus an expositor seeking to understand or explain the sense of a beast emerging from the sea, as in Daniel 7, could know that it represented an earthly power which had come into being from among the peoples or nations of the world.

Although appearing in the text less frequently, a fourth symbol, a woman (e.g., Jeremiah 6:2), was widely held to signify the Church.[34] Hence the woman clothed with the sun in Revelation 12 symbolised the true Church, while the scarlet-clad woman of the seventeenth chapter depicted the apostate Church.

In the fifth place, angels when seen in prophetic vision were to be understood as typifying preachers, or those who proclaimed truth, "God's messengers" on earth, "preachers of the Gospel in the times of Antichrist".[35]

It may be superfluous to add that all these meanings were derived in accordance with the elemental axiom that "the Scriptures are interpreters of the Scriptures, and the meaning of the Spirit is to be found out by his own words",[36] and texts could be produced to prove the correctness of each of the foregoing explanations. To borrow the thought which Richard Bernard had incorporated into the title of his book, these were the keys which could unlock the "secret mysteries" of both Daniel and Revelation.

The master-key to apocalyptic interpretation, however, was not to be found among creatures, natural or supernatural. Important as all the preceding principles unquestionably were to a satisfactory understanding of the prophecies, the crucial issue was the question of time. To have any real

---

31   E.g., Dent, *Ruine of Rome,* 170; Thomas Brightman, *A Revelation of the Revelation* (Amsterdam, 1615), 430.

32   James Durham, *A Commentary Upon the Book of Revelation* (1650), 547; Dent, *Ruine of Rome,* 182.

33   E.g., Bernard, *Key of Knowledge,* 158; Cotton, *Exposition Upon the Thirteenth Chapter of Revelation* (1655), 8.

34   E.g., Napier, *Plaine Discovery,* 33; Mede, *Key of the Revelation* (1643), pt. 2, 33.

35   E.g., Cotton, *Seven Vials,* 21; Pareus, *Commentary,* 337.

36   Bernard, *Key of Knowledge,* 141.

significance, all other principles, rules or suggestions for accurate exegesis were to be understood within the framework of thought which related all the apocalyptic prophecies to a continuous process of history. This period of time had had its beginning in the days when the prophecies were first given, and would end only when everything foretold had been brought to a final consummation. "From the beginning of the captivity of Israel, until the mystery of God should be finished",[37] Mede wrote of the scope of Daniel's visions. This explains the emphasis given by Richard Bernard to the necessity of an adequate knowledge of history as a background to Revelation:

> The matter then of this prophecy is historical, as it cometh to be fulfilled. It is therefore not a spiritual or allegorical, but an historical sense, which in this book we must attend unto, from the beginning of the fourth chapter, to the end of the prophecy. For to John was revealed what things should come to pass here upon the earth, before the worlds end, as far as concerned the Church; and the same he here setteth forth to us, as to him it was revealed. If we then do loose the historical sense, we lose the proper sense of this book.[38]

It was the knowledge of two millennia of history that made the men of the seventeenth century certain that what Daniel and John had written with reference to the future was, in fact, by their day largely concerned with the past. While some events were then in the process of accomplishment and while others remained as yet wholly unfulfilled, the overwhelming consensus of opinion held that the greater part of both Daniel and Revelation had already reached complete and verifiable fulfilment. The past was the masterkey to both the present and the future.

Stephen Marshall's observation that "the whole Army of Protestant Interpreters" agreed "in the general scope and meaning"[39] of Revelation, was nowhere more true than when applied to this historicist view. Both the early and later writers of the time were virtually unanimous in assenting to this fundamental position, which was as pertinent to Daniel's prophecies as to those of John. Of sixty-eight separate works on these two books examined during the course of this study, no less than sixty-four subscribed by statement, argument, or implication to this historicist viewpoint. Thomas Brightman, commenting on Revelation 1:1, explained "the matters should be begun by & by, & should flow from thence with a perpetual course without interruption, although the final consummation should be afterward for many ages".[40] David Pareus stated that the time involved was "from the giving of the Revelation, even unto the end of the world".[41] That the historicist con-

---

37   Joseph Mede, 'The Apostasy of the Latter Times' (1641), *Works*, 654.
38   Bernard, *Key of Knowledge*, 123.
39   Stephen Marshall, *The Song of Moses ...and the Song of the Lamb* (1643), 3.
40   Brightman, *Revelation*, 3–4.
41   Pareus, *Commentary*, Author's Preface, 16.

struction should be applied to Daniel in conjunction with Revelation was argued by both Joseph Mede and William Hicks:

> ... what was revealed to Daniel concerning the fourth kingdom but *summatim* ... was showed to S. John *particulatim*, with the distinction and order of the several fates and circumstances which were to betide and accompany the same ... therefore Daniel's prophecy is not terminated with the first, but reacheth to the second coming of Christ ... [42]

> ... Revelation is no longer a mystery, but a book of history of memorable acts and passages. Wherein is foretold the several changes that shall befall the secular state or Roman Empire, and to the Church of Christ under the dominion of that empire, until it shall, as that stone prophesied of in Dan 2 smite the image on his feet and become itself a great mountain and set up upon the top of all mountains.[43]

It was, then, within the context of the historicist position, which viewed the prophecies of Daniel and Revelation as a panorama of successively unfolding events spanning seventeen centuries or more of the Church's history, that all other principles of interpretation were to be applied and related. Any other approach to the interpretation of apocalyptic prophecy was effectively excluded.

The preterist interpretation, which proposed that the major prophecies had reached fulfilment in the first century or two of the Christian era, and the futurist view, which sought to postpone their accomplishment until the very end of Christian history, were alternative constructions on the scope of the apocalyptic prophecies which had no significant appeal whatever to the Protestant commentators of the seventeenth century. If either of these contrary propositions intruded at all into their thinking and writing, it was only in order that they could be summarily refuted or that the discreditable source of their origin could be brought to the attention of all who sought after truth, as was frequently thought necessary.

The preterist hermeneutic, according to James Durham, had arisen through the influence of a Spanish Jesuit, Luis de Alcasar, who had put forward the argument that the book of Revelation had reference only to the pre-Constantine age and related solely to the experiences of the Church under the Roman Empire.[44] Henry Alford's statement that "the preterist view found no favour and was hardly so much as thought of in the times of primitive Christianity",[45] is equally true of seventeenth-century Christianity. Henry Hammond, who in 1647 had become chaplain to Charles I, appears

---

42   Mede, 'Epistles', *Works,* 787.

43   Hicks, *Revelation Revealed,* Preface, sig. C1v.

44   Durham, *Revelation,* 667; Luis de Alcasar, *Vestigatio Arcani Sensus in Apocalypsi* (1614).

45   Henry Alford, *The New Testament for English Readers* (1866), vol. II, pt. II, 348–49.

to have been the first English writer seriously to have adopted Alcasar's interpretation.[46] Although the work in which his views appeared went through several editions after its first appearance in 1653, there is little evidence of any wider involvement with preterism in pre-Restoration thought. The failure of the preterist position to make any significant impact may be explained by the knowledge of ecclesiastical history which characterised the thinking of most scholars and divines of the time and which naturally precluded any attempt to place all those prophecies of a future bright with hope in a past which frequently had been so hopelessly dark.

Futurism, although it received more comment, made even less impression on English Protestant thought than did preterism.[47] An early attack on the futurist system came from Thomas Brightman, who defined its basic argument and at the same time identified its source of origin. Brightman explained that futurism projected all the prophecies of Revelation into the last three and a half literal years of human history, thereby denying the historicist contention that the book of Revelation had been in the course of progressive fulfilment since the close of the first century AD. If futurism was true, then Brightman wanted to know what comfort the Church had derived, or could derive, from the special blessing promised at the time the book had been written and which was intended for all who would read and accept its prophetic message, which even then was on the verge of fulfilment. "Were men that lived by the space of these 1600 years which are now past ... altogether devoid of this felicity?"[48] he enquired. Brightman named another Jesuit priest, Roberto Bellarmine, as the originator of futurism, although Bellarmine's views have been traced to the Jesuit scholar, Francisco Ribera.[49] This understanding of the origin of futurism was quickly endorsed and accepted by all succeeding expositors.

In harmony with the strong anti-Romanist convictions of the day, many Protestant expositors saw the wisdom of emphasising this ill-concealed attempt to weaken the strength of the historicist arguments. Jeremiah Burroughes expressed the view that the true meaning of the book of Revelation had been deliberately concealed and distorted by papal scholars:

> Hence it hath been, that in the time that Antichrist hath reigned, there hath been so little known of the book of the Revelation, because it hath been applied only in a metaphorical way, and all the glory hath been

---

46 Henry Hammond, *A Paraphrase, and Annotations Upon all the Books of the New Testament* (1653).

47 Except, perhaps, in the writings of Edmund Hall, who places more of the prophecies of Revelation in the future than did most of his contemporaries.

48 See Rev.1:1; Brightman, *Revelation,* 5.

49 L. E. Froom, *The Prophetic Faith of our Fathers* (Washington, D.C.: Review and Herald, 4 vols.), II, 489–493.

interpreted of the glory of heaven ... there hath been a darkness on the
face of the earth in the time of Antichrist's prevailing, and it hath been
the care of Antichrist to darken this.[50]

For Burroughes, these alternative interpretations originated in papal theology "so as to save their Pope and the present Rome" from being depicted as Antichrist.[51] The fact that Roman Catholic scholars had suggested alternative explanations was enough in itself to render those explanations anathema to every good Protestant. Beyond this, however, the appeal of the historicist position lay in the intrinsic strength of its arguments. Carefully reasoned and subjected to the irrefutable witness of history they made historicism the only valid basis for interpretation.

As is now recognised by many historians of the period, a widespread belief in the imminent second coming of Christ existed in the seventeenth century quite apart from the influence of apocalyptic prophecy. Without detracting from the validity of this reality, it is apparent that belief in Christ's second advent was considerably strengthened as interest in prophecy developed and particularly as historicist interpretation increasingly anticipated momentous and impending changes in the present order. It is, therefore, desirable to appreciate how the historicism of the seventeenth century arrived at its major conclusion that the end of the age was at hand.

Hugh Broughton, commenting on Revelation in 1610 had written, "I must advise the reader to learn Daniel before he learn this book".[52] This recommendation was further stressed by Mede in reply to a letter from Thomas Hayne in 1629. Referring to the first two prophetic visions of Daniel, those of the great metal image of chapter 2 and of the four beasts of chapter 7, he argued that together they constituted "The A.B.C. of Prophecy".[53] Mede later amplified this somewhat concise definition by stating that all other prophecy was related to the content of these two visions:

> For the true account therefore of times in Scripture, we must have recourse to that SACRED CALENDAR and GREAT ALMANACK of PROPHECY, the four kingdoms of Daniel, which are a prophetical chronology of times measured by the succession of four principal kingdoms, from the beginning of the captivity of Israel, until the mystery of God should be finished.[54]

Whatever meaning was to be placed on the ensuing visions of Daniel or John, it could be assumed that agreement would prevail with regard to the four kingdoms. The evidence indicates that this assumption was fully justified.

---

50   Burroughes, *Jerusalem's Glory,* 87.
51   Durham, *Revelation,* 667.
52   Hugh Broughton, *A Revelation of the Holy Apocalypse* (1610), 26.
53   Mede, 'Epistles', *Works,* 743.
54   Mede, 'The Apostasy', *Works,* 654.

The four kingdoms were first mentioned in Nebuchadnezzar's celebrated dream which had subsequently been interpreted by Daniel and defined as specifically relating to "the latter days". The dream, it will be recalled, had revealed an image in four main sections composed of differing metals. The head of the image was made of gold, the upper abdomen and arms of silver, the lower abdomen of brass and the legs of iron. The feet of the image consisted in part of iron and in part of clay. The image had been shattered and the fragments dispersed by the wind when a stone of supernatural origin had struck it upon the feet. Commencing with the Babylonian empire of Nebuchadnezzar, represented by the golden head, Daniel explained that three further empires would arise successively upon the earth, the kingdoms represented by silver, brass and iron. The fourth kingdom would ultimately be divided into ten nations and the resultant segments would never unite again until "the God of heaven set up a kingdom".[55]

This divine kingdom had been symbolised in the dream by the stone which had struck the image upon the feet, depicting that God would intervene in human affairs during the time represented by the divided nations of the iron kingdom. "These times once finished, all the kingdoms of this world should become the kingdoms of our Lord and his CHRIST".[56] The assurance that "the interpretation thereof" was "sure" did not pass unnoticed. The four kingdoms again figured prominently in Daniel's second vision. In this instance the types were beasts; a lion, a bear, a leopard and a fourth beast "dreadful, and terrible, and strong exceedingly". In accordance with the accepted rule of interpretation and also in accordance with the text itself, the beasts were taken as symbols of the same four kingdoms which had been represented by the four main sections of the image.[57] Even as the legs of the image had ten toes so the fourth beast had ten horns, again depicting the divisions of the fourth empire.

The counting of time on this "SACRED CALENDAR" presented little difficulty. If the Word of God explicitly stated that Babylon was the first kingdom of the four, past history as well as the text, provided the identity of the remaining three. They were the empires of Medo-Persia, Greece and Rome and succeeded Babylon, and each other, in that order.[58] Many commentators believed that the iron legs of the image symbolised the Western and Eastern divisions of the Roman Empire, but this was not as important as the fact that, in both visions, the fourth kingdom was eventually divided into ten parts. "For about four hundred years, the Roman Emperors continued in their majesty, even until the end of Constantine the Great; and then began

---

55 Daniel 2: 28–45.
56 Mede, 'The Apostasy', *Works,* 654.
57 Daniel 7: 2–23.
58 Mede, 'The Apostasy', *Works,* 654.

effectually to be broken down, and to be dissolved into ten kingdoms",[59] wrote Thomas Parker, adding that the fall of Rome was fully accomplished by AD 456. Mede dated the end of the Roman Empire from the death of Valentinian in AD 455. In practice, few were concerned about exact dates at this juncture, recognising that the important fact was that the prophecy now focused upon those further nations which had arisen following the barbarian invasions of Rome. Strictly speaking, the Roman Empire had not come to an end; it had been divided and the divisions thereof were to continue in separate existence until the advent of the kingdom of the stone.

Daniel's second vision had drawn attention to the emergence of another power, placed in time between the settlement of the divisions of Rome and the inauguration of the kingdom of God. Probably no figure in all the Bible has given rise to so many interpretations, and misinterpretations, as the Little Horn which Daniel now described as arising after the previous ten kingdoms, arrogant in its appearance and presumptuous in its claims, and resolutely bent on a course of action totally opposed to the purposes of God.[60] The majority of expositors saw in this cryptic symbol a definite allusion to the long-awaited and dreaded Antichrist.[61] It was, in brief, either the Pope or the Turk, or a combination of the two. Both had emerged as a threat to the true Church at the time required for a satisfactory interpretation of the prophecy.[62] Again, the Little Horn was fundamentally an extension of the fourth empire which "was to keep the dominion and Lordship of the world" until the final kingdom of prophecy,[63] a development within the era of Rome and not a separate phenomenon beyond it.

In the eyes of seventeenth-century expositors both these major prophecies of Daniel had been in the course of fulfilment for some two thousand years. During that time, in the outworking of the historical process, all the salient characteristics they bore had met unequivocal identification with the single exception of the last, climactic event. If it is remembered that the remaining prophecies of Daniel were regarded as supplying details of further events within the compass of this same time-scale, it is not hard to perceive why Daniel proved that the end of the age was at hand.

If, as Mede had suggested, Daniel was a necessary introduction to Revelation, it was of greater significance that Revelation be considered an indispensable conclusion to Daniel. While the latter contained six chapters

59   Thomas Parker, *The Visions and Prophecies of Daniel Expounded* (1646), 21.

60   Daniel 7: 20–25.

61   E.g., Nathaniel Homes, *Works* (1652), 596; Parker, *Daniel,* 15.

62   E.g., Pareus, *Commentary,* 166; Homes, *Works,* 255. Luther had held this view of a dual Antichrist.

63   Mede, 'Diatribae'(1642), *Works,* 198; Edmund Hall, *Manus Testium,* 13.

of apocalyptic prophecy the book of Revelation had eighteen and naturally enough attracted considerably more attention that the writings of the earlier and shorter book. The resulting stream of commentaries, treatises, sermons and tracts on Revelation, in part or in whole, grew throughout the first half of the century until by the years between 1640 and 1660 it had reached almost flood proportions. This stream, however, did not change in character as it increased in volume. It was still constituted of the same elements and continued to flow in the same direction as before. Understanding of Revelation throughout the seventeenth century was largely the logical development of the historicist interpretation which had been established during the first two decades of the century.

John Napier's *Plain Discovery of the Whole Revelation of St John* was the first work of any significant appeal in the seventeenth century to set forth a well-reasoned approach to Revelation. Napier held that there were two basic prophecies in the book, the first from chapter 4 to chapter 11, and the second from chapter 12 to chapter 22.[64] These prophecies were in a sense repetitive, both covering the entire Christian era from the time of Christ to the last day. The first of these comprehensive prophecies contained the important visions of the Seven Seals of chapters 6 and 7 and the Seven Trumpets of chapters 7–11 which, to Napier, as to all who would follow him, were indispensable to a correct calculation of the age of the world and the expected consummation of history.

Soon after Napier's *Plain Discovery* had appeared in print, Arthur Dent published *The Ruine of Rome* which provided a slightly modified interpretation, although the conclusion remained the same. Dent maintained that there were three basic prophecies in Revelation.[65] In addition to the two suggested by Napier, concerning the importance, scope and relationship of which Dent fully concurred, he also held that the first three chapters were partially prophetic in that they described the condition of the entire Christian Church from its beginning as well as the actual state of the seven churches named.[66] With regard to the seven Seals and seven Trumpets, Dent put forward a view which was adopted by several later scholars, namely, that these two visions were consecutive in their fulfilment. The first six Seals had foretold events which were to transpire from the time of the Apostolic Church until "about some 300 years after Christ, and somewhat more".[67] The seventh Seal included the entire vision of the Trumpets, which "do all belong to the opening of the seventh seal, and are as it were the seven parts thereof".[68] The first

---

64 Napier, *Plaine Discovery,* 155–156.
65 Dent, *Ruine of Rome,* 15.
66 *Ibid.,* 26.
67 *Ibid.,* 68.
68 *Ibid.,* 87, 90.

four Trumpets described the gradual growth of heresy within the Church, making way for the coming of Antichrist and had been accomplished by about AD 600.[69] The fifth and sixth Trumpets respectively foretold the rise and growth of the Papacy and the Turks and were parallel in time and fulfilment, having commenced at the completion of the fourth Trumpet in AD 600. Dent concluded:

> We live under the opening of the seventh Seal, and the blowing of the
> sixth Trumpet, and the pouring forth of the sixth Vial ... Therefore
> when we see all things fulfilled which do belong unto the sixth trumpet,
> it remaineth that we should every hour expect, and look for the blowing
> of the seventh trumpet, and the end of the world.[70]

Dent had reached the same conclusion as Napier, if by a slightly different route.

Six years after *The Ruine of Rome* had first been published Thomas Brightman's *Apocalypsis Apocalypseos* appeared to give a further turn to the interpretation of apocalyptic prophecy. Brightman agreed with Dent in large measure concerning the Seals and Trumpets, but differed in his interpretation of the Vials. The first six Seals extended to the time of Constantine and the seventh included the complete range of the Trumpets, the first six of which reached from Constantine to 1558.[71] The seventh Trumpet, although it contained a review of "things past", was primarily concerned with "modern" times and things to come and included the remainder of the book, again emphasising the seven Vials. Thus, in Brightman's view, the vision of the Vials was not complementary to that of the Trumpets, but rather consecutive to it and was the last of "three notable terms of time, which contain in them the principal changes that are to fall out in the world, even until the coming of Christ ..."[72] Brightman explained:

> It is manifest therefore that this whole space of time from John to the
> coming of the Lord is divided into three periods of time, & that each of
> those periods is again divided into seven members so as the first mem-
> ber of that period which followeth, beginneth under the last member
> of the former, that is so, that as the seven Trumpets have their original
> from out of the last Seal, so the seven Vials have their offspring out of
> the last Trumpet.[73]

Just how near the end of the age really was in Brightman's estimation may be seen from his interpretation of the vision of the seven Churches which, in effect, contained in concise form the entire message of Revela-

---

69   *Ibid.,* 97.
70   *Ibid.,* 124, 144.
71   Brightman, *Revelation,* 203, 236, 388.
72   *Ibid.,* 202.
73   *Ibid.,* 510.

tion and which was amplified by all the later visions. This first vision was to be understood as applying to the Church in general, from its inception to its triumphant conclusion, setting forth under seven ages the decline of the Church from its first purity of doctrine to its subsequent renewal in readiness for the ultimate reward. The last age, symbolised by the seventh Church, had begun in 1547 and Laodicea represented the Church of England.[74]

If one man stood out above the others in moulding subsequent interpretative thought, it was undoubtedly Joseph Mede. Contemporary opinion, as well as the judgement of later scholarship, recognised the significance of his *Clavis Apocalyptica*. John Worthington, Mede's biographer, wrote, "he proceeded upon grounds never traced by any, and infinitely more probable than any layed down by those who before him undertook that task".[75] Mede's great contribution to the study of Revelation was his insistence that a correct interpretation depended on the "synchronisation" of certain prophecies, and an understanding of their relationship to each other. The "Key" to Revelation was, in fact, an explanation of the seven "synchronismes" which he regarded as so essential.[76]

To Mede, there were only two major prophecies in the book, that of the Seals and Trumpets which outlined the destiny of Empires, particularly the Roman Empire, and that of the "Little Book opened" which foretold the destiny of the Church and the Christian religion.[77] Again, these prophecies were parallel in scope, covering the whole Christian era, and the purpose of the "synchronismes" was to correlate certain symbols, times and events within each prophecy. For example, the first synchronism stated that in the first prophecy the seventh Seal which included all seven Trumpets, corresponded in time with the Beasts of chapter 13 in the second prophecy;[78] the second synchronism showed that the battle between Michael and the Dragon took place in the time of the first six Seals and the third placed the seven Vials within the time of the sixth Trumpet.[79] With seven such clear rules to harmonise the various parts of Revelation, Mede believed that it was possible to interpret virtually the entire book.

The first six Seals represent six stages in the history of the Roman Empire, reaching to the time of Theodosius.[80] The seventh Seal, or first six Trumpets, depicts the fall and punishment of the Empire and extends from

74   *Ibid.*, 6, 126, 168.
75   John Worthington in Mede, *Works*, 'The Author's Life'.
76   Mede, *Key of the Revelation*, pt. I, 1.
77   *Ibid.*, 13.
78   *Ibid.*, 14.
79   *Ibid.*, 17.
80   *Ibid.*, 61.

the death of Theodosius in AD 395 to at least the destruction of Constantinople in 1453,[81] with the seventh Trumpet reaching right down to the final consummation of the mystery of God. The second prophecy retraces the whole era, with stress upon events concerning the Church. Thus, the war between Michael and the Great Red Dragon symbolises the hostility between the Church and the Roman Empire in the first three hundred years or so of Christian history, and the Vials signify the destruction of the Antichrist, all within the time of the sixth Trumpet.[82] Three Vials are past, the fourth is now being fulfilled, and three only remain in the future. Apart from that, virtually every other detail in the book of Revelation has been accomplished except, of course, those things which relate to the kingdom of God, which cannot be long delayed.

With all this weight of learning and experience behind them, it cannot be surprising that the men who came later should follow similar patterns of interpretation. With Thomas Goodwin in 1639 to Williams Hicks in 1659 and with the host of those who came between them, the influence of Mede and his predecessors can clearly be seen. Goodwin, who took the position that there were two basic visions in Revelation, wrote:

> These Seals and Trumpets, which do in order succeed one another, do contain a continued Prophecy of Events following one another in a succession of Ages downward ... from the first Seal to the seventh Trumpet, is run over all the Time that the Monarchies and Kingdoms of this World ... should continue and last.[83]

The book of Revelation made it most plain "that we live now in the extremity of times ... we are at the verge, and as it were, within the whirl of that great mystery of Christ's Kingdom, which will, as a gulph, swallow up all time".[84]

William Hicks, in his commentary on Revelation, *The Revelation Revealed*, appealed for moderation to the militant minority of interpreters, such as the Fifth Monarchy Men, stressing that certain prophecies were yet to be completed before God's kingdom could be established.[85] Among the unfulfilled parts of Revelation's prophecies, he named the final downfall of the Antichrist and the completion of the pouring out of the Vials. It was true, however, Hicks added, that Antichrist had begun to fall under the second angel of chapter 14, when the true gospel had been first restored under the

---

81 *Ibid.,* 80, 85, 117.

82 *Ibid.,* pt. II, 32; pt. I, 17; pt. II, 113.

83 Thomas Goodwin, 'An Exposition Upon the Revelation' (1639), in *The Works of Thomas Goodwin, D.D.* vol. II (1682), 19.

84 *Ibid.,* 190.

85 Hicks, *Revelation Revealed,* 341.

Waldenses and the early German reformers.[86] It was true also, that with only three of the Vials remaining to be emptied upon the declining Antichristian power, the end was much nearer "than the world thinks of".[87]

Hicks, then, spoke for all students of biblical prophecy in the seventeenth century, regardless of academic background or ecclesiastical leaning, as indeed he did for virtually all Christian believers of the age when, at the conclusion of his book he proclaimed, "Therefore ye saints of God, lift up your heads, for the Lord is at the door, and the day of your Redemption is nigh at hand".[88] Within the framework of the fulfilling prophecies of Daniel and Revelation, set in the context of established historical fact, no other conclusion was possible.

It would be easy to dismiss seventeenth-century apocalyptic enquiry as an irrelevant obsession. That would, however, be a mistake. The extensive interest in the books of Daniel and Revelation that developed during the seventeenth century and its widespread influence are now widely recognised as phenomena which spread beyond national boundaries and into the prevailing cultures of the day.[89] The influence of apocalyptic thought in England alone was far greater than any of its many exponents could have imagined. Jane Dawson remarks, "Most British Protestants viewed their daily lives and the world in which they lived through the lens of apocalyptic thought".[90] Moreover, this outlook, similarly based on the books of Daniel and Revelation, has persisted well into our own time and extended the influence of our forefathers into the twenty-first century. Three aspects of that influence deserve to be highlighted in concluding this chapter.

Firstly, it confirmed the prevailing Protestant view of the Bible as an inspired book, God's revelation of himself, his will and his purposes for humankind. Few arguments led to this conviction more than fulfilled prophecy. The Bible contained hundreds of predictions about future events, notably the Old Testament predictions about the life, work and death of Christ. Exegetes of the time—and there were many—explained how most of these prophecies had already been fulfilled. In this context, detailed expositions of the prophecies of Daniel and Revelation which appeared in England throughout

---

86 *Ibid.,* 342.

87 *Ibid.,* 343–44.

88 *Ibid.,* 346.

89 For examples of apocalypticism in Continental Europe see Adriaan H. Bredero, "The Announcement of the Coming of the Antichrist and the Medieval Concept of Time", and Johannes van den Berg, "Joseph Mede and the Dutch Millenarian Daniel van Laren" in Michael Wilks, ed., *Prophecy and Eschatology* (Oxford: Blackwells, 1994).

90 Jane E. A. Dawson, "The Apocalyptic Thinking of the Marian Exiles", in Wilks, *Prophecy,* 75.

the seventeenth century convinced men and women from all walks of life that prophecy was being fulfilled in their day, before their very eyes, in their own country, on an unprecedented scale.[91] God was speaking anew to people everywhere through the ongoing fulfilment of the prophecies of Daniel and John. These books spoke immediately to the times, as had the prophets of old. The inevitable outcome of so much identifiable fulfilment of prophecy was increased respect for the Bible *per se*. With so much prophecy being fulfilled around them who could doubt the inspiration and divine authorship of this very special book? Christopher Hill remarked of the times, "The Bible was generally believed to be an inspired book, containing divine truth on all matters".[92] As the seventeenth century unfolded, the fulfilment of prophecies of Daniel and Revelation could only confirm and strengthen this belief.

Secondly, the well-nigh universal identification of the Roman papacy as the dreaded Antichrist of the last days carried with it an impact which spilled over well beyond the pages on which the reasons for such a view were given and the relevant texts carefully explained. In his book, *Antichrist in Seventeenth-Century England,* Hill quotes one of the many prophetic expositors of the time: "Next unto our Lord and Saviour Jesus Christ, there is nothing so necessary as the true and solid knowledge of Antichrist".[93] The identification of Daniel's "little horn" and the "beast" of Revelation with the papacy reverberated from English pulpits and printing presses throughout the seventeenth century and for much of the next two hundred years. It moulded the English mind for generations. It ensured that any and all attempts to re-assert the authority of Rome over the English people were doomed to failure from the start. The defeat of the Spanish Armada in 1588 is one of the better known examples. Hill comments, "For men to be convinced that the Pope was Antichrist had clear propaganda uses for Tudor governments".[94] But that was only the beginning. In the 1680s fear of a return to Catholicism fed by the pretensions of the Catholic James II to the English throne led to the Glorious Revolution of 1688 and the subsequent Bill of Rights enacted by Parliament in 1689, still in effect in Commonwealth countries, which eradicated forever the possibility of a future Catholic monarchy.[95] It is not too much to say that England has remained a Protestant country, if only

---

91   See, for example, the bibliography of primary sources in *A Great Expectation,* pp. 245–259.

92   Christopher Hill, *Antichrist in Seventeenth-Century England* (London: Oxford University Press, 1971), 3.

93   Thomas Beard, *Antichrist the Pope of Rome* (London; 1625), in Hill *Antichrist,* 2.

94   *Ibid.,* 14.

95   See Wikipedia, s.v. "The Glorious Revolution/Legacy"

in name at times, ever since. It can be traced back to the interpretations of apocalyptic prophecy which began to appear in the late sixteenth century[96] and flowed on for decades to come.

Thirdly, the strong desire to understand apocalyptic prophecy gave to the Christianity of the day an unmistakable future orientation. It looked beyond the identification of Antichrist in the present to the ultimate destruction of Antichrist in the future, to the time when right would prevail over wrong and good triumph over evil. It looked forward to the ultimate realisation on earth of the divine purpose for humanity in creation and re-creation. It was in essence a theology of hope rather than fear, of life rather than death, and in that it was one with the early apostolic proclamation of Christ's return, his second coming in glory at the end of the age. It re-asserted the linear, forward-moving understanding of history to a time when the Kingdom of God would be a reality as well as a theological proposition. Thus is the apocalyptic engagement of our seventeenth-century forefathers to be understood. Indeed, only thus can it be understood. If this chapter has succeeded in communicating even some of these truths it will have been worthwhile.

---

96   An influential, late sixteenth-century commentary was that of John Napier, *A Plaine Exposition of the Whole Revelation of St. John* (Edinburgh, 1593). It was reprinted four times in English, twice in Dutch and four times in French all before 1645.

Redemption and Eschatology

"Jesus' 'life, death, resurrection and Parousia belong together as parts of an indivisible whole, as moments in the great and all-decisive movement of God to man now breaking into the world'".
A. L. Moore, *The Parousia in the New Testament* (1966), p. 218.

12. Righteousness and Redemption in the Epistles of Paul[1]

Bryan W. Ball

The essence of Paul's teaching is that there is a righteousness which is redemptive, which lies at the very heart of God's purposes for mankind. Paul's meaning, however, cannot be grasped only from the English words 'righteous' and 'righteousness' as they are commonly understood today. Morris sounds a warning here. "Many have fallen into serious error", he says, "by taking it for granted that everyone knows what 'righteous' and 'righteousness' mean".[2] But as Morris points out, the biblical words do not have exactly the same meaning as their English translations. Paul uses the Greek word *dikaiosune* and its derivatives more than seventy times in ten of his thirteen epistles, eleven of them if we include Hebrews. These Greek words are always translated 'righteous' or 'righteousness' in English. We tend to think mainly of the English meanings of these words - goodness or moral excellence, even holiness - when in fact they inherently mean 'rightness' or 'justice'. They contain a forensic, or legal, meaning. According to standard dictionaries and lexicons, *dikaiosune* and all its five derivatives have this strong legal connotation.[3] Paul can only be adequately understood, in Romans in particular, if we remember the meaning of the original Greek words, as Paul himself would have understood and used them. That in mind, it may be said that Paul's teaching concerning redemptive righteousness can be summarised in seven propositions.

Redemptive Righteousness is Rooted in God.

The concept of righteousness lies at the heart of the divine redemptive purpose, and is central to the traditional Protestant understanding of salva-

---

1 Adapted and expanded from a paper presented at conferences in the UK and Australia in the 1980s. Previously unpublished.

2 Leon Morris, *The Apostolic Preaching of the Cross* (London: Tyndale, 3rd ed., 1965), 269.

3 E.g., William F. Arndt and F. W. Gingrich, *A Greek-English Lexicon of the New Testament and Other Early Christian Literature*, 3rd ed. (Chicago: University of Chicago Press, 2000), s.v. δίκαιος, δικαιοσύνη, δικαιόω, δικαίομα, δικαίως; Alexander Souter, *A Pocket Lexicon to the Greek New Testament* (Oxford: Clarendon, 1960), 66.

tion. It is, of course, not a coincidence that Gordon Rupp's classic study of Luther and his tortuous spiritual journey bore the title "The Righteousness of God".[4] Rupp's study reminds us that Luther came to understand, as many others have since understood, that the righteousness which saves is God's own righteousness. It begins with him, proceeds from him and leads to him. It is the first thing that Paul lays down in his exposition of righteousness in Romans, beginning in chapter 1, where in verse 16 he says that the gospel he is about to explain reveals the righteousness of God.[5] The first six references to righteousness in Romans all affirm that the righteousness which Paul speaks about and is so anxious to explain is the righteousness of God himself.[6] Everything that he later says as his argument develops must be seen in the light of this seminal truth. Luther understood it well, "God does not want to save us by our own but by an extraneous righteousness, one that does not originate in ourselves but comes to us from beyond ourselves, which does not arise on earth but comes from heaven".[7] For righteousness to be redemptive it must be other than human. Paul knew as well anyone Isaiah's all-inclusive assertion, "All our righteousnesses are like filthy rags" (Isa 64:6).

God's righteousness has a twofold character. Firstly, it has a legal dimension. Scripture as a whole reveals that God is just and fair, that the demands of both divine law and divine grace are fully met through the gospel. This is the essence of Paul's argument in Romans 3, climaxing in vs. 21–26, especially vs. 25 & 26, where, speaking of Christ's death on the cross as an atoning act by which sins may be forgiven, Paul says "God offered him … in order to demonstrate that he is righteous". God thus "shows that he himself is righteous [i.e., fair, just] and that he puts right everyone who believes in Jesus".[8] It all flows from the righteousness, the fairness, of a just God. As Luther discovered, God is just or righteous, not because he condemns or punishes sinners but because he saves them. He provides a way of escape from the consequences of sin and broken law. This is the justice, the 'rightness' of God who cannot overlook the inevitable penalty of sin, but who

---

4   Gordon Rupp, *The Righteousness of God* (London; Hodder & Stoughton, 1968).

5   Biblical references are from the *New King James Version* unless otherwise indicated.

6   Rom 1:17; 3:5, 21, 22, 25, 26.

7   The exact wording of this quotation depends on the translation of the original text; cf. Rupp, *Righteousness,* 161, quoting Weimarer Ausgabe *Werke* 56.158.10, and James Atkinson, *The Great Light: Luther and the Reformation* (Grand Rapids, MI: Eerdmans, 1968), 30.

8   Rom 3:25, 26, *Good News Bible.*

enables the demands of the law to be fully met. And he does so because he himself is righteous — fair, and just.

In his commentary on Romans, Lenksi claims it was the "happiest day in Luther's life when he discovered that 'God's righteousness' as used in Romans means God's verdict of righteousness upon the believer".[9] He then adds, "This joy is ours today. *Dikaiosune theou* [the righteousness of God] is the status of righteousness into which faith and the believer are placed by the judicial verdict of God".[10] Lenski then concludes:

> It is fatal to eliminate the forensic idea from *dikaiosune*. This cannot be done linguistically, save by changing the sense; it cannot be done doctrinally, save by rejecting the central doctrine of all Scripture.[11]

The *dikaiosune* of God is the justness of a just God dealing fairly with both broken law and lawbreakers by handing down a verdict of acquittal because the requirements of the broken law have been fully and acceptably met.

The second defining characteristic of God's righteousness is that it is moral. The righteousness of God is what God himself is, not only just and fair, but also good, holy and perfect. It necessarily encompasses his holiness, his goodness, his sinlessness. Thus divine righteousness is the very antithesis of sin. Paul states it in 2 Corinthians 5:21, "For he made Him who knew no sin to be sin for us, that we might become the righteousness of God in Him". The righteous God, having revealed his righteousness at the cross, now requires that liberated sinners become "slaves of righteousness" (Rom 6:18), living a life approved by God, that is a righteous and morally upright life.[12] Paul then goes on to show, in chapter 8, how this can happen through the inner working of the Holy Spirit, i.e., through God himself, by another act of righteous fairness in making possible that which is humanly impossible.

God's righteousness is therefore both justice and holiness. It is like a two-sided coin, with both legal and moral significance, and because both are conjoined, it can never be one without the other. The righteousness of God himself is the righteousness which redeems and in order to accomplish such redemption it is freely extended to sinful human beings as both justice and holiness, the justice and holiness of very God himself.

---

9   R .C. H. Lenski, *The Interpretation of St Paul's Epistle to the Romans* (Minneapolis, MN: Augsburg,1961), 79.

10   *Ibid.*

11   *Ibid.,* 80.

12   J. J. Von Allmen, *Vocabulary of the Bible* (London: Lutterworth, 1964), 375. Morris states "the righteous man is the one who is accepted before God, the one who conforms to His way", *Apostolic Preaching of the Cross,* 269.

God's Redemptive Righteousness is a Response to Sin.

In Romans 3:5 (AV) Paul declares that human unrighteousness "commends", i.e., recommends, the righteousness of God. The *New International Version* says that our unrighteousness "brings out God's righteousness more clearly". It is on account of human unrighteousness that the righteousness of God is declared and becomes available. The human condition is the dark backdrop against which the righteousness of God shines so brightly. Lenski translates the Greek here as "our unrighteousness places God's righteousness into proper light" with the comment "darkness indeed makes light stand out as what it really is, namely light, as the blacker the darkness, the more the light is made to appear as light".[13] So divine righteousness is God's own response to the human condition into which all are born. We note here just one of the many important consequences of this truth.

If the righteousness of God is to be efficacious, dealing effectively with the sin problem in human nature and experience, there must be on the part of the sinner recognition of sin and an understanding of what sin is and what its consequences are. Indeed, God's saving righteousness can only be effective when sin is known, understood, recognised, confessed and, ultimately, forsaken.

This is true not only at the beginning of the Christian life when one becomes convinced of having a sinful nature and a past life of sinful acts and thoughts requiring forgiveness, but also at all times in the future as the Christian life progresses. A fundamental presupposition in Paul's teaching concerning righteousness is that at all stages of human experience men and women are essentially sinful and thus in need of the righteousness which saves. As Lesslie Newbigin so aptly puts it, "to be human is to be sinful".[14] Since we remain human throughout life, we remain sinful to the end and in need of God's redemptive righteousness. God's own righteousness is a continuing divine response to our fallen and sinful nature.

This Righteousness is Revealed in Jesus.

Paul goes on to say that Christ, both in his incarnate life and atoning death, was the visible revelation of God's righteousness. This righteousness must be explained as well as proclaimed. It must be seen as well as heard, demonstrated as well as argued. And it must be revealed before it can be received. Ellen White wrote, "The righteousness of God is embodied in Christ. We receive righteousness by receiving Him".[15] The question, how-

---

13   Lenski, *Romans,* 218.

14   Lesslie Newbigin, *Sin and Salvation* (London: SCM, 1956), 15.

15   Ellen G. White, *Thoughts From the Mount of Blessing* (Washington, DC: Review and Herald, 1956), 18.

ever, is "how?" How is the righteousness of God revealed in Jesus? Again the answer is twofold.

Firstly, as Paul states in Romans 3:24–25, Christ's redeeming death on the cross revealed the righteousness of God. Calvary was the definitive manifestation of God's own righteousness. There God revealed his justice. Through the propitiatory act of the cross, human beings are reclaimed from sin and death. Christ's shed blood, his substitutionary sacrificial death, deals with human sin, guilt and condemnation. So the cross reveals the justice of God by meeting the demands or requirements of the broken law, and this revelation of righteousness at the cross is foundational. It is a demonstration of the fundamental justice of God as well as the love of God, in dealing with a problem which demanded a solution.

Secondly, Romans 5:10 and 19 sets forth the equally basic truth that the life of Jesus also revealed God's righteousness. Christ was obedient not only "unto death" but throughout his life on earth. He revealed the righteousness, the holiness, the very character of God, in his person and in the way he lived. His obedience in its totality is a revelation of God's righteousness and therefore the source of the righteousness that believers can claim as their own.

The twentieth-century New Testament scholar, F. F. Bruce, explains the significance of Christ's obedient life in the scheme of redemption:

> The obedience of Christ to which His people owe their justification and hope of eternal life is not to be confined to His death ... it was a perfectly righteous life that He offered up in death on His people's behalf. The righteous life in itself would not have met their need had He not carried His obedience to the point of death, 'even the death of the cross', but neither would His death have met their need had the life which He thus offered up not been a perfect life.[16]

Edward Heppenstall explores at some length the sinlessness of the Christ who revealed the righteousness of God. He points to the miraculous nature of Christ's incarnation and birth, his divinity united with humanity, his own witness to himself as well as the witness of the New Testament writers, and "his mission to provide a perfect righteousness for unrighteous" men and women, stating that sinlessness is "a life without sin in any respect".[17] Referring to the Greek word *anamartesia* [perhaps a misprint for *anamartetos,* "without sin"?] Heppenstall states, "In Christ there was not the slightest expression of a perverted will at any point ... He was born of the Holy Spirit in complete oneness with the Father".[18] In Paul's words, he "knew no sin", 2 Cor 5:21. Indeed, how could he know sin, if born in complete oneness

---

16 F. F. Bruce, *The Letter of Paul to the Romans* (London: IVP, 1985), 120–21.

17 Edward Heppenstall, *The Man Who is God* (Washington, DC: Review and Herald, 1977), 130.

18 *Ibid.,* 131.

with the Father? This holy being, the only such being ever to have existed on earth, was the living embodiment of divine righteousness — in life and then in death.

The righteousness of God, in both its judicial and moral dimensions, is revealed in the life and death of Jesus. It is difficult to avoid the conclusion that Christ was the fulfilment of Jeremiah's prophecy, made c.600 BC, that a "righteous Branch" would arise in the future from David's line and would be known as "THE LORD OUR RIGHTEOUSNESS"(Jer 23:5,6).

God's Righteousness Revealed in Christ is Received by Faith

We now turn from theology to experience, from understanding to practice. At the heart of Paul's message of redemption is the crucial truth that God's righteousness, revealed and available in Christ, is received by faith. The righteousness which is available in Christ is for all, Jew and Gentile alike, for all have sinned and all may by faith receive the righteousness of God by receiving Christ (Rom 3:21–24). This is the good news for humanity. Faith is the hand that reaches out to accept the proffered gift.

Two things in particular should be noted about the faith which enables sinful men and women of all ages and from every culture and background to receive God's saving righteousness. Firstly, it is a continuing faith. Here we return to that text which is central to the epistle to the Romans, Romans 1:17, which states that the gospel reveals God's righteousness "from faith to faith". This is truly one of the crucial texts of the New Testament. The *NIV* reads "by faith from first to last". The *New Living Translation* puts it "from start to finish by faith". J. B. Phillips translates the original as "a process begun and continued" by faith.[19]

It is necessary to understand what Paul means here. When he says, "the just shall live by faith" does he speak of the present or the future life? When will those who are justified live? Does Paul refer to eternal life in the future or to daily life in the present? These are critical questions. The following chapters of Romans make it clear that Paul is concerned primarily with the life of the justified sinner in the present. God's saving righteousness is effective from the moment of first belief to the end of the believer's life. It is a process begun and continued by faith. The justified person lives by faith from the moment of justification until he or she ceases to live. God's righteousness as revealed in Jesus and as received by faith is an ongoing process "from start to finish".

The second thing we need continually to remember relates to the nature of faith itself. The faith which Paul speaks of is much more than cognitive assent, important though that is. Saving faith goes beyond knowledge. There

---

19   J. B. Phillips, *The New Testament in Modern English*, Rom 1:17.

is something submissive, dependent, trusting, about true faith. It transcends knowledge, evidence, argument and understanding, although of course it does not dispense with any of these. Saving faith is more than what has been termed 'cerebral religion'. It is a trusting faith which receives the righteousness of God as revealed in Jesus by faith at the beginning and receives it continually by faith from the first moment of belief onwards. This is righteousness by faith in theory and in practice. It is authentic Protestantism now as much as it was in the sixteenth century. It is God's way of righting human sinfulness and Satanic distortion. Righteousness is available from Christ "by faith from first to last".

This Saving Righteousness is Realised in Justification

Two words have traditionally been understood among Protestant Christians as summarising the essence of the plan of salvation — justification and sanctification. As we shall be reminded shortly the complete gospel as set out by Paul in Romans includes both. But first it is necessary to consider justification as it stands alone.

Through the process of justification God is revealed as being just and the believing sinner is *declared* just, or righteous. God is demonstrated to *be* just since through Christ's righteousness, his death on the cross and his sinless life, he frees from guilt and condemnation those who are by nature unrighteous but who believe. The believing sinner is thus *regarded* as righteous on account of Christ's righteousness which he or she has received by faith. In justification God's righteousness, revealed and accessible in Christ, is imputed or credited to the believer. This is the reality of the term "righteousness by faith".

Justification, then, concerns the sinner's standing before God. Nothing visible actually happens at this point in the believer's life through God's gracious act of justification. When a sinner exercises faith in God through Jesus Christ he or she is accepted as righteous by God even though he or she may not actually be righteous, or sinless, in reality. God declares that person righteous on account of faith in Jesus. This transaction is called 'imputed righteousness' (Rom 4:6). "To impute" means "to regard as" or "to ascribe to". In justification God regards the believing sinner as righteous, even though up to that point he or she has been unrighteous and is still in actual fact unrighteous. That declaration of God brings the sinner into a new standing or relationship. Whereas previously that person was sinful and guilty, now he or she is sinless, forgiven and guiltless, even though not actually sinless. Luther's oft-quoted words are still pertinent, *simul iustus et peccator,* "at the same time righteous and a sinner". According to James Atkinson, another version reads "Always a sinner, always penitent, always justified".[20]

---

20 Atkinson, *Great Light,* 33. Rupp quotes a further variation, *semper pecca-*

So we can agree with Leon Morris, "Justification is in essence a matter of right status or standing in the sight of God".[21] It is "the name given in the Bible to the changed status, not the changed nature".[22] And it happens as a result of God's own righteousness and on account of the righteousness of Christ imputed to the one who puts his or her trust in Jesus. In justification the believer is accounted righteous. "Christ ... offers to take our sins and give us his righteousness... for his sake you are accounted righteous".[23] Morris further explains that the righteousness of God "is a righteousness which takes men [generically speaking] in their sins, alienated from the mind of God, subject to the wrath of God, and justifies them".[24] This is the very heart of the gospel. But there is more, and it, too, is crucial.

Redemptive Righteousness is Recognisable in the Christian Life

We must now consider what has frequently been referred to as "imparted righteousness". God's righteousness, imputed through justification, also becomes part of the believer's new life and can be seen as such in an authentic Christian lifestyle. Once again this truth is set forth in Romans as well as in many of Paul's other epistles.

Through the years since the Reformation there has been an ongoing debate concerning Romans. Some affirm that Paul's main purpose in this epistle is to expound the doctrine of justification by faith. Romans has often been preached essentially from this standpoint. However, there is a strong case for a broader interpretation. Paul's exposition of justification by faith takes up the first five chapters of the epistle. Beginning with chapter six another emphasis appears, which runs on through chapters seven and eight and reappears in chapters twelve through fourteen. This emphasis is on the life of the person who has been justified. In these chapters Paul talks repeatedly about personal lifestyle, victory over sin, the power and presence of the Holy Spirit, relationships with God, with one's fellow-believers and with unbelievers. This new life which follows justification is evidence that justification is real for it has been accompanied by a change of life and lifestyle.

The inescapable truth of all this is that Paul's gospel is a gospel of both justification and sanctification. The later chapters of Romans are just as much a part of Paul's gospel as are the earlier chapters. This is confirmed

---

tor, semper iustus, "always a sinner, always just", citing Henri Strohl *L' Evolution Religieuse de Luther* (Thesis - Strasbourg, 1922), 4.

21   Morris, *Apostolic Preaching,* 290.

22   *Ibid,* 291.

23   Ellen G. White, *Steps to Christ* (Washington DC: Review and Herald, 1908), 62.

24   Morris, *Apostolic Preaching,* 278.

when we examine some of Paul's other epistles. In I Corinthians 15:34 Paul's call is "awake to righteousness and do not sin". In Philippians 1:11 he admonishes Christians to be "filled with the fruits of righteousness". He urges Timothy to pursue righteousness, linking it with godliness, love and gentleness (I Tim.6:11). It is difficult, if not impossible, to avoid the conclusion that Paul's gospel is one in which the righteousness of God, initially imputed to the one who believes, is then imparted to that same believer, and is clearly evident in his or her life.

How, then, does this happen? In Romans 8 it is abundantly clear that it happens as a result of God's presence and activity in the believer through the Holy Spirit. Because it is the work of the indwelling Spirit, we can say that even when righteousness is imparted it is still the righteousness of God. It comes as the result of the working of the Holy Spirit in the life of the believer. This is what has been known through the Christian ages as sanctification. This too is part of the gospel, the good news that God not only imputes righteousness to us when we first believe, but that he also imparts it to us as we continue to believe, and that he helps us to live in harmony with his will.

It is worth noting, before we pass to the final section of this brief study, that Luther understood perfectly the necessity of sanctification as an integral element in the divine plan. The total separation of justification and sanctification as discrete processes in the outworking of the plan of salvation is an error, as is the imputation to Luther of a totally forensic justification which on its own account is the sum and substance of the gospel. Speaking of the growth in the Christian life that follows justification, Luther wrote, "It is no use for a tree to be living, to blossom, unless fruit comes from the blossom".[25] Rupp says that Luther recognised "a progress in the Christian life which is never complete in this life, but is consummated in the resurrection".[26] And Karl Holl, commenting on Luther's understanding of salvation as including "making righteous" as well as "accounting righteous", writes "As the great artist sees the finished statue in the rough marble, so God sees already in the sinner, whom he justifies, the righteous man that he will make of him".[27]

God's Redemptive Righteousness is Re-affirmed by Hope

There is one final, crowning truth concerning God's redemptive righteousness. In Galatians 5:5 Paul says we "eagerly wait for the hope of righteousness by faith". Barclay translates this text, "by the Spirit and by faith

---

25 Luther, *Werke*, 56.441.14.

26 Rupp, *Righteousness*, 182.

27 Karl Holl, *Gesammelte Aufsätze* (Tubingen, 1948), 125, cited in Rupp, *Righteousness*, 182.

we eagerly expect the hope of being right with God".[28] The *NIV* reads, "by faith we eagerly await through the Spirit the righteousness for which we hope", with the comment "a reference to God's final verdict of 'not guilty', assured presently to the believer by faith and by the sanctifying work of the Holy Spirit".[29] Paul himself further states that believers are sealed by the Spirit "for the day of redemption" (Eph 4:30) and those who now have the firstfruits of the Spirit, eagerly wait for "the redemption of our body" (Rom 8:23). There is clearly in Paul's mind a strong sense of anticipation that the future will bring finality to the redemptive purposes of God. Perhaps it is all a reflection of what Jesus himself said when he admonished those who would see the signs of his second coming to look up and lift up their heads "because your redemption draws near" (Luke 21:28). Righteousness and redemption are constantly re-affirmed in the believer's life by hope. The final chapter in the story of redemption is yet to be written.

In Hebrews it is stated that Noah and other great worthies of the past became heirs of "the righteousness which is according to faith", but that all died not having received the promise. Elsewhere we are reminded of the new earth "in which righteousness dwells" (2 Pet 3:13). There is clearly a strong eschatological dimension to the truth of God's saving righteousness. Its full consummation is not realised through any of the categories traditionally used. It is not totally contained even by the words "justification" and "sanctification", for it is not fully attainable in this life. Kittel's *Theological Dictionary of the New Testament* states that the righteousness which Paul speaks of is "the object of hope", "a hope that looks forward confidently to the final sentence".[30] Possibly this explains why Paul sometimes uses the words "justify" and "justification" in a future tense, and notably in relationship to judgment and the last days.

Perhaps the clearest statement of this end-time dimension of saving righteousness is Paul's statement to Timothy, "Finally, there is laid up for me the crown of righteousness, which the Lord, the righteous Judge, will give to me on that Day"(2 Tim 4:8). There have been many attempts to define precisely what Paul means by a "crown of righteousness". It is clear that he cannot be talking of a literal crown. It is equally clear that there is here a future dimension in the human experience of righteousness which is as important as

---

28   William Barclay, *Letters to the Galatians and Ephesians* (Edinburgh: St Andrews, 1983), 43.

29   *NIV Study Bible* (Zondervan, 1985), 1786.

30   G. W. Bromiley, ed., *Theological Dictionary of the New Testament* (Grand Rapids, MI: Eerdmans and Exeter, UK, Paternoster, 1985), ii:174.

the present. After an extended discussion of this text Lenski summarises his understanding. It refers, he says, to a victory wreath, "which the Lord (the righteous Judge), will duly give ... in or at that day". Then:

> Throughout the Scriptures there runs this double idea: 1) that the righteous are pronounced righteous by a judicial verdict; 2) that the Judge himself must and will be declared righteous for his absolutely righteous verdicts upon both the righteous and the unrighteous ... On that day, when all things are absolutely revealed, his righteousness which is evidenced in all his judgments will appear convincingly as well as the righteousness of all true believers ... when all who have loved the Lord's epiphany will be judged and duly given the victors wreath.[31]

Perhaps even that is inadequate to describe all that Paul means. And perhaps we can only say categorically that the events of the last day will set the seal on God's righteousness, the source and the substance of the plan of salvation which will come to a final consummation in God's own time. What is beyond doubt is that Paul's explanation of the gospel in terms of righteousness and redemption is ground enough for assurance in the present and hope for the future. Therefore we must allow that future to beckon us on, in faith and in hope and with assurance, knowing that the crown, the eternal reward of the righteous in Christ, awaits all who have been redeemed by God's redemptive righteousness, received continually by faith.

---

31 R. C. H. Lenski, *The Interpretation of ... Colossians, Thessalonians, Timothy, Titus and Philemon* (Minneapolis, MN: Augsburg, 1964), 864–65.

13. The Nature of Biblical Eschatology[1]

Bryan W. Ball

Within the Church there has been a growing interest in the future and final events and in what Scripture has to say about the end-time and the kingdom of God. One writer speaks of "an entirely new era" and of "renewed interest in the eschatology of the New Testament".[2] Another even argues that the only future open for theology in the contemporary world is "to become the theology of the future".[3] The Roman Catholic theologian Rudolph Schnackenburg represents a broad spectrum within contemporary thought when he writes, "Shaken by its existence in an atomic age and influenced by biblical theology and modern philosophy, present-day theology has seriously taken up the question of history and eschatology ... We are prepared to hear and consider the eschatological message of Jesus".[4]

The following comment from the German theologian, Jürgen Moltmann, deserves careful thought as it underlies much of what follows in this chapter:

> From first to last, and not merely in the epilogue, Christianity is eschatology, is hope, forward looking and forward moving, and therefore also revolutionising and transforming the present. The eschatological is not one element of Christianity, but it is the medium of Christian faith [which] ... lives from the raising of the crucified Christ and strains after the promises of the universal future of Christ. Hence eschatology cannot really be only a part of Christian doctrine. Rather, the eschatological outlook is characteristic of all Christian proclamation, of every Christian existence and of the whole church.[5]

Moltmann's emphasis on the centrality of eschatology to Christian belief and his warning to the Church that the loss of eschatology "has always been the condition that makes possible the adaptation of Christianity and the self-surrender of faith"[6] are surely of significance at the present time.

---

1 Abridged from two papers presented at three European Bible Conferences in 1977. Previously unpublished.

2 J. P. Martin, *The Last Judgment in Protestant Theology from Orthodoxy to Ritschl* (Edinburgh & London: Oliver & Boyd, 1963), xv.

3 Harvey Cox, *On Not Leaving it to the Snake* (New York & London: Macmillan, 1967), 12.

4 Rudolf Schnackenburg, *Present and Future* (Notre Dame: University of Notre Dame, 1966), 2.

5 Jürgen Moltmann, *Theology of Hope* (London: SCM, 1967), 16.

6 *Ibid.*, 41.

Biblical eschatology can be summarised in terms of two fundamental principles:

1. Faithfulness to the whole of the relevant biblical text, both Old and New Testaments, including apocalyptic prophecy, and
2. Witness to the redemptive purposes of God as revealed in the 'eschatological man', Jesus Christ.

In what follows we will attempt to explore the rich content of these two underlying principles that make the eschatology of Scripture central and so indispensable to the Christian proclamation.

Faithfulness to the Entirety of the Biblical Text

The fundamental argument underlying this paper is that authentic, biblical eschatology has breadth, completeness, wholeness, and is a crucial element in the total revelation of God. It partakes of the essential nature of both Old Testament and New Testaments. It does not superimpose its own eschatological ideas upon Scripture. Rather, it allows Scripture as a whole to speak, and seeks to understand what is said by the application of sound hermeneutical principles. Such hermeneutic recognises the intrinsic relationship between the Old and the New Testaments in the area of eschatological thought, as in other areas of theological enquiry. Thus New Testament eschatology does not stand in isolation. It proceeds from the rich eschatological emphasis which developed in the Old Testament. Of this relationship John Bright says:

> The New Testament rests on and is rooted in the Old. To ignore this fact is a serious error in method, and one that is bound to lead to a fundamental misunderstanding of the Bible message. He who commits it has disregarded the central affirmation of the New Testament gospel itself, namely that Christ has come to make actual what the Old Testament hoped for, not to destroy it and replace it with a new and better faith.[7]

It is this element of hope which appears as a dominant factor in the Old Testament and which, as we shall see, is then carried over into the New Testament. So we must ask, 'What did the Old Testament hope for?' 'And in what way, and to what extent, did Christ make real such hopes?' The biblical answer to these questions will demonstrate the eschatological relationship between Old and New Testaments, thus clarifying our understanding of the true nature of biblical eschatology.

Old Testament Hope

Bearing in mind the fundamental relationship which always exists between various aspects of Old Testament hope, the following elements can be detected:

---

7   John Bright, *The Kingdom of God* (Nashville, TN: Abingdon, 1953), 193.

The Assertion of Divine Authority: Eschatological Power

Firstly, it may be said that the Old Testament looked for a future assertion of divine authority. This hope for the realisation of God's authority in the world is in reality an expectation of *eschatological power.* We must begin, however, in the New Testament and the statement with which Jesus announced the commencement of his ministry, "The kingdom of God is at hand: repent ye, and believe the gospel" (Mark 1:15).[8] Christ's entire life and ministry, his teaching and doctrine, miracles and parables, death and resurrection, the gospel message *in toto,* are to be seen in the light of this seminal statement, specifically repeated by Jesus at such crucial junctures as the sending out of the Twelve, and again at the sending out of the Seventy (cf. Matt 10:7, Luke 10:1). The context in which Jesus' life and message are launched upon the world is that the kingdom of God has come. Yet he does not attempt to explain what he means by this statement. Rather, he assumes that a concept of the kingdom already exists and that it is well understood. Thus Herman Ridderbos states, "The expression 'the kingdom of heaven' was not unknown to those to whom this message was addressed, but was rather calculated to find an immediate response with them".[9] The 'kingdom of God' was something they knew about and awaited.

Throughout the Old Testament the kingship of God is a central feature. "The Lord is King for ever and ever"; "I am the Lord, ... the Creator of Israel, your King"; "For the Lord ... is a great King over all the earth" (Psa 10:16; Isa 43:15; Psa 47:2). God is the ultimate ruler over the earth and in a special sense over his own people, and this kingship is absolute. "Thine, O Lord, is the greatness, and the power, ... and the majesty, for all that is in the heaven and in the earth is thine; thine is the kingdom, O Lord, and Thou art exalted as the head above all" (I Chron. 29:11). This majestic concept of the kingship of God is crucial to our understanding of Israel's theology and mission. But what does this kingship signify? There are two aspects. The most frequently used Hebrew word for "the kingdom" of God in the Old Testament is *malkuth,* the primary meaning of which is authority, as distinct from a geographical or territorial domain.[10] "They shall speak of the glory of thy kingdom and talk of thy power ... Thy kingdom is an everlasting kingdom, and thy dominion endureth throughout all generations" (Psa 145:11–13). The *malkuth* of God is the authority, the power, the rule of God, sometimes in the Old Testament extended in a secondary sense to designate the realm over which a king reigns, but almost without exception when used

---

8　Biblical references from the AV/KJV.

9　Herman Ridderbos, *The Coming of the Kingdom* (Philadelphia, PN: Presbyterian & Reformed, 1975), 3.

10　A. L. Moore, *The Parousia in the New Testament* (Leiden: E. J. Brill, 1966), 7.

in conjunction with God, designating his power, his authority as King, an authority extending over past, present and future.

The second aspect of God's kingship follows. The God of the Old Testament is "the God who comes", the God who is present, who visits his people in order to accomplish his royal purpose and demonstrate his kingship. "The Lord came from Sinai, and rose up from Seir unto them; He shined forth from Mount Paran, and He came with ten thousands of saints". "Understand therefore this day, that the Lord thy God is he which goeth over before thee" (Deut 33:2; 9:3). The God who is King, who has authority, is an active God, an involved God. The God who is King does not remain in heaven — he comes to visit his people, to bless and to judge, to heal and to smite, to rebuke and to forgive, to be presently involved in their midst. The first aspect of Old Testament hope, then, is that the future will vindicate the reality of God's kingship and demonstrate his authority.

The Establishment of the Kingdom: An Eschatological Perspective

Secondly, Old Testament hope anticipated the establishment of a kingdom, an event to be realised at the consummation of history. In this may be seen the development of an *eschatological perspective*. The Old Testament is not satisfied with the God who "comes", the God who now visits his people. The God who *has* come is also the God who *will* come. "Let the heavens rejoice, and let the earth be glad ... before the Lord: for He cometh to judge the earth: He shall judge the world with righteousness, and His people with truth" (Psa 96:11–13). "Sing and rejoice, O daughter of Zion: for, lo, I come, and I will dwell in the midst of thee, saith the Lord. And many nations shall be joined to the Lord in that day, and shall be my people: and I will dwell in the midst of thee" (Zech 2:10, 11). The God who has visited his people at certain specific times in history, through actual events, will do so again in the future. Thus "the day of the Lord" is a central theme in the message of the prophets. God has acted in the past, he is acting in the present, and he will act in the future. History, therefore, is essentially the history of God's salvation and we may "observe with confidence that events are moving toward a destination, an effective terminus beyond which one need not look".[11] There is a land flowing with milk and honey which one day will be ours; some day we shall be a great nation; God will cause us to live in peace and plenty; a mighty leader will one day appear whom all the nations will serve. The future always holds out the hope of final consummation.

So G. E. Ladd observes that in the Old Testament there is "a distinct theology of the God who comes":

> God who visited Israel in Egypt to make them his people, who visited them again and again in their history, must finally come to them in the

---

11 Bright, *Kingdom,* 30.

> future to judge wickedness and to establish his Kingdom. Israel's hope
> is thus rooted in history, or rather in the God who works in history ...
> there are special times of visitation when his royal purposes find con-
> crete expression, the most important of which will be the final visita-
> tion to consummate his will and bring salvation.[12]

This theology of a God who repeatedly comes to his people and who will come again at the end emphasises the importance of time. History has no meaning apart from time. In this context, the most effective visitation of Jahweh will be his final visitation, when his will is consummated and his salvation finally revealed. The *malkuth* of God will finally be established at the end of the historical process. The kingdom foretold in Daniel's visions of world empires is a kingdom which supersedes all earthly kingdoms in a time sequence at the end of history.

The Coming Messiah: The Eschatological Person

A third element in Old Testament expectation is the hope of a Messiah to come, a future Redeemer - hope which focuses on an *eschatological person*. Thus from the early promise of the Seed who would "bruise" the serpent's head (Gen 3:15) to the Messianic prophecies of Isaiah, Jeremiah, Daniel and others, the purposes of God are increasingly linked to One who would come, and upon whom the realisation of future promise is dependent. It is impossible to divorce Old Testament hope from Messianic promise. He is the prophet comparable to Moses who will speak the words of God (Deut 18:18). He is the child who, as Immanuel, will be God with us (Isa 7:14, Matt 1:23). He it is who, at the end of sixty-nine weeks, will make reconcili-ation for iniquity and bring in everlasting righteousness (Dan 9:24, 25). He will preach good tidings to the meek and bind up the broken-hearted (Isa 61:1). It is in this predicted One yet to come, this eschatological Person, that both the eschatological power and the eschatological perspective hoped for in the Old Testament find substance and reality. Much has been said and written through the centuries about Old Testament Messianic expectation and we do not need to linger here. The "Day of the Lord" is a descriptive and recurrent phrase in the prophetic books of the Old Testament, the emphasis being on the person as much as the event.

Redemption and Restitution: Eschatological Purpose

A final aspect of Old Testament eschatology is the hope of redemption and restitution — the redemption of man and the restitution of the world. Here we clearly discern *eschatological purpose*. Redemption and restitu-tion are concepts which pre-suppose a primeval state unmarred by sin to which man and the world will ultimately return. But death and the decay of

---

12   G. E. Ladd, *Jesus and the Kingdom* (London: SPCK, 1966), 47–48.

the world both stand in the way and both require an answer. The Old Testament recognises that these problems are crucial and that they are related. In Hebrew thought there is a fundamental unity between man and nature. The earth is not merely the temporary stage on which man plays out the drama of his existence. It is an essential part of that existence. Man and the world are both the outcomes of creation; both are affected by sin and both are therefore contained within the redemptive purposes of the Creator.

With reference to the future of mankind, the Hebrew concept of human nature is essential to the hope of redemption. This view of man's wholeness is not so much argued as it is assumed throughout the Old Testament, evident in passages which refer to death and the ultimate redemption of the individual. Man is a creature and therefore depends upon the Creator for life and being. But it is the Creator who becomes the Redeemer and man therefore continues to depend upon him for life and being, retaining his fundamental characteristic of creatureliness. The fact that man is a physical creature is not the measure of his sinfulness and therefore a state from which he must be delivered. The conclusion, in terms of redemption, is crucial:

> Salvation for man does not mean deliverance from creaturehood, for it is not an evil thing but an essential and permanent element of man's true being. Salvation does not mean escape from bodily, creaturely existence. On the contrary, ultimate redemption will mean the redemption of the whole man. For this reason the resurrection of the body is an integral part of the biblical hope.[13]

There is no Greek dualism or Gnosticism in the Old Testament hope of redemption for it is redemption of the whole person. Furthermore, the world itself must also be included in redemption. The world is not evil *per se*. Though marred by human sin and consequently cursed, the world is, and remains, God's world. However, the curse means that, without radical transformation, it cannot be the scene of the final realisation of God's purposes. It, too, stands in need of restitution — a restitution to which the prophets bear witness in language which cannot merely be interpreted as poetic symbolism. The final visitation of God means the redemption and renovation of the world. God will create new heavens and a new earth (Isa 65:17). The wilderness will become fruitful and the desert will blossom (Isa 35:1). Peace will return to the animal world (Isa 11:6). Sorrow will be no more and the earth will be full of the knowledge of God (Isa 11:9).

What, then, were the ingredients of Old Testament hope? In the first place, it looked for the realisation of eschatological power, the demonstration of divine authority. Secondly, it demonstrated eschatological perspective, looking for the consummation of God's purposes within history. Thirdly, it anticipated the appearance of an eschatological person, a Mes-

13 *Ibid.*, 59.

siah through whom promise and prophecy would be fulfilled. Finally, it was marked by eschatological purpose, expecting the redemption of man and the restitution of the world. Such hope shaped the Hebrew mind and gave it a strong confidence in the future.

New Testament Witness to the 'Eschatological Man'

From the question, 'For what did the Old Testament hope?' we now turn to a consequent question, 'In what way did Christ fulfil Old Testament hope?' The following comment points to an answer: "The things which God had foreshadowed by the lips of His holy prophets, He has now, in part at least, brought to accomplishment. The *eschaton*, described from afar ... has in Jesus registered its advent".[14] The New Testament affirms that in Christ, Old Testament hope is both fulfilled but also unfulfilled. In him, God has partially brought Old Testament eschatology to fruition. In Jesus the *eschaton* has begun, but it has not ended.

Partial Fulfilment in Jesus: Fulfilment without Consummation

In order to observe this partial fulfilment we must first return to the declaration with which Jesus commenced his ministry "The kingdom of God is at hand". In both gospels where this significant statement is recorded the context reveals that in the person of Jesus, the authority and saving activity of God are immediately and recognisably demonstrated. He calls men from their work to become his disciples and immediately they respond. He heals the sick, casts out devils, cleanses lepers and restores the mentally unstable. What has happened? The kingship of God, the *malkuth* of God, has come. The authority of God over men, over demons and over disease is now being demonstrated. But it is only partial. It is not yet demonstrated universally, over all men, in all lands.[15] Yet what has already happened affirms its reality.

Furthermore, Jesus begins his ministry, not only with the declaration that the kingdom of God is at hand, but also with the affirmation that "the time is fulfilled" (Mark 1:15). Scripture here and elsewhere is careful to set the coming of Christ in the context of time. God has now broken into history in the form of his Son. He has invaded the present time, yet without taking it over completely. A new age has come, but not yet a new order. "Blessed are the eyes which see the things that ye see", Jesus declared, "For I tell you that many prophets and kings have desired to see those things which ye see, and have not seen them; and to hear those things which ye hear, and have not

---

14   W. Manson, 'Eschatology', *Scottish Journal of Theology*, Occasional Papers, No. 2, 1957, 6.

15   See *Seventh-day Adventist Bible Commentary* (Washington, DC: Review and Herald, 1956), V, 318.

heard them" (Luke 10:23–24). He can say this because something unique and unprecedented has occurred. "But if I cast out devils by the Spirit of God, then the kingdom of God is come unto you" (Matt 12:28). In Jesus the kingdom of God has now come close to men and in his person the kingdom actually confronts them, so Ladd concludes: "God's Kingdom, his reign, *has already come* into history in the person and mission of Jesus".[16] History has taken on a new dimension, but it is still history. God's kingdom is here, in time, but it has not yet superseded time.

Thirdly, in Christ the Messianic hope has also been realised. He is the fulfilment of Messianic prophecy and recognises himself as such. Commenting on Isaiah 61 he emphatically declares, "This day, is this scripture fulfilled in your ears" (Luke 4:21). On the road to Emmaus he interprets the Messianic predictions of the Old Testament with reference to himself: "all things ... which were written ... concerning Me" (Luke 24:44). *He* is the fulfilment. Yet not all the promises contained in Messianic prophecy have been accomplished. He has proclaimed the acceptable year of the Lord and preached good tidings to the meek, but the day of vengeance of our God is still future (Isa 61:1). He has trodden the winepress alone, but the wicked have not yet been trodden down (Isa 63:3). The government has been placed upon his shoulder, but the increase of his peace is not yet without end (Isa 9:6–7). In short, the Messiah has come, but he has not yet accomplished all that is expected of him.

Finally, in the outworking of the Old Testament hope of redemption and restitution there is a similar tension between the present and the future. Jesus promises that the meek will one day inherit the earth. Redemption and restitution will finally be fully accomplished. But in the context of Hebrew thought, against which the New Testament must be understood, the restitution of the earth is linked with human redemption and the conquest of death. Jesus therefore demonstrates his power over death and the tomb, both by miracle and through his own resurrection. He who is the 'firstfruits' of them that sleep declares "I am the resurrection and the life; he that believeth in me, though he were dead, yet shall he live" (John 11:25). Victory over death is made available to those who believe, to those who respond to God's initiative in Christ. Yet this victory is not immediately given to all who believe, even as all are not now healed. That is reserved for the future. At the present time, there is only partial restitution, in token of what is to come.

Clearly then, Jesus is the fulfilment of Old Testament hope. He demonstrates eschatological power; he inaugurates the eschatological kingdom; he is the eschatological person; he reveals the eschatological purposes of God. But all this is only in part. In Christ, the *eschaton* has arrived, the eschato-

---

16 Ladd, *Kingdom,* 140

logical age on earth begins, and it will end at some time in the future. In him there is fulfilment, but without consummation.

Anticipation of Complete Fulfilment

How, then, did Old Testament hope, both fulfilled and unfulfilled in the life of Jesus, affect the outlook of the Christian Church? We share the view that the underlying current throughout the New Testament is eschatological and that the New Testament cannot rightly be interpreted apart from its eschatological character. It looks forward as the Old Testament looked forward. But what does it anticipate? Paul, in what is a fundamental text, declares, "For our conversation is in heaven; from whence also we look for the Saviour, the Lord Jesus Christ: who shall change our vile body, that it may be fashioned like unto his glorious body, according to the working whereby He is able even to subdue all things unto himself" (Phil 3:20,21). There can be no doubt that Jesus is able to "subdue all things unto himself". He frequently demonstrated his ability to do that while he was on earth. But he has not yet done so. Indeed, Paul speaks of the time yet future "when all things shall be subdued unto him" and "when he shall have put down all rule and all authority and power" (1 Cor 16:28, 24). Again, God has so exalted the Son "that at the name of Jesus every knee should bow, of things in heaven, and things in earth, and things under the earth" (Phil 2:9–10).

But in the New Testament, as well as in the Old, this has not yet happened. It is still future. The New Testament still looks forward to the final vindication of divine authority. It engenders hope that the future will bring the subjection of all things to Christ and the universal acknowledgement of his power. The demonstration of that power in the life and work of Jesus makes its final consummation more credible. It is, of course, true to claim that the New Testament has an eschatology with a character of its own, not to be explained as a relic of Judaism, but standing in its own right and in relation to God's new revelation in Christ. For all that, the day is still to come in which the authority of earth's rightful King is to be vindicated. The New Testament also looks forward to the unambiguous demonstration of eschatological power.

This is nevertheless to some degree only the introduction to what emerges as the dominant eschatological theme in the New Testament. Jesus, who came once in fulfilment of Messianic expectation, will himself come again. The authority which is to be fully demonstrated at the end time is *his* authority — *he* will "subdue all things unto himself". It is *his* kingdom which is yet to be finally revealed. "*I* will come again", he said. "This *same* Jesus will so come", "The Lord *himself* shall descend" — these are the phrases which characterise the New Testament promises of Christ's return. The emphasis in each case falls on the person rather than on the action. Jesus, who is already the eschatological Person in a veiled sense, will be unveiled as the eschatological Person for all to see and acknowledge, at the end, when he comes again. All that remained unfulfilled at his first coming will be fulfilled at his second coming.

The crucial truth to be derived from the New Testament witness is that it is not merely a future event that has significance, but a future Person. It is not so much the *day* of the Lord to which the New Testament looks forward, as the day of the *Lord.* The event does have immense significance, of course, but only insofar as it is related to the Person. Moore therefore argues in his fine study, *The Parousia in the New Testament,* that it is difficult "to evade the conclusion that the New Testament as a whole works with the concept of a salvation-history of which the *parousia* is an integral part", and concludes that "Jesus' life, death, resurrection and *parousia* belong together as parts of an indivisible whole, as moments in the great and all-decisive movement of God to man now breaking into the world".[17] Here the end is not thought of primarily as an event, the terminal point of the age, but rather in terms of the completed work of the eschatological Person. The redemptive work of Christ has a future because it has a verifiable, though inconclusive, past.

Together with the redemption of mankind and the conquest of death, the New Testament looks forward with equal certainty to the restitution of the world. Peter sees in the prophecies of Isaiah the assurance of a new order to come and uses them to substantiate his argument that this new order will follow the events of the last day. John's sublime vision of new heavens and new earth is completely in harmony with the creative and redemptive purposes of God as revealed throughout Scripture and is essential for the outworking of those purposes. God did not create the earth in vain; he created it to be inhabited. That this eternal purpose might be accomplished, biblical eschatology looks forward to the total redemption of man and the total restitution of the world. Eschatology, therefore, will not stand at the end of the Church's message as an isolated article of faith. It will stand at the beginning, and will shape the content of the whole. It will take its content from both Old and New Testaments and above all will bear its own unwavering witness to Christ as the 'eschatological Person' in whom all God's redemptive purposes are to be fulfilled.

The Essential Features of Biblical Eschatology

Since New Testament eschatology emerges from that of the Old Testament it inherits and perpetuates the same basic expectations. There is, however, another notable dimension. New Testament eschatology "is not to be

---

17 Moore, *Parousia,* 90.

explained as a hangover or relic of Judaism … It stands on its own proper ground, which is the revelation made in the Incarnation, in the love and suffering of Jesus and in the new life begun in him. Christianity is determined by its own nature to reach forward to the consummation of the life in Christ".[18] The new dimension in New Testament eschatology is its witness to God's new revelation in Jesus Christ. Furthermore, only faithfulness to the entire biblical text and the fullness of God's new revelation in Jesus Christ can together defend the Church from the criticism of being eschatologically unbalanced and deviant. Emerging from its claim to be wholly biblical, there are a number of features which characterise true biblical eschatology, and it is to these that we now turn our attention.

Christology

In the first place, biblical eschatology is evidently and strongly Christological. It is totally related to Christ, the 'eschatological Person'. By derivation, the word eschatology is the *logos* concerning the *eschaton* — literally the word concerning the last things. Traditionally this 'logos' has been understood as those doctrines relating to the future, the events which will occur at the end, including the return of Christ, the judgement, the resurrection of the dead and the re-creation of the world. By these events history will be terminated. While liberal theology has in general turned away from the literal view of a future which will culminate in specific events, such a view is still basic to traditional Protestantism and to authentic biblical eschatology. Nevertheless, we must ask again, 'What is the essential 'logos' of eschatology?' If Christ is the divine 'logos' of Christian faith as postulated in John 1:1–3, the 'logos' of Christology, the 'logos' of soteriology, the 'logos' of ecclesiology, he must also be the logos' of eschatology. Without detracting in any way from what has hitherto been regarded as the content of eschatology, we agree that:

> Christian eschatology does not speak of the future as such. It sets out from a definite reality in history and announces the future of that reality, its future possibilities and its power over the future. Christian eschatology speaks of Jesus Christ and *his* future. It recognises the reality of the raising of Jesus and proclaims the future of the risen Lord.[19]

Christ, not the future in itself, is the true 'logos', the content of eschatology. There is no word about the future that is worth proclaiming that does not emerge from him and point to him. The "blessed hope" is much more than an event, however momentous that event may be. The "blessed hope" is also a person.

---

18 Manson, 'Eschatology', 15
19 Moltmann, *Theology*, 17.

There have been few generations within Protestantism which have understood the Christological nature of authentic second-advent hope more than the English Puritans of the seventeenth century. Richard Sibbes, one of the great devotional writers of that age, preached and wrote extensively on the theme of Christ's second coming. We shall have occasion to hear Sibbes again in the following chapter and to sample his profound understanding of the second coming. Here we may just note that he understood it was necessary both for the individual believer and for the Church as a whole that Christ should come again. Also, and perhaps of greater import, Christ's return was for him more than merely an event at the end of time. For Sibbes, eschatology was directly related to soteriology. "The more we have of Christ in us", he said, "the more shall we desire his coming to us".[20] This is, as Paul said, "Christ in you, the hope of glory". The hope is not merely Christ at the end but Christ here and now. He is the hope of glory only to the extent that He now lives in the believer. It is the person of Christ who gives meaning to the event at the end.

It is not surprising that to Sibbes and to most of his contemporaries in the English Reformation, the doctrine of Christ's second coming was not an appendage to Christian faith, but a momentous truth at the very heart of their proclamation. Three hundred years later, theologians would again be talking of the person and work of Christ as having eschatological significance and there can be little doubt that Sibbes and his fellow preachers would have endorsed the view, "It is therefore right to emphasise that Christian eschatology is at heart Christology in an eschatological perspective".[21] Biblical eschatology does not merely analyse the general possibilities of future history. It announces the future of Jesus Christ and speaks of world future in terms of the One who alone makes any future possible.

Redemption and Restitution

A second characteristic of authentic biblical eschatology arises as a direct consequence of its Christological nature. Since God's purposes for humanity are focussed in Christ, all will eventually be realised in him. He is the 'eschatological Person' of promise and prophecy, the One in whom biblical hope is both fulfilled and unfulfilled. Since Jesus is the eschatological Person, the eschatological age commenced with his appearance on earth when he began to fulfil promise and prophecy. Thus, the coming of Christ at the end is not only related to his first coming in a Christological sense, that is by virtue of the *person* involved, but also in a theological sense, by virtue of the *purpose* involved. All the events which are to occur at the end of the

---

20   Richard Sibbes, *The Bride's Longing for her Bridegrooms Second Coming* (London, 1638), 84.
21   Moltmann, *Theology,* 192.

eschatological age — second advent, resurrection, judgement, kingdom — are, in a theological sense, a necessary sequel to the events which occurred at the beginning of the eschatological age — incarnation, death, resurrection and ascension. Biblical eschatology is redemptive in character because it is redemptive in purpose.

Many contemporary writers describe Christ's coming into history and his redemptive work as 'the Christ-event'. The Christ-event is the totality of Christ's work on behalf of man. It is not only the incarnation of Christ, his life, death and resurrection. The Christ-event also includes his ascension, his priestly ministry, his coming again and his future kingdom. It is viewed as a whole, rather than as a series of events. We can therefore agree,

> Without a fundamental distortion of its essential character, the gospel of creation and redemption could not be dissociated from the hope of the Parousia with all its implications. Christians must always look back in time to the event which is history's climax [the crucifixion] and which gives it its significance, and forward to the final event whose character is revealed already in the former.[22]

The Christ-event is the total redemptive work of Christ, culminating in his redemptive activity at the end of time. So Paul declares in looking forward to this culmination, "Now is our salvation nearer than when we believed" (Rom 13:11). The significance of Hebrews 9:28 is surely that it anticipates a conclusion to the redemptive work of Christ initiated on the cross and continuing now in heaven itself.

Without detracting from the immense significance of Christ's redeeming act on Calvary it is worth noting, as F. W. Camfield has reminded us, that Jesus' "life, death, resurrection and *Parousia* belong together as parts of an indivisible whole, as moments in the great and all-decisive movement of God to man".[23] In this sense, eschatology is wholly redemptive since it is part of the one Christ-event. Looking at the work of Christ from this viewpoint we are continually reminded "of the essential unity of God's saving acts in Christ — the realisation that the events of the Incarnation, Crucifixion, Resurrection, Ascension, and *Parousia* are in a real sense one event".[24]

The preceding two statements remind us that while there is in theology a new interest in the second coming, most eschatological schemes jump from the resurrection to the *parousia,* ignoring the time which exists between the two. Biblical eschatology has no such gap. The New Testament doctrine of Christ's mediatorial ministry in heaven, foreshadowed in outline in the Old Testament, is also part of the Christ-event. It is the essential link in the chain, joining together past and future at a point where otherwise they cannot meet.

22 G. W. Lampe, 'Eschatology', 21.
23 F. W. Camfield, 'Man in his Time', *SJT,* 3 (1950), 133.
24 C. E. Cranfield, 'St. Mark 13', *SJT,* 7 (1954), 288.

The priesthood of Christ, developed in the book of Hebrews from the initial reference at Hebrews 1:4, "when he had by himself purged our sins, sat down on the right hand of the Majesty on high", is to be seen against the background of Peter's assertion in Acts 3:21 that heaven must receive him "until the time of restitution of all things". The priestly ministry of Jesus is part of a continuum which proceeds unbroken until its consummation at the end.

Furthermore, eschatology can only be redemptive in the biblical sense if it involves the redemption of the whole man. The resurrection of the body is therefore also a factor which cannot be ignored. In the first hundred years or so of Reformation theology, the emphasis was not placed as emphatically as it was in later centuries on the survival of the soul after death as the final goal of salvation. As a result of the widespread and strong belief in the second coming which emerged in early Protestantism there existed also a corresponding emphasis on the resurrection of the body. Richard Baxter, another great seventeenth-century biblical scholar, may be quoted as representative of Reformation eschatology:

> O hasten that great Resurrection Day! When thy command shall go forth, and none shall disobey; when the Sea and Earth shall yield up their hostages, and all that slept in the graves shall awake, and the dead in Christ shall first arise; ... therefore dare I lay down my carcass in the dust, entrusting it, not to a Grave, but to Thee: and therefore my flesh shall rest in Hope, till Thou raise it to the possession of the everlasting rest.[25]

It is quite clear that there can be no salvation in the full sense until death is finally conquered and the body resurrected.

The resurrection of the body at the last day is a consequence both of the Christological and redemptive aspects of biblical eschatology and is rooted in the resurrection of Jesus himself, the 'eschatological Person'. The literal resurrection of all who believe owes its possibility to Jesus and to his resurrection without which no such possibility could exist. It is to understand and to proclaim Christ's resurrection that provides hope for the future. In Cullmann's words, "It is no longer possible to say, 'We shall arise', without saying at the same time, 'Christ has risen'".[26] The resurrection is not simply a future eschatological event, but it is also part of the redemptive past. The connection between Christ's resurrection and the resurrection to come is neither wholly prophetic, that is to say a future event in time isolated from the past, nor wholly Christological, that is a past event in time isolated from the future. The connection is one in which the future and past are inseparably related. The resurrection of Jesus contains within it the necessity of

---

25 Richard Baxter, *The Saints' Everlasting Rest* (London, 1650), 837–38.
26 Oscar Cullmann, *Christ and Time* (London: SCM, 1951), 235.

a future resurrection for all who truly believe. Only then does redemption become an eternal reality.

Optimism

Also arising from the Christological and redemptive content of biblical eschatology is the fact that it is optimistic. With the apostle Paul who writes of the "hope of the gospel" (Col 1:23) of "the Lord Jesus Christ, our hope" (1 Tim 1:1) and of "Christ in you the hope of glory" (Col 1:27), it recognises that the essential ethos of the gospel is that of hope, directing humanity and the world forward to a better future. The New Testament further points those who believe to a "hope set before" them (Heb 6:18), to a "hope which is laid up ... in heaven" (Col 1:5) and to a hope of resurrection (1 Cor 15:19). Believers are told that they are begotten into a lively hope (1 Pet 1:3), that they are heirs of the hope of eternal life (Tit 3:7), that they are to look for the blessed hope (Tit 2:13). Similarly, the Church is called to account for her hope in the resurrection of the dead (Acts 23:6) and is committed to provide an answer for the hope that she professes (1 Pet 3:15). If the Church proclaims an eschatology which reflects the total biblical revelation, it will inevitably proclaim an eschatology that is positive and optimistic.

The significance of hope as a major outcome of biblical eschatology is its relationship to faith. Faith, being the basis of salvation, binds human beings to Christ by believing that Christ *was* and by trusting in what he has done. But hope is the inseparable companion of faith and binds them to Christ by believing that he *will be* and by trusting in what he will accomplish. Thus faith and hope cannot be separated either in theology or experience. "For by grace are ye saved through faith" (Eph 2:8). This faith "is the confidence of things hoped for, the evidence of things not seen" (Heb 11:1). Therefore Paul again declares, "For we are saved by hope" (Rom 8:24). True faith and true hope are inseparable. Calvin described this relationship well:

> Faith believes that God is true; Hope expects that in due season he will manifest his truth. Faith believes that He is our Father; Hope expects that He will always act the part of a Father towards us. Faith believes that eternal life has been given to us; Hope expects that it will one day be revealed.[27]

More recently Moltmann perceptively commented, "In the Christian life faith has the priority, but hope the primacy".[28] The Church which proclaims true faith in Christ as the basis of salvation will inevitably also proclaim hope.

---

27 John Calvin, *Institutes of the Christian Religion* (Grand Rapids, MI: Eerdmans, 1964), I, 506.

28 Moltmann, *Theology,* 20.

However, it is possible to hold an eschatology which is cataclysmic, negative, judgmental and hence unredemptive and hopeless. Such eschatological schemes have recurred in Christian history since the Reformation and stand as a sombre warning against the proclamation of any eschatology which is less than optimistic and hopeful. William Whiston once predicted the imminent end of the world. Whiston, a theologian and a preacher, based his predictions on prophecy and the appearance of an unexpected comet. The comet was to collide with the earth, under the direction of God, and thereby bring about the anticipated destruction of the wicked and the final fulfilment of all prophecy. For a few months Whiston's message attracted considerable attention, but the final comment must be that of Professor Perry Miller:

> In London, when the populace realised that Whiston's comet had let them off, they expressed their gratitude by going into taverns and breaking up whole hogsheads for joy. They drank, they whored, they swore, they lied, they cheated, they quarrelled, they murdered. In short, the world went on in the old channel.[29]

The conclusion, as Miller rightly judges, is that men cannot be scared into virtue. A pessimistic eschatology is not only unbiblical, it is pointless. It has no purpose and, being unredemptive, is therefore without hope.

The sombre lesson which emerges from this type of eschatology is that it is not only sterile — it is also self-defeating and self-destructive. Whiston, who was a contemporary of Sir Isaac Newton, had the opportunity of partaking of the wholeness which characterised most of the eschatological thought of his time. Similarly, the Fifth Monarchy movement, which announced the imminent end in terms of prophetic fulfilment bringing destruction to the present order, lasted for forty or fifty years. Today, both Whiston and the Fifth Monarchy Men are remembered for their eccentricities. They demonstrate the ease with which it is possible to move from a wholesome, optimistic eschatology to one which is partial and pessimistic. The eschatology derived from the Bible is one which is full of hope because it is totally Christological and totally redemptive.

Chronology

Fourthly, it should be recognised that chronology is an important factor in a complete eschatology. When we have drawn attention previously to the danger of emphasising eschatological events to the exclusion of their redemptive character, it was not to suggest that chronology and the occurrence of specific events in time are to be eliminated entirely. True eschatology is chronological in character, since it is part of God's redemptive plan for mankind and since man himself is a creature of time. Furthermore, it is

---

29 Perry Miller, *Errand into the Wilderness* (Cambridge, MA: Belknap Press of Harvard University Press, 1956), 187.

impossible to overlook the significance of time and chronology in either the Old or New Testaments as the following comments remind us. James Barr observes:

> The Old Testament contains a complete and carefully worked out chronological system, by which a large number of the important events … can be dated in relation to one another, and in particular dated from the absolute datum point of the creation of the world.[30]

The Old Testament can only be understood against its chronological background and can only be interpreted adequately in terms of time.

A similar concept underlies the New Testament. Oscar Cullmann explains,

> The New Testament knows only the linear time concept of Today, Yesterday, and Tomorrow; all philosophical reinterpretation and dissolution into timeless metaphysics is foreign to it. It is precisely upon the basis of this rectilinear conception of time that time in primitive Christianity can yield the framework for the divine process of revelation and redemption.[31]

Cullmann also argues that in later centuries New Testament eschatological expectation collapsed as a result of the Hellenisation of Christian thought. Whereas the biblical concept of time is best illustrated by a straight line, which has a beginning and an end, the Greek concept of time is more adequately expressed by a circle. The Greek spatial concept of time superseded the Hebrew linear concept in post-apostolic Christianity, simultaneously with the growth of natural immortality and continuing life after death, as opposed to the resurrection of the body at the end of time.

From the standpoint of a complete eschatology it is clear that a well-defined chronological system is of fundamental importance for understanding the Bible. Time had a beginning at creation and it therefore will have an ending, when the purposes of creation and re-creation are accomplished. Not only is God's revelation to man in Scripture contained within a chronological structure, but his principal revelation to man in Jesus Christ was similarly made within the framework of time. The 'Logos' appeared in the fullness of time, in fulfilment of Daniel's seventy weeks as predicted, and lived and worked under the Emperor Augustus, the Emperor Tiberius and under the jurisdiction of Pontius Pilate. Christ and Scripture are both God's revelation in time and can be verified chronologically. But since eschatology is also redemptive, part of the redemptive process, it follows that to have any real meaning for man it must be expressed similarly in terms of time.

It is in this context that authentic biblical theology encompasses the exposition of prophecy in general, including interpretation of Daniel and

---

30   James Barr, *Biblical Words for Time* (Napierville, IL: Allenson, 1962), 28.
31   Cullmann, *Christ and Time,* 53.

Revelation in particular. The inclusion of the books of Daniel and Revelation in the canon requires that their meaning be understood and proclaimed. Prophetic interpretation which identifies itself with the moderate, historicist school which emerged during the Reformation and to which virtually all Reformation theologians subscribed is demonstrably biblical eschatology. It was the Counter- Reformation which produced alternative interpretations of biblical apocalyptic. Understood from a Reformation perspective, the books of Daniel and Revelation still provide a chronological framework within which the redemptive purposes of God are being worked out. Biblical eschatology and the Church's proclamation which emerges from it cannot be complete without a chronological dimension and this requires a responsible, historicist interpretation of prophetic chronology.

What has been said thus far about the nature of biblical theology has been largely theoretical. This remains important if the Church is to retain an authentic identity. Self-understanding is essential to effective mission, and self-understanding is posited on a well-defined theology. Yet this in itself is not sufficient. Theology must lead to religion, theory to practice. If eschatology is truly redemptive and related to the Christ-event, it cannot remain purely theological. Thus there are two further characteristics of eschatology which is genuinely biblical.

Ethics

Biblical eschatology has ethical consequences. It leads to right living both in the life of the individual and in the life of the Church. Eschatology cannot evade the implications of John's expected future, "Beloved, now are we the sons of God, and it doth not yet appear what we shall be: but we know that, when he shall appear, we shall be like him; for we shall see him as he is. And every man that hath this hope in him purifieth himself, even as he is pure" (1 John 3:2–3). This is more than mere sermonising. It is true theology and true eschatology. The inevitable consequence of a truly biblical eschatology is what has been called "eschatological living".

We must return here briefly to the doctrine of the kingdom. The concept of the kingdom of God which, as we have previously seen is essential to understanding biblical eschatology, is not a concept of two separate kingdoms. There is not one kingdom now — the kingdom of grace, and another kingdom at the end — the kingdom of glory. There is one kingdom now *and* at the end — the kingdom of grace which will become the kingdom of glory. John Bright again:

> In New Testament theology the kingdom of God is not only the goal of all history and the reward of all believers … it is a new order which even now bursts in upon the present one and summons [believers] to be

its people. Its summons demands response, and that response is obedience and righteousness here and now.[32]

The Church now lives in 'kingdom' time and looks forward in hope to
the fulfilment of all eschatological promise and prophecy. But it lives, during the eschatological age, in relationship to Christ. The New Testament
therefore requires ethical and moral living of a high standard. It is because
of the presence of the Holy Spirit in the Church, now giving power to believers and to the proclamation of the gospel, that holiness is enjoined in
view of the soon-coming of Christ. The presence of the Holy Spirit in the
Church is the new factor. He is the eschatological gift to the Church, he is
the evidence of the new and last age, and believers are called to holiness, to
eschatological living, in the light of his presence and power.

The holiness, the righteous living, to which the New Testament calls believers, is not a holiness which is required because the kingdom is *to come*
— it is a lifestyle which is required because the kingdom is *already here*.
Sanctification is not only a doctrine which enables believers to participate
in a future kingdom; it is an experience which the present kingdom enables
them to share now. We can only conclude that any eschatology which does
not result in eschatological living is not truly biblical eschatology. Peter's
exhortation, in view of the revelation of Christ at the end, is still relevant:
"As obedient children, not fashioning yourselves according to the former
lusts in your ignorance" (1 Pet 1:13–14).

Responsibility and Mission

A further and final aspect of authentic biblical eschatology is that it engenders responsibility. The word 'responsible' has the double sense that it
is causative, that it leads to action, and also that it is under obligation, that it
has a duty to discharge. Both these senses come together in the relationship
of eschatology to mission.

The Church has a commission to "preach the gospel to every creature"
(Mark 16:15) and to do so as long as time lasts. But what is the gospel
which is to be proclaimed? It is the "gospel of the kingdom" which Jesus
preached (Matt 4: 23). It is the same "gospel of the kingdom" which is to be
proclaimed as a witness to all nations before the end (Matt 24:14). In fact,
the gospel which the New Testament speaks of from beginning to end is "the
gospel of the kingdom". It was the arrival of the kingdom which caused the
Church to embark on world mission and it is the continuing presence of the
kingdom which sustains it in that task. The Church's witness is a response to
the causative eschatology already in its midst. This eschatology places upon
the Church a responsibility to bear witness to itself — the kingdom of God

---

32 Bright, *Kingdom,* 223.

in all its richness and fulness, fulfilled and unfulfilled. It bears witness to the authority of God now revealed in Christ and now seen in the Church under the operation of the Spirit. It bears witness to the eschatological Person who has already appeared and who will appear again.

The Church, then, is already an eschatological community, bearing witness to the world, testifying to its present experience of the kingdom and proclaiming faith in its consummation. The theme which recurs in A. L. Moore's study of New Testament eschatology is that the Church's witness is seriously impaired if eschatology is absent. Indeed, he sees the loss of eschatology as the real reason for the ineffectiveness of the Church's witness throughout history. "The intense urgency with which the Church should undertake its tasks of repentance and of missionary proclamation of the gospel, is weakened if not entirely lost", he argues, by the loss or dilution of the eschatological content of faith.[33] A balanced and biblical eschatology is both the cause and content of Christian witness. A sense of responsibility which leads to mission is a major factor in the wholeness of authentic biblical eschatology.

Biblical eschatology in its wholeness results in two challenges to the Church now living in the *eschaton*. The first is to avoid identifying the Church with the kingdom. The Church is not the kingdom. The confusion of Church with kingdom is the result of Augustinian eschatology which replaced New Testament eschatology as Christianity moved away from its biblical basis. Neither does the Church produce the kingdom. The kingdom is already here and produces the Church. The Church, therefore, can only bear witness to the kingdom, to that which is already present and which is still to be realised in its fullness at the end. The Church must fulfil its eschatological mission, it must continually bear witness, but it must remember that the Church is preceded by the kingdom and will be succeeded by it.

The second challenge is to face honestly the implications of eschatological responsibility. Eschatology, as we have seen, is not merely part of the Church's doctrinal confession, a logical conclusion to what precedes it in a statement of faith. Eschatology shapes the content of the whole and also the content of the Church's proclamation, giving it purpose and meaning, and so places upon the Church an awesome responsibility. It must proclaim hope to a generation which lives with a premonition of doom, and provide answers to an age which cries frantically for satisfaction. The unique wholeness of biblical eschatology can, and must be allowed to, motivate the Church living in the end of eschatological time to continuing mission. To neglect this responsibility would be to deny all that biblical eschatology is and all that it requires.

---

33 Moore, *Parousia*, 4.

14. The Second Advent Hope in Puritan England[1]

Bryan W. Ball

The passing of the English crown from the Tudors to the Stuarts was to prove a significant milestone in the development of Protestant thought in England. With the accession of James I in 1603, the Puritan[2] movement, which had taken root in the later years of Elizabeth's reign, came to shape the beliefs of increasing numbers of people, and this notwithstanding the king's early threat to "harry" Puritans out of the land and the later restrictions imposed upon them by the repressive William Laud, Archbishop of Canterbury. William Haller remarks that from this time Puritan preachers "increased in number and influence faster than ever before, finding a growing audience ever more willing to listen".[3] As time passed and the Bible was more and more expounded by Puritan preachers and writers, clergy and laity alike became increasingly aware of a strong eschatological emphasis in Scripture. The hope of Christ's second coming, together with its associated truths, appears as one of the important outcomes of Puritanism's rediscovery of the total biblical message. Probably at no other time in English history has the doctrine of the second advent been so widely proclaimed or so readily accepted as during the years of Puritanism's ascendancy.

It is the broad sweep of eschatological hope in the seventeenth century that emerges as a major conclusion to the study of Puritan literature. From an ecclesiastical standpoint, the doctrine of Christ's second coming was proclaimed by Anglican and Nonconforming Puritans alike. John Durant, the Independent pastor who preached in Canterbury Cathedral, could say in 1653 that among Protestants of every loyalty, "Prelatical or Presbyterian, or

---

1 This chapter, revised and abridged, was first published in V. Norskov Olsen, ed., *The Advent Hope in Scripture and History* (Washington, DC: Review and Herald, 1987). Used with permission.

2 The terms 'Puritan' and 'Puritanism' are used here of English believers in the seventeenth century within and beyond the Anglican Church whose chief concern was for purity of both doctrine and life.

3 London is the place of publication for all 17th-century works unless otherwise stated. Publisher's names are not usually given. William Haller, *The Rise of Puritanism* (New York: Harper, 1957), 50.

Independent or Anabaptist", advocates could be found even of the extremer millenarian eschatology which by that time had appeared. Certainly in the preceding half century or so many influential clergymen in the British Isles had associated themselves with the more moderate advent hope. To those Anglicans of an earlier generation who had preached the doctrine of Christ's coming — Hugh Latimer, Edwin Sandys, John Bradford and John Rogers, among others — could be added the names of James Ussher, Archbishop of Armagh, Patrick Forbes, Bishop of Aberdeen, Joseph Hall, Bishop of Norwich and John Donne, Dean of St. Paul's.

Beyond the ranks of such prominent mainstream Anglicans, the second advent literature was rapidly augmented by works from leading Puritan theologians. The Presbyterians Thomas Brightman, Thomas Hall and James Durham would have differed ecclesiastically from Independents such as Thomas Goodwin, Nathaniel Homes, William Strong and John Owen. The hope of Christ's coming, however, became a prominent factor in their theology, each of them contributing significantly to the advent literature which was read and re-read in England during the seventeenth century. Other great Puritan divines would have agreed that the recovery of truth was of far greater consequence than the arid debate over Church government, and names like Thomas Taylor, Richard Sibbes and Richard Baxter cannot be excluded from the list of prominent Puritans who espoused and proclaimed the advent hope.

Socially the doctrine of Christ's coming was evident on an even broader plane. Innumerable commentaries, expositions, pamphlets and sermons from clergy of every rank were complemented by works of various laymen from a wide cross-section of public and private life. From James I to James Ussher, from the mathematician John Napier and the statesman William Alexander, Earl of Stirling to the seventeenth century poets John Donne, George Wither and John Milton, the advent hope found a lucid and compelling expression. Aspects of second advent doctrine investigated by Sir Henry Finch, the lawyer, Samuel Hartlib the economist and schoolmasters Thomas Hayne, William Burton and James Toppe, were re-examined and restated not only by theologians but by other laymen, by Leonard Busher, for example, the early advocate of religious toleration and by Robert Purnell the devout Baptist elder from Bristol. The readiness with which the English Church as a whole took to itself the hope of Christ's coming is one reason for the warmth of spiritual life so characteristic of the Puritan era.

Geographically, the spread of second advent hope was considerable. Certain areas of the country, in view of their association with early Protestantism and the nascent Puritan movement, might be expected to have been more open to a new biblical emphasis. East Anglia and the South East accordingly provided a number of second advent preachers and prophetic expositors. Joseph Mede studied and lectured at Cambridge; William Bridge had been appointed town preacher at Great Yarmouth and Joseph Hall, nominally at least, was still Bishop of Norwich when he wrote, *The Revelation Unrevealed*. In the West, Richard Bernard, the Anglican rector of Batcombe in Somerset, the Presbyterian John Seagar from Devon and Robert Purnell of Bristol all espoused the advent hope and contributed to its literature. Wales provided the fiery Vavasour Powell and the mystical Morgan Llywd, and Ireland the renowned James Ussher. Among the names that could be cited from Midland counties are Thomas Hall from Warwickshire who wrote at least two books concerning the last events, Robert Bolton from Northamptonshire, author of *The Four Last Things,* and Richard Baxter from Kidderminster in Worcestershire, whose *Saints' Everlasting Rest* is one of the classics of Puritan devotion. Scotland also provided an impressive list of theologians committed to New Testament eschatological hope. James Durham, William Guild and David Dickson were university professors at Glasgow, Aberdeen and Glasgow and Edinburgh respectively. Their writings all convey a deep interest in the events of the last days with a focus on Christ's second coming.

It is clear, then, that many of the most eloquent advocates of the second advent in the British Isles throughout the seventeenth century were prominent theologians loyal to the norms of accepted doctrinal orthodoxy. So Baxter, whose moderation and orthodoxy were widely recognised, is thoroughly representative when he says:

> Christ will come again to receive His people to Himself, that where He is, there they may be also ... The Bridegroom's departure was not upon divorce. He did not leave us with a purpose to return no more; He hath left pledges enough to assure us. We have His Word, His many promises, His sacraments which show forth His death till He come... He that would come to suffer will surely come to triumph ... He that would come to purchase will surely come to possess.[4]

Richard Sibbes, another greatly respected Puritan preacher and writer, concurs with similar certainty: "We must take it for granted that there will be a second, glorious coming of Christ ... God will at length make good what He hath promised".[5]

The Doctrine of the Second Advent

The certainty with which the Church in Puritan England anticipated the *eschaton* is matched only by the clarity with which it understood related

---

4   Richard Baxter, *The Saints' Everlasting Rest* (London, 1650), 45–46.

5   Richard Sibbes, *The Brides Longing for her Bridegrooms Second Coming* (1638), 34.

aspects of second advent doctrine. Samuel Smith, one of the many Puritan divines ejected at the Restoration of the monarchy in 1660, had, in 1618, written *The Great Assize, or, Day of Jubilee*, a popular work which had been through no less than thirty-nine editions by the turn of the century and which was read by many thousands throughout the land. "He shall come as a king", Smith declared, "full of majesty and glory, guarded and attended upon with many thousands of heavenly soldiers, even all His holy angels".[6] There was little deviation in the seventeenth century from the belief that Christ's coming would be literal, personal and glorious, "in the flesh", to quote John Seagar, another Puritan preacher. Seagar's *A Discovery of the World to Come*, an important contribution to the second advent literature at a time when more extreme views were beginning to gather momentum, examined virtually every aspect of the advent hope, emphasising that the bodily and visible return of Christ at the end of the age was to be distinguished from any spiritual "comings" to the individual believer through the presence of the Holy Spirit.[7]

This point was taken up again by Christopher Love, a Presbyterian preacher who also wrote at great length on the advent hope as he found it in Scripture. Love pointed out that the concept of a spiritualised second advent was a third-century deviation introduced by Origen and that it should not be regarded as biblical. Love explains:

> It was the great mistake of Origen, though he holds for the coming of Christ again, that he pleads for the coming of Christ in spirit. Therefore the text where it is said, 'You shall see the Son of Man coming in the clouds of heaven', Origen understands by the clouds, to be the saints, because it is mentioned in Scripture, that the believers are a cloud of witnesses. Now this is to pervert the whole letter of the Bible, and turn all the Scripture into an allegory and metaphorical sense ... I only mention this to confute those that follow the conceit of Origen, merely to make Christ's coming to be but a spiritual coming, a coming in the hearts of saints.[8]

In harmony with many biblical exegetes of the time, Love recognised that the Bible referred to the coming, or appearing, of Christ in different ways.

In another work, *Heaven's Glory, Hell's Terror*, Love drew attention to three apparent comings of Christ mentioned in Scripture, the first in the flesh at the incarnation, another "spiritual" coming through the gospel and the third, a final appearance to judgment at the last day. Love stressed that it was this final coming to judgment which was referred to in both Colos-

---

6   Samuel Smith, *The Great Assize, or, The Day of Jubilee* (1618, 1628 edition cited), 21.

7   John Seagar, *A Discoverie of the World to Come* (1650), 76, 94–95.

8   Christopher Love, *The Penitent Pardoned* (1657), 175.

sians 3:4 and John 14:3, the texts on which his *Heaven's Glory* and *The Penitent Pardoned* were respectively based. Hence, "by Christ's appearing here, is meant that glorious manifestation of Jesus Christ upon earth at the time when He shall come at the last day",[9] and "the same Jesus that you saw ascend, shall descend, so that it cannot be Christ in His spirit, but in His person"[10] who will return at the end of the age.

A part from the certainty with which Christ's second coming was anticipated, there is possibly no point of wider agreement among Puritan theologians than on what Love here describes as "a glorious manifestation". Ussher's description of Christ's coming at the end "environed with a flame of fire, attended with all the host of the elect angels",[11] is matched by Robert Bolton's "coming in the clouds of heaven with power and great glory".[12] John Owen's exposition of the epistle to the Hebrews, written in 1680, speaks of an "illustrious appearance filling the whole world with the beams of it",[13] a late echo of Thomas Taylor's earlier description of the advent as it appeared in his commentary on Titus, published in Cambridge in 1619, in which he describes the event as occurring "in such glory as neither the tongue can utter, nor the mind of man conceive".[14] Few exponents of the second advent doctrine in the seventeenth century transmit a note of hope more than does Richard Baxter as he contemplates the glory of the last day:

> If there be such cutting down of boughs and spreading of garments, and crying hosanna, to one that comes into Jerusalem riding on an ass; what will there be when He comes with His angels in His glory? If they that heard Him preach the gospel of the kingdom, have their hearts turned within them, that they return and say, 'Never man spake like this man' then sure they that behold His majesty and His kingdom, will say "There was never glory like this glory".[15]

In attempting to explain the nature of the second advent, Puritan theologians often compared Christ's second coming with his first coming at the incarnation. "When our Saviour Jesus Christ lived on earth, He came in misery, very base and lowly", said Samuel Smith, "but now, He shall come as a king, full of majesty and glory".[16] Christopher Love, again, is unambiguous in describing the manner of the advent:

9   Christopher Love, *Heavens Glory, Hells Terror* (1653), 32.
10 Love, *Penitent Pardoned*, 176.
11 James Ussher, *A Body of Divinitie* (1645), 477.
12 Robert Bolton, *The Four Last Things* (1632), 87.
13 John Owen, *Exposition of the Epistle ... to the Hebrews* (1680), 470.
14 Thomas Taylor, *Commentary on Titus* (Cambridge, 1619), 480.
15 Baxter, *Saints' Rest*, 776.
16 Smith, *Great Assize*, 21.

> When Christ first appeared, He appeared in the form of a servant; at His second coming He shall appear in majesty as a king. In His first appearing He appeared in contempt in a manger, in His second coming He shall shine in glory in the clouds. In His first appearing, He had only beasts to be His companions, in His second appearing He shall have saints and angels to be His attendants.[17]

Such precise theological statements concerning the manner in which Christ would come had previously been prefigured in Sir William Alexander's epic poem of some fourteen hundred stanzas *Dooms-day, or, The Great Day of the Lord's Judgment*, (1614):

> Who can abide the Glory of that sight,
> Which kills the living, and the dead doth raise,
> With squadrons compass'd, Angels flaming bright,
> Whom thousands serve, Ten thousand thousands praise?
> My soul entranced is ravished with that light,
> Which in a moment shall the world amaze.[18]

If the poetry was not all it might have been, the theology was above reproach, and preachers and people alike widely expected a glorious, visible advent and a personal and literal appearance of Christ at the end of the age.

But when would Christ's second coming occur? In attempting to answer this tantalising question, Puritan theologians and preachers were aware that they were wrestling with a problem that went back to the earliest days of the Christian Church. Thomas Hall is representative of his own age in re-echoing the New Testament note of imminence when he says "The days we live in are the last days. Our times are the last times ... this is the last hour ... and upon us the ends of the world are come".[19] The Puritans of the seventeenth century were essentially children of the Reformation and within the context of Reformation theology, itself contained within the framework of the New Testament, there was but one answer that could be given. Christ would come soon. The end of the present order was imminent. As Hall again points out, "If the apostle thought the day of the Lord was at hand sixteen hundred years ago, we may well conclude that it is near now".[20] The Puritan preachers readily identified with the New Testament emphasis on the imminence of the second advent and Henry Symons speaks for many when he says:

> It will not be long before this Judge comes ... yea, I may say of some here as was said of Simeon, they shall not depart this life before they

---

17 Love, *Heavens Glory*, 38.

18 William Alexander, 'Dooms-day, or The Great Day of the Lord's Judgement' (1614), in *Recreations with the Muses* (1637), 48.

19 Thomas Hall, *Commentary ... upon ...the Latter Epistle to Timothy* (1658), 7.

20 *Ibid.*

shall see the Lord's Christ ... He is on the wing, he will be here before most are aware.[21]

This conviction that Christ's coming was at hand became widespread in England in the seventeenth century, but as Henry Symons and many others plainly demonstrate, it was a conviction which could be held without becoming involved in capricious date-setting or the subjective interpretation of prophecy. When these men and their contemporaries studied the Bible they discovered a recurring eschatological emphasis. They saw that Christ himself had spoken at length of the last days and the consummation of world history and that the early Church had gone forth on its world mission seemingly sustained in the hope of an early fulfilment of Christ's promises. As the Puritan apologist strove to recapture the spirit as well as the letter of New Testament eschatology, he inevitably identified with the hopes of the early Church. Thus to Richard Baxter, the eventful day is "approaching", "not far off" and "comes apace". Thomas Adams, whose prodigious exposition of 2 Peter went to more than sixteen hundred folio pages, explained:

> The time from Christ's ascension to the world's end, is called *dies extrema*, the last day, because it immediately (without any general alteration) goes before it. The end in the apostles' time was not far off, now it must be very near: if that were *ultima dies*, this is *ultima hora*: or if that were *ultima hora*, the last hour, this is *ultimum horae*, the last minute.[22]

Hall was one of many in the seventeenth century who saw the entire post-New Testament age in an eschatological sense. The last days began with the apostolic age, and it behoves good Christians to live always in the expectation of a final fulfilment. In professing the hope of an imminent advent, Puritan preachers clearly felt an affinity with the first disciples of Christ, and Baxter speaks again for many when he exclaims, "How near is that most blessed joyful day? It comes apace, even He that comes will come, and will not tarry".[23]

The Basis of Eschatological Hope

The foundation of eschatological hope in seventeenth-century England was the unqualified acceptance of Scripture as the sole source of faith and doctrine. The Puritan apologist wishing to substantiate a point of doctrine turned instinctively to the Bible. James Ussher argues, "The books of holy scripture are so sufficient for the knowledge of Christian religion, that they do most plentifully contain all doctrine necessary to salvation".[24] Richard Baxter's *Saints' Everlasting Rest* similarly stated, "The Scripture promising

---

21 Henry Symons, *The Lord Jesus His Commission* (1657), 35–36.
22 Thomas Adams, *A Commentary ... upon ...Second Peter* (1633), 1130.
23 Baxter, *Saints' Rest*, 254.
24 Ussher, *Body of Divinitie*, 18.

that rest to us is the perfect infallible word and law of God".[25] Christopher Love exhorts his readers to "Be sure you make the word of God to be the standard by which you try and prove all doctrines that you hear, and if there be anything preached ... that is not according to the word of God, believe it not".[26] To the true Puritan the Bible was authoritative, not only in its record of the past and in its guidance for the present life and doctrine of the believer, but equally so in its delineation of future events.

In his *Penitent Pardoned,* Christopher Love sets out the doctrine of Christ's second advent as an integral element in the historic Christian faith. On John 14:3 Love comments, "This text contains in it the most material and fundamental points of all the doctrine of Christianity", notably "the great doctrine of Christ's second coming".[27] John Owen, the eminent Puritan theologian, similarly argues, "Christ's appearance the second time, his return from heaven to complete the salvation of the church, is the great fundamental principle of our faith and hope".[28] Richard Sibbes, an earlier exponent of the second advent whose works were published posthumously between 1635 and 1650, had suggested that since the coming of Christ was fundamental to Christian doctrine, it should be desired by the Church:

> Such is the disposition of the church, that before Christ was come, good people were known by the desire of his coming. And therefore it was the description of holy men that they waited for the consolation of Israel. O Lord come quickly, come in the flesh. But now the first coming is past they desire as much his second coming, and therefore they are described in the epistle of St Paul, to be such as love and long for the appearing of Christ.[29]

Such expectancy was an essential characteristic of the true Church, the espoused bride of the heavenly bridegroom, and Sibbes adds, "As in civil marriage there is a contract, so here in the spiritual; and seeing there is a contract, there is also an assent to the second coming of Christ; the contracted spouse must needs say 'Amen' to the marriage day".[30]

Since the second advent hope was related to the revealed purpose of God for his people William Jenkyn logically enquired, "If the other predictions in Scripture, particularly those concerning the first coming of Christ, have truly come to pass, why should we doubt of the truth of Christ's second appearance?"[31] Jenkyn's question, rhetorical though it was, had already been answered by Richard Baxter: "As Christ failed not to come in the fullness of

---

25   Baxter, *Saints' Rest*, title page.

26   Christopher Love, *A Christians Duty and Safety in Evil Times* (1653), 82.

27   Love, *Penitent Pardoned*, 115.

28   Owen, *Hebrews*, 471.

29   Sibbes, *Brides Longing*, 55–56.

30   *Ibid.*, 15.

31   William Jenkyn, *An Exposition of the Epistle of Jude* (1652), pt. I, 537.

time, even when Daniel and others had foretold his coming, so in the fullness and fitness of time will his second coming be".[32]

The foregoing statements suggest that a relationship was recognised in Puritan eschatology between the incarnation and Christ's coming at the end. This relationship, in fact, saw the second advent as a necessary and inevitable theological sequel to the first advent. "The first and second coming of Christ are of so near connection", Richard Sibbes argued, "that oftentimes they are comprised together, as the regeneration of our souls and the regeneration of our bodies, the adoption of our souls and the adoption of our bodies, the redemption of our souls and the redemption of our bodies".[33] Christ must come again to complete the work of salvation which he had begun at his first coming. Indeed, many would argue strenuously that the work of redemption could not be complete or efficacious until Christ returned.

The concept that a theological link existed between Christ's two advents and that it related ultimately to the redemptive purposes of God in Christ, was nowhere put more forcibly than by John Durant in his introduction to *The Salvation of the Saints by the Appearance of Christ* (1653). Durant explained that many Christians were content to go no further in appreciating the redemptive work of Christ than in understanding what had been accomplished at the cross. In Durant's view this was unfortunate, since the final and total salvation of humanity depended also on the work which Christ accomplished after his death and resurrection. While it was not to be disputed that the atoning sacrifice of Christ lay at the heart of God's redemptive plan, yet it did not constitute the whole of Christ's work. Although it was the "*medium impetrationis*", it was not the "*medium applicationis*". Salvation had been "purchased" but not "completed". Beyond the cross "there remained a great deal more to be done ... to apply it unto us".[34] Thus the divine redemptive purpose had been furthered through Christ's priestly ministry in heaven, and would culminate at his second coming.

To Durant, as to many other theologians in the seventeenth century, a believer's salvation was now in hope, at a distance, as the rightful, though suspended, inheritance of an heir under age. While accomplished and assured it was not yet a tangible reality, although Durant was careful to point out that it was "as safe as if you had it".[35] The robe had been provided, as had the crown, and at his coming the Lord would deliver both. "Christ keeps the crown till the day of His appearance and kingdom, and in that day He will

---

32   Baxter, *Saints' Rest*, 92.

33   Sibbes, *Brides Longing*, 72.

34   John Durant, *The Salvation of the Saints* (1653), Epistle to the Reader, sig. A7r.

35   *Ibid.*, 221.

give it to you".[36] Sibbes said that at his second coming Christ "shall perfect our salvation". Love stated, "You shall then be saved to the uttermost" and John Owen, with a little more finesse, added "the end of His appearance is *eis soterian*, the salvation of them that look for Him".[37]

Whether it was to effect or complete an individual's salvation, or to make it a reality, or to receive the redeemed to himself, it was clear to believers in Puritan England that the final chapter in the saga of human redemption could not be written until Christ had returned at the end of days as he himself and other biblical writers had promised.

The Soteriological Significance of the Second Advent

William Haller has drawn attention to the theological and experiential sequence by which a believer in the seventeenth century eventually attained to salvation. "Election — vocation — justification — sanctification — glorification was more than an abstract formula", he says. "It became the pattern of the most profound experience of men through many generations".[38] In the understanding of most Puritans, glorification at Christ's coming would set the seal upon his experience in this present life and effectively prepare him for the life to come. John Milton drew an argument for the necessity of the second advent from his understanding of glorification. In his *Treatise on Christian Doctrine* Milton contrasts the "imperfect glorification to which believers attain in this life" with the "perfect glorification which is effected in eternity". Of the latter he states, "Its fulfilment and consummation will commence from the period of Christ's second coming to judgment, and the resurrection of the dead".[39] To Milton a believer's glorification is an essential factor in the redemptive purpose of the gospel. It is a process which begins in this life but which is not fully realised until the second advent.

Other Puritan theologians shared similar views about glorification. To Christopher Love, glorification was essentially the future, eternal state of the believer, "that we shall enjoy with Christ, when the world is ended" and which would become a reality when Christ "shall appear to judge the world".[40] Thomas Brooks, writing in *The Glorious Day of the Saints Appearance*, states succinctly, "when He shall appear the second time ... He

---

36 *Ibid.*

37 Richard Sibbes, *An Exposition of the Third Chapter of the Epistle ...to the Philippians* (1639), 225; Love, *Heavens Glory,* 51; Owen, *Hebrews*, 470.

38 Haller, *Rise of Puritanism*, 93.

39 John Milton, 'A Treatise on Christian Doctrine', in *The Works of John Milton* (New York: Columbia University, 1931), vol. XVI, 337.

40 Love, *Heavens Glory*, 4, 6.

shall appear glorious, and so shall all His saints".[41] To Milton, Love and
Brooks alike, the believer's glorification is bound up with the ultimate purpose of the gospel and is contingent upon the second advent.

Those who lived in the seventeenth century saw another aspect to the
completion of Christ's redemptive work. Not only was it essential that
Christ should finish that work for the sake of believers, it was equally essential as far as he was concerned himself. He had begun a work and it
was unthinkable that he should leave it unfinished. Having undertaken the
restoration of man to the fullness of fellowship with God and having at his
first coming achieved reconciliation between God and mankind through the
atoning act on the cross, it was incumbent on him now to bring everything
to a just and satisfactory conclusion. This he would do, and could only do,
at his second coming. Richard Sibbes had been persuaded by this argument,
suggesting that the second advent would bring to perfection not only the
Church and the individual believer, but even Christ himself. "Christ is in
some sort [way] imperfect till the latter day, till his second coming", Sibbes
stated, explaining:

> The mystical body of Christ is His fullness. Christ is our fullness, and
> we are His fullness; now Christ's fullness is made up, when all the
> members of His mystical body are gathered and united together; the
> head and the members make but one natural body ... Christ in this
> sense is not fully glorious therefore till that time.[42]

The emphasis is almost that of a divine obligation, self-imposed by the very
nature of deity, to bring all to a glorious completion, so Sibbes commented
again that Christ must come the second time "to make an end of what he
hath begun".[43]

A further turn to this argument came from the logic of what may be
described as the continuity of Christ's work for mankind. As Haller's soteriological formula suggests, believers in the seventeenth century came to
realise that Christ's identification with humanity was not be seen merely as
one act at a given time in history, but rather as a continuing involvement.
Christopher Love thus saw the second advent, not as an isolated event at the
end of time, but as part of an unceasing process which moved towards the
ultimate complete and harmonious restoration of fellowship between man
and God. This process, having begun at the incarnation, had continued ever
since and included, in succession, Christ's death on the cross, his ascension
to heaven, his priestly ministry in heaven, his second advent, the resurrection of the dead and "the great doctrine of that everlasting communion that

41 Thomas Brooks, *The Glorious Day of the Saints Appearance* (1648), 6.

42 Sibbes, *Brides Longing*, 50–51.

43 Richard Sibbes, 'The Churches Echo', 107 in *Beams of Divine Light* (1639).

the saints shall have with Christ in heaven".[44] More recently theologians have again recognised the essential truth in this assertion, describing the various aspects of Christ's work as 'the Christ event'.

The writings of both Christopher Love and John Durant suggest that if Christ's ascension and priestly ministry could be shown as necessary parts of this continuous work, then it would naturally follow that the second advent, with its outcomes of restoration and restored fellowship, would be seen in a similar light. Therefore Love, before he discusses the second advent, emphasises the importance in the total work of Christ of his mediatorial ministry in heaven. He "'is entered into the very heavens that He might appear before God for us".[45] Love goes on to argue that the intercessory ministry of Christ in heaven is to be regarded as even more essential than his personal presence on earth. Only as Christ fulfils the office of high priest in heaven can he adequately make intercession for all men. This he could not do by being bodily present on earth, "therefore we have great advantage by Christ's going into heaven".[46]

John Durant drew an analogy from the sanctuary services of Old Testament Israel. In the sanctuary ritual it was not sufficient, Durant argued, for the sacrifice merely to be offered. It was also necessary for the blood of the sacrifice to be taken into the tabernacle itself. The significance of the sacrificial system was incomplete until the shed blood had been administered in that way. Durant then continues:

> When Christ died, the sacrifice was slain, the blood was shed, there was more sacrifice to succeed, all was finished in that respect; but yet all was not done till the blood of Christ was carried into the holy places, which was not until Christ went to heaven, to appear as our high priest.[47]

Having thus established the necessity of Christ's high priestly ministry, both Love and Durant then proceed to discuss the doctrine of the second advent in its logical sequence as the consummation of Christ's work for humanity. He had voluntarily undertaken the salvation of mankind in response to the universal problem of sin, and the moral constraint to complete that work was indisputable.

Another dimension was given to the doctrine of Christ's second coming by Richard Baxter: "Fellow Christians, what a day will that be, when we who have been kept prisoners by sin, by sinners, by the grave, shall be fetched out by the Lord Himself"[48] Baxter suggests here a hope which is

---

44 Love, *Penitent Pardoned*, 115.
45 *Ibid.*, 122.
46 *Ibid.*
47 Durant, *Salvation of the Saints*, 48–49.
48 Baxter, *Saints' Rest*, 47.

related to a definitive event in time. It is "by the grave" as well as by sin, that men have been bound and prevented from enjoying the fullness of fellowship with God for which they were created. Thus only as the grave is conquered and its captive released can the believer enter into eternal life in the widest sense. The limitations of mortality must be overcome and when Baxter speaks of an everlasting rest for the saints he speaks of more than the liberation of the soul from the body at death. To be sure, in Baxter's view the saint's rest begins at death when the soul is liberated from the body, but this is only a partial rest. The fullness of the saint's rest is not achieved until after the resurrection when soul and body are united again, and Baxter looks forward confidently to the day when "perfect soul and body together" come into the presence of God.[49] This essential reunification of body and soul will take place at "that most blessed joyful day", that is at the second coming of Christ. In this assurance Baxter can trustingly commit his whole being to the grave:

> O hasten that great resurrection day! When thy command shall go forth, and none shall disobey; when the sea and earth shall yield up their hostages, and all that slept in the graves shall awake, and the dead in Christ shall first arise ... therefore dare I lay down my carcass in the dust, entrusting it, not to a grave, but to thee: and therefore my flesh shall rest in hope, till thou raise it to the possession of everlasting rest.[50]

Through his redemptive act on the cross "Christ bought the whole man, so shall the whole partake of the everlasting benefits of the purchase".[51] In short, the fullness and blessedness of eternal life can only be realised through the resurrection of the body.

This again is Christopher Love's message when he argues that the "main end of Christ's coming again" is the resurrection of the body.[52] It is what John Durant means when he declares "salvation is only yours at the last day".[53] The doctrine of the resurrection of the body is thus very much a question of a believer's personal salvation. "You are already redeemed in your souls", says Durant, "but your bodies are not yet redeemed ... in that day you shall have not only soul-salvation, but body-salvation".[54] The consensus of opinion in Puritan England was that Christian hope lay less in the survival of the soul after death, as widespread as that doctrine undoubtedly was, than in the new creation of the whole being.[55] When David Dickson spoke

---

49   *Ibid.,* 836.

50   *Ibid.,* 837–38.

51   *Ibid.,* 29.

52   Love, *Penitent Pardoned,* 197.

53   Durant, *Salvation of the Saints,* Ep. Ded., sig. A4v.

54   *Ibid.,* 224–25.

55   On the doctrine of conditional immortality in seventeenth-century England, see Bryan W. Ball, *The Soul Sleepers: Christian Mortalism from Wycliffe to Priest-*

of "the full accomplishment of the salvation of the believers" he spoke in terms of Christ's coming and the resurrection of the body.[56] He who had in the first place fashioned man from the dust of the ground and pronounced him perfect, would yet bring forth from the grave a multitude of men and women with bodies not subject to "diseases and distempers, infirmities and deformities, maimedness and monstrous shapes".[57] Here again is glorification, the hope of personal and perfect salvation, and in professing that hope the saints in seventeenth century England were not ashamed.

Consequences of the Advent Hope

The Puritan emphasis on eschatology and the coming of Christ in glory reminded believers that hope was an essential element of Christian faith. As devout and erudite scholars diligently studied Scripture they learned of a hope set before them, of a hope laid up in heaven, of a hope that the body would be resurrected at the last day. They read that Christian believers were begotten unto a lively hope, that they were heirs of the hope of eternal life and that they were to look for the blessed hope, the glorious appearing of Christ. It all spoke of a future consummation in time, and in professing such hope the saints in seventeenth-century England felt one with those of New Testament times.

It was precisely this hope that encouraged believers along the path to sanctification and ultimate glorification. The goal to be reached by travelling this path was godliness, the evidence of fitness for eternity to be spent in the presence of a holy God and holy angels. "If a man hope for this coming of Christ, he will purify himself for it, even as He is pure. He will not appear in his foul clothes, but ... will fit himself as the bride for the coming of the bridegroom", Sibbes declared.[58] Even as the earthly bride did not spend the time of her betrothal dreaming of bliss to come, but in acquiring apparel suitable for the wedding and in the exacting task of preparation for a new life, so both the Church and the individual believer were to spend the remaining time in preparation for Christ's coming and eternity to follow. As Alexander Nisbet pointed out, belief in Christ's second coming "is a special means to make Christians thrive in grace and holiness".[59] Richard Sibbes emphasised that the converse was also true. If the hope of Christ's coming is not seen to work efficaciously in the present life of the believer, "it is but

---

ley (Cambridge: James Clarke, 2008) and chapter 15 of this volume.

56 David Dickson, *A Short Explanation of Hebrews* (Aberdeen, 1635), 193.

57 Bolton, *Four Last Things,* 129.

58 Sibbes, *Brides Longing,* 73–74.

59 Alexander Nisbet, *A Brief Exposition of ... St Peter* (1658), 330.

a false conceit and lying fancy".[60] Sibbes also notes the positive effect of Christian hope:

> If we say this truly, come Lord Jesus, undoubtedly it will have an influence into our lives. It will stir up all graces in the soul; as faith, to lay hold upon it; hope, to expect it; love, to embrace it; patience, to endure anything for it; heavenly mindedness, to fit and prepare us for it.[61]

True Christians, in Ussher's words, "always live in expectation of the Lord Jesus in the clouds", with oil in their lamps and "prepared for His coming".[62]

All this recaptures both the letter and the spirit of New Testament eschatological hope. Thomas Goodwin is one of many seventeenth century writers who recognised that the Church in the New Testament lived constantly in the expectation of an early fulfilment of Christ's promise to return. The early Church "had that day in their eye", they "walked in view of it", and consequently they were "set forth as a pattern" to succeeding generations.[63] Thus, in Goodwin's view, the whole gamut of eschatological doctrine — belief in Christ's coming, the interpretation of apocalyptic prophecy, the computation of biblical chronology, an understanding of the age, the future of the papacy, the millennium and the kingdom, all, in the last analysis, were to be measured by one criterion. "The only use of knowing them", declared Goodwin, is "to prepare for them".[64] John Durant likewise exhorted "it is your work and wisdom, to cleanse yourselves from all filth, and to perfect holiness in a filial fear of God".[65]

While Puritan believers looked forward to a definitive point in time for the ultimate realisation of their hopes, they also understood that the future emerged from the present. Eschatological hope was not posited solely on an isolated event at the end of time, but rather in the culmination of a divine, age-long process. For the world, this process had been in operation from the beginning of history; for the individual it had begun with the inward working of divine grace at conversion. There was no future, no hope, for those who in the present lived only for the present. The hope associated with the last events led both Church and individual saint towards a future final event only along the path of present and total commitment.

Christopher Love preached ten sermons on the coming of Christ and the glory of the future life from Colossians 3:4, all of them based on the three propositions: that Christ is the life of the believer now, that Christ will ap-

---

60 Sibbes, *Brides Longing,* 73–74.

61 *Ibid.,* 79.

62 Ussher, *Body of Divinitie,* 451.

63 Thomas Goodwin, *The Works of Thomas Goodwin, D.D.,* 5 Vols. 1681–1704, vol. V, pt. II, 25.

64 *Ibid.,* vol. II, pt. I, 190.

65 Durant, *Salvation of the Saints,* Ep. Ded., sig. A5r.

pear in glory at the end of time, and that when he does appear the saints will appear in glory with him. Love's argument is that the saints will appear with Christ in glory at the end only as his holy life is manifest in them now.[66] Richard Sibbes also emphasised the relationship between the believer's present life and the future, using the analogy of the marriage of the bride with the heavenly bridegroom at the end of time. Before this marriage can be finally ratified there is to be a threefold union of Christ with his Church, a union of nature, a union of grace and a union of glory. To Sibbes, the union of nature came through the incarnation when Christ took upon himself human nature. The union of grace comes through the effective outworking of the gospel in human experience, when believers partake of the divine nature. The union of glory will be at the end when the Church, duly prepared and perfected, will be in heaven, in the presence of Christ.[67] The marriage cannot be consummated until this union of glory occurs, but this union itself is not possible without either those of nature or grace. The future, either of church or of individual believer, cannot be isolated from the present. It is part of it, the culmination in time of a process in history and in life.

The reality of this hope in the personal experience of the individual believer finds expression in many ways in the writings of the Puritan Adventists. Richard Sibbes, for instance, sees it as an effective antidote to sin:

> The soul is never in such a tune, as when the thoughts of those glorious times have raised the affections to the highest pitch ... so long as it is so affected, it cannot sin ... so long then, as we keep our hearts in a blessed frame of faith, and in a love of the appearing of Christ, they are impregnable.[68]

To Thomas Goodwin, hope is a barrier against the machinations of Satan. "The devil, the shorter his time is, the more he rages and ... seeing these are the last days ... the more should we endeavour to do God service".[69] To Thomas Brooks, it is a challenge to prepare the whole man for eternity. "Those that have hopes to reign with Christ in glory, that have set their hearts on that pure and blissful state ... they will purify both their insides, and their outsides, both body and soul".[70] It is an incentive to duty and obedience.[71] It is the spring of brotherly love. [72] It is a stimulus to work and to pray for others.[73] It is the root of happiness and contentment in the present

---

66   Love, *Heavens Glory,* 4–5.
67   Sibbes, *Beams of Divine Light,* 102.
68   Sibbes, *Brides Longing,* 105–106.
69   Goodwin, *Works,* vol. I, pt. III, 133.
70   Thomas Brooks, *Heaven on Earth* (1654), 540.
71   Love, *Heavens Glory,* 47.
72   Nathaniel Holmes, *The Resurrection Revealed* (1653), 542.
73   Sibbes, *Philippians,* 230.

life.[74] There is, in short, no aspect of Christian life and doctrine that is not quickened and ennobled by the influence of a positive eschatological hope.

This theology of hope is an effective agent which breaks down the barrier between present and future by bringing the future into the present in a form which is accessible to every aspiring believer. In the language of the time, it is eloquently summarised by Thomas Brooks in the introduction to his *Heaven on Earth*, when he says "Holiness is the very marrow of religion",

> Holiness is God stamped upon the soul; it is Christ formed in the heart; it is our light, our life, our beauty, our glory, our joy, our crown, our heaven, our all. The holy soul is happy in life, and blessed in death, and shall be transcendentally glorious in the morning of the resurrection, when Christ shall say, 'Lo, here am I, and my holy ones, who are my joy; lo, here am I, and my holy ones, who are my crown; and therefore, upon the heads of these holy ones will I set an immortal crown'. Even so, Amen, Lord Jesus.[75]

It is difficult to avoid the conclusion that the advent hope was an indispensable factor, perhaps even the chief factor, in the vitality and spirituality which characterised both the Church and the individual believer in the seventeenth century.

We return again to Richard Sibbes to note the immediate significance of eschatological hope in the life of the believer and in the life of the Church. The fundamental unity of the believer with Christ and the consequential unity of believer with believer within the Church were both seen in direct relationship to a positive belief in the coming of Christ. Sibbes had repeatedly stressed the point: "the contracted spouse must needs say 'Amen' to the marriage day", "it is the disposition of a gracious heart, to desire the glorious coming of Christ Jesus", and "the more we have of Christ in us, the more shall we desire His coming to us".[76] The implications of all this must be understood, Sibbes argues:

> Let us labour to have all the corners of the heart filled up with the spirit of Christ: our understandings with knowledge; our affections with love and delight; and our wills with obedience. The Scripture calls it, being filled with all the fullness of God ... the more we enter into the kingdom of heaven by growth in grace here, the fitter shall we be for it and the more shall we desire it.[77]

To Sibbes, as to a multitude of others, fellowship with Christ in glory was measurably dependent on fellowship with Christ in grace. The relationship was unalterable but not unattainable, and belief in the second advent effectually contributed to the believer's present spiritual condition.

---

74 Taylor, *Titus*, 492.
75 Brooks, *Heaven on Earth*, 606–07.
76 Sibbes, *Brides Longing*, 15, 48, 84.
77 *Ibid.*, 84–85.

Yet the goal of Christian unity was more than a personal relationship between Christ and the individual believer which would culminate at Christ's
coming. The entire Church was to draw a blessing from the second advent
hope, a blessing related to the unity of believer with believer, and it was at
this very point that Sibbes found cause for concern. In the preface to his
Glorious Feast of the Gospel he regrets that many have apparently lost this
necessary relationship: "Alas, Christians have lost much of their communion with Christ and his saints".[78] The very experience upon which the future
glory of both Church and believer rested was being eroded and the reason
was clear: "They have woefully disputed away, and dispirited the life of
religion and the power of godliness into dry and sapless controversies about
government of Church and State".[79] Matters of a secondary consequence
have come to claim the attention of many, and Sibbes' point of concern is
apparent. Let the message of the Church take precedence over its machinery.
Let believers recapture a unity with Christ and with each other through a
rediscovery of essentials.

From this premise, Sibbes went on to set forth the doctrine of the second
advent as an integral part of the total New Testament message. Other influential preachers in the seventeenth century voiced similar sentiments. Edmund Calamy and Stephen Marshall, both moderate and esteemed, deplored
the divisions which had appeared in church and kingdom and Marshall described the multiplicity of sects into which the church had been divided as
an "epidemical disease ... pleasing to Satan".[80] The divisions within the
Church were clearly an obstacle to the realisation of the divine purpose and
while some undoubtedly expected the desired unity to be realised through
acts of parliament and the establishment of a state Church, there were many
whose discernment was more far-reaching. William Strong's eschatological hope of "perfect and sweet communion with one another" is contingent
upon the communion of each individual believer with God, in Christ.[81] The
cure for division, according to the moderator of the Westminster Assembly,
lay in a universal acceptance and an individual application of the essentials
of the Christian faith and the last word thus belongs to Jeremiah Whittaker:

> The way to cure the bleeding distempers of Christendom is for all men
> to endeavour to get inward persuasions answerable to their outward
> professions, for as these main principles are more or less believed, so is
> the heart and life of men better or worse ordered. When the soul is once
> fully persuaded that Christ is God, that He is the true Messiah, that

---

78 Richard Sibbes, *The Glorious Feast of the Gospel* (1650), Preface.

79 *Ibid.*

80 Stephen Marshall, *A Sermon ... The Unity of the Saints with Christ* (1653),
21, 37.

81 William Strong, *The Trust and Account of a Steward* (1647), 29.

there is another life besides this, that the Lord Christ is ready to come
to judgement and His reward is with Him, then the soul begins to seek
and beg an interest in Christ, to flee from wrath to come, to assure the
hopes of heaven, whilst we are on earth. And this hope, when once truly
attained, carries the soul far above the comforts of life, and beyond the
fears of death.[82]

There is more here than mere concern with ecclesiastical politics or Church
structure, more than the unrealistic ambitions of a radical millenarian minority. Hope, the future, Christ's coming, eternal life — these, in the context of
a complete Christocentric gospel and in the experience of each believer, are
the basis of a valid ecumenism, the assurance of an ultimate triumph. Many
in the seventeenth century died in that hope and counted it a privilege to do
so. They had not received the promises, but with the eye of faith had seen
them afar off, and the Church in Puritan England was stronger for the advent
hope it cherished and for its effect on the lives of those who embraced it.

---

82   Jeremiah Whitaker, *The Christian's Hope Triumphing* (1645), Ep. Ded.

15. Sixteenth-Century Continental Conditionalists[1]

Bryan W. Ball

Note: In its original setting in *The Soul Sleepers* this chapter provided a Continental context for the development of mortalist thought in England during the sixteenth and seventeenth centuries. Those who held mortalist views rejected traditional belief in the soul's separate existence and innate immortality. They have been variously known as mortalists, conditionalists, or more particularly in their own day, as soul sleepers. They were mortalists because, it was said, they believed in the death of the soul as well as the body, although many of them, notably in the early years of the Reformation, did not quite go that far. They were conditionalists because they held that immortality derived from the work of Christ, personal faith in him, and the resurrection at the last day, and soul sleepers because they considered that death was a sleep during which the soul was non-existent or, in the less extreme view, unconscious though still alive.

Both in Europe and later in England as the Reformation developed, two distinct forms of Christian mortalism developed, known since as psychopannychism and thnetopsychism. Psychopannychists believed in a separate, immaterial soul in common with those who held the traditional view of the soul's immortality, but maintained contrary to them that after death the soul slept until the resurrection. Thnetopsychists did not believe in the soul so defined, maintaining instead that the soul was best understood as the mind, or more usually as the whole person,

---

1 First published as ch. 1 in Bryan W. Ball, *The Soul Sleepers: Christian Mortalism from Wycliffe to Priestley* (Cambridge: James Clarke, 2008), and reprinted here by permission of James Clarke & Co, Cambridge, UK, with a new title and a revised introduction containing material from the original Introduction to *The Soul Sleepers*.

Abbreviations used in the references:

CFF L. E. Froom, *The Conditionalist Faith of our Fathers* (Washington, DC: Review & Herald, 1965)

CM N. T. Burns, *Christian Mortalism from Tyndale to Milton* (Cambridge, MA: Harvard, 1972)

LW Martin Luther, *Luther's Works* (St. Louis, MO: Concordia, 1958–86)

ME *The Mennonite Encyclopedia* (Scottdale, PA: Mennonite, 1955–90)

NCE *The New Catholic Encyclopedia*, 2nd edn, 2003

ODCC *The Oxford Dictionary of the Christian Church* 3rd edn, 1997

RR G. H. Williams, *The Radical Reformation* (3rd edn, Kirksville, MO: 1992)

Original English works were published in London unless otherwise indicated.

which existed as the result of the union of breath and body. The soul, therefore, died or 'slept', metaphorically, between death and the resurrection, since the union of breath and body then no longer existed. While both forms of the mortalist 'heresy' were anathema to the majority of the mainstream Reformers, thnetopsychism was clearly more deviant from traditional orthodoxy. Mortalism in both forms appeared early in both the Continental and English Reformation and we will meet them frequently as this chapter unfolds.

The extent to which developing post-medieval doctrine in England was influenced by contemporary European thought remains largely an unresolved question. It is clear that much Reformation and post-Reformation English theology emerged from the independent thinking of strong English minds open to the catalytic and powerful texts of Scripture recently made available in the original languages and in the vernacular, and interpreted against the prevailing moods and conditions. On the other hand, the presence in England of individuals and congregations fleeing from repression on the Continent, and an awareness of Continental ideas cannot be overlooked. The two-way flow of English and Continental believers across the Channel from the earliest days of the Reformation inevitably enhanced the accessibility and credibility of ideas current on the Continent. A. G. Dickens referred to "substantial examples of transition from Lollardy to Lutheranism" in London during the early 1500s, and more recently Alister McGrath noted the influence of Luther on Tyndale's New Testament.[2] Many of the influential English mortalists of the sixteenth and seventeenth centuries had European contacts of one kind or another which, in terms of the exchange of ideas, were mutually beneficial. The least that can be said is that English beliefs, including mortalism, in the Reformation and immediate post-Reformation era developed with some understanding of what was happening in Europe.

***

In 1597 John Payne, an English refugee in Haarlem, warned against the mortalist beliefs of Dutch Anabaptists,[3] and in 1646 Friedrich Spanheim alerted his English readers to the deviant views of German Anabaptists who taught that the souls of the dead "sleep with their bodies until the last day … deprived of all knowledge, both intellectual and sensitive".[4] In 1653 John Biddle translated into English Joachim Stegmann's *Brevis Disquisitio* (1633) which, among other concerns, queried "whether the dead do properly live", asserting that the traditional affirmative answer constituted "the grounds of the greatest errors among the Papists".[5] In reality, however, it

---

2 A. G. Dickens, *The English Reformation* (London: Batsford, 1964), 33; Alister McGrath, *In The Beginning: The Story of the King James Bible* (London: Hodder & Stoughton, 2001), 72–3.

3 [John Payne], *Royall Exchange* (Haarlem, 1597), 19, 22.

4 Friedrich Spanheim, *Englands Warning by Germanies Woe* (1646), 36.

5 John Biddle (tr.), *Brevis Disquisitio; or, A Brief Enquiry Touching a Better Way Then Is commonly made use of, to refute Papists, and reduce Protestants to certainty and Unity in Religion* (1653), 26. See also *CFF*, II, 177.

was not only Anabaptist or Continental Socinianism that may have helped English mortalism on its way. The psychopannychism of the German reformers Luther and Carlstadt gave Continental mortalism an early degree of respectability which it's later and less respectable associations with Anabaptists and other radicals could never wholly take away. It is, therefore, to Luther and Carlstadt and their rejection of long-standing medieval doctrines which had undergirded so many of the abuses germinal to the Reformation, that we will turn first. But before that, it will be helpful to note developments concerning the soul's immortality in the years preceding the Reformation.

Consolidation of the Traditional Doctrine

It is easily forgotten that the doctrine of the immortality of the soul had appeared relatively late in the development of traditional Catholic theology.[6] Two events in particular may be said to have precipitated a more definitive formulation of the medieval belief in the soul's immortality and hence the later but consequent appearance of an alternative mortalist eschatology. These events were outcomes of the Council of Florence, 1438–45, and the Fifth Lateran Council, 1512–17, relating to the developing doctrines of purgatory and the immortality of the soul. Even before that, however, there had been hints of uncertainty over the nature of the soul and its state after death from within the higher echelons of the Church itself, which may have reflected things to come as well as past doubts and ambiguities.

In 1312 the Council of Vienne, reacting to continued philosophical assertions in some academic circles of the soul's mortality, denounced as heretical and "inimical to the truth of the Catholic faith" certain ideas which appeared to question the superiority of the soul over the body and the possibility of its independent existence.[7] John XXII, the first of the Avignon popes, for some years held the view that the departed souls of the righteous dead do not see God until after the last judgment.[8] He is said to have written a work on this theme prior to his election to the papal throne in 1316. After becoming Pope he continued to advance these ideas in sermons as late as 1332,[9] arousing considerable opposition, particularly from the theology faculty at the University of Paris, to the point that he was actually accused of heresy. Under pressure from his theological advisers to conform, he eventually withdrew

6   Philippe Aries notes that the concept of an immortal soul, long cultivated in clerical circles, began to spread "from the eleventh to the seventeenth century, until it gained almost universal acceptance", Philippe Aries, *The Hour of Our Death* (New York: OUP, 1981), 606.

7   G. H. Tavard, *The Starting Point of Calvin's Theology* (Grand Rapids, MI & Cambridge, UK: 2000), 22–3.

8   *ODCC, s.v.* John XXII, states that he maintained this opinion until his death.

9   Tavard, *Calvin's Theology*, 18.

his divergent views in favour of the more orthodox Catholic position, declaring that his earlier beliefs had been merely a personal opinion.[10] Clearly this was not the mortalism of the Reformation era, but it is difficult to agree entirely with Burns here that the earlier position of John XXII "does not even approach psychopannychism"[11] since it shared one of psychopannychism's major tenets, denial of heavenly glory until after the last judgement.

In 1439 the Council of Florence clarified and declared canonical a belief which had already existed for some time, the doctrine of purgatory, with its essential presupposition that the souls of the dead are conscious and "capable of pain or joy even prior to the resurrection of their bodies",[12] and its corollary that prayers for the dead are valuable and necessary. Few doctrines of the medieval church provoked such widespread opposition from the early Reformers and those who followed them than this idea of an intermediate state between death and a future life where those who had died would undergo purification and punishment prior to the resurrection and the last judgement. The abuses deriving from belief in purgatory were to become one of the major concerns of Luther's Ninety-Five Theses, with his open attack on the sale of indulgences and the "audacious" claim that souls could be released from purgatory thereby. Luther would ultimately conclude that the underlying doctrine of the soul's substantiality and immortality was "a monstrous opinion" emanating from Rome's "dunghill of decretals".[13]

Meanwhile the consolidation of purgatory as a major tenet of the Western Church by the Council of Florence had provided the impetus for a renewed focus on the question of human existence with particular emphasis on the nature of the soul. Interest in such philosophical and theological matters was naturally strong in the universities, where in Italy the discussion came to centre on Aristotelian and Platonic views. At the University of Padua in 1509 it was propounded that Aristotle had taught the mortality of the soul.[14] Pietro Pomponazzi, successively professor at Padua, Ferrara and Bologna, eventually articulated his interpretation of the Aristotelian view in his *On the Immortality of the Soul* (1516) and *Apologia* (1517), maintaining that it was possible to conclude from reason not only that the soul was individual and transient, but that it was also mortal. In so doing, Pomponazzi also asserted that his philosophical conclusions, mere "deductions of hu-

---

10　*NCE*, VII, 932, where it is claimed that John XXII's views "threatened the theological foundation of the papacy".

11　*CM*, 152.

12　*NCE*, V, 770; *RR*, 65.

13　*CFF*, II, 73; R. H. Bainton, *Here I Stand, A Life of Martin Luther* (New York: Mentor,1950), 54; E. G. Rupp and B. Drewery, *Martin Luther* (London: Arnold, 1970), 19–25.

14　*RR*, 65. See also Tavard, *Calvin's Theology*, 28–30.

man reason", were transcended by the divine revelation of a resurrection to come and needed to cause no offense.[15] Girolamo Cardano of Milan shared Pomponazzi's doubts about the soul, if not his reluctance to cause offence. Cardano's *De Animi Immortalitate* (1545) began by considering "whether human souls are eternal and divine or whether they perish with the body", and proposed fifty-four reasons for concluding that the soul was not immortal.[16]

Any hopes that Pomponazzi may have had of avoiding conflict were clearly naive. The ecclesiastical hierarchy had, in fact, already reacted against the new ideas which had been emanating from Padua for some years. In 1513 the Fifth Lateran Council dealt with the problem caused by the proposition that the soul was mortal, denouncing it as a "very pernicious error" and re-asserting that each individually created soul is "truly, and of itself... immortal" and capable of existence after death prior to the resurrection. Williams notes that "this importation of *natural* theology into Catholic dogma" was in actual fact "much closer to Platonic philosophy than to the Bible"[17], and then comments more fully on the pronouncement of the Fifth Lateran Council:

> The natural immortality of the soul had become so integral a part of the massive penitential and liturgical structure of Catholic moral theology that the philosophical threat to it moved Leo X, in the first year of his pontificate, to condemn in 1513, at the eighth session of the Fifth Lateran Council, the philosophical proofs and disproofs of immortality in the universities ... and academic circles ... Leo in council asserted that the soul is naturally immortal and, as the substantial form of the body, is susceptible both of the pains of hell and purgatory, and the bliss of paradise.[18]

Those who were soon to deny the soul's immortality, both on the Continent and in England, could never doubt the importance of this doctrine to the entire structure of Roman theology or, perhaps, of the consequences which such denial might incur.

---

15 *ODCC,*. s.v. Pietro Pomponazzi; *RR*, 66. A more detailed account of Pomponazzi's theology of the soul can be found in Don Cameron Allen, *Doubt's Boundless Sea* (Baltimore: John Hopkins,1964), 29–45. Allen proposes that it was Pomponazzi who "revived the Athenian disease of doubt".

16 Allen, *Doubt's Boundless Sea*, 56. On Cardano, see Allen, 45–58.

17 *RR, 66*. The much revised entry on 'soul' in the third edition of *ODCC* claims that "there is practically no specific teaching on the subject in the Bible", stating that in the post-Nicene era "a modified Platonic view" of the soul gained acceptance.

18 *RR*, 66–7. The 'Apostolici regiminis', the document by which the Council's official judgment was promulgated, re-asserted the immortality of the soul as necessary dogma. See also *NCE*, I, 595.

Luther and Carlstadt

Luther's views on the state of the soul after death, arising in large part from his respect for biblical authority over that of the Church, began to appear in his response to Leo X's Bull of 1520, *Exsurge Domine*, which re-affirmed papal endorsement of the now established doctrine. In his defense of the propositions he had earlier put forward and which Leo's Bull had condemned, Luther argued that the church's official doctrine of the soul as a spiritual but substantial substance and the "form" of the human body, was only a papal opinion.[19] While this was clearly not yet an outright expression of the mortalism he was shortly to declare, it nevertheless demonstrated his profound unease with the prevailing doctrine. This fundamental divergence over the soul and its condition after death would, with the exception of Carlstadt, set him apart from the other major Continental Reformers. Indeed, Luther and Carlstadt alone of all the early Reformers seem to have entertained the doctrine of soul sleep, while Calvin, Bullinger and Zwingli were all advocates of the traditional view and strongly opposed any alternative. Luther's essential mortalism has been questioned, but the evidence seems indisputable that, with occasional lapses towards an inherited medieval view, he held a psychopannychist position for most of his life following his break with Rome.[20]

Certainly this was the understanding of the later Anglican mortalist, Francis Blackburne, who added to his historical survey of mortalism, first published in 1765[21], an appendix entitled *An Inquiry into the sentiments of Martin Luther concerning the state of the Soul between Death and the Resurrection.* Blackburne maintained that Luther had been incorrectly accused of thnetopsychism by Cardinal du Perron, but also noted a letter from Luther to Amsdorf in 1522, commenting that in it Luther appeared "much inclined to believe that the souls of the just sleep to the day of judgement, without knowing where they are".[22] This earliest known indication of mortalism in Luther's thought appears to confirm a psychopannychist position as opposed

---

19 *Ibid.,* 197.

20 *CFF*, II, 76. Williams maintains that Luther's occasional ambivalence had a significant outcome: "Little by little within Lutheranism the doctrine of the sleep of the soul was replaced by the idea of a natural immortality", *RR*, 197.

21 Francis Blackburne, *A Short Historical View of the Controversy Concerning An Intermediate State and The Separate Existence of the Soul Between Death and the General Resurrection* (1765). An expanded second edition appeared in 1772 with the same title but for the word *Short*. Unless otherwise stated the 1772 edition is cited in this study. The appendix remained the same in both editions.

22 Francis Blackburne, *An Historical View of the Controversy Concerning an Intermediate State and the Separate Existence of the Soul Between Death and the General Resurrection* (2nd edn., 1772), 344, 348.

to the thnetopsychism which du Perron had mistakenly seen and which manifested itself shortly thereafter in the thinking of other Continental mortalists. Blackburne was convinced that Luther remained a psychopannychist to his dying day, using the doctrine to refute medieval teachings of purgatory and the invocation of saints in his definitive struggle with the papacy.[23]

But Luther must be allowed to speak for himself. When he does so, two things are readily apparent: the strength of his convinced psychopannychism, and the distinction between it and the thnetopsychism which was soon to appear elsewhere on the Continent and which would find ready and articulate advocates in radical circles, notably among the Italian Evangelical Rationalists, and which would later flower across the Channel as the mature expression of English mortalist thought. Although it has largely been ignored since, Luther's psychopannychism was recognised and challenged in its own day. In England, Sir Thomas More responded to it in his well-known *Dialogue* with Tyndale in 1529[24], thereby providing Tyndale with the opportunity of defending Luther and at the same time airing his own conclusions. We must, however, first note Luther's own views. Tyndale's opinions and the subsequent and more widespread thnetopsychism of the radical Continental reformers will be considered later.

Despite moments of hesitation and occasional ambiguities, even contradictions, Luther's psychopannychism cannot for a moment be seriously doubted. It is expressed too frequently and too emphatically. Indeed, it is hard to find anywhere a more concerned or enthusiastic spokesman for psychopannychism, either on the Continent or in England, throughout the Reformation and immediate post-Reformation periods. All the essentials of mortalism as interpreted in psychopannychism can be found in Luther's writings, and most of them occur repeatedly: the separate existence of the soul, its unconscious sleep after death, its exclusion from heavenly bliss until the resurrection, and the vital importance of the resurrection of the body and the re-unification of body and soul at the last day as the way to immortality and eternal life. The meeting point between Luther's psychopannychism and the more developed thnetopsychism is their shared emphasis on death as an unconscious sleep[25] and the necessity of the resurrection. In 1526 in his lectures on Ecclesiastes Luther noted that the dead are "completely asleep" and do not "feel anything at all". "They lie there not counting days or years; but when they are raised, it will seem to them that they have only slept for

---

23 *Ibid.*, 14, 15.

24 Generally known as *The Dialogue Concerning Tyndale*, although an introductory note to the 1529 edition begins with the words "A Dialogue concernynge heresyes and matters of religion".

25 Psychopannychism's literal sleep of the soul as opposed to thnetopsychism's figurative use of the term has been noted previously. It is an important distinction.

a moment".[26] Commenting on Ecclesiastes 9:5 Luther said that he knew
of no more powerful passage in Scripture showing that the dead are asleep
and unconscious. Verse 10 was another text proving "that the dead do not
feel anything", since they are "completely asleep".[27] In his commentary on
I Corinthians 15 he argues that what was prior to Christ's resurrection "true
and eternal death" is now no longer death: "It has become merely a sleep".
And for Christ "it is but a night before He rouses us from sleep".[28] Again,
the saints who died in faith "died in such a manner that after they had been
called away from the troubles and hardships of this life, they entered their
chamber, slept there, and rested in peace".[29] For Luther, death is always a
sleep, a time of rest and waiting.

The soul, however, is a separate entity which leaves the body at death.
Luther says, "After death the soul enters its chamber and is at peace; and
while it sleeps, it is not aware of its sleep".[30] In the lectures on Psalms, he
states "The crossing of Jordan is the departure of the soul from the body".[31]
Of the Old Testament patriarchs, notably Abraham, Isaac and Jacob, Luther
says that each was "gathered to his people", to rest, to sleep, to await "resurrection and the future life"[32]. The same is true of all who thus sleep, "There
is no doubt that those who have been gathered to their people are resting...
There is a place for the elect where they all rest...The human soul sleeps
with all senses buried, and our bed is like a sepulchre ...they rest in peace".[33]
Luther holds that we cannot now know the exact nature of the intermediate
state, but is sure that the disembodied soul is "freed from the workhouse
of the body".[34] Moreover, "it is sufficient for us to know that the saints in
the Old Testament who died in faith in the Christ who was to come and the
godly in the New Testament who died in faith in the Christ who has been
revealed" are safe in the hands of God, "gathered to their people".[35] But "we
do not know what that place is, or what kind of place it is".[36] So for Luther
both body and soul rest after death, the body in the grave and the soul, still
alive but asleep, in some appointed but undefined place, to await the last day.

---

26 "Notes on Ecclesiastes", in *LW*, 15 (1972), 150.
27 *Ibid.*, 147.
28 "Commentary on I Corinthians 15", *LW*, 28 (1973), 109–10.
29 "Lectures on Genesis, Chapters 21–25", *LW*, 4(1964), 312–13.
30 *Ibid.*, 313.
31 "First Lectures on the Psalms 1–75", *LW*, 10(1974), 327.
32 "Lectures on Genesis 21–25", *LW*, 4, 309–10.
33 "Lectures on Genesis, Chapters 45–50", *LW*, 8(1966), 317–18.
34 "Lectures on Genesis 21–25", *LW*, 4, 329.
35 "Lectures on Genesis 45–50", *LW*, 8, 317.
36 *Ibid.*

Despite the moments of doubt, Luther's psychopannychism appears to have been well settled in the years leading up to his death in 1546. In his massive commentary on Genesis, published in 1544, he states more fully, yet still with a degree of mystery, that after death the soul "enters its chamber and is at peace" and

> while it sleeps it is not aware of its sleep. Nevertheless, God preserves the waking soul. Thus God is able to awaken Elijah, Moses, etc., and so to control them that they live. But how? We do not know. The resemblance to physical sleep – namely that God declares that there is sleep, rest, and peace – is enough. He who sleeps a natural sleep has no knowledge of the things that are happening in his neighbour's house. Nevertheless, he is alive, even though ... he feels nothing in his sleep."[37]

Yet we know that the sleeping dead will live again and, at least to an extent, how it will happen:

> And so the Christians who lie in the ground are no longer called dead, but sleepers, people who will surely also arise again. For when we say that people are asleep, we refer to those who are lying down but will wake up and rise again, not those who are lying down bereft of all hope of rising again. Of the latter we do not say that they are sleeping but that they are inanimate corpses. Therefore by that very word "asleep" Scripture indicates the future resurrection".[38]

> For since we call it [death] a sleep, we know that we shall not remain in it, but be again awakened and live, and that the time during which we sleep, shall seem no longer than if we had just fallen asleep. Hence, we shall censure ourselves that we were surprised or alarmed at such a sleep in the hour of death, and suddenly come alive out of the grave and from decomposition, and entirely well, fresh, with a pure, clear, glorified life, meet our Lord and Saviour Jesus Christ in the clouds ...[39]

The resurrection at the last day will terminate the sleep of death and bring to reality eternal life and, through the re-unification of soul and body, the fulness of immortality for those who believe. In fact, Luther goes as far as to say of the resurrection that it is "The chief article of Christian doctrine".[40] So Francis Blackburne was undoubtedly correct in saying that Luther's "sleeping man was conscious of nothing", and in concluding that

---

37   "Lectures on Genesis 21–25", *LW*, 4, 313.

38   "Commentary on I Corinthians 15", *LW*, 28, 110.

39   Luther, "Sermon, the Twenty-fourth Sunday after Trinity", cited in H. T. Kerr, ed., *A Compend of Luther's Theology* (Philadelphia: Westminster, 1943), 242.

40   "Commentary on I Corinthians 15", *LW*, 28, 94. More than one hundred and twenty-five references to death as a sleep and the unconscious state of the dead are said to be found in Luther's writings. The count is based on an analysis in J. G. Walch (ed), *Martin Luther's Sammtlichte Schriften* (1904).

Luther held to "total suspension of thought and consciousness during the interval between death and the resurrection".[41]

Luther found a ready ally for his psychopannychism in Andreas Carlstadt,[42] his unpredictable co-labourer in the German Reformation. The psychopannychism of both Luther and Carlstadt was closely bound up with a strong biblical eschatology, indicating perhaps that a more consistent interpretation of the biblical text as a whole confirmed belief in the sleep of the soul. This was undoubtedly true of Luther. In Carlstadt's case, however, there was possibly more. His psychopannychism may have been generated, in part at least, while a student at Sienna, 1516–17, through contact with the Paduan challenge to the doctrine of immortality, and may therefore have been tinged with the philosophical overtones which characterised Padua's revised Aristotelianism and which, as we have seen, incurred the indignation of the Fifth Lateran Council.[43] Also, Carlstadt's relationship with the radicals of the Reformation was stronger than Luther's, and here again, notably in the case of the Evangelical Rationalists, for whom the immortality of the soul was inconsonant with reason, mortalism was a common denominator.

Like Luther, however, Carlstadt found that psychopannychism was an effective weapon with which to attack purgatory and the elaborate system of indulgences which had grown up around it, together with the pivotal Roman doctrine of the Mass. Carlstadt's psychopannychism was first articulated in the context of his radical reinterpretation of the Mass as commemorative rather than sacramental, based on a more literal biblical foundation.[44] It is also probable that the depiction of purgatory as spiritually purgative in the present rather than as punitive in the future, as advocated in a contemporary Wittenberg publication,[45] helped to clarify Carlstadt's convictions regarding the sleep of the soul. In any event, by 1523 Carlstadt had published in favour of psychopannychism, although it is only fair to say that he does not appear to have given it as much emphasis as did Luther. It should also be said that Carlstadt's understanding of soul sleep, at least at this point, appears to have been just that, i.e. psychosomnolence, rather than the more radical thnetopsychism of some of his contemporaries.[46] Advocates of psychopannychism in Germany at the same period include Gerhard Westerburg in Wittenberg and Frankfurt, and the more radical Augustine Bader, c.1530.[47] Wes-

---

41   Blackburne, *Historical View,* 355, 359.

42   Carlstadt is unaccountably missing from Froom's *Conditionalist Faith of our Fathers.*

43   *RR* (1st edn.,1962), 104.

44   *ME,* I (1955), 519–20; *RR,* 110–20, 196.

45   Wessel Gansfort, *Farrago Rerum Theologicarum* (Wittenburg, 1522).

46   *RR,* 197.

47   *Ibid.,* 196–8, 298.

terberg, a colleague of Carlstadt, may have derived his mortalist eschatology from Carlstadt's 1523 publication. Both were exiled from Saxony in 1524, and in 1526 Westerberg was condemned for his teachings on purgatory and the sleep of the soul.[48]   With Westerberg, of course, we have already moved into the ranks of the radicals.

The Continental Radicals

Before we turn to Calvin and his crucial participation in the mortalist debate, it is necessary to trace in more detail the position of the radicals of the Continental Reformation. Opposed vehemently by Calvin,[49] their well-attested opposition to the doctrine of innate immortality may ultimately have contributed more to the continuity of mortalism as a legitimate Christian hope, both on the Continent and in England, than did either Luther or Carlstadt. Williams, in his comprehensive analysis of the radical Reformation, maintains that mortalism in its various forms was a crucial element in the theology of many radicals, equally as important to their identity as anti-Trinitarianism or a revised soteriology. He distinguishes between three types of radicals: Anabaptists, Spiritualists, and Evangelical Rationalists,[50] believing that "some" of the Spiritualists, "many" of the Anabaptists, and "almost all" the Evangelical Rationalists adhered to the doctrine of "the sleep or death of the soul prior to the resurrection".[51] This, as we have previously noted, Williams rather loosely terms "psychopannychism", and care is sometimes needed in determining whether at a given point he means psychopannychism or thnetopsychism. Mortalism in either of its two more recognisable forms, psychopannychism, more precisely defined as psychosomnolence, or thnetopsychism was "a recurrent feature of the Radical Reformation".[52] Tavard argues that by the time Calvin wrote the first draft of the *Psychopan-*

---

48   *ME*, IV(1959), 930–1; *RR*, 198.

49   Notably in his *Psychopannychia* (Geneva, 1545), which was first published in Strassburg in 1542 with the title *De statu animarum post mortem liber, quo asseritur Vivere apud Christum non dormire animos sanctos, qui in fide Christi decedunt:Assertio,* but which was almost certainly first composed in 1534, Willem Balke, *Calvin and the Anabaptist Radicals* (tr. William Heynen, Grand Rapids, MI: Eerdmans, 1981), 26. Heynen's translation reads "Dissertation about the state of souls after death, proving that the saints who died in faith in Christ now live with Christ and are not asleep as far as their souls are concerned".

50   The Spiritualists should not be confused with those called by the same name who arose in the nineteenth century. Those of the sixteenth century emphasised the inner, contemplative life as essential to authentic Christian faith. Williams defines the Evangelical Rationalists as "a fusion of Italian humanism or critical rationalism with selected ingredients of ...Anabaptism and visionary Spiritualism", *RR*, 836.

51   *Ibid.,* xxxi, 70.

52   *Ibid.,* 69.

nychia in 1534 he had been aware for some time of the existence of "false" doctrines about the soul that had "gained considerable ground among some advocates of the reform movement",[53] specifically among the radicals of the Continental Reformation.

The Anabaptist psychopannychists were well represented in Austria in the mid-1520s by three disciples of John (Hans) Hut, or Huth: Leonhard Schiemer, John (Hans) Schlaffer and Ambrose Spittelmaier. Hut himself believed in the imminence of the second coming and preached on the prophecies of Daniel and the book of Revelation, anticipating the imminent end of the world, the resurrection, judgement and the kingdom of Christ.[54] Schiemer, Schlaffer and Spittelmaier, likewise "confident in the imminence of Christ's second advent", maintained a belief "in the sleep of the soul pending the resurrection and the last judgement".[55] Another follower of Hut, Augustine Bader of Augsburg, also held to soul sleep in the context of the general resurrection at the last day.[56] In Switzerland the Anabaptist leader Michael Sattler was burned in 1527, convicted of numerous charges of heresy, including denying the efficacy of the intercession of the Virgin Mary and the saints since, like all the faithful they were asleep, awaiting the judgement. It would certainly have been of great concern to the Catholic establishment to be told that Mary "must with us await the judgment".[57] Psychopannychism was known to leading spokesmen of the Reformation, and equally reprehensible to them. Both Zwingli and his successor at Zurich, Bullinger, attacked the doctrine of soul sleep, Bullinger publishing against it as early as 1526.[58] A later English translation of a work by Bullinger testified to the existence of Swiss Anabaptist psychopannychism: "They say that the souls, after the death of the body (if they do depart in faith), do sleep in the bosom of Abraham till the day of judgment, and that then they enter into everlasting life".[59]

Among the Spiritualist radicals who advocated psychopannychism we have already noted Carlstadt. The sixteenth-century Libertines of the Netherlands, some of whom, Anthony Pocquet among them, were psychopan-

---

53 Tavard, *Calvin's Theology,* 41.

54 *ME,* II (1956), 846–48.

55 *RR,* 266–7, 279–80.

56 *Ibid.,* 298.

57 *ME,* IV, 431; A. M. Mergal and G. H. Williams eds, *Spiritual and Anabaptist Writers* (Philadelphia,1957), 140.

58 Balke, *Calvin,* 32.

59 H. Bullinger, *An Holsome Antidotus ... agaynst the pestylent heresye and secte of the Anabaptistes* (tr. J. Veron [1548]), sig. N vi *r.*

nychists, should also be considered in this connection.[60] Pocquet, a former priest and doctor in canon law, had worked out an elaborate scheme of history in which the world passed through seven stages, the last being the paradisic age. Within the seven phases of history Pocquet developed a mystical, spiritualised interpretation of the redemptive work of Christ, culminating in the resurrection of the righteous. Believers who had died in anticipation of the resurrection were asleep in the grave, to be "awakened to the life of the redeemed at the end of the seventh age".[61] Pocquet, it seems, also promulgated psychopannychism in France and Navarre, sympathetic, perhaps, to the "French evangelical Paduans", and became one of the principle targets of Calvin's *Psychopannychia* shortly to be published.[62] In a chapter entitled "Sectarianism and Spiritualism in Poland" and in an earlier chapter, Williams discusses the thnetopsychism of Faustus Socinus, pointing out that "the second basic principle of his theology" was the natural mortality of man, and drawing attention to a soteriological scheme which culminated in "resurrection in a spiritual body at the Second Advent of Christ".[63] Whether or not Socinus was truly a Polish Spiritualist,[64] his mortalism deserves to be noted for at least two reasons. It was decisively thnetopsychist in character, and it laid a foundation for the later Unitarian mortalists in Poland and Transylvania. We shall return to Socinus shortly.

The Evangelical Rationalists, essentially Italian in origin though by the latter half of the sixteenth century spread across Eastern Europe, took mortalism to what Williams convincingly calls its "extreme" position of thnetopsychism.[65]The Evangelical Rationalists themselves, with their insistence that reason must prevail in the interpretation of Scripture, and for that matter the later English thnetopsychists of the eighteenth century, might have preferred to call it the most logical and consistent formulation of mor-

---

60   Pocquet is not included in Froom's *Conditionalist Faith*. Of all the radical mortalists mentioned in this section, only Camillo Renato is treated adequately by Froom. Laelius and Faustus Socinus are mentioned briefly, although Froom recognises the importance of Socinian mortalism in general, *CFF*, II, 86.

61   *RR*, 538.

62   In a letter to Margaret of Navarre in 1545, Calvin warned the queen of the dangerous influence of Pocquet and his associate, Quintin Thieffry, estimating that they had 10,000 followers; cited in Balke, *Calvin*, 22.

63   *Ibid.,* 980, 1162.

64   Williams elsewhere defines him as an Evangelical Rationalist, but notes also that ultimately the Polish churches adopted many features of his Christology and soteriology, *RR*, 1253, 1162.

65   *Ibid.,* 1149.

talist theology. The Italian Evangelical Rationalists were well represented by Camillo Renato, their most prominent and articulate sixteenth-century spokesman. Wilbur describes Renato as "a man of keen and fertile mind", well-educated and "persuasive and adroit in discussion". It was widely believed in his day that Italian Anabaptism in its entirety could be traced back to him.[66]

Renato had worked through the problems of human nature and mortality to reach a thnetopsyschist position.[67] One of the four main accusations brought against him at his trial in Ferrara in 1540 was his teaching that the souls of "both the righteous and the wicked expire at the death of the body and have no abiding place until the resurrection and the last judgment".[68] Renato's ideas had unsettled many erstwhile more moderate Protestants in Northern Italy, the Republic of Rhaetia and bordering parts of Switzerland. The Anabaptist Council of Venice, 1550, called to settle disputed points of doctrine among the radicals of Northern Italy, Rhaetia and the affected Swiss cantons, all but unanimously agreed on a ten-point statement of belief which stated "that the souls of the wicked die with their bodies; that for the unrighteous there is no hell except the grave, and that after the death of the elect their souls sleep till the day of judgment".[69] That this represented something of a retreat from Renato's fully-developed thnetopsychism to accommodate the psychopannychistic position should not be allowed to minimise the endorsement of radical Italian mortalist doctrine by the delegates of some thirty conventicles.

The influence of Italian Evangelical Rationalism was felt further afield, particularly in Eastern Europe. In Poland and Lithuania the mortalist cause was advanced by Laelius Socinus, who left among his papers a work concerning the resurrection, *De resurrectione corporum*, which, "following Camillo Renato ... attempted to replace the V Lateran teaching of the natural immortality of the soul" with what he believed to be a more biblical, mortalist alternative.[70] Socinus was followed by Gregory Paul who, again

---

66   E. M. Wilbur, *A History of Unitarianism: Socinianism and its Antecedents*(Cambridge, MA: Harvard, 1945), 103–4.

67   *Ibid.,*105. On Renato, see also G. H. Williams, "Camillo Renato (c.1500 – ?1575)" in J. A. Tedeschi, ed., *Italian Reformation Studies in Honour of Laelius Socinus* (Florence, 1965), 105–183.

68   *RR*, 841–2.

69   *Ibid.,* 872.

70   Wilbur, *History of Unitarianism,* 247. Williams describes Renato as the *praeceptor, dux,* and *informator* of the young Laelius, *Italian Reformation Studies,* 108. Laelius later visited England briefly, 1547/8, at the invitation of Cranmer, E. M. Wilbur, *A History of Unitarianism in Transylvania, England and America* (Cambridge, MA: Harvard,1952), 170; *ODCC,* s.v. Socinus.

following Renato, taught that the soul, like the body, is mortal.[71] This sounds like thnetopsychism once more. There is no possible ambiguity, however, with the energetic Simon Budny, the anti-Trinitarian leader in Lithuania and Little Poland, who in 1576 openly advocated a form of thnetopsychism, declaring that the soul was nothing more than the life of the body and had no independent existence.[72] Already in 1572 a group of students had returned to Transylvania from the university of Padua, with similar views to those of Gregory Paul and Camillo Renato, notably "psychopannychism with a lively expectation of being resurrected" as loyal followers of Christ.[73] Despite the pronouncements of the Fifth Lateran Council, Paduan doubt over the immortality of the soul and the reasonable alternative proposed by the Italian Evangelical Rationalists seem to have taken root well beyond the borders of Northern Italy and the Venetian Republic.

We may now return to Faustus Socinus, 1539–1604, whose own theology was influenced both by his uncle, Laelius, and by Camillo Renato. Laelius Socinus, who we shall meet again in an English setting, had also studied at Padua and had himself been influenced by Renato, in particular by Renato's robust thnetopsychism,[74] which he later used to good effect in discomfiting Calvin over the future state of the righteous. Faustus himself came to hold the Paduan view of man's natural mortality and the death of the soul with the body, a conviction which was central to his influential work *De Jesu Christo servatore*, published in 1578.[75] In the context of this important work, Williams comments on the significance of the whole theological system worked out by Faustus Socinus:

> In his Christology, thnetopsychism, and conception of sanctification, Socinus brings together with memorable clarity and baffling simplicity a doctrine of the atonement and justification which (more than any other work thus far discussed) shows how sectors of the Radical Reformation, in various thrusts and tentative endeavours, differed profoundly from the Magisterial Reformation."[76]

We must not allow the close relationship of Socinus' thnetopsychism to his soteriology to escape us here. While not necessarily agreeing with the soteriology itself, it was a relationship that later thnetopsychists, including

---

71 Williams, in *Italian Reformation Studies,* 105.

72 *RR,* 1149.

73 *Ibid.,* 1122.

74 Williams's references to Renato's mortalism as "psychopannychism", e.g., *RR,* 880, are best explained by his willingness to use the term to describe both psychosomnolence and thnetopsychism. In fact, there can be no doubt about Renato's thnetopsychist position, which Williams himself acknowledges elsewhere, e.g., pp. 841–2. See also Wilbur, *History of Unitarianism,* 105.

75 *RR,* 983–4.

76 *Ibid.,* 989.

Trinitarians, would defend with equal conviction. It is also worth pointing out again that although the spokesmen of the Radical Reformation differed profoundly in many respects from their counterparts in the mainstream Reformation, there were those on both sides who found in mortalism, in whichever form they expressed it, a statement of authentic eschatological hope.

As for Faustus Socinus himself, his thnetopsychist doctrine of man's essential mortality, already embodied in the theology of the early Polish Racovians from about 1570, was to become an important element in the later, reshaped Unitarian system better known as Socinianism. Williams concludes that almost every aspect of Socinus' theology "would soon be taken over by the Minor Church",[77] notably his "hermeneutical and epistemological principles (and) his doctrine of natural mortality" with its thorough-going mortalist emphasis on the resurrection of the righteous.[78] But with Polish Socinianism fully articulated we have reached the seventeenth century and a point beyond the scope of this brief survey of Reformation and immediate post-Reformation Continental mortalist thought. We must now briefly retrace our steps.

Calvin, Servetus and the *Psychopannychia*

It is clearly evident that Christian mortalism in both its forms was widely known and promulgated across the European continent for much of the sixteenth century. But it should not be thought that the Continental radicals practised or preached their faith, mortalist or otherwise, unimpeded. Spurned and stigmatised for the most part by the leaders of the mainstream Reformation, hunted down frequently by the Inquisition and turned over to the secular authority to be dealt with as deemed expedient, and sometimes betrayed without warning from within, the radicals and their beliefs survived at considerable cost.[79] With respect to mortalist theology in particular, few demonstrated their hostility more consistently than the French reformer John Calvin, both in his treatment of the radical Spaniard, Michael Servetus, and through his own first major theological work, *Psychopannychia*. It is with Calvin, and his contemporary Henry Bullinger, as we shall later observe, that we find clear indications that there may have been a link between the mortalism of the Continental radicals and English mortalism in the sixteenth century.

---

77   The Minor Reformed Church is the name given to the Polish anti-Trinitarian, anti-paedobaptist radicals of the sixteenth century.

78   *RR*, 1174.

79   E.g., the betrayal by the former priest turned Anabaptist Peter Manelfi of many who had subscribed to the conclusions of the Synod of Venice, and the subsequent activities of the Inquisition, *RR*, 871–3

The episode concerning Servetus which ultimately led to his execution in 1553 is notoriously well-known and has been the subject of much comment. Servetus's psychopannychism, however, appears to be less well-known. Of three quite different lives of Calvin selected at random,[80] all refer to Servetus' life and teachings in some detail but none mentions his psychopannychistic views as one of the several heresies of which he was accused. Even Tavard, who traces the development of Calvin's *Psychopannychia*, seems unaware of the connection. Williams associates Servetus with Camillo Renato as "early representatives" of Continental radical psychopannychism "and the apocalyptic eschatology" in which it was generated. He points out that a meeting arranged between Calvin and Servetus in 1534, for which the latter did not turn up, was to have taken place shortly before the first draft of the *Psychopannychia*.[81] More to the point, perhaps, is the assertion that one of the four main charges brought against Servetus' "matured theological system" was that of psychopannychism, and that at the trial itself Calvin questioned Servetus about his psychopannychistic beliefs.[82] Together with Laelius Socinus, Gregory Paul, John Hut and Camillo Renato, Servetus had advocated his mortalism in the context of an apocalyptic eschatology which anticipated an imminent consummation of history, with the last judgment and the resurrection of the righteous dead at hand. It was this total biblical witness to the future that gave Servetus and those who thought like him their deep eschatological convictions and mortalism its strength and its appeal in sixteenth-century Europe.

Calvin, of course, was not of the same mind at all. He saw mortalism in any form as heresy, and a threat to the order he sought to bring to the Reformation and to the reformed church which he was in the process of shaping and which he fervently hoped would endure into the future. He called mortalists, particularly psychopannychists, "Babblers" and "Hypnologists", and mortalists in general soul-killers, "*psuchoktonoi*, assassins of the soul".[83] Calvin clung to the traditional, prevailing view of immortality, believing in the soul's separate existence and its continuing consciousness after death. The term 'psychopannychia' means literally 'the watching wakefulness' of the soul after death, Calvin's own defined position. The title of his now fa-

---

80   J. Mackinnon, *Calvin and the Reformation* (London:Longmans,1936); E. Stickelberger, *Calvin: A Life* (Richmond, VA: Knox, 1961); F. Wendel, *Calvin* (London: Collins,1965).

81   *RR*, 70, 903.

82   *Ibid.*, 929, citing Calvin, *Opera quae supersunt omnia* (1863–1900), vol.8, cols. 739–40.

83   Balke, *Calvin,* 29; Tavard, *Calvin's Theology* , 41. Tavard seems to be unaware of Balke's earlier comments on Calvin and the *Psychopannychia*, in Balke, *Calvin,* 25–34.

mous work against psychopannychism, therefore, has come to represent the doctrine he opposed rather than the position he advocated, namely both "the doctrine of the death of the soul (thnetopsychism) and the unconscious sleep of the soul (psychosomnolence) pending the resurrection".[84] As we have already noted, the first draft of the *Psychopannychia* is believed to have been written as early as 1534, with a subsequent draft in 1536, before the first printed edition in 1542, and the first edition under the title of *Psychopannychia* in 1545.[85] It is immediately apparent that Calvin was concerned about the development of mortalist views over a period of several years early in his career and early in the history of the Reformation as a whole.

Moreover he clearly understood, by the time his thoughts on the matter were finally committed to print, that there were two mortalist camps advocating different positions. One group, the psychopannychists, as already noted, believed that the soul existed as a separate entity but that it slept during death and thus lost consciousness temporarily. The other group, the thnetophychists, held that the soul was not an entity separate from the body, and that it existed only as long as the body was alive, but that it could and, in the case of the righteous, would exist again following the resurrection. Calvin wrote with commendable clarity and fairness:

> Our controversy, then, relates to the human soul. Some, while admitting it to have a real existence, imagine that it sleeps in a state of insensibility from death to the judgment day, when it will awake from its sleep; while others will sooner admit anything than its real existence, maintaining that it is merely a vital power which is derived from arterial spirit on the action of the lungs, and being unable to exist without the body, perishes along with the body, and vanishes away and becomes evanescent till the period when the whole man shall be raised again.[86]

These were the views which Calvin vigorously set out to combat in the *Psychopannychia*. With some reservation, perhaps, concerning the attempted scientific explanation of thnetopsychism, they fairly represent developing mortalist thought in Europe throughout the period.

Williams suggests that the original draft of the *Psychopannychia* may have been directed against Servetus and his mortalist fellow-believers in

---

84   *RR*, 902.

85   Wendel believed that the 1534 version may have been published, *Calvin*, 43; cf. *RR*, 900. Froom also states that the 1534 edition was published, but incorrectly gives the later title, *CFF*, II, 113. Balke, Tavard and Lane maintain that the first known printed edition was that of 1542, Balke, *Calvin*, 26–7; Tavard, *Calvin's Theology*, 1; A. N. S. Lane, *John Calvin: Student of the Church Fathers* (Edinburgh: T & T Clark, 1999), 70.

86   Calvin, "Psychopannychia", in H. Beveridge (tr.), *Calvin, Tracts Relating to the Reformation* (Edinburgh: Calvin Translation Society, 1844), III, 419; cf. Tavard, *Calvin's Theology*, 54–5.

Paris c.1534.[87] In 1537, much to Calvin's chagrin, psychopannychism was openly advocated in Geneva by two Anabaptist teachers from the Netherlands, Herman of Gerbehaye and Andrew Benoit of Engelen. Calvin's concern apparently arose from the fact that the people of Geneva were "responsive to their preaching". In the following year, while at Strassburg, and perhaps not for the first time, he became aware of French psychopannychists preaching the sleep of the soul, including that of the Virgin Mary.[88] We have already noted that at about this same time, Anthony Pocquet was teaching psychopannychism in France and Navarre. It was all the tip of a dangerous iceberg. "Horrified by the extent of the Anabaptist and Spiritualist movements", with their psychopannychist and thnetopsychist emphases, and seeing in them a serious threat to the stability of the Reformation, Calvin was at last persuaded to publish *Psychopannychia* which appeared, under its earlier title, in Strassburg in 1542.[89] It was, it might be judged, rather too late.

One further fact concerning the *Psychopannychia* must be noted, particularly in relation to Calvin's pending influence in England. It was originally written, if not before Calvin's final conversion to the Reformed faith, then certainly at a time of transition, turmoil and personal stress.[90] Tavard, in fact, argues persuasively that the point of Calvin's actual conversion may have been after the first draft of *Psychopannychia* had been composed.[91] Whatever the truth may be, it is certain that Calvin's reaction to the growing Continental mortalist threat faithfully reflected the traditional medieval view of the soul, a pre-Reformation eschatology which "does not exhibit a reforming orientation".[92] Balke correctly states that in the *Psychopannychia* "there is no evidence that Calvin was at variance with the Roman Catholic Church".[93] In Tavard's opinion, Calvin, the humanist, "entertained a thoroughly Platonic conception of the soul" which he did not surrender "when he became a biblical scholar".[94] Indeed, a critical evaluation of the *Psychopannychia* reveals that Calvin "has retained Plato's thesis that the soul is a stranger to the body that imprisons it during the present life".[95] It was this

---

87   *RR*, 903. The circumstances surrounding the writing of the *Psychopannychia* are covered in some detail by Williams, *RR*, 899–904

88   *Ibid.*, 916. Calvin may also have been aware of the earlier psychopannychism of Otto Brunfels in Strasburg, c.1530, *ibid.*, 309.

89   *Ibid.*, 918. Both the Reformers Bucer and Capito had urged Calvin not to publish until the time was more propitious, Balke, *Calvin*, 27.

90   Tavard, *Calvin's Theology*, 10, 39.

91   *Ibid.*, 10, 41.

92   *Ibid.*, 113.

93   Balke, *Calvin*, 34.

94   Tavard, *Calvin's Theology*, 53.

95   *Ibid.*, 77.

view of the soul and its destiny that found its way into Calvin's influential *Institutes*[96](where the influence of Plato is evident, e.g. Bk. I, ch. XV), the first draft of which was being written at the same time that Calvin was revising the *Psychopannychia* for publication and while the questions of mortalism and the soul were still major issues in his mind.[97] There were profound and lasting implications here for both Continental and English Protestantism in their formative years.

The young Calvin's lingering attachment to certain aspects of medieval theology and patristic authority is further evident in his treatment of the relevant biblical texts which, within the scholastic tradition, is undergirded by frequent appeals to the interpretations of these texts by the Greek and Latin fathers. In addition to Tertullian and Augustine, there are recurring references to Irenaeus, Origen, Cyprian, Chrysostom and Jerome, *inter alios*, those who, in Calvin's mind, "have reverently and discretely handled the mysteries of God".[98] Other considerations aside, if this was the case it is not surprising that the *Psychopannychia* failed to impress those whom it sought to counter, or that it did little to stem the rising mortalist tide across Continental Europe. Such unconcealed respect for the opinions of the fathers would surely have undermined Calvin's impact on more radical minds attracted to the pure word of God and whose own hermeneutic required a "total disregard of the Augustinian and ... mystical traditions".[99]Arguing that Calvin's "anti-Roman stance" was adopted after he had first written against mortalism and soul-sleep, Tavard concludes that while the *Psychopannychia* betrayed Calvin's hostility to the radical wing of the Reformation, it was not in itself a reforming document. "The position it defended was identical with Catholic teaching, and it did not contain one word that was critical of the medieval church or the papacy".[100]   Clearly there are significant implications here for English mortalism and the repeated attempts of its opponents in England to suppress it, as well as for the wider eschatology which would later dominate the English-speaking Protestant world. Indeed, we may find

---

96   See Calvin, *Institutes of the Christian Religion*, Bk. I, ch. XV and Bk. II, ch. XXV.

97   Tavard, *Calvin's Theology*, 7, 9.

98   John Calvin, *An excellent treatise of the Immortalytie of the Soule* (tr. Thomas Stocker, 1581), *passim* and 63. Lane emphasises Calvin's "great respect for the teaching of the fathers" from which "he did not lightly depart", although his "refusal to accord them authority on a par with Scripture" should not be overlooked. Lane also appears to endorse the older view that the *Psychopannychia* was Calvin's first post-conversion work, Lane, *John Calvin*, 35, 38, 28, 31.

99   Tavard, *Calvin's Theology*, 112.

100   *Ibid.*, 149.

in all this a hint of the solution to a question that has remained largely un-answered for four hundred years or more - why mainstream Protestantism, both in England and on the Continent, which in its formative years so em-phatically repudiated what it considered to be the doctrinal legacy of the medieval church, retained what was arguably the central plank in the entire dogmatic and liturgical structure of late medieval Catholicism, belief in the immortal soul.[101]

It is enough for now to observe that the confrontation with Servetus and the entire sequence of events which ultimately led Calvin to publish the *Psychopannychia* are indications of the growing strength of mortalist views on the Continent during the first half of the sixteenth century, and of their wide appeal to many European Christians who had been unsettled by the new Reformation theology. The fact that mortalism steadily gained ground and the attention of leading thinkers among the Continental radicals was not, of course, due to Calvin's *Psychopannychia*, but rather in spite of it. It is ironic that the mortalist radicals appealed for their authority to precisely the same court that Calvin, and the English Reformers who followed him, all invoked – God's Word in Scripture. The very least that can be said of the surprisingly widespread dissemination of mortalism across Europe by the middle of the sixteenth century in relation to the development of mortalist opinion in England, is that it confirmed what English tongues and pens were already beginning to articulate.

---

101   See also *The Soul Sleepers*, ch. 2, 64–68.

16. The Decline of the West: Myth, or Reason for Hope?[1]

Bryan W. Ball

The conviction that Western civilisation is in irreversible decline surfaced with Oswald Spengler's much-read book *The Decline of the West,* published in 1918 and available in English since 1926. It has been called "one of the most widely read and most talked about books of our time".[2] Spengler compared the life of a civilisation to the seasons of the year, stating that by the early twentieth century Western civilisation had already come to its winter, its spring and summer, the seasons of birth and growth, now past. He also spoke metaphorically of the "twilight" of the West, that short period of gathering darkness between day and night, a gradual process rather than the sudden descent of night. Spengler's word for "the West", which appeared in the title of his book, was *Abenlund,* literally "evening land". Spengler said "the future of the West is not a limitless tending upwards and onwards for all time", but "a single phenomenon of history, strictly limited", and covering only "a few centuries" in duration.[3] In his day, he believed, the limit had almost been reached. Spengler's view was widely criticised in his time and for the next 50 years or so as being too pessimistic and too narrow in its Teutonic view of the world.

The passing of time, however, seems to have vindicated him. In 1959 Helmut Werner, who edited an abridged edition of *The Decline,* wrote, "everywhere an irresistible conviction has been making itself felt that Spengler 'might have been right after all'".[4] Since then a steady stream of similar works has continued to appear, the titles of which tell their own story, among them: *The End of History and the Last Man* (1992), *Slouching Towards Gomorrah* (1996), *The Wreck of Western Culture* (2004), *Architects of the Culture of Death* (2006), *The Death of Christian Culture* (2008) and, to bring into focus the real issue before us, *How the West Really Lost God*

---

1 Previously unpublished.

2 The *San Francisco Chronicle,* cited on back cover of the OUP 1991 abridged edition of Spengler's work.

3 Oswald Spengler, *The Decline of the West* (abridged edition, H. S. Hughes, ed., Oxford: OUP, 1991), 30.

4 *Ibid.,* xxxv.

(2013) – all written by articulate scholars, each delivering Spengler's message in their own words and from their own standpoint. The West is on its way out. The greatest civilisation known to man is dying and cannot be revived. Can this really be true? Can the civilisation which split the atom, conquered gravity, put men on the moon and brought them back, invented the micro-chip, decoded the gene, and produced Michelangelo, Rembrandt, Beethoven, Bach, Shakespeare, Newton, Milton, and Einstein *et al* have come to its end? It sounds preposterous, bizarre, impossible, the meanderings of unbalanced minds.

So what is the evidence? What do these writers and others like them have to say? What are their reasons for insisting that the West is in irretrievable decline? Could they be wrong, monumentally mistaken, perhaps? And if they are correct, what does it mean for us, for our children and grandchildren? Is there anything beyond the dark midnight? Even a glimmer of hope? Or is life in our time, as many have said, absurd, pointless, and not worth living? The questions are many and momentous, and will not go away. And there is one more: Is there any hope to be gained from placing this great dilemma of our time in the context of biblical and prophetic perspectives?

The West

For there to be any meaningful consideration of the West's decline it is first necessary to understand how the West came into being and what makes Western civilisation what it is or, if the prophets are correct, what it was. Perhaps the most obvious truth about the West is that, strictly speaking, it is no longer the West. What began in Western Europe and quickly spread to North America, before it had even fully developed in Europe, has grown to include significant segments of the East, most of the North and much of the South. The Western world-view and way of life, with national and regional adaptations, has increasingly dominated the world for the past four hundred years or so, achieving an influence its predecessors would not have dreamed possible. It is all the more imperative, therefore, to know precisely what we mean by the 'West' and if the assertion that the West is in decline is in fact sustainable.

The consensus of historical thought is that the roots of Western civilisation are derived from the Greco-Roman era. In his acclaimed *History of the World,* J. M. Roberts states that the achievements of ancient Greece, particularly those of the mind, "made Greece the teacher of Europe, and through it, of the world".[5] There was democracy, clearly significant, but the emphasis on rational thought, the necessity of reason and the challenge

---

5   J. M. Roberts, *The Penguin History of the World* (6th edn., ed., O. A. Westad, London: Penguin, 2014), 189.

"to irrationality in social and intellectual activity", Roberts says, was "the greatest single Greek achievement".[6] It can be summarised in one word, *nous* [mind]. Rome's contribution to the West was law, *lex,* bringing order, a natural consequence it might seem of rational thought applied to the development of social cohesion. The legendary *Pax Romana,* based on just laws strictly applied, held the far-flung Roman Empire together for several centuries, giving to those who lived within its borders a stability and peace that had never before been seen across so wide an area, a social order which is still one of the hallmarks of civilisation. Athens and Rome, *nous* and *lex,* are appropriate symbols of the Greco-Roman roots of the West.

A somewhat broader view was more recently suggested by George Weigel, who reminds us that the West "did not just happen". Athens still symbolises "Greek rationality, which taught the West that there are truths embedded in the world and in ourselves" which can be accessed by reason. Rome stands for "Roman jurisprudence, which taught the West the superiority of the rule of law over the rule of brute force and sheer coercion".[7] But Jerusalem, in addition to Athens and Rome, is also a necessary symbol in understanding what ultimately contributed to the rise of the West. Jerusalem represents "biblical religion [i.e., Judaeo-Christian faith], from which the West learned the idea of history as a purposeful journey into the future".[8] Weigel holds that it was "the fruitful interaction of Jerusalem, Athens and Rome" which provided the soil "for the taproots of our civilisation".[9] In the final analysis, however, it might prove to be Jerusalem which provided continuity in the West for so long. Hope for the future is crucial to continuity.

All this, however, relates only to the foundations of the West — its roots — not to the completed, majestic building or the mature tree. It takes no account of the Dark Ages in medieval European history, traditionally an epoch of approximately a thousand years following the collapse of the Roman Empire and the disappearance of Greco-Roman culture, when knowledge disappeared and the collective memory of the glories of Greece and Rome were forgotten. Modern historical thinking is that the medieval period was not as 'dark' as once thought, and that glimpses of light were seen at various times and places. Even if correct, they do not much alter the overall picture. No amount of historical revisionism can hide the fact that for much of this long period the vast majority of Europe's people were illiterate, unable to read or write, economically disadvantaged and subject to poor health, dis-

---

6 *Ibid.*

7 George Weigel, 'The Handwriting on the Wall', *National Affairs,* No. 11 (2012), cited in Mary Eberstadt, *How the West Really Lost God* (West Conshohocken, PA: Templar, 2013), 219

8 *Ibid.*

9 *Ibid.*

ease and early death. If that is not dark, it is difficult to envisage what is. John Senior called that age the "Dark Night of Christendom".[10] The Greco-Roman foundations of the West, hidden for centuries, had to be uncovered before the building could be erected.

If a date or an event is required for the beginning of the West as traditionally perceived, it would not be inappropriate to suggest the invention of movable-type printing in Germany in 1439. It was a measurably defining moment in human history. Within a few years printing presses were springing up all over Europe, signifying a new era and the availability of knowledge on a hitherto unprecedented scale, knowledge that would never again be lost and that would revolutionise human existence. The development of printing gave rise to two of the most significant movements in European and Western history, the Renaissance and the Reformation. The Renaissance, literally rebirth, specifically the re-birth of knowledge and learning, was a time of intense intellectual activity and cultural advancement resulting, among other things, in the rediscovery of the history of classical Greece and Rome and with it the roots of Western civilisation. Without the Renaissance, it is doubtful if the West would have existed, so we need to exercise care in claiming too much for the Greco-Roman contribution *per se* to the West. It is doubtful that we would have known much about it but for the Renaissance.

Nor must we lose sight of another notable fact arising from the printing revolution. The first book to be printed was the Bible, the justly famous Gutenberg Bible, a work of high quality and relatively low cost. Soon Bibles were available in all the languages of Europe. They were immediately best-sellers. No other book has so influenced the world as the Bible, a fact that cannot for one moment be doubted but that is often too easily forgotten or merely conveniently ignored. The printed words of the Bible consistently bore witness to the "Word of God", a phrase used repeatedly in both Old and New Testaments. In the New Testament it is presented as *logos*, the "word", a seminal word and concept in the Christian declaration, and thus *logos tou theou*, "the Word of God". The open *logos* led to *charis, pistis, agape, zoe, elpis* and *photos* – grace, faith, love, life, hope and light — the core of Christian belief and Christian life for two thousand years, and the substance of civilised life in the West until very recently.

Logos is a word with profoundly rich significance. In addition to "word", it is translated in the New Testament with more than twenty different English words.[11] It inherently contains meanings of reason, purpose and revelation. In all these usages it is a common noun. But in John 1:1–3 it becomes

10   John Senior, *The Death of Christian Culture* (Norfolk, VA: IHS, 2008), 170

11   See, for example, Young's *Analytical Concordance to the Holy Bible* under 'Logos'.

a proper noun, a name, the original "Word", the *Logos* who had been with God in the beginning, who *was* God, who had been made flesh (John 1:1–3, 14), who "dwelt among us" (v.14) and who was seen and heard by untold thousands in the early decades of the first century AD. His existence was confirmed by Greek and Latin sources outside the Bible and his coming had been repeatedly foretold in the Old Testament, his life and teachings recorded in the New Testament. John thus affirms the pre-existence and divine nature of this eternal *Logos,* the divine-human redeemer. He is "the One who gives and is this Word, not only in His addresses, but in His whole earthly manifestation ... He is the Word ... the eternal Word".[12] Here is the very essence, the core of Christian truth from its beginning and through all subsequent ages – God made flesh to redeem fallen humanity. It was this belief, with its collective and personal consequences, which undergirded the post-Renaissance West as it eagerly fed on the opened Bible, growing rapidly to become the dominant world outlook for more than four centuries.

But there is in the New Testament another profound truth concerning this incarnate Word. In Philippians 2 Paul offers practical counsel to the young Christians at Philippi concerning attitudes and relationships. In this context Paul also speaks specifically of the incarnate redeemer. This divine, pre-existent Christ did not consider divinity, his status as God, as something to be "held on to", something to be "grasped". Rather, he "made himself nothing" (Phil 2:7, NIV), "of no reputation" (NKJV), "he humbled himself", coming "in human likeness" and "appearance" (Phil 2:1–5). This entire passage is often thought of as a Christological statement, referring principally to the nature of Christ. Yet the essential truth here is not that of pre-existence or incarnation, but of humility, condescension, self-abasement, self-sacrifice, even to the point of painful and humiliating public death. This, too, is of the essence of authentic Christianity, always hard to understand, but never more so than by twenty-first century men and women addicted to materialism and dedicated to the seemingly unlimited gratification of self.

All this and everything that pertains to it as recorded in the Bible is the essence of Christianity and the substance of Western civilisation as it developed in Europe following the sixteenth-century Reformation with its emphasis on the Bible as the source of truth. In his 12-volume world history, the twentieth-century historian, Arnold Toynbee, wrote much of the nexus between Christianity and Western civilisation. He regarded Christianity as being at the heart of Western civilisation, attributing the "problems of Western civilisation to its breaking away from Christianity and embracing false

---

12   G. Kittel, ed., *Theological Dictionary of the New Testament* (trans. G. W. Bromiley, Grand Rapids, MI: Eerdmans, 1981), IV, 129.

idols".[13] As we shall shortly observe, many other informed thinkers in more recent times have taken a similar view. To the rediscovered *nous* and *lex* of ancient Greece and Rome and the teleological understanding of history, *teleios*, which emanated from Jerusalem, was added the *logos* of the New Testament and all that *logos* stood for and became. We can only truly understand the decline of the West as we grasp what the West really was and how it came to be.

The Decline

Toynbee (1889–1975), was one of the most distinguished and influential men of the first half of the twentieth century. His own history is a pertinent illustration of the decline of the West. A graduate of Balliol College, Oxford, he was appointed tutor and fellow there in 1912, later becoming Professor of International Studies at the London School of Economics in 1925, a position he held until his retirement in 1956. He was also director of studies at the Royal Institute of International Affairs at the Foreign Office, serving as advisor to the British Government, notably during the later years of World War II and immediately thereafter. The author of many books and hundreds of articles, he was best known for the twelve-volume *Study of History* in which he examined in great depth the rise and fall of the 23 civilisations known in human history. He appeared on the front cover of *Time* magazine in 1947, was a regular commentator on the BBC on history and foreign affairs, and lectured frequently at home and overseas, often to large audiences. As the dominant intellectual figure in the first half of the twentieth century, his influence was immense, "the world's most read, translated and discussed living scholar".[14]

Today Toynbee's work is seldom read or quoted, his ideas since the early 1960s regarded as *passé* in academic circles and the media and hence in the popular mind, his name largely unknown to anyone under the age of fifty. It was a remarkably rapid loss of prestige for such a respected writer who in his day had appealed widely to both academia and the general public, and it raises a fundamental question. Why? Why Toynbee and not Spengler? The reason is now broadly agreed on and it illustrates the parallel between Toynbee and the decline of the West — his views on the relationship of Western civilisation and Christianity, the underlying thesis of much of his work, particularly the *Study of History*. Marvin Perry assessed it well:

---

13   Marvin Perry, *Western Civilisation: Ideas, Politics and Society* (10th edn., 2012), 789.

14   Michael Lang, 'Globalisation and Global History in Toynbee', *Journal of World History*, 22/4 (2011), 747.

> Toynbee attributed the problems of Western civilisation to its breaking
> away from Christianity and embracing false idols ... The secular values
> of the Enlightenment, divorced from Christianity, cannot restrain hu-
> man nature's basest impulses. For the West to save itself, said Toynbee,
> it must abide by the spiritual values of its religious prophets.[15]

It is likely that Toynbee would have seen in his own demise confirmation of
his rejected world view.

If a time or an event is required for the last fading of the light in the West,
it would almost certainly be the Sixties, the decade of "revolution in social
norms", and any one of the following: My Lai, Woodstock, the rise of the
drug culture, campus revolution and riots, civil disobedience, availability
of the Pill, radical feminism, blatant pornography, escalating violence and
brutality, demonstrations for gay and lesbian rights, vocal minorities claiming to speak for the majority. Together they were, in the words of a later
analyst, "harbingers of a new culture that would shortly burst upon us and
sweep us into a different country".[16] Toynbee, like the civilisation he represented and sought to explain, was caught up in this tsunami-like sea change
that swept across the West, tossed up like detritus from the ancient past
and left to expire on the shores of this strange and irrational new world. Of
course, the ground had been prepared and the seed sown in earlier decades,
to change the analogy, for the upheaval of the Sixties and the denouement
of the West. Naziism, World War II, the Holocaust, Hiroshima and Naga-
saki, and Nietzsche's nihilistic 'God is dead' philosophy had all played their
part. Twilight finally and inevitably yielded to darkness and by the end of
the decade, *Abenlund,* "evening land", had virtually become the land of the
sunless midnight.

It is significant that this is precisely how several others have seen it.
Robert Bork, former US Solicitor General and Court of Appeals Judge,
in his masterly analysis of the West at the end of the twentieth century,
Slouching Towards Gomorrah, asserted that belief in the God of Christianity "is probably essential to a civilised future".[17] Paul Johnson had written
in his *History of Christianity* (1976), "with public Christianity in headlong
retreat, we have caught our first distant view of a de-Christianised world,
and it is not encouraging".[18] Bork agreed. Twenty years later he had seen it
more closely and concluded, "Large chunks of the moral life of the United
States, major features of its culture, have disappeared altogether, and more

---

15   Perry, *Western Civilisation,* 790.

16   Robert Bork, *Slouching Towards Gomorrah* (New York: Regan/Harper Collins, 1996), 1.

17   *Ibid.,* 295.

18   Paul Johnson, *A History of Christianity* (New York: Simon and Schuster,
1976), 517.

are in the process of extinction".[19] One assessment claims that as early as 1948 England was "a pagan country in any ordinary sense of that term".[20] In North America there were similar fears that the old order was disintegrating. Carl Henry, soon to be the first editor of *Christianity Today*, was in the 1940s Professor of Theology at Fuller Theological Seminary where he felt that Fuller's mission should to challenge "the humanist presuppositions that underlay Western civilization".[21]

A more recent interpretation of Western decline appeared in 2004 with John Carroll's brilliantly written *The Wreck of Western Culture: Humanism Revisited*, "in essence, the spiritual history of the modern West",[22] to quote the author himself. Carroll was professor of sociology at La Trobe University in Melbourne at the time of writing. We shall return to Carroll shortly, but here we note comments in the Prologue to his book referring to "The weakening of Christian faith" and the determined attempt "to find a credible alternative to Christ crucified".[23] The book is essentially an evaluation of the Enlightenment when "at last the ties to Christianity — Catholic or Protestant — were cut ... denouncing it as superstition, a barbarian shackle on the triumph of rational humanity".[24] The "main shackle to be cast off was religion", in the process of which "the eighteenth-century men of reason turned with venom against Christianity", undermining "traditional Christian orientation" and the biblical revelation in particular. The consequence was predictable and inevitable. "The authority of the Bible began to diminish",[25] and both the undermining and the diminishment have continued unabated until the present time. Nietzsche, one of the last Enlightenment spokesmen, became with time "more and more contemptuous of the darkness of faith, and more caustically anti-Christian", declaring that Protestantism "must be killed off completely".[26] He must be credited at least with a Herculean attempt to do just that, even if he went mad in the process.

Lesslie Newbigin had already assessed the consequences of Enlightenment thinking and the nature of the new West that had appeared in the second half of the twentieth century. The goal of a secular society, free from the "shackles" of the religious past had more than been achieved. "The result

---

19   Bork, *Towards Gomorrah*, 12.

20   Brian Stanley, *The Global Diffusion of Evangelicalism* (London: IVP, 2013), 12.

21   *Ibid.*, 32.

22   John Carroll, *The Wreck of Western Culture: Humanism Revisited* (Melbourne: Scribe, 2004), 8.

23   *Ibid.*, 6.

24   *Ibid.*, 135.

25   *Ibid.*, 139.

26   *Ibid.*, 194, 191.

is not, as we once imagined, a secular society. It is a pagan society, having been born out of the rejection of Christianity" and far more resistant to the gospel than the pre-Christian paganism that Christianity had conquered in the early centuries.[27] Even Bultmann's attempt to connect with this new West, in which the thinking of the majority was now shaped by a different plausibility structure, by demythologising the Bible, had failed. "In the end, the reductionist program takes the modern world-view as ultimate and must eventually jettison even those parts of the Christian tradition Bultmann was seeking to safeguard".[28] Little now remains of the West as traditionally understood. "One does not need Jesus in order to embrace the existentialist view of life".

In 2009 Melanie Phillips wrote from London in *The World Turned Upside Down*, another well-researched and well-written examination of Western civilisation, of the "unravelling of British culture", stating that Britain had become "an increasingly post-Christian society", in large measure a result of "the erosion of the building blocks of Western civilisation"– Christianity and the Hebrew Bible.[29] Like many of the writers cited, Phillips laid much of the blame for Britain's religious decline on the prevailing educational system:

> The teaching of Christianity gave way not just to other religions but to pagan cults, which were given equal status. In 2009, the government announced that pupils would learn about the rituals and teachings of the Druids, Moonies and Rastafarians for a new 'religious studies' 16-plus exam [taken at age 16], along with atheism and humanism. A draft outline of the new exam also included rap music, Stonehenge, human rights, gender equality, GM crops, multiculturalism in Britain, cloning and the effect of the internet on religion.[30]

The truth of the old adage "as the twig is bent, so grows the tree", attributed to Alexander Pope, appears to have been confirmed. The kind of irrational revisionism evident above has been seen elsewhere in the Western world of late, where extreme left-wing idealists have manipulated educational curricula to reflect their own political agendas.

An even more recent evaluation of Western decline came from the pen of Mary Eberstadt, senior fellow at the Ethics and Public Policy Centre in Washington. In 2013 she published a well-researched account of the collapse of Christian faith in the West, unambiguously entitled *How the West*

---

27 Lesslie Newbigin, *Foolishness to the Greeks* (Grand Rapids, MI: Eerdmans, 1986), 20.

28 *Ibid.,* 12.

29 Melanie Philipps, *The World Turned Upside Down* (New York and London: Encounter, 2010), 339, 343–44, 356–59.

30 *Ibid.,* 346

Really Lost God, at many points confirming much that Carroll had written from the other side of the world. With reference to "The dramatic decay of Christian belief and practice" and the arrival of the "post-Christian" era in some parts of the world, Eberstadt writes:

> In addition to being "post"-Christian, some parts of this landscape are also notably *anti*-Christian – as a lengthening list of public events disfigured by aggressive atheist or secular protests goes to show. Some observers have even used the term "Christophobic" to capture the vehemence with which some Europeans, including high-ranking public figures, have come to renounce the influence of Christianity on the Western present and past.
>
> For Western Europeans, the waning of religious belief has transformed practically every aspect of life from birth to death: politics, laws, marriages (or lack thereof), arts, education, music, popular culture, and other activities ... A growing number of Western individuals greet the milestones of life with no religious framework at all. They are born without being baptised; they have children without being married; they contract civil marriages instead of religious ones ... and upon dying their bodies are incinerated and scattered to the winds, rather than prayed over whole in the ground as Christian ritual and dogma had hitherto commanded.[31]

It seems difficult, if not impossible, to deny the reality of Western decline, or that this decline can be traced to the loss of its Christian roots.

Callum Brown, Professor of Modern European History at the University of Glasgow, says "It is in my lifetime that people have forsaken formal Christian religion, and the churches have entered seemingly terminal decline", adding "It matters that we understand why".[32] John Senior, formerly professor of Classics at the University of Kansas argued that Christianity had lost its identity in the modern world, saying without qualification towards the end of his book, *The Death of Christian Culture*, that "the declining West is ruined Christendom".[33] Perhaps the most chilling comment of all comes from Michael Craven, who provides another critique of Toynbee's *Study of History*. Arguing again that the present-day troubles of the West began with the Enlightenment, Craven cites Toynbee as saying that the Enlightenment produced a tolerance "based not on the Christian virtues of faith, hope and charity but on the Mephistophelian maladies of disillusionment, apprehension and cynicism".[34] It would be entirely in keeping with the biblical revelation itself to think that a Satanic influence was at work in the destruction

---

31 Eberstadt, *How the West Really Lost God*, 7.
32 Cited in Eberstadt, v.
33 Senior, *Death of Christian Culture*, 164.
34 Michael Craven, "Theology and the Church', June, 2011, www.battlefor-truth.org/ArticlesDetail.asp?id=434

of Christianity and the demolition of the West but that, of course, would be completely unacceptable and naive to the modern mind.

We have surveyed, albeit briefly, the views of several highly-qualified men and women, writing over the last thirty years from three continents and differing backgrounds — Christian, Jewish and secular, Catholic and Protestant, each addressing the most momentous issue of our time, the declining state of our civilisation. They do so from various perspectives — historical, theological, sociological and biblical — and they all reach essentially the same conclusion. We now live in the fading twilight of Western civilisation. The decline is evident and irreversible. The West has become "the culture of death". Surely, it is inconceivable that these scholars, having carefully weighed the evidence, could all be wrong, seriously and culpably mistaken. So how did the West lose its original identity and the nature that made it what it was for at least five centuries, now racing "lemming-like toward inevitable destruction"?[35] One of the writers previously cited remarked, "It is important that we know", and that is not difficult to determine.

The Ascent of Humanism

It was not so much a false idol that the West had embraced, but a new religion, a new philosophy. Born, or re-born perhaps, in the Renaissance, coming of age in the Enlightenment, and reaching its maturity in the late nineteenth and early twentieth century, the new religion is Humanism. The first Humanist Manifesto of 1933 specifically called it a religion, a replacement for the old, outdated and irrelevant Christianity which had shaped the past.[36] The second Humanist Manifesto of 1973 claimed "no deity will save us; we must save ourselves". Commenting on this Manifesto a noted humanist, John Dunphy, wrote:

> I am convinced that the battle for humankind's future must be waged and fought in the public school classroom by teachers who correctly perceive their role as proselytizers of a new faith ... The classroom must and will become an arena of conflict between the old and the new — the rotting corpse of Christianity, together with all its adjacent evils and misery, and the new faith of humanism.[37]

It is evident that humanism has been driven by these convictions ever since.

Two writers in particular deserve our attention if we are to understand this new religion, its god, its beliefs and its consequences. John Carroll we have already mentioned. His *The Wreck of Western Culture: Humanism Revisited* was first published in 1993 with the title reversed: *Humanism: The Wreck of Western Culture*. The original title seems preferable since it puts

---

35 Senior, *Death of Christian Culture*, 11.
36 Humanist Manifesto I, www.en.wikipedia.org/wiki/Humanist_Manifesto
37 Humanist Manifesto II, www.em.wikipedia.org/wiki.Humanist_Manifesto

the horse before the cart, cause before effect, as Carroll clearly demonstrates. A decade before Carroll's perceptive study, Francis Schaeffer's collected works had been published in five volumes, the last of which bore the title *A Christian View of the West.* Both Carroll and Schaeffer are essential reading for all who would know the truth about humanism and its far-reaching and demoralising impact on Western civilisation. Carroll describes humanism as a myth, "a myth that failed".[38] Schaeffer says that already in the eighteenth century it began to dawn on some humanists that their philosophy had failed. Its stance had "changed from optimism to pessimism".[39] But it was already too late to change course, too late to re-lay the shaken foundations of the civilisation they had sought to destroy.

What exactly are we to understand by the term 'humanism'? It is a substantial and sometimes inadequately understood concept which, like a giant octopus, has spread its tentacles in many directions. We may reduce various definitions to two — secular humanism and Christian humanism, so called, the latter largely an unsuccessful attempt to combine secular thought with Christianity, an enterprise by no means yet abandoned. It is secular humanism, however, that has by and large prevailed, affecting contemporary society and which, although now in its old age and expiring with the culture it has created, is still evident across the landscape of the entire Western world.

Carroll begins his book with a bold assertion, "We live amidst the ruins of the great five-hundred-year epoch of humanism. Around us is that colossal wreck".[40] We can agree with Carroll's time-frame if we recognise that humanism established itself during the Renaissance but did not attain its majority until the Enlightenment and only reached its zenith in the two centuries following. Carroll says that now, living at the end of that epoch, "Our culture is like a dying god, its altar unattended ... its rage turned to indifference".[41] Schaeffer is more specific. The humanistic elements which had risen during the Renaissance came "to floodtide in the Enlightenment",[42] and it is this matured humanism, the calculated alternative to Christianity, that concerns Schaeffer through most of the five hundred pages of his analysis of the West in the years following.

Schaeffer makes a perceptive observation on Renaissance humanism, often thought to be primarily concerned with the rediscovery of classical learning and its relevance to the new society emerging from the Dark Ages. Most specialists agree that Michelangelo was probably the most significant

38 Carroll, *Wreck of Western Culture,* 2.
39 Francis Schaeffer, 'A Christian View of the West', *Works* (1985), 5, 172.
40 Carroll, *Wreck of Western Culture,* 1.
41 *Ibid.*
42 Schaeffer, *Works,* 5, 148.

exponent of Renaissance ideals through art. Referring to Michelangelo's magnificent statue of David, carved in 1504 and universally acknowledged as one of the greatest achievements of Renaissance art, Schaeffer points out that *David* "was not the Jewish David of the Bible" but merely a title for the sculpture. Furthermore, and to the point, Schaeffer observes "Michelangelo knew his Judaism, and in the statue the figure is not circumcised".[43] Most who have seen this amazing piece of Renaissance sculpture will not have noticed this detail. Schaeffer has, and he comments, "We are not to think of this as the biblical David but as the humanistic ideal. Man is great".[44] Michelangelo's *David* was oversize, with disproportionate hands and exaggerated muscles, bigger and better than the original David, a hero of the Judaeo-Christian tradition. Schaeffer again, "The *David* was the statement of what humanistic man saw himself as being tomorrow ... man waiting with confidence in his own strength for the future".[45]

We are now ready to define humanism more precisely, to understand just what Renaissance humanism was and what it bequeathed to the Enlightenment humanism of the eighteenth and nineteenth centuries. Schaeffer puts it well, "The humanistic cry was, 'I can do what I will; just give me until tomorrow'".[46] Carroll is more descriptive, defining humanism as the attempt to "turn the treasure-laden galleon of Western culture around", to put that ship off course, to divorce it from Christianity and thus change its very nature. Carroll explains, "It attempted to replace God by man, put humans at the centre of the universe — to deify them ... to found an order on earth ... without any transcendental or supernatural supports — an entirely human order".[47] Further, in the humanist view,

> Humans are all-powerful if their will is strong enough. They can create themselves. They can choose to be courageous, honourable, just, charitable, rich, influential, or not. They are creator and creature in one. Out of their own individual wills they can move the earth. The great individual stands alone ...[48]

In short, humanism is the belief "that man is his own measure, autonomous, totally independent",[49] as even a cursory reading of the Humanist Manifestos makes abundantly clear. The humanist god is man himself.

Carroll and Schaeffer are not the only voices raised against the baleful and pervasive consequences of Enlightenment humanism. In his illuminat-

---

43 *Ibid.*, 114.
44 *Ibid.*
45 *Ibid.*
46 *Ibid.*, 116.
47 Carroll, *Wreck of Western Culture*, 2.
48 *Ibid.*, 3.
49 Schaeffer, *Works*, 5, 109.

ing study of twentieth-century art as a reflection of the culture of its time, H. A. Rookmaker, Professor of the History of Art at the Free University of Amsterdam, argued in *Modern Art and the Death of a Culture* (1970) that as humanism had grown in influence since the Enlightenment, so Christianity had grown weaker:

> The Enlightenment was to change the world. It is a period in which we today are still living, though at its end. Its aims have been fulfilled. The world is different. What started in the philosopher's study is now in the hearts and minds of the whole western world.[50]

Rookmaker had not seen the evidence which the final decades of the twentieth century and the first years of the twenty-first century would provide, but his conclusions were, nonetheless, essentially accurate, as later writers would demonstrate.

It would be impossible to cite all that those already quoted have written about the Enlightenment and post-Enlightenment humanistic culture in the West. One final foray into the massive amount of material available will suffice. Schaeffer claims with Robert Bork that moral degeneracy is one of the most evident consequences of humanism's attempt to re-shape the West after its own image. The change can be seen in literature, art, music, the media, and in society as a whole. It can be seen on the streets of all the major cities of the West, in London, New York, Sydney, Paris and as Schaeffer points out, in Amsterdam and Copenhagen too. Those who have been there know exactly what he means. "Pompeii has returned. The marks of ancient Rome scar us: degeneracy, decadence, depravity, a love of violence for violence's sake. The situation is plain. If we look, we see it".[51] Bork wrote at the beginning of his book, "A nation's moral life is the foundation of its culture", and at the end, after several chapters of evidence, "We must take seriously the possibility that perhaps nothing will be done to reverse the direction of our culture, that the degeneracy we see about us will only become worse".[52] That was in 1997. Those who have lived through the last twenty years and are willing to look objectively at the evidence must surely agree. It is, indeed, "the colossal wreck" of humanism's new West that surrounds us, the old West dead or in its final death throes.

It remains to bring to bear on this assessment of humanism and its role in Western decline, two relevant passages from the book that humanism so emphatically rejects. The first is from the account of human origins in Genesis, chapter 3. The key text is found in verse 5 where the serpent says to Eve that as soon as she eats the forbidden fruit "your eyes will be opened,

---

50   H.R. Rookmaker, *Modern Art and the Death of a Culture* (London: IVP, 1970), 41.

51   Schaeffer, *Works*, 5, 226.

52   Bork, *Gomorrah*, 12, 332.

and you will be like God". In whatever way this encounter is interpreted, metaphorically or literally, the fundamental issue remains the same. The first temptation to assail humans was not to eat a forbidden fruit, but to "be like God". It was a dazzling idea, an irresistible temptation, but also a false promise, a lie, wonderful to contemplate. To be God, even to be like God, is the ultimate temptation and, as we have observed, it lies at the very heart of the humanist vision. As long as human beings believe that they can be like God, whatever it takes, they will never forget the promise. To be like God eliminates the need for God. The West is in its present state of decay because humanism has offered the old lie over and over again and because humanity has willingly believed it.

The second passage comes from the New Testament, from Paul's description of the "perilous times" that will come in "the last days" (2 Tim 3:1–5). Paul lists nineteen symptoms that will mark the last age and they are all human characteristics. There is nothing here about wars, earthquakes, pestilence, famine, or preaching the gospel throughout the world. This list is entirely a description of the human character and human behaviour in the end time. The list includes brutality or violence, materialism or love of money, youngsters out of control – "disobedience", a preference for evil over good, arrogance, and the ceaseless search for pleasure, frequently without self-control. It all sounds like last night's news bulletin. Carroll, Schaeffer, Eberstadt, Bork and Senior, *inter alia*, have written many chapters describing the scenario, often in great detail. Merely to read much of it leaves one feeling contaminated. The characteristics Paul lists describe what happens every day on the streets, in the offices, in the homes and in the schools of virtually every country in the Western world.

Yet none of this is the real issue. The key text is verse 2, in which Paul declares at the outset, "Men will be lovers of themselves". This is the first of the nineteen characteristics, and it is the spring from which all the others flow. The NIV and other translations are more gender inclusive, "People will be lovers of themselves". The real issue here is narcissism. In our time Narcissus has reappeared and come of age. Today's 'selfie' is Narcissus dressed up in modern garb, obsessed with his or her appearance, expectations and compulsion to be noticed. Narcissism, self-love, precedes love of money in Paul's list. Scott Peck argues that "malignant narcissism" is "at the very root of evil".[53] The love of money is in reality a manifestation of the narcissism from which it springs, as is the case with all other indications of self-absorption and self-gratification. Bork argues that narcissism leads to nihilism. It is a connection that deserves consideration. "The one who is absorbed in himself and his sensations, believing in few or no moral or religious principles,

---

53 M. Scott Peck, *People of the Lie* (London: Arrow, 1990), 89.

in nothing transcendental, is a nihilist. A culture that preaches narcissistic nihilism is asking for trouble".[54] Bork's case is that this is exactly what has happened over the last thirty years or so and that it is happening on an ever-increasing scale today. Little wonder that trouble of all kinds surrounds us everywhere. We have asked for it.

The point in all this is that this defining mark of our culture, narcissism, is the very antithesis of the incarnate *Logos* whose existence in human form lay at the heart of Western civilisation as traditionally understood. The Jesus who must be abolished to make way for humanism's new god, emptied himself, made himself of no reputation, thought that being God was nothing to be grasped, clung to, cherished. So he renounced it, to enter the arena of human existence. That is so alien to contemporary thought as to be incomprehensible. At the heart of his teachings, which in turn lie at the heart of the Christian West, were the twin principles of self-denial and the welfare of others. The contrast between the old, Christian West and the new, humanist West could not be greater. The options are self-abnegation or self-glorification, self-sacrifice or self-gratification, humility or hubris, the culture of life or the culture of death, God in Christ or Narcissus by himself. If we have correctly understood the prophetic voices of our time and comprehended the meaning of the evidence that surrounds us, we know that Western civilisation is in decline, and we know why.

A Prophetic Perspective

We now return to Jerusalem and the teleological, forward-moving understanding of history which re-appeared in the Reformation as a significant factor in the Protestant world-view. It is most clearly enunciated in two outlines of successive world empires set out by the prophet Daniel and referred to by one early English expositor as "the A.B.C. of prophecy",[55] i.e., the starting-point for understanding all subsequent biblical prophecies. They are Daniel's first two symbolic visions, the great metal image in chapter 2 and the four beasts in chapter 7, widely held to be complementary outlines of world history from Daniel's time to the final establishment of God's kingdom on earth. This linear understanding of history affirmed by these chapters was not, however, the sole prerogative of Reformation and post-Reformation biblical scholars. It came to be the standard Protestant interpretation for several centuries, still valid today and finding its way, complete with diagram and dates, into the *NIV Study Bible* published by Zondervan in 1985.[56] This long-established view of prophecy and history provides a final

---

54 Bork, *Gomorrah,* 125–26.

55 *Supra,* ch. 11, 'Early English Apocalyptic Interpretation', 13–15.

56 *NIV Study Bible* (Grand Rapids, MI: Zondervan, 1985), 1311.

prism through which it is possible to understand in context the decline of the West and to grasp its full significance.

Limitations of space require that we focus on the prophetic outline in Daniel 2:28–45, assuming that readers will be familiar at least to some extent with the text and Daniel's interpretation. As previously noted, this prophecy covers in outline the entire course of Western history from Daniel's time to the establishment on earth of the kingdom of God. The sequence of events is symbolised by a great image composed of four different metals — gold, silver, bronze and iron — depicting the four empires that would successively rule the Western world from the end of the 6th century BC onwards: Babylon (626–539 BC), Medo-Persia (539–331 BC), Greece (331–168 BC) and Rome (168 BC–AD 476). The fourth empire, Rome, would be divided, first into two parts, East and West, Constantinople and Rome, symbolised by the legs of the image, and ultimately into ten kingdoms, symbolised by the toes of the image and also by the ten horns of the fourth beast of Daniel's second prophecy in chapter 7. Many commentators agree that it is not necessary to understand this as a literal number, even though it is possible to identify ten such nations.

Some of the nations into which the Roman Empire was divided were strong and some were weak, as indicated by the feet and toes of the image which were made of iron mixed with clay (vv. 33, 42). These divided nations would last until the kingdom of God was established, bringing to an end all earthly kingdoms as predicted in the vision by a great stone or rock of supernatural origin. This rock would strike the image upon its feet, i.e., in the time symbolised by the feet and toes, becoming "a great mountain" and "filling the whole earth" (v.35), or in the words of the interpretation, "in the days of these kings, the God of heaven will set up a kingdom which shall never be destroyed" (v.44). Thus would human history and earthly time yield to eternity.

Beyond the identity of the four empires there are at least three further facts that emerge from the text and its fulfilment in the course of history. In specifying them it is recognised that we are attempting the impossible in seeking to condense several centuries of rich history into just a few paragraphs. That aside, it is clear firstly that the main focus of this prophecy is on the time represented by the feet and toes of the image. In the interpretation of Nebuchadnezzar's dream, Daniel gives one verse, sometimes only part of a verse, to each of the four empires, while four verses are given to the events to take place in the time of the feet and toes. Even the mighty Roman Empire which had lasted for six centuries is passed over in a single verse. It is as though the text must reach its apogee as quickly as possible. The kingdom of the stone is, of course, the ultimate climax of the prophecy, but in terms of what transpires on earth and leads ultimately to the kingdom of God, it is undoubtedly what happens on earth in the period designated by the feet and toes of the image that is of greatest significance.

The identity of the nations into which the Western Roman Empire was divided is obviously also of crucial importance. Roberts describes what happened: "The last western emperor was deposed by a Germanic warlord, Odoacer, in 476, and formal sovereignty passed to the eastern emperor"[57] [in Constantinople]. Odoacer was leader of the Ostrogoths, one of many tribes which descended on Rome from the north during the 4th and early 5th centuries, eventually settling in what had been the Western Roman Empire. Often thought of as barbarian, many of these tribes, the Ostrogoths included, were in fact Arian Christians. Roberts again, specifically of the origins of Western Europe, says:

> People, customs and concepts that had been developed on the Central Eurasian steppe were part of the foundation for the new kingdoms that emerged, either through peoples such as the Goths, Alans and Huns, or through the influence they had on the Germanic tribes who had encountered them. It was a new world for those who lived on the continent.[58]

Another account reflects the turmoil of the age, "The period was one of great upheaval, confusion, and change, during which a large number of states secured their independence".[59] Three of the tribes which invaded Rome, the Heruli, Vandals and Ostrogoths, were themselves destroyed by 538, those remaining from the conquest of Rome settling down across the lands of the old Empire and eventually giving rise to the nations which now comprise Western Europe. The crucial fact emerging from this all too brief account of what was a long and often confusing sequence of events over many centuries is that the feet and toes of Daniel's image represented the nations of Western Europe as they emerged after the fall of the Roman Empire.

The final point of note is that all four empires represented in the prophecy, beginning with golden Babylon, made a significant impact on the world of their day. The details are not mentioned in the text, but can easily be ascertained from any reliable history. Rome is a prime example. A vast and well-ordered empire, Rome dominated the world of its time for several centuries bequeathing to posterity an understanding of law and order as the basis for peace and prosperity. We are thus led to a final and critical question. What contribution did the nations represented by the feet and toes make to the world of their day? What impact did Europe, Western Europe in particular, have on the course of history? Roberts suggests the answer in a chapter

---

57 Roberts, *History,* 279.

58 *Ibid.*

59 *Seventh-day Adventist Bible Commentary* (Washington, DC: Review and Herald, 1955), 4, 826.

entitled, 'Christianity and the Western Transition'. Noting that Christianity came of age in the old Roman Empire, Roberts recognises Christianity's significance to the developing European mind and ethos and to Europe's subsequent character:

> Often disguised or muted, its influence runs deep in the countries that were shaped by it; almost incidentally, it defined Europe. That continent and others are what they are today because a handful of Jews saw their teacher and leader crucified and believed he rose again from the dead.[60]

The influence of Christianity on European history and therefore on the West is incalculable and widely recognised. As Europe developed so did Western civilisation, built initially and firmly on Christian principles and values. That the United States has also played a significant role in the making of the West is undeniable, but so is the fact that early America was settled by immigrants from many European countries, not least among them the founding Pilgrim Fathers from England, taking with them their Christian beliefs and deeply held convictions of the Bible as the basis for a coherent and ordered society. Europe initially gave the world what we now know as Western civilisation and until recent times Europe has been a staunch defender and promulgator of Christianity. Christianity, 'the essence of western civilisation', came to maturity in Western Europe with the latter-day descendents of the feet and toes of Daniel's vision of world history.

We can be even more precise concerning recent events. Melanie Phillips, reminding us once again of the most significant battle of our time, 'The Attack on Western Civilisation', writes, "Christianity is under direct and unremitting cultural assault from those who want to destroy the bedrock values of Western civilisation".[61] Specifically, "Christianity and the Hebrew Bible have come under explicit attack".[62] Toynbee was right in asserting that the survival of the West was directly related to "the spiritual values of its prophets". We now live in a different world, however. Humanism and secularism have for most people destroyed belief in the prophets whose values undergirded the original West. As Newbigin explains, "The real world is not the world of the Bible", but a world "that can be explained without reference to the hypothesis of God".[63] The old prophets have gone, their voices muted and disregarded, the culture they shaped changed for ever. So Phillips can conclude, "The attack on Western civilisation at its most profound level is an attack on the creed that lies at the very foundation of that civilisation".[64]

---

60   Roberts, *History,* 246.
61   Phillips, *World Turned Upside Down,* 312.
62   *Ibid.,* 98.
63   Newbiggin, *Foolishness to the Greeks,* 67.
64   Phillips, *World Turned Upside Down,* 316.

And it has all come about at the very end of Daniel's depiction of world history, in the final stages of the times represented by the feet and toes of the image.

Carroll argues that in order to succeed, humanism had to "create out of nothing something as strong as the faith of the New Testament that could move mountains".[65] But humanism failed. The results of that failure lie all around us, "the wreck of Western culture", in the end-time of human history as foretold by Daniel. Yet that is not the end, if we take seriously the final assertion of the prophet, which reason tells us we must do in view of the fulfilment of all that has preceded it over the course of many centuries. "In the time of those kings, the God of heaven will set up a kingdom that will never be destroyed" (v. 44).

On this positive note we must conclude what has been for the most part a sombre and sobering analysis of our time and our culture. While we feel compelled by the evidence to agree with those who have said there is no going back to the past, no way to reverse the changes that can be seen all around us, there is a way forward — the kingdom of the stone, the kingdom of God, the kingdom which the incarnate *Logos* himself proclaimed and to which the biblical prophets consistently bear witness. We are told that the "kingdom of God was the central message of Jesus", a kingdom "both present and future".[66] It was manifest in the incarnate *Logos* himself, the one who was and is, in his very being, in his life and teachings, but it is not completely fulfilled until the end of the age. If this is true, then all that the *Logos* is and all that he says demands a future, the final fulfilment of the prophetic vision that has been unfolding for two and a half millennia.

In this context it is possible to look forward with assurance to that final fulfilment - the arrival of the kingdom signified by the stone, the kingdom of God. Here is anticipation in place of despair, light to dispel the gloom, the brightness of a new day to follow the twilight and darkness that has descended on a confused and culpably misled and misinformed world. The irreversible decline of the West, in reality no myth, is in fact a welcome harbinger of hope.

---

65 Carroll, *Wreck of Western Culture*, 3.
66 G. E. Ladd, *A Theology of the New Testament* (London: Lutterworth, 1975), 57, 59.

17. Jesus and the Great Commission[1]

Bryan W. Ball

In his widely-read book *On Being a Christian,* Hans Küng reminds us that the "most fundamental characteristic of Christianity" is that it regards Jesus as "definitive" and "ultimately decisive". In answering the question "Which Christ?" of the many versions of Jesus currently available, Küng declares that it is the "concrete," "historical" Jesus, whose history can be "located" and "dated,"[2] crucified yet alive, who still calls men and women to faith and discipleship. Thus it will continue until the end of time if those who call themselves his followers today will take seriously Jesus' last words to his first disciples —his command to go into all the world with the gospel.

We now face an urgent and insistent question: How should we respond? What are we to do with this Jesus who cannot be ignored without compromising our own integrity or identity? Jesus himself has already provided the answer to this most pressing question. His last recorded words to the disciples who had witnessed firsthand all that he said and did, including his death and resurrection, contain the answer for us as it did for them. Jesus commanded them to go into all the world with the gospel message and make more disciples. The exact words of the Great Commission are unambiguously simple: "Go therefore and make disciples of all nations, baptizing them in the name of the Father, Son and Holy Spirit, teaching them to observe all things that I have commanded you" (Matt 28:19, 20, NKJV).

The Great Commission raises three fundamental questions, each of them requiring urgent attention if we are serious about Jesus and his will for the church and for the world. What does the Great Commission mean? Who does it include? And how can it be accomplished? In attempting to answer these questions and explore their relevance for professing Christians in the twenty-first century, we must first accept that mission is foundational to the very nature of the church as well as to Christ's own declared purposes. Jon Dybdhal observes, "If the church ceases to be missionary, it has not simply

---

1   First published as the final chapter in Bryan W. Ball and William G. Johnsson, *The Essential Jesus* (Boise ID: Pacific Press, 2002. Abridged and used by permission.

2   Hans Küng, *On Being a Christian* (London: Collins, 1978), 123, 146, 148.

failed in it's task, but has actually ceased from being the church".[3] It would not be difficult to find a dozen similar statements. The church exists for mission.

Before we explore these questions, a word about terminology. Three related words appear in the following pages. Two of them, "mission" and "witness", are used frequently, and often synonymously, although strictly speaking mission is broader than witness. Mission is the task of the church. Witness is what the church and Christians do in order to accomplish mission. Witness can take many forms, one of them being evangelism in both its broad and narrower senses. We shall argue that as witness is essential to mission, so evangelism, both broadly and narrowly understood, is essential to witness. Since all are applicable and necessary everywhere in the world, Max Warren can say that "the word 'missionary' is to be understood as applying to anyone, anywhere"[4], who is motivated by the Great Commission.

Rediscovering the Great Commission

What does it mean, then, this final word from Jesus to his disciples? How shall we understand it, initially as it was given to the first disciples and then for ourselves, his disciples in the contemporary world? Only as we listen to it carefully, coming direct from Scripture, free from the weight of tradition, bias, or denominational pride, can we grasp again its immense and compelling significance.

The words of Jesus recorded in Matthew 28:19, 20 were delivered at one of several post-resurrection appearances, at most of which Jesus spoke of the task awaiting his disciples. Parallel passages are Mark 16:15–18 and Luke 24:46–49. They reflect similar words spoken by Jesus on other occasions between the resurrection and the ascension, as do also John 20:21-22 and Acts 1:8. Matthew 24:14 is also particularly relevant. These passages all relate to the Great Commission and Christ's intention for his disciples, and they need to be studied together, although Matthew 28:19, 20 remains the basic text.

While the Authorised Version at Matthew 28:19 begins with the familiar words, "Go ye therefore, and teach all nations", most modern versions agree that the word here rendered "teach" should be translated "make disciples of". The Revised Authorised and New International Versions both retain the imperative and read, "Go and make disciples of all nations". Lenski says that

---

3 Jon L. Dybdahl, "Adventist Mission Today", in Jon L. Dybdahl, ed., *Adventist Mission in the 21ˢᵗ Century* (Hagerstown, MD: Review and Herald, 1999), 18.

4 Max Warren, *I Believe in the Great Commission* (London: Hodder & Stoughton, 1976), 173.

"teach" is an "unfortunate and even misleading translation" for those who do not have access to the original.[5] Howard Snyder insists that "disciple-making" means "teaching believers to follow Jesus and live the life of the kingdom that he taught and lived before them", while according to another view discipleship requires "belief in Jesus and transformation of life"[6]. So more than instruction is enjoined by the Great Commission. It also calls for decision and commitment. It encompasses the entire process of leading men and women to become authentic disciples of Jesus, "obedient followers", to borrow Lenski's pithy phrase.

The other side of this coin, however, is equally significant. Making disciples also includes teaching or the impartation of knowledge. To pass over the debate as to whether this instruction should precede or follow baptism (the answer surely is both), the essential point to grasp here is that true Christian faith is rooted in understanding. A disciple is a person who has been instructed and enlightened in coming to faith. The Greek word in verse 20 (from *didasko*) clearly means to teach, but even the word in verse 19 (from *mateteuo*) carries with it the underlying idea of instruction. Kittel refers to the "unambiguous" sense of teaching or instruction, "the impartation of practical or theoretical knowledge" implicit in this passage and says of verse 20, "the risen Lord made the continuation of this task the life work of his people"[7]. It is not possible to be a true disciple of Jesus with an empty mind.

Some contemporary Christian writers are speaking again of apologetics, the defence or explanation of Christian faith. The concept is crucial if the Great Commission is to be accomplished in the Western world. Apologetics proposes the reasons for believing in Christ and for being his disciples and suggests answers to possible objections. Informed Christians become informed through the process of apologetics. Alister McGrath declares that one of the important tasks of apologetics is "explanation", in the context of a secular society that is increasingly ignorant of the basic truths of Christianity and in which "half-truths, misconceptions, and caricatures abound"[8]. The world needs to hear, loud and clear, repeatedly and uncompromisingly, what Christian faith really is.

---

5   R. C. H. Lenski, *The Interpretation of Matthew's Gospel* (Minneapolis, MN: Augsburg, 1964), 1172.

6   Howard Snyder, *Liberating the Church* (Downers Grove, IL: IVP, 1983), 24; Donald Senior and Carroll Stuhlmueller, *The Biblical Foundations for Mission* (Maryknoll, NY: Orbis, 1983), 252.

7   G. Kittel ed., *Theological Dictionary of the New Testament* (Grand Rapids, MI: Eerdmans, 1964), II, 138, 135, 145.

8   Alister McGrath, "Starting Where People Are", in Michael Green and Alister McGrath, *How Shall We Reach Them?* (Milton Keynes, UK: Word, 1995), 20.

In Acts 1:8 we find three further elements of the divine mandate for mission. Jesus also said to his disciples, in the context of the promised Holy Spirit, "You shall ... be witnesses to Me ... to the end of the earth" (NKJV). We shall return later to two of these crucial factors. For the present, the key word here is "witnesses". It has been pointed out frequently that this word refers to those who testify from personal experience. One of the most trusted New Testament exegetes of the twentieth century says that it "denotes one who declares facts directly known to himself", one who speaks from "his own direct knowledge" about people or events he has observed personally[9]. The disciples of Jesus were to be witnesses to facts, but also to the meaning of those facts. Their word was to be testimony and evangelistic confession.

The facts in question "are the facts of the history of Jesus ... which took place in the clear light of history at a specific time and place, facts which can be established and on which one can rely". They must be attested to and their significance must be explained.[10] Those are qualified to be witnesses who could, and who still can, vouch for the objectivity of these facts and explain their continuing redemptive significance. They are witnesses in the legal and biblical senses. On their testimony the lives of others may depend. This is what Acts 1:8 means when it speaks of witnesses.

Further relevance may be found in John's account. On the evening of the resurrection day Jesus met with a small group of his disciples and began immediately to point them toward the future. "As the Father hath sent me, I also send you", he declared (John 20:21, NKJV). This is probably the genesis of the Great Commission which finds its fullest expression at a later meeting between Jesus and a larger group of disciples and which, as we have noted, is recorded in Matthew 28:19, 20. Lenski relates this text specifically to the Great Commission and renders it, "As the Father has commissioned me, I, too, am sending you".[11] While his death and resurrection are still vivid in their minds, on the day of the resurrection and on the first occasion thereafter when Jesus met with the disciples, he focuses their attention on what their response must be to these momentous events. It shows just how vital mission was both to him and to them.

There is more here, however, that relates to effective witness. Jesus sends his disciples into the world "as the Father" had sent him. It is not coincidental that this particular emphasis is found in John's account. It reflects the earlier emphases in this same Gospel where there is repeated reference to the "sending" of the Son by the Father (John 3:16, 17; 6:38, 39; 9:4; 12:49,

---

9   Kittel, *Theological Dictionary* (1967), IV, 492, 489.

10   *Ibid.,* 492.

11   R. C. H. Lenski, *The Interpretation of St. John's Gospel* (Minneapolis, MN: Augsburg, 1943), 1368–69.

50). These texts are all to be seen in the light of John's unique and powerful first chapter where the sent Word becomes flesh and comes down to his own for their enlightenment and redemption. Jesus' own mission has an incarnational character. He was sent from the Father to be one with humankind, to identify and be identified with them. It is a truth of the utmost significance for those who are now sent by Jesus into the twenty-first-century world. To be sent as Christ was sent is to be sent incarnationally into the world. We ignore this truth at great loss, even to ineffectiveness.

Matthew 24:14 presents us with a further factor of great significance in attempting to grasp the intent of the Great Commission for mission in our time. Here, where Jesus refers to the final, end-time gospel proclamation, a particular phrase is used to describe the gospel that is then to be proclaimed "as a witness to all nations". It is not merely "the gospel" without clarification. It is specifically the gospel "of the kingdom". Again, this can be understood adequately — and must be so understood — only in the light of what Matthew has said previously.

Matthew has already written much about the kingdom. There are more than fifty such references in his Gospel, many of them sayings of Jesus himself. Matthew even uses this same phrase, "the gospel of the kingdom", on other occasions (4:24; 9:35). It was in fact this "gospel of the kingdom" which Jesus himself proclaimed, the good news that God's kingdom had already arrived in his person and which figures prominently in his own proclamation. As has been shown repeatedly over the past fifty or sixty years, this was the central thrust of Jesus' own teaching — the kingdom of heaven is at hand (Matt 4:17; 10:7; Mark 1:15); it has, in Jesus himself, already "drawn near". The parables of the kingdom (Matt 13 and 25) are parables of a kingdom that, while yet to come in its finality, is also ready present. It is *this* kingdom that is at the heart of the gospel. It is the good news concerning *this* kingdom that is to be preached as a witness to all nations in the end-time proclamation.

We must not allow the force of this essential truth to elude us any longer. The kingdom of the future emerges from a kingdom that is already present. They are one and the same kingdom, now in time, then in eternity. To preach only, or even mainly, a future kingdom is to distort the very gospel of Jesus. The church exists as the agent to bring this kingdom continually into being, to demonstrate the presence and the nature of this kingdom and to extend it by mission.

The kingdom, therefore, becomes the focus of true mission, the genesis, the vehicle, and the consummation of the gospel and the Great Commission itself. Beyerhaus understands the church's responsibility to be to "hasten the visible establishment of Christ's kingdom on earth", noting the relationship of this task to the coming of the Lord. "Only when this work is complete will Christ come to redeem the groaning creation from its present bondage".[12] The gospel *of the kingdom*, proclaimed throughout the world, makes this ultimately possible. We must in all honesty ask ourselves if we have been faithful to the gospel that is described in Matthew 24:14. Or have we been content with something less, the message of half a kingdom, the kingdom which is yet to come, perhaps?

Finally, the extent of the task confronts us again: "Witnesses ... to the ends of the earth", "to all nations", to the "end of the age". For two millennia the church has, more or less, been driven by this vision. Christian believers can now be found all over the world. It would be easy to think that the task is almost done, and indeed it may be. But we must not forget that the command to preach the gospel and make disciples in all nations applies to peoples and localities where the church already exists, as well as those over the seas. It includes new generations in countries and cultures that have been regarded as Christian for centuries but in reality are not so any longer. In this respect it is imperative to hear again the cry of the lost in the Western world. It is here more than anywhere that the Great Commission needs immediate resurrection. The Christian church here is having little, if any, effect on society. Adventist missiologist, Jon Dybdahl, speaks of the "mission malaise of the First-world church", specifically in Western Europe, North America, Australia, and New Zealand.[13] The secular humanist and the secular materialist are as far removed from the Christ of Scripture as the devout Hindu, the Moslem fundamentalist, and the unenlightened Animist. They, too, must hear.

This chapter then is largely and unapologetically a response to this noxious malaise. It is a condition which must be countered rapidly if the church, indeed Christianity as a whole, is to remain what it claims to be, the body of Christ with a message for all humankind. While much of what is said here, of course, will also be relevant to the church elsewhere in the world, the "appalling lostness" of the secular millions in the West,[14] to borrow John Stott's evocative phrase, cannot go unheeded.

So from these seminal passages in Matthew 28, Acts 1, John 20 and Matthew 13 and 24, we can recapture what it is that Jesus wanted his disciples to accomplish. There is much more that can be drawn from these texts and

---

12 Peter Beyerhaus, "World Evangelisation and the Kingdom of God", in J. D. Douglas ed., *Let the Earth Hear His Voice* (Minneapolis, MN: World-Wide, 1974), 285.

13 Dybdahl, *Adventist Mission,* 18.

14 John Stott, *Christian Mission in the Modern World* (London: Falcon, 1975), 108.

others that are also relevant, and some of it will be said later. But can we not confidently declare that in essence Jesus commanded his disciples to go incarnationally into the world with the gospel of a kingdom already present as well as yet to come; that he bade them witness to all nations and cultures, making other disciples — men, women and young people who would come to understand who Jesus is and why he came to earth, and who would gladly respond affirmatively to his gospel invitation and in turn become witnesses and disciple-makers? There may indeed be more, but certainly nothing less than this is acceptable, either in understanding the Great Commission or in putting it into effect. It is this momentous task that remains "the central mission", the "great charter" of the church.[15]

Refocusing on Responsibility

We must now turn without flinching to the question of responsibility. It arises inevitably from the very nature of the Great Commission, especially when applied to our own time and to our specific location, wherever that may be. To whom is the Great Commission given? Who are those who are commanded by Jesus to go and make disciples? Are any excluded?

It is helpful here to remember the relationship between kingdom and church. The church is the created community of the kingdom and this community is the agent of the kingdom. Snyder says that the church "exists for the kingdom of God"[16], a position we can accept more readily when we remember also the eschatological future of that kingdom. Bonhoeffer stated "the Church is the Church only when it exists for others"[17], i.e. to extend the kingdom on earth by intentional, focused mission and witness by which others accept Jesus and become his disciples. Although Jesus spoke much more about the kingdom than he did about the church as such, he nonetheless envisaged the church's existence and its future in declaring that the gates of hell would not prevail against it and that he had entrusted to the church the keys of that kingdom (Matt 16:18, 19). *The church now has the keys to this kingdom.* It is an awesome responsibility that many voices throughout the Christian centuries have emphatically sought to underline, including many in our own time. We must not ignore them.

Charles van Engen deplores the current situation in which, in the minds of many Christians, "church" and "mission" are often seen as distinct and

---

15   Roger Hedlund, *The Mission of the Church in the World* (Grand Rapids, MI: Baker, 1991), 190; *Seventh-day Adventist Bible Commentary* (Hagerstown, MD: Review and Herald), 5(1956), 557.

16   Snyder, *Liberating the Church*, 24.

17   Dietrich Bonhoeffer, *Letters and Papers from Prison* (New York: Macmillan, 1953), 203.

conflicting ideas. He contends emphatically that to understand the church as principally a missionary organization "is not optional", proposing that the church "is being obedient when it can be found out in the main thorough-fares and the streets, inviting everyone to the eschatological wedding feast of the Lamb".[18] Roger Hedlund insists that "we cannot escape the obligation to carry the gospel to the nations", declaring that the Great Commission is "the essential mission of the church".[19] Michael Green says it is "incumbent" upon Christians to spread the good news.[20] Some see a negative attitude to mission in the Western church manifesting itself in a "Little Bo-Peep" mentality which believes that the lost sheep will come home on their own.[21] Clearly, they will not. They must be brought home.

Much of the foregoing reminds us of a statement made many years ago but which now seems remarkably pertinent once again: "The church is God's appointed agency for the salvation of men. It was organized for service, and its mission is to carry the gospel to the world".[22] Few would actually disagree with that. Most, in fact, would wholeheartedly agree in theory. The challenge comes in translating theory into practice, particularly for churches in which it has become comfortable to be nominally Christian and where it is easier for the majority of members to sit in the pews during the worship service and remain silent for the rest of the week.

Perhaps the problem and its resolution lie in part at least in the balance between nurture and mission. In recent years there has been an increasing emphasis on nurturing activities designed to keep alive the often-flickering flame of the local congregation. At a time when secularism and materialism increasingly erode the foundations of the faith, it is entirely understandable. The argument that nurture is an essential prerequisite to witness is persuasive. But how far does it go before the balance becomes untenable? Snyder believes that the church "gets into trouble whenever it thinks it is in church business rather than in kingdom business".[23] The point is clearly valid. It is possible to become more concerned with the life of those in the local congregation than with the death of those in the surrounding community. By "kingdom business" Snyder means activities which are specifically directed

---

18   Charles van Engen, *God's Missionary People* (Grand Rapids, MI: Baker, 1991), 28, 76, 81.

19   Hedlund, *Mission of the Church,* 188, 190.

20   In David Watson, *I Believe in Evangelism* (London: Hodder & Stoughton, 1976), 9.

21   Cited in David Haney, *The Idea of the Laity* (Grand Rapids, MI: Zondervan, 1973), 141–42.

22   E. G. White, *The Acts of the Apostles* (Mountain View, CA: Pacific Press, 1911), 9.

23   Snyder, *Liberating the Church, 11.*

at extending the kingdom of God by sharing the good news of Jesus and the kingdom with those who have not yet heard it or not yet responded.

Gavin Reid, an Anglican who became disillusioned with the failure of his congregation to make any significant impact on the community, wrote a book having the provocative title *The Gagging of God*. Proposing that the church, by its ineffectiveness, was actually preventing God's message from reaching the community, Reid suggested three reasons for this situation, the third of which is "the accelerating introversion of practically all forms of Christian activity".[24] If this was true a couple of decades ago, it is more than ever true today. Nurture is the "in" word now. It has climbed the agenda, become more fashionable, more time-consuming and, dare we say it, more congregationally chic, than mission.

It would be easy to conclude that those who spend most of their time and energy, even financial resources, on structure, the nature of ministry, the social life of the congregation, maintenance committees, and the seemingly endless round of camps, conferences, retreats and workshops have really lost the plot. That might be a harsh judgment since there is nothing intrinsically wrong with any of these concerns or activities. They are in fact all quite legitimate. It is simply that they take up so much time and energy and the best available personnel that there is little left to invest in the reason for the church's existence. Consequently the church becomes increasingly inward-looking and self-centred, which is the very antithesis of authentic Christian life and the church's reason for being. This unhealthy and unbiblical nexus must be corrected if we are serious about our mission responsibilities. David Watson complains impatiently of the "moribund, introverted ranks" of many churches, and observes painfully but truthfully, "we have a private dialogue with ourselves while man plunges suicidally on into absurdity and despair".[25]

It is also necessary to address with purposeful intent the issue of function within the church. The idea that ministry is the sole prerogative of the ordained pastor simply will not do any longer. It is not a biblical view, as has been said frequently in recent years. Some local churches may have caught on, but the truth still has a long way to travel before it permeates the whole body of Christ. Ministry is the task of the entire believing community, pastor and people together. Michael Green, in one of his many perceptive and helpful books on the life and work of the church, says in *Evangelism Now and Then* that every-member involvement in the mission of the church is "the

---

24   Gavin Reid, *The Gagging of God* (London: Hodder & Stoughton, 1969), 125.

25   Watson, *Evangelism,* 136.

biggest difference between the New Testament church and our own". Then he adds, "It is not until church members have the enthusiasm to speak to their friends and acquaintances about Jesus that anybody will really believe that we have got good news to tell".[26]

Walter Douglas believes, with substantial reason, that we have "a great deal of catching-up to do" with respect to lay involvement in the mission of the church and in ministry to the waiting world. "It is not more or less organization of church structures or the refining or redefining of church polity that we need", he says. *"What is desperately needed is the laicization of the church"* (emphasis supplied). It is a conclusion that many from across the Christian spectrum have reached as they have studied the New Testament teaching on church, mission and ministry. "Members in the local congregation must be taught that when God calls them into his church, he calls them to serve in the mission of the church".[27] This message has been preached widely now for years, but it is still far from being implemented in many parts of the world. So where does responsibility lie for ensuring that the Great Commission is fulfilled? It lies, as it always has, with all who are disciples of Jesus.

Regaining the Initiative

Further direction from Jesus can be found in Luke 10, a chapter that invites scrutiny by all who are serious about the Great Commission. In appointing the seventy Jesus said, "The harvest truly is great". There is timeless truth here, relevant to every age in which disciples are called to go out into the highways and byways, as they still are today. To Jesus, the harvest is always great. There are always those who, for whatever reason, are ready to hear the gospel and are willing to receive it. Some may have been opposed or hostile on previous occasions. But now their minds and hearts are open. The Spirit has been doing his silent work. And, of course, witness must be faithfully borne to those who are still ignorant, hostile, or apathetic, regardless of any immediate outcome, since they too might respond later.

How, then, shall we proceed? What can be said that will direct us towards a more successful fulfilment of Christ's commission? It is impossible to answer that question in any detail, and in any case it is not the purpose of this chapter to suggest strategies or methodology. Basic attitudes and underlying principles must come first and must undergird all strategies and methods. The following five principles are critical to successful mission now as al-

---

26 Michael Green, *Evangelism Now and Then* (London: Daybreak, 1992), 117, 35.

27 Walter Douglas, "Vocation as Mission", in Dybdhal, *Adventist Mission,* 111.

ways, as we proceed into the twenty-first century. Without them any hope of true success is at best minimal.

Witnesses to Jesus

Acts 1:8 contains two further truths essential to the fulfilment of the Great Commission. Firstly, the disciples were to be "witnesses unto Me" (NKJV), although some other contemporary versions prefer "witnesses for Me". Lenski is rightly all-inclusive: "Called to witness by me, for me, about me, yea, all about me".[28] Jesus was the supreme focus of the apostolic witness. He still is.

How often we have heard that, and how often we have forgotten it in our enthusiasm to witness about our church, our congregation, our distinctive beliefs, our world mission program, our institutions, even our diet. Jesus is the focal point of authentic witness, no matter how valid it is to speak of other things on the appropriate occasion. John Stott adds perceptively that we are not at liberty to communicate a Christ of our own predilection who is not recorded in Scripture, "nor to embroider or manipulate the Christ who is in Scripture, but to bear faithful witness to the one and only Christ there is … the authentic Jesus, the Jesus of history who is the Jesus of Scripture".[29] This is the "irreducible minimum of the apostolic gospel".[30]

In his book, *I Believe in the Great Commission,* Max Warren speaks of the "recovery of nerve".[31] He means attempting to fulfil the Great Commission in an age that is outwardly more sceptical and apathetic than any other in history. In this context Warren calls for obedience in discipleship and to Christ's command. "Obedience" is not a popular word today. It contradicts the individualism pervading the popular culture that surrounds us, the culture to which we must bear witness and which so easily infiltrates the church. Yet obedience is non-negotiable for the true Christian, especially obedience to the commands of Jesus, if witness and mission are again to become a priority. It is, of course, the obedience of love, but obedience nonetheless — specifically obedience to the mission imperatives of Jesus.

In describing the content of authentic witness, David Watson refers to the "objective, historical events" upon which Christian faith is built, pointing out that to concentrate on the "purely subjective side of the Christian faith … is but one step away from confusion, deception, agnosticism or even atheism". The strength of the gospel is that it is "firmly rooted in the true,

---

28 R. C. H. Lenski, *The Interpretation of the Acts of the Apostles* (Minneapolis, MN: Augsburg, 1961), 32.

29 Stott, *Christian Mission,* 48.

30 John Stott, *Explaining the Lausanne Covenant,* Lausanne Occasional Paper, 3 (London: Scripture Union, 1975), 13.

31 Warren, *Great Commission,* ch. 7, "The Recovery of Nerve".

historical events of Golgotha and the empty tomb".[32] Citing John Stott, Watson declares, "If the cross is not central in our thinking, it is safe to say that our faith, whatever it may be, is not the Christian faith".[33] It is what Michael Green means when he says so incisively, "Mission is Jesus-shaped".[34] It is witness to Jesus that is true witness. Anything other, or anything less, must be abandoned immediately and forever.

Yes, it takes nerve to witness to Jesus, deliberately and uncompromisingly, in a post-Christian, post-modern culture, but no more than it did for the first disciples in a pagan Roman or traditional Jewish culture. In spite of all perceived hazards and hostility, Jesus says to his disciples today, as he did in sending out the seventy, "I send you out as lambs among wolves" (Luke 10:3), specifically to be witnesses to him, "to all nations" and "to the end of the age". The prospect may sometimes be confronting, but it does not release us from our obligations or from his expectations.

A Persuasive Lifestyle

It is almost possible to sense the unease arising in the minds of many as they read the preceding paragraphs. All the old fears and feelings of inadequacy, even guilt, are flowing again. Let me attempt to bring some comfort. We do not need special training, an extrovert personality, facility with words, endless free time, or the latest equipment in order to fulfil Christ's command. Most of us can do it without saying anything. Jesus calls us to *be*, before he calls us to *say* or to *do*. In the Sermon on the Mount he spoke about shining lights and good works leading others to glorify God (Matt 5:16). Light and good works are both inaudible.

In a culture in which many people have become word-resistant, we can witness simply by what we are. In fact, it is impossible to communicate the gospel effectively with words if those words are not substantiated by a corresponding lifestyle. As the relentless pressure of media exposure creates expectations of a good image, the most effective images are still real people. It is what the atheistic enemy of Christianity, Nietzsche, had in mind when he wrote so scathingly, "His disciples have to look more saved if I am to believe in the Saviour".[35] Michael Green puts it more positively, "If we are not thrilled with Christ and being changed by Him, we can have all the techniques in the world and get nowhere".[36]

---

32 Watson, *Evangelism,* 68–9.

33 *Ibid.,* 71.

34 Michael Green, *Matthew for Today* (London: Hodder & Stoughton, 1988), 112.

35 Cited in Watson, *Evangelism,* 104.

36 Green, *Evangelism,* 22.

Few have understood this challenge better than the late Francis Schaeffer. In *The Church at the End of the Twentieth Century*, Schaeffer spoke of the need for integrity in the profession of the Christian faith. He says we "must practice truth" as well as proclaim it. In an age like ours, he argues, we have "removed our credibility before the non-Christian, post-Christian, relativistic, sceptical, lost world" if we compromise our Christian profession by a lifestyle that is less than totally Christian.

> If you think that those who have rejected the plastic culture and are sick of hypocrisy are going to be impressed when you talk about truth and at the same time practice untruth, you are wrong. They will never listen. You have cut the ground from under yourself. We live in a generation that does not believe that such a thing as truth is possible, and if you practice untruth while talking about truth, the real thinkers will just say, "Garbage!"[37]

And, we might add, not only the thinkers. The same conclusion can and will be drawn by anyone. Jon Paulien's chief concern here is that the prevailing secular culture is already producing a lifestyle within the first-world church that is barely distinguishable from that which prevails within the culture itself.[38]

Arguing that affluent Christians are a contradiction in terms and "out of sequence" with the times Snyder claims, "We have forgotten, or rejected the values of simplicity, plainness and frugality held by our forefathers and most of the world's peoples".[39] He then confronts the church with "a difficult choice":

> To follow the way of easy affluence that leads almost inevitably to spiritual poverty or to take seriously the demands of the gospel and become a covenant community that risks taking a counter cultural stand at every point where Christian faithfulness is at stake.[40]

Whether or not we agree, the need for a transparent and consistent lifestyle is beyond question if our witness, corporate or individual, is to be more than "garbage" in the eyes of the watching world. It is a witness that all can bear from now on, even if they never say another word.

Social Responsibility

Jesus also said that believers are to be the salt of the earth and the light of the world. In the context of this passage (Matt 5:13–16), Stott comments on the two sayings of Jesus known as the Great Commission and the Great

---

37   Francis Schaeffer, "The Church at the End of the Twentieth Century", in *The Complete Works of Francis Schaeffer* (Westchester, IL: Crossway, 1982), 4, 33.

38   Jon Paulien, *Present Truth in the Real World* (Boise, ID: Pacific, 1993), *passim.*

39   Snyder, *Liberating the Church*, 206.

40   *Ibid.*, 194.

Commandment, observing that the Great Commission "neither explains, nor exhausts, nor supersedes the Great Commandment". This commandment to love our neighbour is an "urgent Christian dimension". Stott refers to man as "a psycho-somatic being", pointing out that our neighbour "is neither a bodyless soul that we should love only his soul, nor a soulless body that we should care for its welfare alone", thus reminding us of our responsibility for our neighbour's "total welfare", the physical as well as the spiritual. While such interaction brings credibility to a gospel that otherwise lacks "visibility", that gospel is always defined by "simple, uncomplicated compassion".[41]

For those committed to words and proclamation, the equation of compassion with communication has been a hard lesson to learn. It is much easier to talk than to be involved. Yet it is impossible to study the New Testament objectively without concluding that concern for the needs of others is the hallmark of true Christian faith. A religion which majors only in words, written or spoken, to the exclusion of actual involvement in meeting the needs of the disadvantaged is never authentic Christianity, regardless of how articulate its advocates may be. The incarnate Christ has been described as "the unwearied servant of man's necessity", and the work of his disciples now, as always, is "to feed the hungry, clothe the naked, and comfort the suffering and the afflicted".[42] Social concern and involvement are of equal importance in fulfilling the Great Commission as is verbal proclamation.

This conviction led to the inclusion of a statement regarding Christian social responsibility in the Lausanne Covenant on world evangelization, a document that still shapes the thinking of many in the evangelical world.[43] Both social action and evangelism "are necessary expressions of our doctrines of God and man, our love for our neighbour and our obedience to Jesus Christ".[44] Commenting on this clause in the Covenant, John Stott declares, "We must seek not only the spread of the kingdom itself, nor only to exhibit its righteousness ourselves, but also to spread its righteousness in the midst of an unrighteous world. How else can we be the salt of the earth?"[45] The question refuses to go away.

---

41 Stott, *Christian Mission,* 29–30.
42 E. G. White, *The Ministry of Healing* (Mountain View, CA: Pacific, 1942), 17, 106.
43 The definition of 'evangelical' has changed in recent times; see David F. Wells, *No Place for Truth: Or Whatever Happened to Evangelical Theology?* (Grand Rapids, MI and Cambridge, UK: Eerdmans, 1993) and Brian Stanley, *The Global Diffusion of Evangelicalism* (Nottingham: IVP, 2015).
44 Stott, "Lausanne Covenant", clause 5, Lausanne Occasional Paper, 3, 15.
45 *Ibid.,* 17.

Evangelism and Growth

It hardly needs to be said that evangelism and growth are crucial to the life and mission of the church. Yet both have attracted unfavourable comment in recent times from some within the church, quite unjustifiably it may be said. In the unambiguous words of one thoughtful and convinced practitioner, "The church is in the growth business, or it will die".[46] This forthright statement calls for serious reflection, particularly as many congregations in some parts of the world are already dying and as the church as a whole in the Western world is more or less stagnant, at best. It is our contention that evangelism, in its broadest sense and as one form of mission and witness, still leads to growth.

It is important to qualify the foregoing by explaining that growth includes spiritual growth and growth in maturity as well as statistical growth. All are essential to the well-being and therefore the functionality of the body of Christ. The church *must* grow spiritually *and* in numbers, or it will die. Both are critical. Membership growth there must be if congregational death, and ultimately even denominational death, is to be avoided. It is evangelism in the narrow as well as the broad sense that will bring growth, if we understand the word of God aright (Isa 55:11). It is crucial that we rediscover our passion for evangelism, for it is both biblical and necessary.

Evangelism is suspect in some minds primarily because of its perceived emphasis on numbers. It is a difficult logic to follow given the many New Testament references to quantity (Luke 15; Acts 2:41, 47; 5:14). Using the phrase "yearning for growth", van Engen asserts that "yearning for numerical growth is an essential mark" of the true church. It is a biblical concept, "by which the church has always expressed her nature in 'yearning' to incorporate more and more men and women within the bounds of God's grace". Seen like that, there can be no convincing argument against either growth or evangelism. In fact, where this yearning and subsequent rejoicing over the recovery of the lost are missing van Engen says, "we must ask ourselves whether something is not wrong at the very centre of the church's life".[47]

Recovery of the evangelistic imperative begins with Jesus' own ministry, in his delivery of the Great Commission and in his vision of the church yet to come. The various Greek words used to record these situations all carry the inherent idea of public comment or proclamation of the gospel. This is what Jesus himself did and what he required of his disciples (Luke 4:43; Mark 16:15; Matt 4:17). The Greek word from which we derive the word "evangelism" is used in the New Testament of the verbal proclamation of

---

46   Michael Harper, *Let My People Grow* (London: Hodder & Stoughton, 1977), 20.

47   van Engen, *Missionary People,* 81–2.

the gospel. For those who regard dialogue as a preferred method for today, it is also worth noting Watson's additional comment, "Before any profitable discussion or debate can take place we need to declare the gospel of Jesus Christ".[48]

Lest there be any doubt about the nature of the evangelism here envisaged, it has been clearly defined as "The proclamation of the historical, biblical Christ as Saviour and Lord, with a view to persuading people to come to Him personally and so be reconciled to God". The results of such evangelistic proclamation "include obedience to Christ, incorporation into his church and responsible service in the world".[49] It is intentional, focussed, and insistent. Proclamation and persuasion lead to discipleship, obedience, church membership, service and growth. The outcomes are as assured as the process itself is necessary. We do it or, ultimately, we die.

The Holy Spirit

We have left until last what is arguably the most important single factor necessary to effective witness. It is the *sine qua non* of everything the church undertakes in the name of Jesus — the presence and the power of the Holy Spirit. To do justice to this profound and indispensable theme would require a whole volume in itself. It is possible here only to underline again the essentials of what we have known, at least in theory, for decades.

The necessity of the Holy Spirit in witness begins with Jesus himself. On the evening of the resurrection day when he first met with his frightened and uncomprehending disciples, he "breathed on them" and said "Receive the Holy Spirit" (John 20:22; with Luke 24:44–48). Lenski makes the important point that this was not, as many have supposed, an "in earnest" bestowal of the gift that would come in its fullness at Pentecost, but a full and real impartation of the Holy Spirit then and there. It had a different purpose from the Pentecostal bestowal. The Spirit was here given to the disciples "for him to work in them personally", to comprehend and internalize all that had happened in the preceding few days and to grasp what it was that Jesus now wanted them to do.[50] It is a critical distinction. Those who are to receive the power of the Spirit in witnessing must first be open to him and have their minds changed by his presence. The Spirit does his work in the disciples *before* they can do their work in the world.

The definitive reference by Jesus to the Holy Spirit in relation to the Great Commission is recorded in Acts 1:4–8. The disciples were to receive the Spirit before being witnesses to Jesus throughout the world of their day.

---

48 Watson, *Evangelism,* 27, 46.
49 Lausanne Covenant, clause 4, "The Nature of Evangelism".
50 Lenski, *John's Gospel,* 1373–74.

The inference is clear enough. Without the Spirit they could not be witnesses, at least not effective witnesses, and experience tells us that there is a world of difference between witness and effective witness. The book of Acts is the record of what happened as a result of the fulfilment of this promise at Pentecost. Lenski, again, commenting on this text refers prophetically to Christ's witnesses "speaking to the end of time in a great apostolic chorus".[51] It is all made possible, and only made possible, through the presence and operation of the Spirit.

Stott refers to the "language of human activity" in his book *Christian Mission in the Modern World.* He says pointedly it "is seriously misleading" if such language is taken to mean that "mission is a human work and conversion a human achievement". Speaking of the person yet to receive Christ and enter the kingdom Stott affirms that "only the Holy Spirit can open his eyes, enlighten his darkness, liberate him from bondage, turn him to God and bring him out of death into life".[52] Michael Green observes that the Spirit is "the author, the controller and the energizer of Christian mission".[53] Jon Paulien states the Spirit's role is "essential to all effective outreach", calling for sensitivity "to the leading of the Holy Spirit" in all such activities.[54]

The final chapter of Philip Samaan's book, *Christ's Way of Reaching People,* is entitled "By His Spirit". It is a fitting conclusion and an essential emphasis. Samaan speaks of the "pivotal relationship between the Holy Spirit and witnessing", saying, "The New Testament inextricably links the Holy Spirit with the sharing of the gospel". We are compelled to agree. It is impossible, as Samaan together with those cited above and a host of others affirm, to witness effectively without the Spirit's abiding presence, his guidance, and his power. So we ask again with Samaan, "How can we ever think that we can bear witness to Christ without the infilling of the Holy Spirit?"[55] It is perhaps the most pressing question for our time and our church.

Despite promises of the Spirit's empowering presence "to the very end of the age", witness to Jesus and his kingdom is a daunting task, particularly in cultures that for the past half century or more have appeared to reject the gospel in favour of more "enlightened" alternatives, or even alternative versions of Christ. But some claim that times may be changing, that there may be hope, and on this optimistic note we conclude this reconsideration of Jesus' last command to his disciples.

---

51   Lenski, *Acts,* 32.

52   Stott, *Christian Mission,* 123–24.

53   Michael Green, *I Believe in the Holy Spirit* (London: Hodder & Stoughton, 1975), 64. The entire chapter "The Spirit in Mission", is helpful.

54   Paulien, *Present Truth,* 23, 140.

55   Philip Samaan, *Christ's Way of Reaching People* (Hagerstown, MD: Review and Herald, 1990), 144, 146.

Michael Green and Alister McGrath, two of the most informed and articulate contemporary advocates of Christian mission and of the biblical message itself, believe that a new day is dawning, "a day of renewed confidence in the truth of the Christian story". Noting the "barrenness of materialism" and the "hunger for spirituality" evident in our day, Green sees a "massive cultural shift" beginning to take place and believes that "the dogmas of the Enlightenment, which have dominated Western thought for two centuries, are in full retreat". "We are standing", he declares, "at one of the turning points of human thought". It is a "fascinating time to be alive". In this context, McGrath asserts that apologetics and evangelism "are the key to the future of Christianity as it stands poised to enter its third millennium".[56]

While the grip of secularism and materialism remains strong in many quarters, there is evidence that these hopes may be justified. In Jesus' view they are always justified. For him the fields are always ripe for harvest, particularly now at the end of time (John 4:35; Matt.13:39). We may therefore confidently declare our position. Never before has the potential harvest been so plentiful. Never before have the fish been waiting in such abundance to be gathered in. Never before have the sons and daughters of Adam in so many corners of the world been made so aware of the devastating effects of disordered and sinful human nature and the ineradicable hopelessness of the human predicament as in recent times. Each passing year brings increasing evidence.

Against this background, at the same time full of insecurity and abundant with offers of assurance, full of despair and full of hope, Jesus says, "Go *ye* into all the world, and make disciples". What better time, then, than now for unreserved commitment to a revitalized, refocused, Christ-centred, Spirit-inspired and thoroughly biblical proclamation of the Great Commission? We must not hesitate or prevaricate any longer. We *must* go. We must *all* go. The survival of the faith, the church, and the destiny of yet unenlightened millions depend on it.

---

56 Green and McGrath, *How Shall We Reach Them?* 7, 12.

Responses

18. Response to Bryan Ball's Biblical and Theological Chapters

Steven Thompson

Avondale Seminary

It is a privilege to offer a written response to the chapters on biblical and historical theology in this volume of essays by my one-time department chair, and long-time fellow theologian and personal friend, Bryan Ball. Reading (in most cases re-reading) his chapters has provided a refreshing heads-up from my usual focus on exegetical minutiae, to view several "big picture" biblical and theological concerns which remain perpetually at the centre of Christianity.

Chapter 2 "Revelation and the Authority of Scripture"

Chapter 2 argues the inadequacy of the "encounter" view of the doctrine of divine revelation, and offers a view that accounts more adequately for the evidence available in Scripture itself. While it is customary to combine study of the doctrine of revelation with the doctrine of biblical inspiration, the two are treated separately by Ball, with the doctrine of inspiration being the topic of chapter 5, "The Sufficiency of Scripture".

After an opening look at the enduring "crisis" (p. 14) in understanding the doctrine of revelation, he poses his key question: "Do words, spoken or written, play any part in the revelatory process" (p. 18). He answers by putting forward a case for "Special Revelation as Rational Proposition" (p. 26). In other words, the Bible reveals the will of God for his people, not only by encounter, but also through logical, rational content.

After briefly sketching the history of the doctrine from the New Testament church to the present, Ball concludes by highlighting the need for Christians to recognise and reaffirm that divine revelation includes rational, logical content which can be stated in propositions. Readers of Scripture encounter not only God himself, but also God's will expressed through *logos* and *ethos*, to guide and instruct the willing reader. Only thus can we resist the damage done by humanism and liberalism to our confidence that we can know God's will through his Word, the Scriptures.

Significant Old Testament evidence could have been cited to strengthen his thesis, such as the Hebrew verb *gālāh* and its Aramaic equivalent *gᵉlāh*, "to reveal", which together occur more than 25 times in the Old Testament in reference to God's revelation of himself, including specific information, to his people. This word is especially prominent in connection with king Nebuchadnezzar's dream in Daniel chapter 2 (cited by Ball), where it occurs seven times, a significant number. Another common Hebrew formula for "revelation" is "word of the LORD" which in its 270 occurrences distributed widely through the Old Testament clearly includes propositional content.[1] In the New Testament, "word of God", employing Greek *logos*, occurs more than 40 times. The main definition of *logos* in the standard New Testament Greek lexicon is: "a communication whereby the mind finds expression."[2] In other words, the "mind of God" (if one can speak of God in such anthropological fashion) expresses itself to the mind of humans. This is certainly more "*logos*-enriched" than even the most awe-inspiring "encounter"—it is the language of "rational proposition". Ball's thesis is clearly supported by the biblical evidence. While "encounter" is a component of divine revelation in Scripture, God's *logos* and *ethos* are at the heart of Scripture.

Chapter 3 "The Birth of the English Bible"

On the Day of Pentecost, the "birthday" of Christianity, it became clear that the Christian proclamation should not be restricted to a single "sacred" language, but was to be available to "every man in our own tongue, wherein we were born" (Acts 2:8, KJV). In continuation of this precedent, the Bible has become available in the languages of many of the world's people. The clear but unstated aim of this chapter is to trace the birth and the first 300 years of the history of the Bible in English, plus a brief sketch of history of the Bible in Anglo-Saxon from about 700 CE.

What happens to a Christian society which is denied access to the Bible for a considerable period of time? Ball's brief answer is "ignorance and corruption" among both laity and clergy. A major cure for both, in the British Isles, was to make Scripture available in the language of the people, a dangerous mission undertaken successfully by John Wycliffe, and which produced the Bible translation named for him. Very recent scholarship indicates the so-called "Wycliffite Bible" was even more popular and more widely available to English readers than believed in sources Ball cited.[3]

---

1   The less frequent phrase "Word of God" carries the same meaning.

2   F. W. Danker, editor, *A Greek-English Lexicon of the New Testament and Other Early Christian Literature*. 3rd edition (Chicago: University of Chicago Press, 2000), λόγος.

3   Scholarship on the Wycliffe Bible has experienced considerable recent advancement, summarized by Laura Light in her review of Kathleen Kennedy, *The Courtly and Commercial Art of the Wycliffite Bible* in *The Medieval Review* 15.05.35 (downloaded 29 May 2015 from tmrl=Indiana.edu@mail16.atl91.mcsv.

The Protestant Reformation was aided by a revolution in communication spurred on by the invention of printing by moveable type. This greatly accelerated the pace of Bible translation, and increased the demand of readers for the Bible in their own language. "When it pleased God to move King James to that excellent work, the translation of the Bible..."[4] With these words, the seventeenth-century biographer Anthony Walker began his account of the work of John Bois, the only translator of the KJV whose personal recollections and diary provide first-hand insight into the work which went into the translation and production of this most influential of English versions.

Ball closes by cautioning against attempts to enthrone any one translation as "the" correct and final form of God's Word. He does so, first, by sketching the history of revisions of the KJV. He could have informed readers that they do not have access to the KJV of 1611, but the KJV as it had been revised several times, including the major revision in 1769, which among other things, increased the number of personal pronouns such as "thee", "thou", "thine", "ye" in the text! Ball endorses the use of contemporary Bible translations, but does not mention that their multiplication is no longer justified by changes to the English language, or even by increasing knowledge of the Bible's original languages, but by the hope of publishers to score a best-seller![5]

Chapter 4 "The Enduring Influence of the Authorised Version"

Chapter 4 continues charting the impact of the Authorised King James Version of the Bible, not only on English-language Christianity but also on the English language itself.[6] Just as Martin Luther's Bible translation helped standardize the German language, so the KJV helped standardize English. Its impact on literature, art, education and civilization in general would be hard to over-estimate. The single most poignant image capturing its vast and

---

net). She opens her review by declaring "There were probably more bibles copied in the vernacular in the fourteenth and fifteenth centuries than there were Bibles copied in Latin."

4 Anthony Walker, *Life of John Bois*, chap 5, par 6, cited in Ward Allen, *Translating for King James* (Nashville, TN: Vanderbilt University Press, 1969), 139. Bois's own notes on the process of translation constitute another valuable part of this publication.

5 For an evaluation of recent translations, see Lorinda Bruce and Steven Thompson, "Does it Really Matter? Choosing a Bible Translation for Schools" *Teach Journal of Christian Education* 7 (2013): 34–41.

6 This chapter depends mainly on McGrath, Scroggie and Bragg. Another, more recent and comprehensive collection of essays on the KJV is by Philip H. Towner, David G. Burke and John F. Kutsko, editors. *The King James Version at 400: Assessing Its Genius as Bible Translation and Its Literary Influence* (Atlanta, GA: Society of Biblical Literature, 2013).

varied impact, to this writer's mind, is that of the young Abraham Lincoln reading his family's treasured copy by flickering firelight in an isolated Kentucky log cabin, storing up its message and values for that future time when he could make his mark on civilization.

The KJV has also had an impact on entertainment, especially in the United States. One thinks for example of Fulton Oursler's 1949 book, *The Greatest Story Ever Told: A Tale of the Greatest Life Ever Lived*, which became the basis of the 1965 movie of the same title.[7] Earlier Hollywood Bible-influenced productions include *The Ten Commandments* (1923) and *Ben Hur* (1959). In these and other movies, KJV-redolent language and imagery have impacted viewers.

But the Bible is more than a source of great stories; it *is* a great, inspiring, challenging and character-forming story, the greatest ever told. Ball appeals to readers to "cherish, defend, promulgate and exemplify the values and ideals of this quite amazing book..." (p. 64). He then concludes with an unexpected and foreboding reference to the decline and collapse of western culture, probably to prepare readers for chapter 16.

Chapter 5 "The Sufficiency of Scripture."

Chapter 5 addresses a question that has faced Christians of all ages—deciding the valid source of religious authority and Christian duty. Ball at the outset declares what he takes to be the correct reply, and warns the Christian reader against "the danger... of assigning authority to the establishment rather than to Scripture" (p. 68). He aims to defend the Bible as the supreme authority for Christian doctrine and life. He starts with what he considers a defining characteristic of Puritanism: to discover, understand and adhere to the "real" meaning of Scripture, and to let it instruct the life.

Major topics include Scripture's inspiration, purpose and authority. Ball highlights the importance of recognizing the bi-level nature of Scripture's authority: on one hand, authority for the church in her formulation of doctrine; on the other hand, authority for the individual believer's faith and life—one's "duty" according to seventeenth-century Puritan divines. Correct methods of studying Scripture lead to correct understand of God's will, and prevent misunderstanding of the plan of salvation caused by uninformed tradition and by the speculative philosophy that creeps in when Christian belief is not properly based on Scripture.

Ball summarises classic arguments for Scripture's inspiration: its survival in face of attack and neglect; its accessibility to the honest reader, who can discern its inspiration through its unity of theme, overall message, internal agreement on its central themes, fulfilled prophecy, and especially

---

7 Doubleday, 1949.

through its accounts of the life of Christ, and its continuing source of life-changing power.

What is known today as "verbal inspiration" was considered, but rejected, by leading Puritan divines. They distinguished between the *words* of Scripture recorded by "God's penmen" (one of their preferred expressions) on the one hand, and the *substance* and *matter* of Scripture on the other, which is the plan of salvation.[8]

The chief points of the Puritan doctrine of Scripture are central to Ball's goal for this chapter. Scripture's main purpose is to lead people to Christ and to salvation in Him. It is therefore the responsibility of all believers to read and seek to understand Scripture for themselves, guided by the Holy Spirit. The Spirit that inspired Scripture's authors will guide the seeking reader to a knowledge of salvation. A necessary component of the individual's understanding of Scripture is reason. Obstacles to rightly understanding Scripture include prejudice, previously held opinions, the grip of tradition, and the long reach of ancient Greek speculative philosophy, still obvious and influential during the Puritan epoch. Although he does not explicitly state it, Ball implies, on the chapter's final page, that the Puritan sense of living in the last days was a contributing factor to their understanding of Scripture.

This theologically concentrated essay at the heart of this volume concludes with a too-brief section on "Progressive revelation" (pp. 83–5), a belief close to the theological heart of several Puritan divines. It is an important topic, but seems better suited to chapter 2.

Chapter 6 "The Origins of Genesis Reconsidered"

Nearly 80 years ago a bold and original theory of the compilation of the book of Genesis was put forward, based almost exclusively on first-hand literary evidence which was then coming to light as a result of archaeological discoveries. If accepted, it would cut directly across the path of the so-called "Documentary Hypothesis" for the origin of the Pentateuch, which dominated biblical scholarship at the time. Ball introduces this remarkable theory through the experience of its main proponent, P. J. Wiseman, supported more recently by his son the Orientalist D.J. Wiseman, and the Old Testament scholar R.K. Harrison.

Attributing the authorship of Genesis to a single person, traditionally Moses, has problems: how could the records have been preserved accurately by memory? A bigger problem emerged for those with a high view of the inspiration of Scripture in the latter half of the nineteenth century, when critical biblical scholars developed the Documentary Hypothesis. They argued

---

8 The author's point in this paragraph could have been supported by reference to A.T.B. McGowan, *The Divine Inspiration of Scripture: Challenging Evangelical Perspectives* (Nottingham, UK: Apollos, 2007), especially 114–122.

that Genesis as we know it was the product of an editor working a thousand years after the time of Moses, who drew on sources which preserved diverse and sometimes contradictory accounts of origins and of the patriarchs.

The crucial question prompting the quest for the origin of Genesis is whether today's Bible readers can rely on the authenticity of its narratives. Are they based on actual records from the time of Moses and before? Or were those narratives the product of long periods of oral transmission which had become fictionalised in the process, and which were extracted from different and sometimes contradictory earlier sources?

Wiseman began his defence of the antiquity and therefore reliability of Genesis by highlighting the antiquity of the high civilizations of the Near East, including the antiquity of their literary conventions and traditions, which survive in the huge quantity of documents, many written in cuneiform script on baked clay tablets. Since many of these date to the time assigned by historians to Moses, they provide contemporary, reliable, first-hand insight into his times.

Wiseman theorised that much of Genesis was originally written in cuneiform, on clay tablets, following literary conventions of the time (p. 97). As evidence he cited the occurrence of Babylonian vocabulary in the Hebrew of chapters 1–11, the Egyptian flavour of chapters dealing with the Israelites in Egypt, later (possibly Mosaic) glosses in Genesis explaining place names which had already become redundant by the time of Moses, and finally, so-called "catch-lines" which open and close the genealogies of Genesis, and which originally would have "joined" the source tablets used by Moses.

While Wiseman did not argue that Moses actually composed all of Genesis, he made a case for him as its compiler, using records which had been preserved, most likely in cuneiform writing, by previous generations. The strength of Wiseman's hypothesis lies in its locating of Genesis in the world dominated by Babylon and Egypt during the time of the Hebrew patriarchs, something that the Documentary Hypothesis, dating the composition of Genesis nearly a thousand years later, failed to do.

One objection raised against Wiseman's hypothesis centres on the so-called *toledot* passages, or genealogies, of Genesis. There are eleven of them, and they seem to come at the beginning of relevant sections of Genesis, rather than at their conclusion, as they do in ancient cuneiform documents. The clear exception to this is the first *toledot*, Gen 2:4a, which refers to what has gone before. While the Wiseman hypothesis removes the need for the Documentary Hypothesis, and makes a clear case for a single compiler, it does not specify that Moses was that compiler. It does however point to the time of Moses as the most likely date of compilation for Genesis.[9]

---

9 Reference to the "early Hebrew scholar Gesenius" (p. 99) needs supple-

Chapter 12 "Righteousness and Redemption in the Epistles of Paul"

This chapter opens with a recognition of the impact of the life and work of Australian theologian Leon Morris, and an acknowledgement of Ball's dependence, for this chapter, on Morris's well-known book *The Apostolic Preaching of the Cross*. The key question is the meaning of "righteousness" in the Pauline epistles. There is no New Testament word more central to the Gospel, more loaded with potential for misunderstanding, and whose meaning is more contested than "righteousness." This chapter wades into this charged topic with Ball's usual focus on the identify and pursuit of a core Christian concept. Ball develops seven propositions which, taken together, explain and expound the legal as well as the moral aspects of what he repeatedly terms God's "redemptive righteousness":

1) Redemptive righteousness, because it is rooted in God, has a moral aspect. He is "fair and just, good, holy and perfect" (pp. 196, 197);
2) It responds to human sin, enabling humans to comprehend their sinfulness in its light;
3) It is revealed in the life and in the death of Jesus;
4) It is received by faith which, according to Paul, is ongoing: "from faith to faith" (Rom 1:17). It is also relational: trusting, believing, dependent, submissive;
5) It is realised in justification. Justification by faith is the core Protestant term which indicates the believer's initial, unearned "change of status" before God, which is made possible by commitment to Christ. The technical term "imputed righteousness" expresses this initial redemption by faith in God's righteousness;
6) It is recognisable (under its more familiar labels "imparted righteousness" or "sanctification") through the visible changes to a believer's life resulting from God's presence through the Holy Spirit;
7) Finally, it is reaffirmed by hope. Righteousness has an eschatological dimension, the anticipation of the splendour and wonder of the future redeemed life awaiting all who remain faithful.

It is hard to fault this fluent and well-rounded treatment of New Testament righteousness. However, the chapter does not develop the term "redemptive", even though the word occurs eleven times, and "redemption" occurs ten times. The concept and practice of redemption, as understood by Paul and his early readers, would contribute another significant component to our understanding of the all-important concept of righteousness.

---

menting. Heinrich Friedrich Wilhelm Gesenius (1786–1842) was probably his generation's most prominent specialist in ancient Near Eastern languages and literature. His Hebrew lexicon provided the lasting foundation for subsequent biblical Hebrew lexicons.

Chapter 13 "The Nature of Biblical Eschatology"

In this chapter Ball challenges Christians to achieve and maintain balance in understanding biblical eschatology, first by giving balanced attention to the eschatology of both Testaments, and second, by recognizing the place of eschatology in God's redemptive purposes in Jesus Christ, God's "eschatological man" (p. 208). Christians have struggled repeatedly to achieve and maintain the balance and wholeness called for in this chapter, which outlines five crucial truths about biblical eschatology that must be in place in order to achieve the essential balance. First, true biblical eschatology is Christ-centred, not just tacked on to the end. Second, eschatology's Christ-centredness requires recognition that "the last days" of the New Testament began at Christ's first coming, so our present age is already in some sense part of the eschaton. Third, Ball advocates the acceptance of what he terms a "moderate historicism" and "responsible historicist interpretation of prophetic chronology" (p. 223), especially when interpreting Daniel and Revelation.[10] Fourth, there is an ethical dimension to biblical eschatology, calling for what Ball terms "eschatological living" (p. 224). "Eschatological living" is not a requirement in order to be ready to enter the kingdom at some future date; it is part of current life in the kingdom. Biblical eschatology's fifth and final component is mission. "Preach!" "witness!" "proclaim!" are key New Testament terms expressing what Christians do with their Christ-given eschatological message.

Ball concludes with two challenges that face the church. The first is for the church not to repeat its past mistake of identifying itself with the kingdom. The church is not the kingdom, and does not produce the kingdom; rather, the kingdom produces the church! The second is for the church to develop and proclaim the element of hope at the heart of biblical eschatology to a world where hope is in short supply.

Chapter 15 "Sixteenth-Century Continental Conditionalists"

What happens to the human person at death? Behind this question is the more fundamental one, what is human nature? What are the human's constituent components? Matter only? Spirit only? Or a uniting of matter and spirit? Once this question is settled, a more insistent and personal one immediately emerges: what, if anything, survives death? Ball's knowledge of the

---

10   Historicism, as developed and applied to the biblical apocalypses, differs from that used by social critics such as Karl Popper in his *The Poverty of Historicism*, 2nd ed. (London: Routledge & Kegan Paul, 1960). For a summary of biblical historicism see William Johnsson, "Apocalyptic" in Raoul Dederen, editor. *Handbook of Seventh-day Adventist Theology* (Silver Spring, MD: Review & Herald, 2000), 784–814.

Christian debate surrounding this topic becomes evident; he has published a monograph on it.[11] His findings in this chapter are therefore a significant, original contribution towards the solution of an issue which has long divided Christians.

The question whether an eternally living soul is housed in a material body was pivotal to the Protestant Reformation, which included a reaction against the fairly recently developed doctrine of purgatory, official Roman Catholic dogma only since 1439 CE. Many readers will be surprised to learn that Luther believed the human soul to be mortal. This belief prompted his abhorrence of, and strong reaction against, the sale of indulgences which, it was claimed, would shorten the time that the conscious souls of the dead would suffer in purgatory. Calvin on the other hand was committed to the doctrine of an immortal soul. This strongly held doctrinal position on this issue contributed to his willingness to authorise the execution of Servetus for heresy, a fact that has escaped the attention of several recent treatments of Calvin, but revealed by Ball's research.

The close connection between the doctrine of soul sleep/mortalism and belief in the imminent return of Christ is another striking feature disclosed in this chapter. This connection was demonstrated especially in the case of Servetus, whose theology embraced and integrated both beliefs.

The question of the presence or absence of conscious awareness in death has emerged very recently in response to what has become a stream of books from evangelical Christian publishers recounting what has become termed "heavenly tourism"; accounts of journeys to heaven by those who have recovered from a near-death experience. Perhaps the best known is *The Boy Who Came Back From Heaven*.[12] At the book's heart is six year-old Alex Malarkey's account of what he experienced as the result of a terrible automobile collision. A decade after his accident and four years after the publication of his book, Alex confessed in an open letter "I did not die. I did not go to Heaven."[13] This has refocused Christian attention on the meaning of the biblical concept of "resurrection" and the biblical position on the state of persons in death. There is hope that Alex's confession will lead Christians back to the biblical position on the state of the person in death, and its accompanying belief in the resurrection of the dead at Christ's return.

---

11   Bryan W. Ball, *The Soul Sleepers: Christian Mortalism from Wycliffe to Priestley*. Cambridge: James Clarke, 2008.

12   The subtitle is telling: *A remarkable account of miracles, angels, and life beyond this world.* Carol Stream, IL: Tyndale House, 2010.

13   Alex Malarkey, "An Open Letter to Lifeway and Other Sellers, Buyers, and Marketers of Heaven Tourism, by the Boy Who Did Not Come Back From Heaven." (Downloaded 8 May 2015 from http://pulpitandpen.org/2015/01/13/the-boy-who-came-back-from-heaven-recants-story-rebukes-christian-retailers/)

Chapter 16 "The Decline of the West: Myth, or Reason for Hope?"

The hypothesis of progress has been a centrepiece of the long-standing western humanist and enlightenment assumption that human beings, and with them human society, are on an evolutionary "up escalator" to even more-highly evolved persons, and ever higher civilization.[14] Although expressed at least since the time of Plato (427–347 BCE), this evolutionary view has been a prominent component of western humanism for the past five hundred years. Recently it has encountered major ideological competition in the form of an opposing "down escalator" hypothesis that western society is not ascending at all, but descending into decline and decay. Articulated prominently early in the twentieth century by Oswald Spengler, this theme of western decline has been taken over and updated by John Carroll.[15] Is Western civilization "going up" or "going down"? In either case, what comes next?[16]

What should be the attitude of Christians to the announcement of western civilization's decline? Rejoicing? Welcoming? Lamenting? Working to counter it? This question is addressed only briefly by Ball. He does not call for Christian activism of the type done, for example, by Jim Wallis and his Sojourner movement, who engage socially and politically to "hold back the winds of strife" by efforts to repair western society. Nor does he advocate isolation and withdrawal into sheltered Christian communes to await the end.

Ball enters this complex debate only far enough to explore a single facet, the decline of western Christianity. While the validity of the hypothesis of declining Western civilization can be debated, the decline of western Christianity and its impact on society is easily documented. It was already detected in nineteenth-century literature by J. Hillis Miller in his *The Disappearance of God*.[17] Ball's main authorities include John Carroll and Francis Schaeffer, plus more recent proponents of declining western Christian influence, which

---

14   The analogy between the popular notion of ever-advancing evolutionary progress and an "up escalator" comes from Mary Midgley, *Evolution as a Religion: Strange Hopes and Stranger Fears*. Rev. ed. (London: Routledge, 2002), 33–39.

15   *Humanism: The Wreck of Western Culture*. London: Fontana, 1993. Carroll's view, but not his basic thesis, has been modified in subsequent revisions of this book in 2004 and 2010, which are titled *The Wreck of Human Culture: Humanism Revisited*.

16   The debate was summarized by Raymond Tallis, *Enemies of Hope: A Critique of Contemporary Pessimism*. New York: St Martin's, 1997. His fundamental thesis is that "the [Enlightenment] hope of progress is well founded..." (p. 64).

17   J. Hillis Miller, *The Disappearance of God: Five 19th-Century Writers* (Cambridge, MA: Harvard University Press, 1963; revised edition New York: Schocken, 1965).

it is said is due largely to the humanistic shouldering-aside of Christianity and exaltation of post-Christian humanity.

Ball concludes with a very brief call for renewed attention to the biblical apocalypses, especially chapters 2 and 7 of Daniel. A reminder of the main assumptions of biblical apocalyptic would have improved the chapter at this point, William Johnsson's seven-point summary of biblical apocalyptic's core assumptions come to mind: God is sovereign over this world; He has genuine foreknowledge; apocalyptic visions/prophecies have a cosmic sweep rather than a focus on Israel; biblical covenant echoes are absent from apocalyptic narratives; predicted epochs extend through time, and are continuous, covering all of earthly history; in the future divine intervention will break into this world from outside and in total independence of earthly processes.[18]

The contentious issue of the present state and future fate of western civilization is not easy to address in a single essay, but Ball provides what he acknowledges is a "sombre and sobering analysis of our culture" (p. 288) which demands that Christians take a fresh look at what can be learned about our times, and our future, in light of Scripture's apocalyptic visions.

Chapter 17 "Jesus and the Great Commission"

Ball appropriately concludes this collection of essays with an exposition of the Gospel Commission. Following brief exegesis of the New Testament accounts of Jesus' commissioning his disciples, the chapter takes up three questions: what does the Great Commission mean? Who is included in it? How will it be accomplished?

The Commission was first delivered to those who witnessed Christ's ministry and resurrection, making them irreplaceable. Christ, not the church, must remain the subject of all Christian witness. Church and kingdom are not identical. The church is a valid part of the kingdom only when it exists to further that kingdom. Ball cites a range of leading thinkers on church and mission in support of this church-to-kingdom relationship. For the second time in this volume Ball reminds readers that "this kingdom" which Christ spoke about in the Gospel Commission is already present, as it has been with his followers since his resurrection.

Responsibility for mission rests "with all who are disciples of Jesus" (p. 298). A truly balanced witness to Christ demands that his followers live a "persuasive lifestyle" (p. 300) and demonstrate "social responsibility" (p. 301). A major burden of Ball is the challenge of carrying out mission "at home" in post-Christian societies. He points to the tendency in many churches towards a "nurture-mission" (im)balance in favour of nurture. He

---

18   William Johnsson, "Apocalyptic", 790, 795–99.

closes by sketching the essential role of the Holy Spirit in carrying out the Gospel Commission.

Ball repeats the importance and centrality of the concrete, historical, objective facts about the Jesus of Nazareth, including his crucifixion and resurrection, as the content of today's Christian witness (pp. 292, 299, 303), but he could develop more the importance of sharing also one's personal, subjective experience of the risen Christ as part of the individual believer's witness—in the words of hymn writer Fanny Crosby, "this is *my* story, this is *my* song, praising *my* Saviour all the day long."

If this chapter were to be written today, one would expect reference to the impact of megachurches on witness and evangelism. Their growing presence and influence would also be acknowledged and dealt with in exploring the role of the Holy Spirit in witness. Many megachurches have emerged from the Assemblies of God and similar Pentecostal denominations, which have their own distinctive understanding of the reception of the Holy Spirit.

There is need today to acknowledge postmodernity's distrust of metanarratives, including the Christian metanarrative of salvation history. How can witness and evangelism best be conducted among postmoderns who prefer the personal above the institutional, the local above the national, the immediate above the future? These criticisms do not detract from the chapter's powerful encouragement for every Christian disciple first to understand the Gospel Commission—its source, its components, its goals, and its empowering by the Holy Spirit. And with that understanding, to *go* on the mission that Christ assigns, whether across the world or across the street, to hearts and minds that are open to the message of salvation through Christ.

19. Bryan Ball as Historian

Daniel Reynaud

Avondale College of Higher Education

'To review the historiography of Puritanism is to review the history of early modern England,' wrote historian Peter Lake in his overview of the field.[1] Yet one can go a step further when reviewing the historiographical output of Bryan Ball, for while much of his historical research and writing explores Puritan thought in early modern England, it is also written with an eye on the history and theology of the Seventh-day Adventist church, though that denomination dates only from the mid-nineteenth century. This capacity to illuminate two periods of history through shedding light on the one is a distinctive feature of his historical writings. The selected chapters in this volume illustrate well the kind of historical coverage that Ball has achieved in his work.

The field of studies in Tudor and Stuart history has been a popular one, and rightly so, given the impact those eras have had on later British, European and indeed world history right up to the present. Religion played a central role in shaping the period and, therefore retrospectively, in understanding it. In particular, as Lake noted, Puritanism formed a critical part of the discourse of those times, and to study Puritanism is to enter into the essence of many of the key historical events that made the Tudor and Stuart eras seminal in history. Leading historians over several centuries have shed light on the personalities, events and issues of these times, but only relatively recently have historians began to plumb the diversity of religious belief that characterised the movement collectively badged as Puritanism, an imprecise label that covers an astonishing diversity of beliefs and practices while encompassing all social classes, even having its adherents within the official Church of England, so often typified as a bulwark of conservative thought and practice.

The notable historian Christopher Hill was a leader in broadening scholarly attention from the centres to the margins of secular and clerical power. His work from the 1950s onwards was seminal in bringing the marginalised

---

1   Peter Lake, 'The historiography of Puritanism', in John Coffey & Paul C. H. Lim (eds.) *The Cambridge Companion to Puritanism* (Cambridge: Cambridge University Press, 2008), 346.

versions of Protestantism to the attention of both historians and the public. As a Marxist historian, he sought not only to find economic causal factors in the religious history of the day, but also to explore the ways in which alternative views challenged the bastions of power in the seventeenth century. In his footsteps, other historians expanded the studies of the marginalised, alternative and regional variations within Tudor and Stuart history.

It is firstly in this context that Ball's contribution as a historian of Puritanism has been significant. Puritanism has long been easy to caricature and stereotype, from contemporary Sixteenth and Seventeenth Century literary figures like William Shakespeare (whose character, the joyless prig Malvolio in Twelfth Night, embodies the clichéd Puritan) and Ben Jonson (in a satire indicting Puritan theology and hypocrisy in The Alchemist, which includes mocking its views on the book of Daniel). Ball begins by asserting the validity of Puritan thought, demonstrating that far from being promoted exclusively by extremists, it was promoted by many respected and respectable figures within the Establishment, even if their advocacy of certain Puritan positions put that respectability at risk at times. He discusses insightfully the difficulties in defining Puritanism as a movement, noting that the term has been 'persistently misunderstood and misused'.[2] He emphasises that Puritanism initially developed as part of the diversity of Anglicanism. It was not until later, particularly during the reign of Charles I, through the Civil War, the Interregnum and Restoration, that there was a more distinct and formalised divide between Anglicanism, which became increasingly narrow and exclusive, and Puritanism, which became more aggressive in seeking 'a means for the recovery of true doctrine and the preservation of the true Christian way of life.'[3] In fact, the narrowing of Anglicanism and the stridency of Puritanism were directly related, each being reactions to the behaviour of the other.

In several chapters in this volume, Ball notes the ways in which Anglican divines and prominent lay people in society advocated beliefs that were distinctly Puritan. Chapter 8 features pocket biographies of two Anglicans who had Puritan leanings: Joseph Mede and Samuel Bold. Mede is recognised for the quality of his scholarship and his wide influence in the field of biblical eschatology, and Ball names him as the father of English millenarianism. He expands on Mede's contribution to eschatological studies in Chapter 11, where the prominence of apocalyptic thought in England in the sixteenth and seventeenth centuries is given more detailed attention. Bold's career was a little different from Mede's in that his advocacy of both religious toleration and of the doctrine of mortalism made him controversial

2   Bryan W. Ball, Chapter 7, 'Puritans and Puritanism', 112.
3   Ball, 'Puritans and Puritanism', 112.

in the Restoration era, where he was one of the few Anglicans who dared voice heterodox opinions in an atmosphere of paranoid repression intended to eliminate any whiff of Puritanism within the Establishment.

The inter-related subjects of eschatology and the second advent of Christ are generally supported by mainstream opinion of the era, as Ball notes in Chapters 8, 11 and 14. Royal support came in the person of King James I, who fancied himself an amateur theologian and published a volume on demonology. Archbishop of Armagh James Ussher and Bishop of Norwich Joseph Hall published on Daniel and Revelation, adding weight to the popularity of studies on eschatology which had begun in the early days of the Reformation. Ball notes that their publications were successful and that four significant scholars in the area of eschatology—Thomas Brightman, John Napier, Arthur Dent and Joseph Mede—laid the foundations for future interpretations of Daniel and Revelation, evidenced by the repeated reprinting of their work, and their constant referencing in the works of later scholars. Ball credits the widespread advocacy of the doctrine of the Second Coming among both Anglicans and Non-Conformists as accounting for the warmth of Puritan spiritual life, the driving force of sanctification and the provider of Christian hope.

On the subject of the seventh-day Sabbath, Ball finds Anglican cleric Theophilus Brabourne's writings to be 'convincing apologetic literature.' His impressive output influenced later Sabbatarians, though for his views on this more controversial topic, Brabourne was imprisoned as a Judaiser. On another controversial doctrine, that of the soul's sleep after death, Ball finds support not from mainstream English reformers but from Martin Luther himself, as well as his more radical colleague Andreas Carlstadt. Ball discerns in Luther's writings evidence that he held to psychopannychism — that the soul slept after the death of the body, until reawakened and reunited with the body at the Resurrection. So also Carlstadt, and Ball argues that this understanding was closely connected to their eschatology. He does note, however, that mortalism in general was more characteristic of the radical Anabaptists, Spiritualists and Evangelical Rationalists, being hotly opposed by Calvin as constituting an intolerable heresy.

While Ball is able to demonstrate sectors of Anglicanism that promoted Puritan thought, naturally he does not consider this to be the limits of Puritanism, nor even its major manifestation. The more radical wing of Puritanism was apparent in various forms, ranging from mild Non-Conformism through to revolutionary and anarchist expression. Socially repressive Puritanism, as well as extremism which manifested itself in many bizarre and cultic versions, has more easily grabbed the imagination, typecasting the whole of Puritanism as simultaneously being both repressive and 'kill-joy' on the one hand and, on the other, socially radical, attempting to eliminate class divisions, government, private property, even marriage and clothing in its more extreme forms. It became easy to reduce Puritanism collectively in all of its diversity to an ideology that posed a threat to the spiritual, emotional, moral and political well-being of the nation, and hence to persecute anyone of that label, even if their actual ideas were in themselves unthreatening. While radical (and often tiny) Puritan groups such as Fifth Monarchists, Muggletonians, Ranters, Diggers, and Adamites have attracted scholarly attention and popular notoriety, both then and now, other groups who were persecuted at the time have since attained a level of respect and even influence. Quakers and Anabaptists, for example, equally feared and persecuted at the time, have birthed modern manifestations whose views have become tolerated and in some cases have even entered mainstream religious and secular opinion.

Ball takes particular interest in the latter groups of the Puritan tradition, highlighting that they canvassed some modern theological concerns. His chief interests are in Sabbatarianism and soul-sleep, as well as eschatology, which was also a passionate concern of radical Puritans. Associated with these beliefs came concerns over the nature of biblical inspiration and the role of reason in interpreting Scripture. Ball explores Anabaptists' opposition to the doctrine of the immortality of the soul and their advocacy of psychopannychism in contrast to the Spiritualists, who tended to argue for a more radical version of mortalism, thnetopsychism, in which the soul has no separate existence from the body, being quite simply the breath that departs at death.

In this volume's chapters, Ball also investigates several radical individuals whose theology stood outside the mainstream of the time. Clement Writer, an uneducated radical who belonged to the rather vague group called 'Seekers', argued for mortalism and against a professional, formally educated clergy, believing that reason enlightened through the individual's connection with the Spirit was the best way to interpret Scripture. Three men, the poor weaver John James, the prosperous merchant Joseph Davis Snr, and the gentleman Francis Bampfield, are noted for their contribution to Sabbatarianism, though their fates were different. James was wrongly associated with Fifth Monarchists and suffered the horrific death of being hanged, drawn and quartered, while his congregation was persecuted. Davis was able to endow Sabbatarian groups with church property and pensions for ministers, which helped to ensure their survival for some time. Bampfield's effective preaching won him large congregations, but also imprisonment in conditions harsh enough to hasten his death.

While Ball's scholarship has advanced our knowledge of the nuances of Puritan thought in the sixteenth and seventeenth centuries, his interest in the area has not been purely academic. As an influential theologian in the Seventh-day Adventist Church (his career has included major leadership roles in the SDA church in England and Australia, including a stint as president of an Adventist college in Australia, as well as the presidency of the South Pacific Division of the world-wide church), he has sought to enlighten thinking on matters of theological interest to the church. Hence, his selected focus on the doctrinal issues of Puritanism which find their echo in the more distinctive elements of the theology of Adventism. He makes this link overt in his study of English Puritanism, which is subtitled *The Puritan Roots of Seventh-day Adventist Belief*, but the link also underpins most of his other historical writing, where this connection is more often implicit.[4]

It is here that Ball has made his second great contribution to historical scholarship. By tracing the antecedents to Adventist theology, he is able to locate Adventism in a deeper historical context than has generally been done, and in doing so he seeks to validate Adventism's distinctive emphases as beliefs with a long history in Christianity rather than as the innovations of the enthusiasms (both words with pejorative connotations with regard to religion in the seventeenth and eighteenth centuries) of a recent minor American sect. He endows apparently new Adventist doctrine with the credibility of reformers from the beginnings of Protestantism, thus upholding Adventism's claim to be true heirs of the Reformation movement.

This theme underpins the historical chapters in this volume, beginning with Chapter 7, where he emphasises the importance of paying attention to the Puritans precisely because their influence continued into the early twentieth century. As already noted, Ball's focus in Puritan history is predominantly with doctrines of Sabbatarianism, mortalism and eschatology, three areas of importance to Adventist thought and belief. His study of English Sabbatarianism in Chapters 9–10 identifies the role of a number of leading seventeenth-century Sabbatarians in establishing and fostering the notion of a biblical seventh-day Sabbath, and shows how the scholars of the era distinguished Christian Sabbatarianism from heretical Judaising.

In Chapter 11, which pays attention to Puritan eschatology, Ball notes many key ideas which recur in Adventist thought. He highlights the understanding that the Puritans had of the special role of the books of Daniel and Revelation in speaking 'with meaning and authority' to their present time in ways which other biblical prophecies (such as Jeremiah, Ezekiel and Zechariah) did not—a Puritan concept that is familiar to Adventist exegetes who hold those books to continue to apply to the present age.

---

4   Bryan W. Ball, *The English Connection; The Puritan Roots of Seventh-day Adventist Belief* (Cambridge: James Clarke and Co., 2nd edition, 2014 [1st edition, 1975]).

Ball claims the authority of the Puritans for Adventism's basic approach to eschatology, detailing their application of Historicism to Daniel and Revelation, and their interpretation of five fundamental symbols of prophetic literature: the day-year principle, the representation of earthly kingdoms and powers by the beasts, whose horns symbolise kinds of governments, the use of seas and waters to represent peoples, and the use of women to symbolise the church. He also traces the sound Puritan roots of common Adventist interpretations of the Antichrist, the kingdoms of Daniel 2 and 7 and the understanding of the basic structure of Revelation, in particular the visions of the seven seals and seven trumpets.

For added emphasis, he shows how the Protestant commentators of the seventeenth century dismissed both Preterist and Futurist views of prophecy (largely the fruits of Jesuit Catholic scholarship) thus anchoring Adventist eschatology firmly in the traditions of Protestant interpretation. In order to locate it further into the mainstream, he notes the risks identified in Puritan times for the discipline to lead to hasty and strained misinterpretation, suggesting that Adventist eschatology, by sharing its key features with that of Puritanism, had managed largely to steer clear of the dangers of lunatic interpretations.

On the related topic of the Second Advent of Christ, Ball again highlights Puritan beliefs that coincide with Adventist thought. The notion of a literal, visible, personal, imminent and glorious second coming was commonly held by Anglicans and Puritans alike. Likewise, the second coming governed their understanding of the whole Christian age, giving it eschatological significance, filling the Christian with hope and providing motivation for character transformation. Ball draws out how some thinkers of the era connected the first and second advents through the high priestly ministry of Jesus in heaven, paralleling Jesus' work to that of the high priest in the Old Testament sanctuary in bringing to full completion the work of redemption—again a notion which is at the heart of the Adventist doctrine of the investigative judgment of Christ in the heavenly sanctuary.

In his examination of the shades of conditionalist or mortalist doctrine in Chapter 15, Ball is less obviously foreshadowing Adventist thought, for he gives more or less equal emphasis to both psychopannychism and thnetopsychism, the latter reflecting more closely the Adventist doctrinal position. In drawing other parallels between the seventeenth and nineteenth century, he notes the Puritan use of the term 'Present Truth' to applications of prophecy in each generation as counter to falsehood, a term that recurs in Adventist literature. Similarly, the Puritan notion of progressive revelation has its manifestation in Adventism, as do the concepts of religious toleration and religious liberty.

While the main focus of Ball's historical work is on the doctrinal connections between selected Puritan thinkers and those of the Adventist movement of roughly two centuries later, he takes the time to observe that the family tree of thought patterns precedes the Puritan era, in many cases being traceable as far back as early Christian doctrine and practice. Essentially, he argues that Puritan ideas were themselves not innovations, but rather had their origins in the ancient Christian church. More specifically, he locates Puritan Sabbatarianism as grounded in the beliefs and practices recorded by Athanasius and the Council of Laodicea, fifth-century church-historian Socrates, and the Celtic church, which depended on Scripture rather than popes and councils for its authority. This desire to return to primitive Christianity's simplicity of practice and purity of doctrine which Ball locates in Puritan attitudes is also part of the rhetoric of Adventism, revealing its Restorationist roots.

Perhaps where Ball is at his weakest is in chapter 16, where he moves from historian to contemporary commentator and even futurist. His brief overview of the history of dominant thought from Greek and Roman times to the present offers a picture of a decline in the fundamentals of Western civilisation to the point of it now being pagan. While he claims that the decline is due to the abandonment of Christianity from its high point in the logo-centric era of the advent of the printing press and Protestantism, his argument in fact begins with the implicit value of Greek logic and Roman law—legacies of pagan societies which he also sees as bedrocks of the heights of Western civilisation. The appeal to pagan Greek and Roman heritage undermines his argument of the centrality of a Christian Western heritage which he sees as in irretrievable decline. This loss, he states, has come through the influences of violent ideologies such as Fascism and Communism and the values-levelling emphasis on multiculturalism, while secular humanism has made autonomous humanity the new centre of attention. The governing metaphor is the multi-medium statue in the prophecy of Daniel 2, where the feet of iron and clay indicate a failure of secular politics and society to provide the necessary unity to ensure a future. In this pessimistic view of the contemporary world, Ball sees hope because these developments are the harbinger of the return of Christ and the establishment of his eternal kingdom.

There is much of merit in Ball's analysis, but what is unsettling is the blending of a Eurocentric with a Christocentric worldview. The relegation of one's traditions and history from the limelight to the footlights is not in itself a sign of end. Ball implies, almost certainly accidentally I believe, that had the West maintained its Christian heritage, the Second Advent would be less necessary or immediate. I share his view of the trajectory of world history and its imminent conclusion in the triumphant return of Christ, bringing to an end the tragic history of sinful humanity's cruelty and suffering. However, I do not necessarily believe that virtue has resided in Western civilisation and that danger lurks in other cultures. Most societies have been blessed by insight into how to live well in some respects, and cursed by a fatal blindness in many others. The history of the Christian West is shamefully littered with too many examples of unchristian behaviour, even from those professing Christ. Christian doctrine has even been used to justify violence and abuse towards others, Christian and non-Christian alike. In many respects, recent exposure to other cultures has allowed the West to develop greater empathy and reduce bigotry—a move in harmony with the Gospel. And the challenge that 'Present Truth' demands of us living in a less Eurocentric world is to understand the prophecies of Daniel and Revelation according to today's global, rather than yesterday's Euro-American, perspectives.

I do agree with him that the Christian legacy has been a strength of Western civilisation, but that torch has now been passed on to vast numbers in other parts of the world, where Christianity is an increasingly important cultural influence even as it diminishes in the West. The illness of the world at large is not so much an abandonment of Western society as it is a lack of Christian love, on which Western society has had neither monopoly nor mortgage. And so, by a slightly different path, I end up agreeing with Ball— bring on the return of Christ.

This is not to diminish the accomplishments of Ball's scholarly work as historian. Where the bulk of Adventist historians have mostly ploughed the narrow field of the history of the denomination, especially in America, and have published largely within the Adventist press to a parochial audience, Ball's work has broadened the scope of Adventist historical research, has been published primarily through reputable non-denominational scholarly publishers, and has reached a wider scholarly audience. Of course, there are advantages in not researching immediate Adventist history: he has been able to avoid the denominational political controversies that have dogged some of his contemporaries who have produced research that challenged Establishment hagiography.[5] But his output has also helped to reduce the narrowness of Adventist historical focus. By drawing denominational attention to the Puritan past, he has helped expand an Adventist understanding of its own origins, drawing attention to the doctrinal precedents of Adventism, and blazing a trail for others to tease out the legacies of earlier reformers in the Adventist movement. For example, current research in a better under-

---

5   Daniel Reynaud and Arthur Patrick, 'Idealisation, Conflict and Maturation: The development of Seventh-day Adventist Historiography.' *Lucas: An Evangelical History Review,* 2:3, June 2011, 11–18.

standing of Adventism's debt to the Seeker network is building and expanding on the foundations that he laid.[6]

His work has provided a necessary filling of gaps in understandings of Puritan thought and influence, and has also proved to be a valuable correction to previous histories that overlooked or underplayed aspects of Puritan theology.[7] Consequently his writings have received plaudits from academics and his books have received excellent reviews, with only the occasional carping caveat. A reviewer described one of his books as offering 'a detailed and balanced assessment' of Puritan Sabbatarianism, while his study of Puritan mortalism was praised as 'a fascinating study of a neglected minority theological position and the controversy surrounding it.' The reviewer concluded that 'Ball is to be commended for bringing this movement more fully to light, as its witness influenced mainstream Christian thought in significant ways that we may not have previously understood.'[8]

In short, Bryan Ball as historian has been innovative in exploring the origins of Adventist belief through the lens of Puritan thought, belonging to that small group of Adventist historians, mostly of English or European heritage, whose work has been grounded in the European socio-religious context of advocating a minority view in the face of powerful state-endorsed religions. He has been rare among Adventist historians in working in an area of religious history which has attracted the attention of mainstream historians. His work demonstrates both sound scholarship and an ability to frame the potentially dull minutiae of late English Reformation theological hair-splitting in a language that is accessible to a literate laity. His contribution as a scholar is invaluable both to Adventism and to the broader community of historical endeavour.

---

6   See Garry Duncan, 'Converging edges of the Midnight Cry: A journey of select Seeker and Rogerene descendant faith paths in mid-state Connecticut,' paper presented at *Adventism and Adventist History: Sesquicentennial Reflections*, Silver Spring, MD, January 6, 2014.

7   Bryan W. Ball, *The Seventh-Day Men: Sabbatarians and Sabbatarianism in England and Wales, 1600–1800.* Oxford: Clarendon Press, James Clarke & Co, 2009, 39n; Bryan W. Ball, *The Soul Sleepers: Christian Mortalism from Wycliffe to Priestley* (Cambridge: James Clarke, 2008), 16–18.

8   W. M. Spellman, review of Bryan W. Ball, *The Seventh-Day Men. American Historical Review* 101 (1996) 479; Charles Hambrick-Stowe, review of Bryan W. Ball, *The Soul Sleepers. Christian Mortalism from Wycliffe to Priestley. Journal of Ecclesiastical History* 60 (2009) 167.

Appendix

Major Publications of Bryan W. Ball

Books

As Sole Author:

A Great Expectation: Eschatological Thought in English Protestantism to 1660, Leiden: E. J. Brill, 1975; Vol. XII in 'Studies in the History of Christian Thought', ed. Heiko A. Oberman.

The English Connection: The Puritan Roots of Seventh-day Adventist Belief. Cambridge UK: James Clarke, 1981; 2^d ed., revised, Cambridge, UK: James Clarke, 2014

The Seventh-day Men: Sabbatarians and Sabbatarianism in England and Wales, 1600–1800, Oxford, UK: Clarendon, 1994; 2^d ed., revised and expanded, Cambridge, UK: James Clarke & Co, 2009.

Living in the Spirit, Warburton, Victoria: Signs Publishing Co., 1997.

Can We Still Believe the Bible? And Does it Really Matter? Warburton, Victoria: Signs Publishing Co., 2007; Spanish edition, Buenos Aires, Argentina: Asociacion Casa Editora Sudamerica, 2010; Latvian edition, Riga, LV: Patmos, 2010; 2nd Edition, revised and enlarged, Warburton, Victoria: Signs Publishing Co, 2011.

The Soul Sleepers: Christian Mortalism from Wycliffe to Priestley, Cambridge, UK: James Clarke, 2008.

As [Joint] Editor and Contributor:

The Essential Jesus: The Man, His Message, His Mission, Boise, ID: Pacific Press, 2002; second edition, Nampa, ID: Pacific Press, 2011, in the Adventist Heritage Library. [Co-edited with William G. Johnsson.]

In The Beginning: Science and Scripture Confirm Creation, Nampa, ID: Pacific Press, 2012; Portuguese Edition, Tatui, SP, Brazil: Casa Publicadora Brasileira, 2014.

Chapters in other books, Reference Works, etc

"Eschatological Hope in Puritan England", Ch. 7 in V. Norskov Olsen ed., *The Advent Hope in Scripture and History,* Washington DC: Review and Herald, 1987.

Six entries in *The Oxford Dictionary of National Biography*, Oxford University Press, 2004:
Theophilus Brabourne, 1590-1662;
Samuel Bold, 1649-1737;
Nicholas Byfield, 1578/9-1622;
Christopher Feake, 1611/12-1682/3;
Joseph Mede, 1586-1638;
Clement Writer, fl. 1627-1658.
"Through Darkness to Light: Post-Restoration Sabbatarianism: Survival and Continuity", Ch. 3 in Richard Bonney and D. J. B. Trim, eds., *The Development of Pluralism in Modern Britain and France*, Bern & Oxford: Peter Lang, 2007.
"Towards an Authentic Adventist Identity", Ch. 3 in Borge Schantz and Reinder Bruinsma, eds., *Exploring the Frontiers of Faith*, Lueneberg: Advent-Verlag, 2010.
"Saving Righteousness," *Ministry* June 2010, 10-13.
"The Immortality of the Soul: Could Christianity Survive Without it?" *Ministry* March 2011, 10-14; May 2011, 14-17.
"The Enduring Influence of The King James Bible", in Nikolaus Satelmajer, ed., *The Book That Changed the World*, Nampa, ID: Pacific Press, 2012.

Contributor to Peter Bishop and Michael Darton, eds., *The Encyclopedia of World Faiths: An Illustrated Survey of the World's Living Religions*, London & Sydney: Macdonald Orbis, 1987.
Advisor to 3rd edition of *The Oxford Dictionary of the Christian Church*, Oxford, Oxford University Press, 1997.
Contributor to the on-line edition of *The Oxford English Dictionary*, 2003, ongoing.

Acknowledgments

Avondale Academic Press would like to extend thanks to:

Clarendon Press, for permission to republish "The Roots of English Sabbatarianism" from Bryan W. Ball, *The Seventh-day Men: Sabbatarians and Sabbatarianism in England and Wales, 1600–1800* (Oxford: Clarendon Press, 1994).

E.J. Brill, for permission to republish "Early English Apocalyptic Interpretation" from Bryan W. Ball, *A Great Expectation: Eschatological Thought in English Protestantism to 1660* (Leiden: Brill, 1975).

James Clarke and Company Ltd, for permission to republish "The Sufficiency of Scripture," and "Puritans and Puritanism," from Bryan W. Ball, *The English Connection: The Puritan Roots of Seventh-day Adventist Belief* (Cambridge: James Clarke, 1981); and in its revised 2nd edition, also published by James Clarke, 2014; and for permission to republish "Sixteenth-Century Continental Conditionalists" from the introduction and Chapter 1 of Bryan W. Ball, *The Soul Sleepers: Christian Mortalism from Wycliffe to Priestley* (Cambridge: James Clarke, 2008).

Oxford University Press, for permission to publish the profiles of Joseph Meade, Samuel Bold, and Clement Writer from the 2004 edition of Oxford Dictionary of National Biography.

Pacific Press Publishing Association, for permission to republish "Revelation and the Authority of Scripture," and "The Origins of Genesis Reconsidered," from Bryan W. Ball, ed., *In the Beginning: Science and Scripture Confirm Creation* (Pacific Press, Nampa, ID, 2012); as well as "The Enduring Influence of the Authorised Version," from "The Enduring Influence of the King James Version" in Nikolaus Satelmajer, ed., *The Book That Changed the World: The Story of the King James Version* (Nampa, ID: Pacific Press, 2012); and "Jesus and the Great Commission" from Bryan W. Ball and William G. Johnsson, eds., *The Essential Jesus* (2002 Nampa, ID: Pacific Press, 2002).

Peter Lang, for permission to republish "Through Darkness to Light: Post-Restoration Sabbatarianism, Survival and Continuity" from Richard Bonney and D.J.B. Trim, eds., *The Development of Pluralism in Modern England and France* (Oxford, Bern, New York: Peter Lang, 2007).

Review and Herald Publishing Association, for permission to republish, "The Second Advent Hope in Puritan England" from V. Norskov Olsen, ed., *The Advent Hope in Scripture and History* (Washington, DC: Review and Herald, 1987).

Signs Publishing Company, for permission to republish, "The Birth of the English Bible," in Bryan W. Ball, *Can We Still Believe the Bible? And Does it Really Matter?* (2nd revised edition; Warburton, Vic: Signs, 2011).

Made in the USA
Las Vegas, NV
02 August 2024

93253995R00187